A NEW INTRODUCTION TO ISLAM

A NEW INTRODUCTION TO ISLAM

Second Edition

Daniel W. Brown

WILEY-BLACKWELL

A John Wiley & Sons, Ltd., Publication

This edition first published 2009

Blackwell Publishing was acquired by John Wiley & Sons in February 2007. Blackwell's publishing program has been merged with Wiley's global Scientific, Technical, and Medical business to form Wiley-Blackwell.

Registered Office
John Wiley & Sons Ltd, The Atrium, Southern Gate, Chichester, West Sussex, PO19 8SQ, United Kingdom

Editorial Offices
350 Main Street, Malden, MA 02148-5020, USA
9600 Garsington Road, Oxford, OX4 2DQ, UK
The Atrium, Southern Gate, Chichester, West Sussex, PO19 8SQ, UK

For details of our global editorial offices, for customer services, and for information about how to apply for permission to reuse the copyright material in this book please see our website at www.wiley.com/wiley-blackwell.

Library of Congress Cataloging-in-Publication Data
Brown, Daniel W., 1963-
A new introduction to islam / Daniel W. Brown. — 2nd ed.
p. cm.
Includes bibliographical references and index.
ISBN 978-1-4051-5807-7 (pbk. : alk. paper) 1. Islam. 2. Islam—Essence, genius, nature. I. Title.
BP161.3.B76 2004
297—dc22

2008049848

A catalogue record for this book is available from the British Library.

Set in 10/12.5 pt Meridian
by Graphicraft Typesetters Ltd, Hong Kong.
Printed in Singapore.

11 2016

CONTENTS

ILLUSTRATIONS

Figures

Maps

PREFACE TO THE SECOND EDITION

Any serious introduction to a field of study should take into account the most significant ideas being debated in that field. This has not been the norm in the field of Islamic studies. Many of the most interesting debates in the field over the last thirty or so years have been slow to find their way into introductory texts. It is rare, for example, to find John Wansbrough's work on the Qur'ān mentioned in a college textbook, even though his studies continue to exert enormous influence twenty-five years after their publication. Wansbrough's work is so technical that perhaps the omission can be excused, but what of Joseph Schacht or Ignaz Goldziher? Some of the questions these and other scholars raised are deeply controversial, calling into question the traditional story of Muhammad's life, how the Qur'ān came into being, and the nature of early Islam. Yet no student, Muslim or not, should come away from an introductory course in Islam without knowing these names and understanding something of the challenges they have posed to traditional understandings of Islamic origins. To ignore them is like teaching a college-level New Testament course without mentioning Rudolph Bultmann or discussing form criticism. Consequently, my aim in the first edition of this book was to introduce students to critical questions in the field in an original and lively way.

In this second edition, while retaining this goal, I have set out to fill some of the gaps in the first edition. Changes begin with an entirely new introductory chapter which aims to give students a sense of the diversity of the contemporary Islamic world and which introduces the key themes of the book. The early chapters of the book have been reordered to more closely match the usual order of topics in introductory courses on Islam. In particular, I have shifted chapters on Muhammad and the Qur'ān forward, and moved discussion of the Islamic conquests and the geographical expansion of Islam to a separate section. Throughout the book I have given greater attention to everyday Muslim practice, and especially to the experience of women in Muslim societies. A revised final chapter on Islam in the twenty-first century surveys the most important currents in recent Islamic thought, including discussions of Islamic liberalism, Islamic feminism, and Islam in the West.

While the changes in this new edition are substantial, the basic thrust of the book remains unchanged. My major aim has been to raise questions that are too seldom addressed in introductory texts, and the teachers and students who will find this book most useful will be those who are looking for a critical introduction to the major issues in the field of Islamic studies.

I am grateful to the many readers who have taken the trouble to comment on the first edition. I appreciate their many suggestions, and especially their correction of errors, and I regret that I have been unable to incorporate all of their valuable suggestions. The errors that remain are my own.

I am, as always, more in debt to my wife Carol than I can hope to express. This work is dedicated to her and to my children, Sarah, Ruth Anne, and Stephen.

SOURCE ACKNOWLEDGMENTS

The editor and publisher wish to thank the following for permission to use copyright material.

A. J. Arberry, 1955. *The Koran Interpreted*. New York: Macmillan and London: Allen & Unwin. Reprinted by permission of HarperCollins Publishers Ltd © 1955 Arthur J. Arberry

P. Crone, 1987. *Meccan Trade and the Rise of Islam*. Copyright © Princeton University Press. Princeton, NJ. Reprinted by permission of Princeton University Press

O. Grabar, 1996. *The Shape of the Holy: Early Islamic Jerusalem*, p. 55. © Princeton University Press, Princeton, NJ. Reprinted by permission of Princeton University Press

O. Grabar, 1996. *The Shape of the Holy: Early Islamic Jerusalem*. p. 58. © Princeton University Press, Princeton, NJ. Reprinted by permission of Princeton University Press

R. Hattox, 1988. *Coffee and Coffeehouses: The Origins of a Social Beverage in the Medieval Near East*. © University of Washington Press, Seattle, WA. Reprinted by permission of The University of Washington Press

A. H. Johns, 1987. Tarique. In *Encyclopaedia of Religion*, ed. Mircea Eliade, vol. 14, p. 346

R. Nicholson, 1959. *The Kashf al-Mahjub of al-Hujwīrī*, p. 195. London: Luzac

Qushayrī, 1990. *Principles of Sufism*, trans. B. R. von Schlegell. pp. 14, 49, 116, 170, 177, 207, 274, 316–17, 327–8, 343. Berkeley, CA: Mizan Press

M. Sells, 1989. *Desert Tracings: Six Classic Arabian Odes*, pp. 48–56. © Wesleyan University Press, Middletown, CT. Reprinted by permission of the Wesleyan University Press

Every effort has been made to trace copyright holders and to obtain their permission for the use of copyright material. The editor and publisher will gladly receive any information enabling them rectify any error or omission in subsequent editions.

Unless otherwise noted, quotations from the Qur'ān are from Yūsuf 'Alī, *The Meaning of the Holy Qur'ān*, 6th edn., revd. Beltsville, MD: Amana Publications, 1989.

PART ONE

THE FORMATION OF THE ISLAMIC TRADITION

1

ISLAM IN GLOBAL PERSPECTIVE

The Problem of Defining Islam

The student who sets out to learn about Islam will soon face a problem something like this. If we were to draw a circle and designate the contents of that circle as the complete set of phenomena that fall under the rubric of Islam, how would we decide what would be included within the circle and what must be excluded? Provocative examples are easy to find. Do the actions and motivations of those who destroyed New York's World Trade Center or the London Underground bombers fall within the circle of Islam? Or should "true" Muslims abhor and repudiate such actions? To phrase the question in the terms of popular debate, is Islam a "religion of peace," or does it somehow promote violent action? The issue need not be limited to the question of violence, of course. Did the rigorous constraint of women's rights by the Ṭālibān of Afghanistan (or the present regime of Sa'ūdī Arabia) belong in the circle? And if so, how can the ideas of Muslim feminists like Amina Wadud or Fatima Mernissi also fit there alongside them? Was Elijah Muhammad, twentieth-century Prophet of the Nation of Islam, a Muslim? Did his assertion that the white man is the devil and the black man God represent a manifestation of Islam? Reaching back into Islamic history we can multiply the examples. Do the doctrines of Shī'īte Muslims who taught that 'Alī was an incarnation of God fall within the circle of Islam? What of the speculations of the Islamic philosophers who held that the universe is eternal and treated revelation as no more than philosophy for the masses? Were the targeted assassinations of the Nizārī Ismāʿīlīs "Islamic"? What of the modern Aḥmadiyya movement, rejected as heretical by many Muslims, but whose members insist they are a part of the Islamic community?

This exercise is useful because it quickly exposes a common confusion. For the believing Muslim the question is meaningful. It is essential and proper for the believer to determine where the boundaries of his faith community lie and to decide what represents Islam and what does not. But for those, whether believers or not, who seek to understand Islam as a movement of people and ideas in history, this way of thinking will not do. Whether we take an anthropological, historical, or religious studies perspective, all of the phenomena I have listed belong within the realm of the study of Islam.

But this raises a further problem that is rather central to the object of this book. If such conflicting movements of people and ideas all belong in the circle of Islam, how is one to go about introducing the whole lot of them? How is it possible to "introduce" such a diverse, indeed contradictory, set of phenomena? One common answer is that the attempt is in itself misleading and fruitless; the idea of "Islam" with an upper-case "I" is a false construct; we should rather speak of many different "islams" which must be examined as separate phenomena. To paraphrase a political maxim, all religion is local, and to imagine that all these different "islams" have something in common which can be labeled "Islam" is to imagine something that has no reality. Since I have already written several hundreds of pages in which I have tried to introduce Islam with an upper-case "I," it is too late for me to take this perspective. Nor am I inclined to do so.

My own perspective is best introduced by analogy. When a student sets out to study a language, Arabic for instance, she will soon learn that there are many quite different varieties of Arabic. Yet she will not normally trouble herself with the question of whether such different linguistic phenomena deserve to be called "Arabic." And she is quite right not to be troubled. Arab grammatical police might worry about demarcating the precise boundaries of true "Arabic," but from a common-sense perspective it is clear that all of the different dialects and varieties of the Arabic language rightly share the family name. Even if speakers of Maghribī and Palestinian Arabic may have some difficulty communicating, they all belong within the circle of Arabic speakers. In particular, the dialects they speak share sufficient common roots, sufficient common vocabulary, or a close enough grammatical structure to make it clear that they belong to the same family. It would be perfectly reasonable for a linguist to set out to survey the common structures, lexicon, and heritage of the whole family of dialects that are called Arabic, and so to introduce Arabic.

It is in that spirit that I have set out to introduce Islam here, and this book might be seen as an attempt to explain the evolution of the common grammar and vocabulary of Islam. Thus the Islamic feminist and the Ṭālibān both belong here, for although they are diametrically opposed in their conclusions, they make use of a common vocabulary. Similarly the Muslim pacifist and the suicide bomber, the Nizārī "assassin" and the Sunnī religious scholar who condemns him, are responding (albeit in very different ways) to a shared heritage – indeed, they are contending for control of that heritage.

Mapping the Islamic World

To restate the argument to this point, the set of phenomena that we label "Islam" is exceedingly varied, and there is enough complexity in the literatures, history, philosophy, theology, ritual, and politics of Islamic civilization to engage many lifetimes of study. Oversimplifying will not do. But keeping that danger in mind, we can still attempt to gain some sense of the big picture before our attention is consumed by details. There is a place, in other words, for the global view that excludes most detail as well as for the street-level view that includes it all.

A map turns out to be a useful starting point. If we peruse a map of the contemporary Islamic world, what will we notice? We can begin with a simple demographic survey. Map 1 is a simple map of the world's Muslim population by country. The first thing to notice about this map is that it includes the entire world. The time when we could depict the Muslim world on a single hemisphere is long past, although many cartographers have yet to catch on. The contemporary Muslim community, the umma, is worldwide. Muslims live, work, raise families, and pray everywhere, from China to California, from Chile to Canada; there is almost no place on earth where Muslims have not settled. This simple fact turns out to be both easily forgotten and immensely important to understanding contemporary Islam. The modern Muslim diaspora is shaping the course of Islam, and of the world. Many critical issues facing contemporary Muslims arise precisely because so many influential Muslims are German, French, British, Canadian, Dutch, or Australian. Muslims work throughout the world as scientists and scholars, teachers and doctors, lawyers and entrepreneurs, farmers and factory workers. Their responses to this geographical mobility and the pluralism of the varied societies in which they live fuel rapid change in Muslim communities, and significant conflict among Muslims as well as between some Muslims and their non-Muslim neighbors. The experience of Muslims as a truly worldwide community has stimulated new and pressing discussions of the relation of Islam to women's rights, human rights, bioethics, religious diversity, tolerance, and freedom of expression.

The worldwide controversy stirred by the publication in 2006 of inflammatory cartoon images of Muhammad in the Danish newspaper *al-Jostens* is a case in point. The publication of the cartoons, and the varied Muslim responses, were a product of a Muslim community that spans the globe. The cartoons were

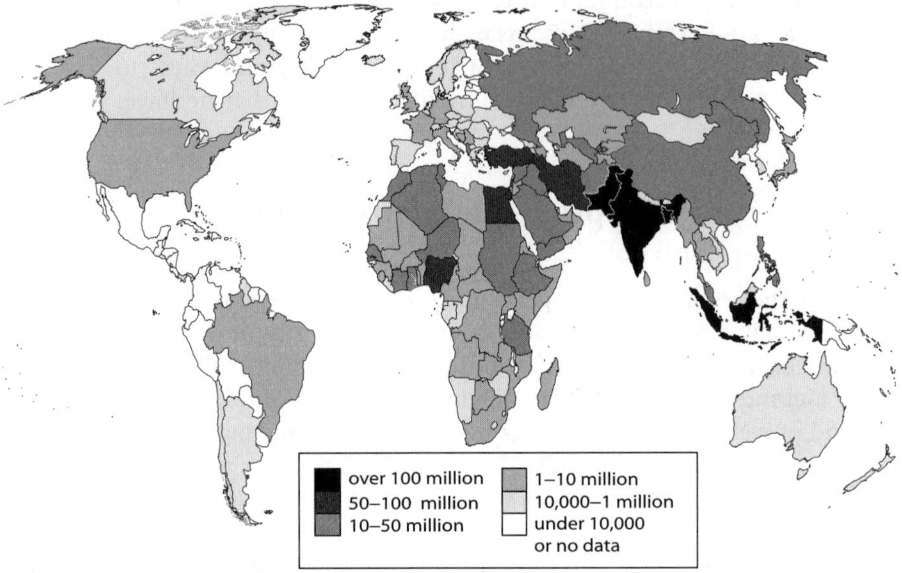

Map 1 Distribution of Muslim population by country
Muslims are concentrated in Asia, but significant numbers of Muslims now live on every continent. This map should be read with caution, however. Russia, for example, has a population of more than 14 million Muslims, but this population is not evenly distributed throughout its vast territory as the map seems to suggest, nor does Alaska have significant numbers of Muslims. China has a large Muslim population, but there is a great deal of uncertainty about its actual size. Population figures used for this map were drawn from the database at adherents.com.

published in the first place because the Muslim community in Europe is sizeable enough to motivate fierce debate about the compatibility of Islam with European cultural and political tradition. Authors like the pseudonymous Ba't Yeor raise the specter of "Eurabia," a Europe held hostage to Islamic radicalism because Europeans have failed to recognize the threat to freedom and to European tradition posed by Islam. The Muslim response to the cartoons was worldwide, however, and the fiercest reactions came from outside of Europe.

But while Islam is worldwide, our map also gives rise to a second, paradoxical observation: Muslims are heavily concentrated in Asia and Africa. More than 50 percent of the world's Muslims live in just eight countries: Indonesia, India, Bangladesh, Pakistan, Nigeria, Iran, Turkey, and Egypt. This list is surprising for two reasons. First, the majority population of only one of these, Egypt, is Arabic speaking. The range of cultures and languages for which the most populous Muslim countries are home is staggering. More than twice as

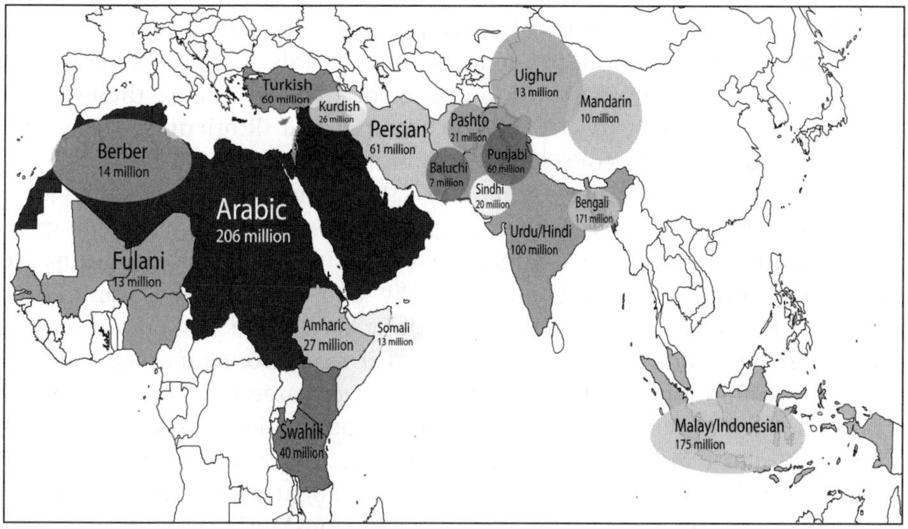

Map 2 Major languages spoken by Muslims
The map shows something of the linguistic diversity of the Muslim world. For a catalogue of all of the hundreds of languages spoken by Muslims, see the source from which the data for this map was drawn, Raymond G. Gordon, Jr., ed., 2005. *Ethnologue: Languages of the World,* 15th edn. Dallas, TX.: SIL International. Online version: http://www.ethnologue.com/.

many Muslims speak Indonesian, Bengali, or Urdu as speak Arabic. Map 2, portraying the major languages spoken by Muslims, hints at this cultural and linguistic diversity but also grossly understates it by leaving out hundreds of smaller languages.

The second surprise is that a great many contemporary Muslims live in religiously plural societies. In India, Muslims are, despite their numbers, dwarfed by the size of the majority population. China, with 40 million or more Muslims, presents a similar case. In both countries the Muslim minority faces real or perceived threats from the majority. Nigeria, too, is religiously divided. About 50 percent of its population is Muslim, 40 percent Christian, and 10 percent animist. Communal tensions there are high. Many other nations with significant Muslim populations – Sudan, Lebanon, the Balkan nations, Malaysia – are also multi-ethnic and religiously plural. Consequently a large number of contemporary Muslims do not live in Muslim majority societies. Rather, they live in societies in which they must live, work, and worship amongst non-Muslim neighbors.

We can add a final observation: among these most populous Muslim countries, most are former European colonies, and all faced significant economic and social upheavals in the twentieth century. During the last fifty years all have contended with high rates of poverty, uneven distribution of wealth, and the accompanying political turmoil. In other words, the vast majority of Muslims in the contemporary world live in societies which bore the brunt of colonialism, and which have experienced rapid and disorienting social and economic change in the course of decolonization.

To summarize: the Muslim community – the umma – truly spans the globe, and thus faces all of the challenges of globalization and pluralism; in a great many countries Muslims are a minority community; and, finally, Muslims are demographically concentrated in politically and economically tumultuous regions of the world. Gathered together, these varied facts make for a turbulent picture. We should hardly be surprised if many contemporary Muslims view their community as embattled and besieged. Large numbers of Muslims have suffered a great deal at the hands of European colonizers, Chinese communists, Hindu zealots, and homegrown tyrants. Many are not free to order their lives as conscience or community norms might dictate, either because they live as minorities in societies dominated by non-Muslims or because, even in Muslim-majority societies, they suffer under repressive regimes.

Arabs and Non-Arabs

But dwelling, as we have, on the diversity of the Islamic world, begs an important question. If the majority of Muslims are Indonesian, Indian, Bengali, Pakistani, Nigerian, or Chinese, then why *do* we tend to think first of Arabs and Arab culture when we think about Islam? And why do textbooks like this one spend so much space making the obvious point that non-Arab Muslims vastly outnumber Arabs, when we know quite well that much of the book will inevitably focus on the Arabic-speaking Middle East? Stereotypes become stereotypes for a reason, and in this case the reason is fairly simple. Because Islam originated in Arabia, because the Qur'ān is in Arabic, because the classical intellectual tradition of Islamic civilization was recorded in Arabic, and because Islamic religious ideas and cultural norms were rooted first of all in Arab culture – for all of these reasons Arabs exert and will continue to exert an influence on Islam disproportionate to their demographic strength. Important as it is, and although it is spoken by nearly 200 million Muslims, Indonesian will never be the classical language of Islam or the lingua franca of Islamic scholarship. Jakarta will never be the worldwide center of pilgrimage. It is too late for that. So long as Muslims continue to read the Qur'ān, study Islamic law, and value their heritage, Arabic and the Arabic-speaking world will remain of critical importance. This should be no more surprising than the observation that the Vatican, a tiny city-state in

Italy that still publishes documents in Latin, has an outsize influence on the worldwide community of Christians.

The reality, then, is that a relatively small population of Arabs exerts an outsize influence on the religious and intellectual culture of a far larger population of non-Arab Muslims. The result is a dynamic interaction between a centripetal pull toward uniformity and the centrifugal forces of cultural and linguistic diversity. We see this tension in medieval Muslim travel writers like Ibn Battuta. There was no end to the strangeness that Ibn Battuta encountered as he traveled through India, China, and Indonesia. Yet wherever he went he also found himself on familiar ground. Throughout Islamic history, and continuing into the contemporary period, Muslim practice has been constantly shaped by local environments, while local variations of Islam are constantly under pressure to conform to a uniform standard. We will see this pattern especially in the growth of ṣūfism, which is often adaptive to local practice, in contrast with the spread of various forms of fundamentalism, which favor uniformity with some ideal norm.

Sunnīs and Shīʿītes

There is more to the diversity of Islam than language, culture, and geography. In fact, the Muslim world is split by a major sectarian fault line. Roughly 80 percent of Muslims identify themselves as Sunnīs. About 18 percent call themselves Shīʿītes. Shīʿītes are themselves divided into several communities, and small sects make up the remaining 2 percent. Such a major schism seems to demand explanation, and among the first questions students of Islam ask is "What's the difference?" The short answer is that Shīʿītes and Sunnīs are divided over the questions of leadership and authority within the umma. The division is rooted in the early years of Islamic history when Muslims faced the urgent question of who should succeed Muhammad as leader of the Muslim community. Shīʿītes supported the leadership of Muhammad's cousin, ʿAlī, and his descendants. They came to see authority, both religious and political, as vested in divinely appointed leaders, beginning with ʿAlī. By contrast, Sunnīs adopted a pragmatic political stance. The Sunnī theory of the caliphate required that the leader of the Muslims be male, a member of the Prophet's tribe of the Quraysh, and meet certain basic qualifications for fitness. Beyond these broad expectations, it was up to the community to decide. Moreover, although the Sunnī caliphs had religious obligations and were expected to guard and defend Islamic values, they did not come to be viewed as sources of religious authority in their own right. Authority, for Sunnīs, came to be vested in texts – the Qur'ān and the Sunna – whereas for Shīʿītes it was focused on the family of the Prophet and its descendants, humans especially chosen by God to represent him on earth. Many other differences – in law, ritual, attitudes toward suffering, and eschatology – grew out of this basic difference over leadership. In particular Shīʿītes make martyrdom and redemptive suffering central values, and these values are given dramatic shape in annual celebrations during the month of Muḥarram.

These differences between Sunnīs and Shīʿītes are significant, but they would be easy to overplay. The two groups share more than divides them, and throughout most of Islamic history Shīʿīte communities were demographically dispersed amongst the majority Sunnī population. It was only after the emergence of the Safāvid empire in the sixteenth century that Iran and southern Iraq came to be almost exclusively Shīʿīte. Even in the contemporary Islamic world, where conflicts between resurgent Shīʿītes and Sunnīs are once again becoming important, it is striking how much the two communities have in common, and this raises a broader question: in the face of the stunning diversity among Muslims, what holds Islam together? Is there anything that *all* Muslims agree on, whether Sunnīs and Shīʿītes, Arabs and Indonesians, twelfth-century theologians and twentieth-century scientists? A simple reversal of our map exercise will focus the question. When we survey a map, we place ourselves at some imaginary point in space from which we pretend we can see all. And from that vantage point, we cannot help but be struck by the scope and variety of the world of Islam. But suppose we descend from our imaginary lookout and zoom in on one particular place at one particular time – a local mosque at the time of Friday prayers. This is a field trip that most readers will have little difficulty arranging. On such a visit, what will we notice? And in particular, what will we notice that will be more or less the same regardless of geography, ethnicity, or historical era?

Islamic Ritual

The first thing we are likely to notice, often before even arriving at the mosque, will be heard not seen. The voicing of the call to prayer, the adhān, whether by the unaided human voice or broadcast over loudspeakers, is part of the universal experience of Muslims. For many Muslims, these were the first words whispered into their ears. The words of the call (although not its intonation) are always the same, and always in Arabic. The founder of modern Turkey, Mustafa Kemal Atatürk, tried to change this, imposing a call to prayer in Turkish in the early part of the twentieth century. Only an iron hand could enforce such a policy, however. After 1950 democracy undid the change. Now, five times each day, should they choose to listen, Turks, along with Bengalis, Malays, and Canadians, are summoned to worship with the same Arabic words that Muslims throughout history have heard:

Allāhu akbar	God is great (repeated four times)
ashhadu anna lā ilāhā illa Allāh	I testify that there is no god but God (repeated twice)
ashhadu anna Muḥammadan rasūl Allāh	I testify that Muhammad is the Prophet of God
ḥayya 'ala al-ṣalāt	Hasten to prayer (repeated twice)
ḥayya 'ala al-falāḥ	Hasten to success (repeated twice)
[aṣ-ṣalāt khayrun min an-nawm]	[Prayer is better than sleep] (Sunnīs; morning only)
[ḥayya 'ala khayr al-'amal]	[Hasten to the best of works] (Shī'ītes only)
Allāhu akbar	God is great (repeated twice)
lā ilāha illa Allāh	There is no God but God (Sunnīs once, Shī'ītes twice)

It is worth noting the subtle differences between Sunnī and Shī'īte practice. These differences are sufficient to mark out a separate communal identity without, however, negating the essential unity of Muslim experience. It is also worth noting that the call to prayer incorporates the most elemental of Muslim credal statements, the Shahāda, or confession of faith. With the call to prayer we would seem to encounter the Islamic belief system at its most elemental, stripped of commentary or controversy: God is One and without rival, the messenger of the One God is Muhammad, and worship is God's most basic requirement of his creatures. We will have plenty of opportunity to complicate this picture as we proceed, but at this point it may be worth pausing to admire the simplicity and directness of this message. A person who takes this message to heart is bound to live with a certain seriousness and focus.

If the visitor heeds the summons of the adhān to come to prayer, he will arrive at the mosque to be greeted at the entrance by a collection of shoes. Here is an image with universality that extends well beyond even the Muslim community. The removal of shoes marks the borderline between sacred and profane space. As we enter the mosque the shoes remind us that we are leaving the marketplace and the mundane world behind, entering what Mircea Eliade calls sacred space and sacred time.

The mosque itself has few universal features. It may or may not have a dome, minarets, a pulpit, a source of flowing water for ritual ablutions, or a niche, the miḥrāb, indicating the direction of prayer. The mosque, at its most basic, is simply a place of worship as its Arabic designation, masjid, communicates. Any space can be transformed into a masjid, whether a rectangle marked out in the sand, an empty office, or a rented church basement. Mosque architecture has been remarkably varied through Islamic history, although modern times and Sa'ūdī Arabian money have brought increasing pressure toward uniformity.

Figure 1.1 A Muslim father whispers the call to prayer to his newborn child. Ideally, the words of the adhān are the first words heard by a Muslim infant, and will be heard at the start of every act of worship throughout his life. Photo: World Religions Photo Library/Alamy

What goes on once the worshiper enters the sacred space and joins other worshipers for prayer is also remarkably uniform, and like the call to prayer, is part of the universal experience of Muslims. We will have occasion to describe the detailed requirements of Muslim prayer in chapter 10. For now it is sufficient to note that believers face the same direction, toward Mecca, they recite the same passages of the Qur'ān that generations of Muslims have recited, and they follow a prescribed pattern of movements and prostrations that has

Figure 1.2 Shoes outside a mosque in Xian, capital of Shaanxi province, China. The removal of shoes is a visible indicator for Muslims of entry into sacred space and time. Photo: Eitan Simanor/Alamy

remained uniform for centuries. The ritual prayer, in other words, is a universal aspect of Muslim experience, even for those Muslims who may have abandoned it. It is a ritual that any Muslim, whether Sunnī or Shīʿīte, whether from the tenth century or the twenty-first, will immediately find familiar not just in broad outlines, but in specific detail.

The uniformity of practice demonstrated in the ritual prayer is mirrored in other aspects of Muslim religious practice. The rites followed by pilgrims to Mecca when they perform the Ḥajj and the rules followed by Muslims when they fast during the month of Ramaḍān, are all remarkably uniform. So too is the value placed on charitable giving, zakāt. Indeed, it is with good reason that every introduction to Islam begins by outlining these so-called pillars of Islam. Like pillars in a mosque, the words of the Shahāda, the practice of ṣalāt, the rules for fasting, the rites of pilgrimage, and the value of generosity enshrined in the notion of zakāt seem to remain fixed, solid, and unchanging. In contrast with many other aspects of Muslim experience, essential Muslim religious duties have remained remarkably stable over time and across cultures.

How can we account for this picture, at once so diverse and so valuing of uniformity? On the one hand, the Islamic world is dizzyingly varied, and one

Figure 1.3 Variations in mosque architecture in Indonesia. Above, the Jepara masjid in Indonesia, showing the influence of Javanese Hindu architecture; below, the Grand Mosque in Banda Aceh (the photograph was taken before the mosque was inundated by the 2004 tsunami). Photos: Jepara masjid © Bettmann/CORBIS; Grand Mosque: © Kees Metselaar/Alamy

cannot presume to know what any given Muslim values or believes without first asking. Indeed, the most practical nugget of advice I usually offer newcomers to the study of Islam is not to assume that one's textbook will be reflected in reality. A new Muslim acquaintance may, in the modern world, be influenced quite as much by Marx as by Muhammad. Yet in the face of all of the diversity of the Muslim community Islam still offers Muslims a remarkably stable set of core practices – what I called earlier in this chapter a common vocabulary and grammar of Islam – that would be recognizable as in some sense "Islamic" by any Muslim of any cultural origin or any historical period.

What to Expect from This Book

How this came about – how Islam came to be what it is today in all of its variety and its paradoxical unity – is the story I have set out to tell in this book. It is a story that is first of all rooted in history, and to begin to explore that history we begin well before the rise of Islam. Part I explores the historical and religious context of the rise of Islam, and surveys the central elements of the Islamic tradition. We begin with pre-Islamic Arabia, and are immediately faced with a critical question: how significant is the Arab background for understanding the rise of Islam? Is sixth-century Arabia a credible context for the rise of a new, vigorous monotheistic faith and a vibrant civilization? And, if not, where should we look for the "cradle" of Islam? These questions will lead us, in chapter 3, on an exploration of Near Eastern civilization and religion before the rise of Islam.

With chapter 4 we begin to examine the sacred history of Islam, beginning with the key narrative in that history, the life of Muhammad. The story of Muhammad, we will find, is far more colorful and fantastic than many modern treatments of his life allow and it is rooted squarely in the religious context of the Near East. Chapters 5 and 6 take on the two thorniest questions in the field of Islamic studies – how the Qur'ān came into its present form, and the authenticity of the ḥadīth literature on which the traditional story of Islamic origins, including the life of Muhammad, is based. It is in these chapters that we will have to contend with two centuries of critical scholarship that has increasingly brought into question the traditional account of how Islam came into being.

In part II we turn from sacred history and the formative elements of Islam to the complex historical context in which Islamic civilization grew to maturity. We begin with the Arab conquests. The conquests stand as one of the great turning points of world history, but how much really changed in the Near East? Less, it turns out, than we sometimes imagine. Chapter 8 examines the worldview of the early Arab conquerors. In this formative phase in the shaping of Islamic identity, what did these new rulers of the world believe, what motivated them, and how do we know? Finally, in chapter 9, we follow the story forward to the rise of the ʿAbbāsid caliphate, the maturing of Islamic political thought, and the emergence of the major schisms in Islam.

Part III surveys the great institutions of Islamic civilization in its maturity, beginning with Islamic law in chapter 10. The elucidation of God's law preoccupied the greatest minds of the Islamic world, and the resulting system was a signature achievement of Islamic civilization. The ideals of Islamic law continued to give the world of Islam unity and coherence long after it had fragmented politically. By comparison with the law, and in contrast with its status as the queen of sciences for Christians, Islamic theology was a lowly stepchild. But it is in the field of theology that we most clearly see the articulation of a distinct Sunnī worldview. Finally, in chapter 12 we turn to the spiritual center of Islam, ṣūfism. These three great institutions – the law, theology, and ṣūfism – are the defining features of Islam in its maturity. In combination they gave it the coherence, the brilliance, and the resiliency that marked Islamic civilization at its height.

This resiliency would be severely tested in history, however, especially in the modern period. Part IV examines Muslim responses to the challenge of history and patterns of renewal and reform in Islam. The ways in which Muslims met the challenges of the Crusades and the Mongol invasions are both of intrinsic interest and illuminating for our understanding of what would follow. What did follow was first of all a florescence of great Islamic empires on the eve of modernity. The great "gunpowder empires" – Ottoman, Safāvid, and Mughal – arose simultaneous with the first foreshadowings of Western power, and the religious environment in these empires had a profound effect on Islamic responses to Western imperialism. From the eighteenth century on, the power and pervasiveness of Western civilization has proved to be a challenge unlike any in Islamic history. The heart of the final section is an examination of the varied responses of Muslims to the West, and the effects that the encounter with the West has had on developments in Islamic law, theology, and worldview. The concluding chapter 5 surveys the major challenges facing Muslims in the twenty-first century, particularly the challenges of pluralism, of violence, and of feminism.

Essential Resources for the Study of Islam

The *Encyclopaedia of Islam* (*EI*) will be the student's best friend in any serious study of topics related to Islam. This massive work is difficult to get to know, but will abundantly repay the effort. *EI* comes in two editions, and the second, only recently completed and recognizable by its oversized green volumes, is naturally more up to date and thus preferred. Most college libraries will have a copy, and an electronic version is now available from the publisher, E. J. Brill. For those who cannot access the full *Encyclopaedia*, an abbreviated volume of excerpts from the first edition is available in *The Shorter Encyclopaedia of Islam*.

So much for the good news. The bad news for the newcomer to the field is that headwords in *EI* are given in transliterated Arabic. Thus if one is interested in Islamic mysticism, one must know to look under *Taṣawwuf* rather than *Ṣūfism*. Consequently, non-specialists will need to make frequent use of the subject index. The *Encyclopaedia* also has other peculiarities. The system for transliterating the languages of the Islamic world, for instance, uses "dj" rather than the now more common "j," and "Ḳ" rather than "q." Once these hurdles are overcome and the desired entry found, the articles themselves will prove dense and daunting. They are written by specialists for specialists. Still, many of the entries represent the definitive word, sometimes the only word, on their particular topic and all of the articles supply extensive bibliographies.

Serious research on Islam is unimaginable without *EI*. But in addition to the *Encyclopaedia of Islam*, there has recently been a frenzied rush to publish other encyclopedias with relevance to Islam; some of them are quite good and draw more heavily on the work of younger scholars than the staid and ponderous *EI*. Among these John Esposito (ed.), *The Oxford Encyclopaedia of the Modern Islamic World* (1995) and the *Encyclopaedia of Islam and the Muslim World* (2004) are worthy of mention. A number of reference works, while not specifically focused on Islam, provide excellent coverage of topics related to Islam, sometimes in a much more accessible manner than *EI*. Among these Mircea Eliade (ed.), *The Encyclopaedia of Religion*, and André Vauchez (ed.), *The Encyclopaedia of the Middle Ages*, stand out, often providing a convenient starting point for many topics.

For the beginning student searching for a guide to the most important books on Islam, Charles Adams's *Reader's Guide to the Great Religions* (1977) provides an excellent starting point, although it is now dated. Stephen Humphries provides a more recent and somewhat more technical bibliographical introduction to the field, geared toward graduate students, in his *Islamic History: A Framework for Inquiry* (1991). Other bibliographical guides include Derek Hopwood and Diana Grimwood-Jones's *The Middle East and Islam* (1972), Jean Sauvaget's *Introduction to the History of the Muslim East* (1965), and George Atiyeh's *The Contemporary Middle East 1943–1973* (1975). It will not be long, however, before most serious students of Islam will have to face J. D. Pearson's *Index Islamicus, 1906–1955* (1958) and its many supplements. *Index Islamicus* lists just about every article written about Islam in a European language. The trick is to decipher its idiosyncratic organization. The index is arranged topically, with the list of topics given at the front of each volume, and because there are many separate volumes without a comprehensive index the print edition is laborious to use. An electronic version is now available, making bibliographic research in Islamic Studies a great deal easier.

Two of the best short introductions to Islam are H. A. R. Gibb's *Mohammedanism* (1969) and a rejoinder to Gibb's book by one of his most gifted Muslim students, Fazlur Rahman's *Islam* (1972). Among more ambitious surveys of Islamic history, Marshall Hodgson's three-volume *Venture of Islam* is unrivaled. Other such surveys include Ira Lapidus, *A History of Islamic Societies* (1988) and Gustave E. von Grunebaum's three volumes, *Classical Islam* (1970), *Medieval Islam* (1953), and *Modern Islam* (1962). Classics in the field include Bertold Spuler's *The Muslim World: A Historical Survey* (1960) and Carl Brockelmann's *History of the Islamic Peoples* (1947). *The Cambridge History of Islam*, edited by P. M. Holt, and Ann K. S. Lambton (1970) is also worth a look. A handy chronology, although confined to the Middle East, is available in Jere L. Bacharach, *A Middle East Studies Handbook* (1984). Much more detailed chronological tables are found in Clifford Bosworth's *The Islamic Dynasties: A Chronological and Genealogical Handbook* (1967).

Many anthologies of Islamic texts in translation are now available, among them F. E. Peters, A *Reader on Classical Islam* (1994c), A. J. Arberry, *Aspects of Islamic Civilization as Depicted in the Original Texts* (1964), Bernard Lewis, *Islam: From the Prophet Muhammad to the Capture of Constantinople* (1987), and James Kritzeck, *Anthology of Islamic Literature* (1964). Finally, for lovers of maps, several good atlases are available, including Harry W. Hazard's *Atlas of Islamic History* (1954) and R. Roolvink's *Historical Atlas of the Muslim Peoples* (1957).

If this list seems rather daunting for the beginner, it is perhaps worth reminding ourselves that the development of Islam spans fourteen centuries, that the Islamic world encompasses a vast range of languages and cultures which now span the globe from China to North America, that about one-fifth of the world's people call themselves Muslims, and that many of those billion-plus people disagree vehemently with one another on the most basic matters of faith and practice. One cannot begin to study such a subject without some effort. Those who shy away from complexity had better stop here.

2
ARABIA

The story of Islam begins in the Arabian peninsula, and the great puzzle of early Islamic history is the sheer unlikeliness of its beginnings. A thoughtful Arab living in Mecca a short time before the rise of Islam would have had every reason to laugh out loud at the suggestion that Arabs would soon be world rulers, representatives of a new universal faith, and purveyors of a vibrant civilization. What would such an Arab observer have seen as he looked around at his world?

Geography

Our imaginary observer would, first of all, have seen desert. Two huge deserts fill almost a quarter of Arabia. If we imagine the Arabian peninsula as a great ax blade slicing into the Arabian Sea, its northern edge, where the ax handle might connect, is joined to the fertile regions of Syria and Iraq by one great desert, the Nafūd. To the south, the notched blade edge stretches from Oman in the east to the Yemen in the west and is separated from the rest of the peninsula by a great and forbidding desert, the Rubʿ al-Khālī or empty quarter. Two geographical features break the pattern. First, the thick top of the ax blade along the peninsula's western edge, a narrow coastal region called the Ḥijāz, is punctuated by oases. The biggest of these – Yathrib, Najrān, and Tabūk – are sufficient to support agriculture and a sizeable sedentary population. Second, the southern coastal region of the Yemen – an area the Romans called Arabia

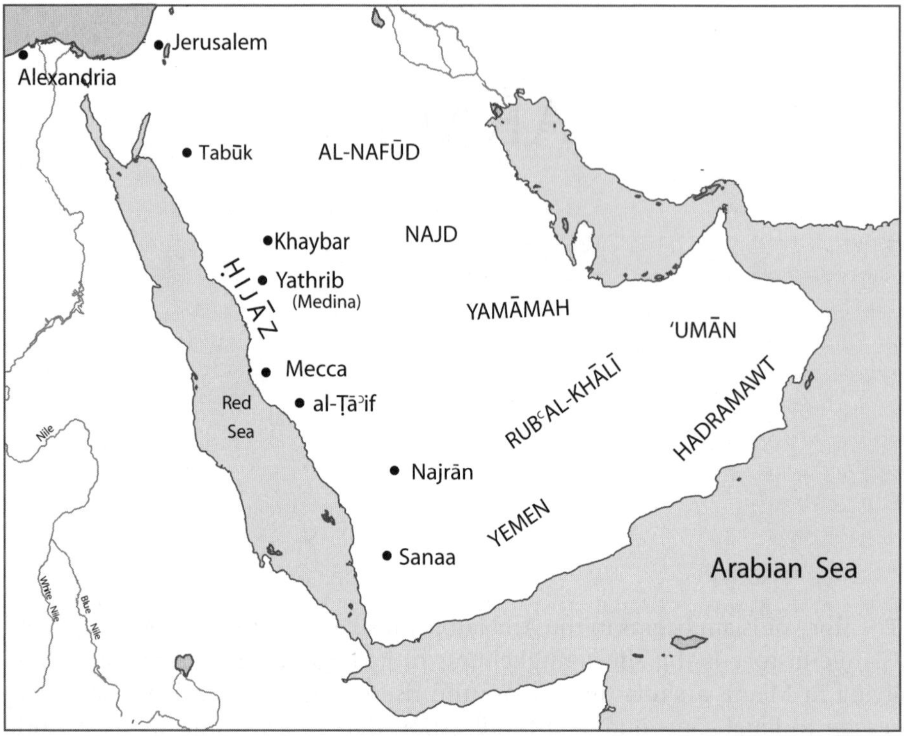

Map 3 Major regions and settlements of the Arabian peninsula, ca. 600 CE

Felix (Happy Arabia) – enjoys monsoon rains and is the only region of the peninsula to support a significant agrarian civilization prior to the rise of Islam.

If our sixth-century Arab observer was to feel any suspicion of significant events looming, we might expect him to look south. There, at least, a significant agricultural economy was possible which might support a sizeable agrarian state. In fact the south was the site of Ḥimyar, Arabia's only significant pre-Islamic state. Moreover, southern Arabia was better integrated, economically and politically, with surrounding civilizations – Abyssinia, Rome, and Persia – than any other region of the peninsula. But even in the south the prospects for sixth-century Arabs were hardly promising. In the two or three centuries before the Arab conquests the agriculture of Yemen experienced a marked decline. Irrigation infrastructure was crumbling, culminating in the destruction of the famous Ma'rib dam, and the region had become a pawn in regional politics, enduring invasions first from the Persians and then the Abyssinians. As it turned out, southern Arabia played a minor role in the Arab conquests or the rise of Islam. The only other agricultural regions, the oases of the Ḥijāz, turned out to be more significant, but for reasons unconnected with agriculture.

Aside from settled agriculture, the Arabian peninsula offered a rather limited range of economic options: camel and sheep pastoralism, and trade. We will turn to the important question of trade below, but first something needs to be said about pastoralism, and particularly camel herding, an occupation for which the Arabs are stereotypically famous. The Arabs are themselves to blame for this stereotype. The very word *'Arab* refers, in the first instance, to a Bedouin nomad, and the adoption of the label Arab as a self-designation elevates pastoral nomadism to a sort of ethnic ideal.

Pastoralists, of course, live off the produce of herds: milk, meat, bones, and hides, along with whatever can be made from these. Many pastoralists move around in regular patterns to find grazing lands for their herds – in which case they are not mere pastoralists, but nomadic pastoralists. Pastoralists also tend to be fairly heavily dependent on sedentary communities to supply them with anything that cannot be milked or manufactured from a sheep, goat, or camel. Consequently, although pastoral life has a romantic reputation, it is not a natural path to wealth. Nor do pastoralists tend to leave much of a cultural legacy. From the perspective of more settled peoples, pastoralists are at best symbols of a simpler and nobler life, at worst parasites.

Pastoralists depend on, feed off, and occasionally overrun civilizations. They are not famous for creating them. There was nothing in the pattern of sixth- and seventh-century Arab Bedouin life or culture to suggest an exception. The Bedouin Arabs of pre-Islamic times left few material remains for us to remember them by. The one legacy they seem to have left behind in large quantity is poetry. This is not surprising. Poetry weighs little, is easily passed on, and, under the right conditions, is remarkably enduring.

Pre-Islamic Poetry

Early Arabic poetry follows a set form known as the qaṣīda, which is best introduced by example. The following excerpts are from one such qaṣīda, the *Mu'allaqa* of 'Antara rendered here by a gifted translator, Michael Sells. This (and every qaṣīda) includes certain set thematic units, and begins with a description of an abandoned campsite.

> Have the poets left anywhere
> in need of patching? Or did you,
> after imaginings,
> recognize her abode?
> O abode of 'Abla in al-Jawā'i,
> speak! Morning greetings,
> abode of 'Abla,
> peace!
> There I halted my camel mare,

Figure 2.1 Bedouin children in northern Arabia. The Bedouin are pastoral nomads and their patterns of life have shaped images of the Arab culture since before the rise of Islam. Photo: Dorothy Miller/Saudi Aramco World/PADIA

towering like a fortress above me –
to consummate the care
of one who lingers.

The nostalgia of the abandoned campsite triggers recollections of the beloved – recollections which give rise to a rich depiction of the beloved in nature imagery:

She takes your heart
with the flash edge of her smile,

her mouth sweet to the kiss,
sweet to the taste,
As if a draft of musk
from a spiceman's pouch
announced the wet gleam
of her inner teeth,
Fragrant as an untouched meadow,
bloom and grass
sheltered in rain, untrodden,
dung-free, hidden.

In the next thematic unit of the qaṣīda recollection of the beloved gives way to an account of the poet's journey, intertwined with, sometimes displaced by, a celebration of his camel or horse – a celebration which rivals and sometimes mirrors descriptions of the beloved:

At evening and at dawn she travels
on a pillow
while I spend the night
on a bridled black stallion,
My cushion the saddle
over his thick-legged,
full-flanked,
barrel-girthed frame.
Will a Shadanīyyan mare,
shut off from nurslings,
udders dry,
carry me to her dwelling?

In the final thematic unit of the qaṣīda the poet boasts of his strength, skill, and exploits:

If you let your veil down before me,
know that I am skilled
in seizing the horseman
in his coat of mail.
Praise me
as you knew me,
manner easy
until wronged.
Given wrong
I give it back,
rough as a taste
of bitter apple.
. . .

> How many an unadorned beauty's lover
> have I left thrown flat,
> jugular vein twitching
> like the mouth of a harelip.
> My hand beat him to it
> with a quick thrust,
> and a spray of blood
> the color of ʿAndam crimson.
>
> (Sells 1989: 48–56)

Through such poetry the Arabs left a literary legacy of haunting beauty that takes its place among the great works of world literature. Pre-Islamic Arab poetry is often made to bear a greater burden, however, pressed into service as the primary documentation of pre-Islamic Arab thought, religion, and culture. Much of what historians know, or think they know, of the pre-Islamic Bedouin they know from this poetry. And, as one historian has wryly commented, "the classical ode of the Arab is poor stuff for history" (Peters 1973: 45). Moreover, what we know of pre-Islamic poetry is what ninth- and tenth-century Arab editors knew and thought worth passing on. Consequently, the task of reconstructing the cultural and spiritual life of pre-Islamic nomadic Arabs is like reconstructing the cultural and spiritual life of nineteenth-century New England from an assortment of Emily Dickinson's poems selected and rather freely edited by an unsympathetic scholar. Dickinson's poems no doubt tell us something of the culture in which she lived, but are hardly sources of choice for historians.

Keeping in mind, then, that what we have of pre-Islamic poetry was recorded two centuries after the Arab conquests, in an environment as alien to the life of desert nomads as our own, and by Muslim scholars for whom this poetry was evidence of the spiritual bankruptcy of pre-Islamic Arabia, what picture does it give us? We will not be shocked to find that the nomadic Arabs sound like godless hedonists, as A. J. Arberry's translation of the famous *Ode of Ṭarafa* illustrates:

> Unceasingly I tippled the wine and took my joy,
> unceasingly I sold and squandered my hoard and my patrimony
> till all my family deserted me, every one of them
> and I sat alone like a lonely camel scabby with mange;
> yet I saw the sons of the dust did not deny me
> nor the grand ones who dwell in those fine, wide-spread tents.
> So now think, you who revile me because I attend the wars
> and partake in all pleasures, can you keep me alive forever?
> If you can't avert from me the fate that surely awaits me
> then pray leave me to hasten it on with what money I've got.
>
> (Arberry 1957: 86)

Montgomery Watt (1953: 24) imaginatively describes the complex of values and virtues reflected in such poetry as "tribal humanism." Among the chief of these virtues is muruwwa, manliness, which encompasses all that will display and protect a man's honor: courage, loyalty, generosity, sexual prowess. The poets value intense loyalty to clan and tribe, and are not at all squeamish about violence and vengeance. Honor, strength, and heroic deeds are the stuff of life. The heroic is tinged with the tragic, however. Much of this poetry, like the selection above, displays a striking pessimism with regard to time, death, and fate. These people are noble but world-weary, courageous but hedonistic, without hope and without God in the world.

The overall impression one gets from pre-Islamic poetry is that the pre-Islamic Arabs are in desperate need of Islam. Again, we should hardly be surprised. This poetry is preserved and passed on by later Muslims as part of an Arab national conversion story. "This is what we Arabs were like in the jāhiliyya, the time of ignorance," it suggests, "Wonderful poets to be sure, and courageous warriors, but shockingly godless and lawless barbarians." The Qur'ān presents a similar portrait of the Arabs, charging them with unmitigated pessimism. "There is nothing but our present life," they say, "we die, and we live, and nothing but Time destroys us" (45:24). Consequently, our image of the pre-Islamic Arabs is indelibly and pervasively colored by this national conversion narrative and the juxtaposition of jāhiliyya and Islam, barbarism and enlightenment.

Arab Religion

Other literary data on the pre-Islamic Arabs reinforce this contrast between jāhiliyya and Islam in a somewhat different way. A prolific eighth-century Muslim scholar named Ibn al-Kalbī produced a sort of encyclopedia of Arab religion which he called the *Kitāb al-Asnām*, or *The Book of Idols*. Ibn al-Kalbī's work reveals several purposes. Some of the gods and goddesses he describes are mentioned in the Qur'ān and much of the information he gives is intended to make sense of Qur'ānic allusions – the goddesses Allāt, Manāt, and al-'Uzza (now of *Satanic Verses* fame) who make a cameo appearance in Sūra 53:19–20, are dealt with prominently. Manāt was goddess of fate, al-'Uzza, the Arabian Venus, was the chief deity of the Quraysh tribe, and Allāt was a mother-goddess figure akin to the Babylonian Ishtar. Additionally, gods and goddesses appear in pre-Islamic Arab names and Ibn al-Kalbī had more than a passing interest in Arab tribal genealogy. But the dominant effect of *The Book of Idols* is to document the depths of religious corruption into which the Arabs had fallen since the founding of the Ka'ba, Mecca's temple and subsequently the most sacred of Muslim shrines, by Abraham and Ismā'īl, the biblical Ishmael.

Ibn al-Kalbī's catalogue of gods and goddesses subtly ridicules the vulgarity of Arab religion: the goddess Allāt was a cubic rock beside which a certain Jew used to prepare his porridge (Ibn al-Kalbī 1952: 14); whenever a traveler stopped for the night, he would select four stones, pick the best to be his god, and use the other three to support his cooking pot (ibid. 28). One pair of idols, Isāf and Nā'ila, had been lovers who committed adultery in the Ka'ba. They had been turned into stone for their crime (ibid. 24). The moral is clear. These are people desperately in need of a prophet to destroy their idols and to drag them out of ignorance.

Ibn al-Kalbī's attitude toward pre-Islamic Arab religion is not entirely without nuance. This is especially clear with regard to significant pre-Islamic ritual practices that were continued by Muslims. Three kinds of ritual are important carryovers: animal sacrifice, the circumambulation of sacred sites, and pilgrimage. These are connected, by Ibn al-Kalbī and other early Islamic sources, with Abrahamic monotheism, and the continuation of these practices by Muslims is thus justified as legitimately Islamic. In other words, anything that the Muslims retained from the time of the jāhiliyya – of which there was a good deal – could not possibly have originated in the jāhiliyya, but must have more ancient monotheistic roots.

Women in Pre-Islamic Arabia

The image of pre-Islamic barbarism passed on to us is especially pronounced in the depiction of women prior to Islam, a depiction that survives as a major topic in modern Muslim apologetics. Ibn al- Kalbī's work hints at the theme. Goddess worship is a particular mark of how far the Arabs had fallen, and the worst of the idols were goddesses. Along similar lines the Qur'ān ridicules the pagan Meccans for choosing female gods while preferring male children for themselves. The Qur'ān also harshly and repeatedly denounces the jahiliyya practice of burying female children alive. The resulting picture is grim. Pre-Islamic Arab women endured a hellish existence. If a girl survived to adulthood, she would find herself essentially the property of her father, then her husband, with no economic or social independence or rights. The poets' tendency to conflate the sexual charms of a woman with the qualities of his camel seems bound to offend both modern Western and Muslim sensibilities. Judged against this grim background, the rise of Islam brought a stunning improvement in women's status. The Qur'ān not only repudiated female infanticide, but gave women economic and legal status independent of their husbands and guaranteed daughters a share of inheritance.

While we have no reason to doubt the essentials of this account, the Islamic tradition itself gives us reason to think that there is more to the story.

Muhammad's first wife, Khadīja, is a case in point. Before her marriage to Muhammad, Khadīja was an independent and wealthy widow. She was, in fact, in a position to employ Muhammad as her agent, and it was Khadīja who proposed marriage. If we accept this account it is clear that there were some pre-Islamic Arab women who did quite well for themselves. Moreover, although pre-Islamic poetry treats women primarily as sexual objects, there is also a certain freedom and wildness about the portrayal that hints at a bigger picture.

Mecca and the Quraysh

If we take at face value the picture of the Arabs passed on to us by Ibn al-Kalbī and other later Muslims then the rise of Islam could only have come about by an act of God. Which, of course, is a good part of their point. Most modern historians have been reluctant to allow God to bear this burden alone, however. If neither South Arabian agricultural civilization nor nomadic pastoralism seem likely incubators for Islamic civilization, there must be some other possibility. For the majority of writers on Islam, the smoking gun is trade. The Arabs, we are told, were great traders. We are further told that in the century or so before the rise of Islam, overland commerce had transformed the economic and social life of the Arabs, particularly the Arabs of the Ḥijāz. In this economic transformation, the town of Mecca played a unique role, one particular tribe, the Quraysh, was uniquely placed to benefit, and one minor member of the Quraysh, Muhammad, was uniquely affected.

The seventh-century city of Mecca allegedly had three features which rendered it suitable as the birthplace for a new religion and civilization: an important religious shrine, the Kaʿba; an annual pilgrimage connected with the shrine; and a tribal ruling elite, the Quraysh, who adroitly leveraged control over shrine and pilgrimage to political and economic advantage. The first of these features, the Kaʿba is, according to the Qur'ān, almost as old as creation itself; Adam built the original. Abraham and his son Ismāʿīl rebuilt the shrine after Noah's flood (2:125–7). After Ismāʿīl, the Kaʿba fell into pagan use for centuries until Muhammad cleansed it of idols. Between Ismāʿīl and Muhammad, Muslim historians remember two significant events. First, the shrine came under the control of Muhammad's tribal ancestors, the Quraysh. Second, a city grew up around it. Later Muslims credited both of these developments to one Qusayy, descendant of Ismāʿīl, unifier of the Quraysh, and ancestor of Muhammad. Sometime around 400 CE Qusayy became "King" of Mecca and he and his descendants become guardians of the Kaʿba (Peters 1994a: 13–14).

As guardians of the Kaʿba, the Quraysh controlled the annual pilgrimage, forerunner of the Muslim Ḥajj. This pilgrimage seems to have included many of the same ritual elements known to later Muslims: circling of the Kaʿba on foot, a procession of pilgrims to Mount ʿArafāt outside of Mecca, and an animal sacrifice at the nearby town of Minā. Not much is known of the meaning or origin of these rituals. But even if the religious roots of the pilgrimage remain somewhat obscure, the commercial opportunities were allegedly clear and abundant. The Ḥajj doubled as a sort of North Arabian trade fair. Not only did it provide a peninsula-wide marketplace by gathering far-flung tribes together, it also provided sanctuary from tribal conflict through a "truce of God" observed during pilgrimage months.

On the eve of the rise of Islam, during the late fifth century, a descendant of Qusayy named Hāshim finally put the pieces together and established the Quraysh as the center of a far-flung commercial empire. Hāshim allegedly inaugurated the long-range caravan trade which would figure so prominently in the story of the rise of Islam. Meccan caravans ranged from Syria in the north to Yemen in the south. By the time of Muhammad, according to this account, trade had produced all of the necessary ingredients for the birth of a new religion and civilization: astounding commercial prosperity, sustained contact with civilizations and religions outside of Arabia, a disruption of traditional Arab social and religious norms, and an accompanying spiritual angst. The Meccan Arabs were outgrowing the confines of their desert world. All that was needed was a catalyst – a spark to ignite the explosive potential that trade and prosperity had built up (Rodinson 1991; Watt 1953).

Plausible as it may sound, this story will not survive scrutiny. Certainly the Arabs did trade, the Meccans were surely involved in this trade, and Muhammad was, by all accounts, a merchant. But we have no evidence that this trade was particularly lucrative, and no indication that it was the cause of any social or religious upheaval. Recent scholarship has convincingly demolished any great optimism we might have about knowing what, how, and with whom the Meccans traded. That the Meccans did trade is not in dispute, but the evidence suggests that this trade was not in luxury goods or spices, but in the sort of goods that one might expect in the Arabian environment: leather and dates, for instance (Crone 1987a: 149–67). It was not the sort of trade that would put Mecca on the map (ibid. 134).

To summarize: a sixth-century Arab observer, as he looked about him, would have observed a good variety of interesting things: a fascinating nomadic and tribal society, some fine poetry, interesting religious rituals, and a small trading economy. He also would have noticed the growing influence of monotheism in the form of Jewish and Christian communities, and perhaps even some native experimentation with a sort of generic Arab monotheism. He may have taken note of a significant Christian presence in southern Arabia, concentrated at Najrān, and he might have been familiar with a number of Jewish tribes, most significantly in the oasis of Yathrib. But none of this would have suggested that the Arabs had the resources, not just to dominate, but also to dazzle the world with the vibrancy of their religious vision and the brilliance of their civilization.

The story of the rise of Islam in Arabia sounds implausible because it is implausible. There was simply nothing in Arabia to predict this outcome. It had none of the religious, cultural, or economic resources to nurture a great civilization or a great literary religious tradition. In the middle of the twentieth century H. A. R. Gibb, one of that century's great historians of Islam, contended that, in the formation of Islamic civilization, the desert played no creative part (Gibb 1969: 1). Gibb's judgment accords with common sense. Religions and civilizations do not emerge fully formed out of the desert; nomads are not transformed overnight into theologians, jurists, lexicographers, and political theorists. If we look to Arab history, Bedouin culture, or Meccan trade to explain the rise of Islam as a creative force in the world, we are bound to be disappointed. That Arab armies conquered much of the Mediterranean world is obvious. It is not at all obvious that what they brought with them was a fully formed religious tradition, let alone the seeds of a brilliant civilization.

The Gifts of the Arabs

So what did the Arabs bring? To properly evaluate the place of pre-Islamic Arabia in the development of Islam, we must modify our perspective. Rather than asking how Islam emerged from Arabia, it makes better sense to ask how Arabia came to loom so large in Islam. To adapt our perspective: if you move forward three centuries and imagine yourself an intelligent tenth-century Muslim surveying the world around you, what legacies of pre-Islamic Arabia would you have noticed?

The first and most important legacy of Arabia to Islam was Classical Arabic. Arabic is a Semitic language, part of a family of languages that includes Hebrew, Amharic, and Aramaic. All of these share common grammatical structures, most notably a system whereby most words can be traced to three letters that communicate the basic root meaning of the word. The origins of Arabic are ancient, and like other languages it has been and continues to be characterized by a diverse array of dialects. At some point – exactly when and how is a matter of dispute – a common literary language evolved which crossed tribal and geographic boundaries and which the Arabs called fuṣḥā or clear Arabic, meaning, presumably, Arabic that could be clearly understood by any Arab who knew anything. Our earliest texts in Classical Arabic are the qaṣīdas of the pre-Islamic poets and the Qur'ān. These were the "classics" which ninth- and tenth-century philologists and grammarians relied upon to formulate the standards of usage for Classical Arabic. Consequently, our judgment about when and how Classical Arabic developed will depend largely on the conclusions we reach about how and when the Qur'ān and pre-Islamic poetry originated (Wansbrough 1977: 85–118).

By the tenth century the triumph of Arabic in the lands conquered by the Arab armies was virtually complete. Other literary traditions – most notably Persian – continued to thrive, but Arabic dominated. Arabic became the language of statecraft, of law, of literature, and of scholarship of every kind. For our tenth-century observer, whether ethnically Arab or not, Classical Arabic – al-fuṣḥā – was as central to status and success as English was to a twentieth-century scholar. Indeed, Classical Arabic was not just the medium of scholarship, but its very focus. The root of early Islamic intellectual activity was philology, the meaning of words. To know anything was first of all to know Arabic. This dominance of Classical Arabic has shaped Islam throughout its history.

A second legacy of Arabia for later Muslims was a geographical orientation. As surely as English settlers in North America, Muslims knew where they had come from. Long after it had faded into political and economic insignificance, Mecca remained, psychologically and spiritually, the true center of the world and the axis around which it turned. For our tenth-century Muslim, all roads no longer led to Rome, or even to Jerusalem, but to Mecca. It would be difficult to overestimate the importance of this reorientation, psychologically and culturally. When Muslims look to their roots, no matter their homeland, no matter how distant culturally or linguistically, they look to Arabia. It is an orientation reaffirmed at least five times a day, every time a Muslim faces toward Mecca in worship. The geography and place names of Arabia are part of the vocabulary of Islam. Bengali poets, centuries and cultural light-years away, write verses in praise of Medina, the city from which Muhammad ruled. From Indonesia to Morocco, Muslims dream of going on pilgrimage to Mecca. Just as an Asian American might look to his ancestral home as the place of his roots, self-consciously appropriating Asian influences, so too Muslims and Arabia.

Finally, the Arabs bequeathed to Islam their tribal genealogy. Arab society was organized, and in large part continues to be organized, along tribal lines. What this means in practice is that the individual's identity and place in society are defined primarily by affiliation with a clan or tribe. Membership in a clan or tribe is, in turn, determined by real or imagined descent from a common ancestor. Thus the Banū Hāshim, the sons of Hāshim and the clan into which Muhammad was born, believe themselves to be common descendants of a certain Hāshim and distinguish themselves from the Banū Umayya, the sons of Umayya. Both the Banū Hāshim and the Banū Umayya believe themselves to share a common ancestor, however, and thus together belong to the tribe of Quraysh and call themselves Banū Quraysh. Group solidarity and loyalties are defined by tribal affiliation, and the tribe is the individual's chief source of protection. If a member of one's clan or tribe is killed or injured it is incumbent on other members of the clan or tribe to avenge the wrong.

This way of thinking – a sort of tribal ethos – continued well after the Arabs had taken their place as conquerors and imperial rulers. This is particularly evident in the early political history of Islam, to be discussed in greater detail in chapter 8, in which inter-tribal rivalry and warfare loom large. The earliest non-Arabs to become Muslims had to explicitly opt into this tribal system by becoming adopted members of an Arab tribe. A convert was labeled a mawla (pl. mawālī) or client, and had to have the patronage of a bona fide Arab to gain entrance into the community of Muslims. Even long after such explicit manifestations of tribal organization had faded, the tribal ethos continued in more subtle and enduring patterns. Many Muslim names, for instance, continue to reflect Arab tribal roots, so that an Indian Muslim might well call himself Qurayshī, making a claim to be affiliated with the Quraysh tribe. More significantly, when the brilliant fourteenth-century historian, Ibn Khaldūn (d. 1406), set out to analyze the social and political dynamics of Islamic societies in his *Muqaddimah,* he made tribal solidarity, ʿasabiyya, the centerpiece of his theory.

Arabic language, Arabian geography, Arab genealogy – these were the major bequests of the Arabs to Islam. They are insufficient to account for the central features of Islam, but they are among the raw materials out of which Islam was formed. Arabs wrote the story of the origins of Islam, beginning in the eighth century, and they wrote in Arabic and on Arab terms. When Syrian Christians, Iraqi Jews, Arameans, Persians, Africans, Turks, Mongols, Bengalis, Indonesians, and Chinese became Muslims and made their own peculiar contribution to the growth and definition of Islam, they had to find and accept their places in an essentially Arabo-centric metanarrative. Arabs were by no means the sole authors of the metanarrative – Persians in particular made a major contribution – but it was Arabic language, Arabian geography, and Arab genealogy which provided the basic materials for the story of the origins of Islam as it would begin to crystallize and be recorded in the eighth and ninth centuries. What the Arab environment manifestly did not bequeath to later Muslims was the law, dogma, or ritual – and perhaps not even the scriptural canon – that together came to define the Islamic tradition. All of this came together outside of the Arabian peninsula. Arabia gave to Islam the language in which the Islamic tradition was to be composed, but Islam in any form that we would recognize as such was the product not of the Arab environment, but of the creative interaction of Arabs with the religious and political environment of the Mediterranean world.

Resources for Further Study

The most elegant and readable general introduction to Arab history is Albert Hourani's *A History of the Arab Peoples* (1991). Hourani's interest leans heavily toward the modern period, and can be usefully supplemented by older surveys, especially Bernard Lewis' *The Arabs in History* (1966) and Philip K. Hitti's *History of the Arabs* (1963).

A number of good translations of pre-Islamic Arabic poetry are now available. Among the most elegant is Michael Sells, *Desert Tracings: Six Classic Arabian Odes* (1989) from which I have quoted above. Others include Arthur J. Arberry, *The Seven Odes: The First Chapter in Arabic Literature* (1957) and Charles J. Lyall, *Translations of Ancient Arabian Poetry* (1981). Our most extensive Muslim source for pre-Islamic Arab religion, Ibn al-Kalbī's *Kitāb al-Asnām* (*The Book of Idols*) is available in a translation by Nabih Amin Faris (Ibn al-Kalbī 1952). The most accessible surveys of Arabic literature are Reynold A. Nicholson, *A Literary History of the Arabs* (1998) and Hamilton A. R. Gibb, *Arabic Literature: An Introduction* (1963). On the development of Classical Arabic see John Wansbrough's *Quranic Studies* (1977).

Montgomery Watt's two volumes, *Muhammad at Mecca* (1953) and *Muhammad at Medina* (1956), present the conventional scholarly account of pre-Islamic Arabia based on Muslim sources. For a devastating critique of one aspect of that account, see Patricia Crone, *Meccan Trade and the Rise of Islam* (1987a). For important specialized studies see M. J. Kister, *Studies in Jāhiliyyah and Early Islam* (1980), M. M. Bravmann, *The Spiritual Background of Early Islam* (1972), and R. B. Serjeant, *Studies in Arabian History and Civilization* (1981).

3

THE PRE-ISLAMIC NEAR EAST

While the traditions of Islamic origins point to Arabia and the Arabs, to find the religious and cultural context in which Islam took shape we must turn north. The true incubator of Islam was the rich civilization of the Near East. On the eve of the rise of Islam the Near East was dominated by two great empires, the Eastern Roman, or Byzantine empire, centered on Constantinople, and the Persian, or Sāsānian empire, with its capital at Ctesiphon near present-day Baghdad. The two empires were remarkable for their success in maintaining political and administrative unity, for their intense military rivalry with one another, and for a growing role as patrons and protectors of religious orthodoxies. Both had become, by the time the Arabs arrived, confessional empires – the Byzantines as protectors of Orthodox Christianity and the Sāsānians as patrons of Zoroastrian orthodoxy. For all of these reasons – their success, their unity, their rivalry, and their confessional stance – it is tempting to imagine the Near Eastern world of late antiquity in black and white, divided between two great monolithic states engaged in a sixth-century version of the Cold War and pitting Greek against Persian, Christian against Zoroastrian, civil state against militarist, West against East.

The reality is not so neat, and far more colorful. In fact, by the end of the sixth century the great empires were an increasingly threadbare backing to a dazzling and dizzying patchwork of ethnicities, languages, and religious allegiances. The Byzantine emperors reigned over Greek, Syriac, Aramaic, Arabic, and Coptic speakers, while, as befitted rulers of the New Rome, they conducted their own business in Latin (Brown 1971: 138). Besides Orthodox Dyophysites, loyal to the official imperial creed, Christian subjects of the empire included significant numbers of Jacobite Monophysites, Coptic Monophysites, and Nestorians. Other small but widely distributed heresies dotted the religious landscape, among them Donatists, Montanists, Marcionites, Melitians, Quartodecimans, and Luciferians. In the Persian empire, Aramaic speakers outnumbered Persian speakers, and imperial subjects included Arabs, Armenians, Daylamites, Khwarazmians, and Kurds. The official creed of the empire, Zoroastrianism, had to contend with Nestorian Christians, Monophysite Christians, Jews, Manichaeans, Buddhists, Hindus, and followers of the fifth-century communist prophet, Mazdak. If we are to understand the religious environment in which Islam grew to maturity, it is not to the comparatively simple and uncluttered desert world of Arabia that we should look, but to this colorful and complex patchwork of creeds, sects, prophets, and saints that made up the religious life of the Near East.

Christianity in the Near East

Christianity dominated the Near Eastern religious patchwork, but it was a Christianity divided into three large pieces, and countless smaller ones. For three centuries Christians had been a persecuted minority in the Roman empire. The faith began when Jewish followers of a Palestinian teacher, Joshua son of Joseph, made the startling claim that their rabbi was the expected Messiah, and the more shocking assertion that he had risen from the dead. The followers of Jesus Christ (as Greek speakers called him) were galvanized by this certainty, and they fanned out to Jewish communities throughout the Roman empire spreading the good news of a Messiah and Savior who had defeated death. A brilliant follower of Jesus, Saul of Tarsus, vigorously argued that this Gospel, or "Good News," was for Gentiles as well as Jews. Paul (his Greek name) became a tireless missionary, and by the end of his life Christian communities had sprung up in almost every major urban center of the Roman empire. Three centuries after Paul the Emperor Constantine became a Christian, and a once provincial Jewish sect became the official creed of the empire.

When Constantine conquered Byzantium (later renamed Constantinople) in 324, he came there as the first imperial protector of the Christian faith, but it was a faith in danger of being torn apart by theological controversy. Controversy centered on the question of the relative weight of divinity and humanity in the person of Jesus. Records of the life of Jesus preserved in the Gospels left no doubt that Jesus was truly human; he had a real body, he ate, he drank, he slept, he suffered real pain, and he died. The Gospels and other early Christian writings also left no doubt that Jesus claimed divinity, that his followers believed him to be divine, and that his resurrection from the dead proved it. But how could Jesus be both man and God, both finite and infinite, mutable and immutable?

Arius, an Alexandrian priest, argued on the basis of the uniqueness, self-existence, and immutability of God that Jesus, who is mutable, cannot be God. To Arius and his followers, Jesus, although the Son of God and worthy of worship, was a created, finite being and did not share attributes unique to God. In 325 Constantine convened the Council of Nicaea to consider Arius' challenge and became the first in a long line of imperial dabblers in theology. The Council roundly condemned Arius and established the foundations of an orthodox Trinitarian theology. Christ, as Son of God, was affirmed to be *homoousion tō Patri*, of one substance with the Father, and thus fully divine.

The creed of Nicaea won the day, although not without struggle, and the Arian heresy was snuffed out, at least in Eastern Christendom, by the end of the fourth century. But the Nicene solution opened a Pandora's box of other problems, and in the fifth century the Christological controversy again rose to the level of crisis. If Jesus was fully divine – of one substance with the Father – how should the relationship between his divinity and his humanity be understood? The issue was raised in practical terms: after Nicaea, pious Christians were in the habit of honoring Mary, the mother of Jesus, with the title Theotokos, Mother of God. But in 428 the bishop Nestorius, only recently appointed patriarch in Constantinople, began to preach that Mary could not be called Mother of God, but only Christokos, Mother of Christ. She gave birth to a human being, not to God, and to suggest otherwise was blasphemous. By means of such arguments, Nestorius came to distinguish sharply between the human and divine *natures* of Jesus. According to Nestorius, God used manhood as a means of his self-manifestation and Jesus, a true man, was like a temple in which the fullness of God dwelt.

Nestorius' opponents, led by Cyril of Alexandria, saw in his teachings an undermining of the unity of Jesus' personhood. It seemed to many that Nestorius rendered Jesus more or less schizophrenic, dividing him into two *persons*. Nestorius repudiated the charge, but to no avail. He was already sufficiently disliked for other reasons and in 431 Emperor Theodosius II called a council at Ephesus to consider the case against him. The proceedings were inconclusive, marred by intrigue on both sides, but the eventual result was Nestorius' exile to the Egyptian desert. In 451 the Council of Chalcedon took up the unfinished work of Ephesus by unequivocally condemning Nestorius' teachings and affirming that all true believers must affirm that Mary was, indeed, Mother of God.

Nestorianism was not eradicated from Byzantium without leaving its mark in the form of a deep-rooted reaction against it. The followers of Cyril of Alexandria, Nestorius' nemesis, were not content with a simple disavowal of Nestorianism. While Nestorius might have overemphasized the humanity of Jesus, Dioscorus of Alexandria and Eutyches of Constantinople thought they could do without it altogether. They argued that Christ's humanity was so completely swallowed up in the divine that he did not have two natures, but rather a single, divine nature. By virtue of this reaction, Nestorius, indirectly and quite unintentionally, became the instigator of Monophysite doctrine.

The teachings of Eutyches and Nestorius represented the poles of fifth-century Christian doctrine, and the differences were not merely academic. This was a contest between two ancient Christian centers, Antioch and Alexandria; a contest between different styles of piety; and a contest over the relative weight of philosophy and scripture. The style of popular piety was as much at issue as intricacies of doctrine. The Christians of Alexandria were not about to undermine their adoration of the God-man by thinking of him as a Jewish carpenter, nor were they willing to reduce Mary to the level of just any mother. For the theologians of Antioch, such piety came at too great a cost, for it seemed to them a departure from the plain sense of the Gospels.

In the end, the pope trumped both Eutyches and Nestorius. The Emperor Marcian called a council at Chalcedon in 451 which, under the influence of Pope Leo, adroitly avoided a solution, opting instead for a confident affirmation of what was, to Monophysites and Nestorians alike, an absurdity: "Jesus Christ, at once complete in Godhood and complete in manhood, truly God and truly man . . . one and the same Christ in two natures, without confusion, without change, without division, without separation."

The cost of so affirming the unity of Christ's person was an enduring division of the church. The creed of Chalcedon became the official Christianity of the Byzantine empire, and dissenters scornfully labeled the bishops who toed the official line Melchites, emperor's men. Alexandria, on the other hand, remained true to the Monophysite teachings of Cyril and Eutyches, and took almost all of Egypt and much of Syria with it. Monophysitism also became the national creed of Armenia. Nestorians, pushed out of the Byzantine empire, became the church of the Persian empire.

Besides the big three – Orthodox Chalcedonians, Monophysites, and Nestorians – Christendom was dotted with numerous smaller sects. Marcionites, for instance, rejected the Old Testament and taught that the God of the Old Testament, the creator of the material world, was in fact an evil being. Melitians, Luciferians, and Donatists broke with the main body of the church over the question of whether those who apostatized under persecution could be readmitted to the church. According to these groups, the acceptance even of repentant apostates threatened the purity of the church. The largest of these groups, the Donatists, was limited to Africa, but for a time they dominated the church there. They suffered severely under official persecution in the fifth century, but bounced back in the sixth, and were thriving at the time of the Arab conquests. Manichaeans and other Gnostics also continued to influence Christian thought. The origins and doctrines of

Manichaeism will be dealt with more fully in the context of Persian religion, but despite its Zoroastrian roots, Manichaeans within Byzantine territory often represented their faith as a version of Christianity. Manī, the founder of the faith, had declared himself to be the Paraclete, the comforter promised by Jesus (see, for example, John 14:26). He also taught that the death of the historical Jesus on the cross was an illusion, a position distantly echoed in Islamic teaching (Widengren 1983).

Finally, there were several varieties of Near Eastern Christianity that are marked by Jewish influence. Jacob Neusner suggests that a "Jewish Christianity" was an important influence in the Near East, and that the influence of these Jewish Christians was especially strong in the Persian Nestorian church. Evidence from the Babylonian Talmud, completed shortly before the rise of Islam, suggests that a major threat to Rabbinic Judaism came from Jewish converts to Christianity (Neusner 1968, 3:12–16). Some brands of Christianity, in turn, displayed a strong Jewish influence. The Quartodecimans, for instance, distinguished themselves by insisting that Easter be synchronized with the Jewish Passover, celebrated on the 14th of Nīsān. The Elkesaites, an Iranian sect, displayed their Jewish–Christian roots by making a point of circumcision and Sabbath-keeping and condemning the apostle Paul.

In a frenzy of self-criticism, later Christians have been eager to blame the extraordinary success of the Arab conquests on these deep religious schisms within the Byzantine empire. There is something to the argument. Constantinople's suppression of schismatics was often severe. Churches were confiscated, meetings banned, and clergy fined or deported. The death penalty was rarely invoked, but under the Emperor Justinian heretics were declared incapable of making wills and debarred from public service (Jones 1986). Many provincial citizens had no particular reason to respond to Constantinople's distress with loyalty or love. Thus it should come as little surprise when we hear allegations of Egyptian Monophysites lending their support to the Arab invaders against their distant overlords in Constantinople.

What is perhaps more important from our perspective is that these theological squabbles had an enduring influence on the intellectual and theological environment of the Near East. Muslims were not immune and quickly caught the bug. As we will have ample opportunity to note, the Qur'ān itself makes a major foray into the Christological disputes of the day, forcefully advocating a position that emphasizes the humanity of Jesus and that sides with Manichaeans and Docetists. We need not accept any grand claims about particular influences on the Qur'ān in order to acknowledge that it is a document that clearly fits snugly into the Near Eastern environment and engages Near Eastern monotheism in all its variety. With the development of Islamic dialectical theology the effects of the Near Eastern intellectual environment become difficult to ignore. As we will see in later chapters, Muslim theologians discussed the Qur'ān in terms drawn from Christological disputes, and Muslim jurists studied God's law like rabbis.

Saints and Relics

To allow our image of Near Eastern religious life to be built entirely of creeds, church councils, and rarefied doctrinal disputes would be to miss more than half the picture. Near Eastern Christians were as preoccupied with saints, relics, and miraculous cures as with theology. The bones and bodies of saints, hermits, and martyrs, "cured the sick, gave children to barren women, protected travelers, detected perjurers and foretold the future" (Jones 1986: 957–64). Consequently, such relics were a hot commodity, and the search for bodies of famous saints and martyrs was sometimes frenzied. In at least one case recounted by Jones, villagers are reported to have anxiously awaited the death of a particular hermit, ready to pounce on his body as soon as he expired. The remains of the cross on which Jesus was crucified played an important role in the final round of wars between Byzantines and Persians.

This preoccupation with saints and relics was the popular outgrowth of the flowering of Christian asceticism. It was a tradition particularly strong in Syria and in Egypt, where St. Anthony had set the trend when he withdrew into the desert in 269. The colorful stories of St. Anthony's contests with the devil established the standard for later would-be saints. But it was Syrians who became what Peter Brown calls the "stars" of the ascetic movement. Two centuries after Anthony, St. Simeon (d. 459) inaugurated a uniquely Syrian fashion in asceticism by sitting atop a 50-foot-high pillar for forty years. In the following years such pillar saints proliferated. The tradition of asceticism and of wild-eyed holy men in the Near East did not end with the rise of Islam. Muslim ascetics and mystics, called ṣūfīs, would enthusiastically continue these Near Eastern patterns of ascetic piety.

Zoroastrianism

The religious environment of the Persian empire is nicely captured in a third-century inscription. Kartīr, the head of the Zoroastrian priesthood and an unabashed self-promoter, composed the following in the year 280:

> And afterwards, when Bahrām, the king of kings, the son of Shāpur, died, Bahrām, the king of kings, the son of Bahrām, the generous, the just, the friendly, the beneficent and pious in the empire, came to reign. And for the love of Ohrmazd

> and the gods, and for the sake of his own soul, he raised my rank and my titles in the empire . . . And in all the provinces, in every part of the empire, the acts of worshiping Ohrmazd and the gods were enhanced. And the Zoroastrian religion and the Magi were greatly honored in the empire. And the gods, "water," "fire" and "domestic animals" attained great satisfaction in the empire, but Ahriman and the idols suffered great blows and great damages. And the [false] doctrines of Ahriman and of the idols disappeared from the empire and lost credibility. And the Jews, Buddhists, Hindus, Nazarenes, Christians, Baptists, and Manichaeans were smashed in the empire, their idols destroyed, and the habitations of the idols annihilated and turned into abodes and seats of the gods. (Boyce 1990: 112–13)

As a Zoroastrian priest, Kartīr saw himself as responsible for the religious purity of the empire and the stamping out of heresy. It was a big job, but Kartīr was up to it so long as he had the support of the Shāh. His inscription reflects two important features of the Sāsānian situation. First, Zoroastrianism was inseparably linked with imperial rule; second, the Zoroastrian establishment felt itself threatened by numerous challengers.

Figure 3.1 Zoroastrian fire ceremony. Zoroastrianism, the religion of ancient Persia and the official religion of the Sāsānian empire, was almost entirely displaced by Islam. Photo: HASAN SARBAKHSHIAN/AP/PA Photos

Zoroastrianism, or Mazdaism, is frankly dualistic, a feature which marks it as unique among Near Eastern religions. In Zoroastrian cosmology the spiritual world is characterized by a cosmic struggle between good in the form of Ahūra Mazda (Ohrmazd in Pahlawi) and the evil Ahriman. Like the other major Near Eastern religious traditions, however, Zoroastrianism is also a prophetic and scriptural tradition. The founder and prophet, Zarathustra, lived about 1000 BCE and his teaching was incorporated into the Avestas, the sacred texts of the Zoroastrians. It is a testimony to how thoroughly Islam displaced Zoroastrianism in Iran that the earliest surviving manuscripts of the Avestas date to the thirteenth century and include only about a third of the original scriptures. The chief symbol of the religion is fire, and the chief rituals make heavy use of fire, hence the Muslims incorrectly labeled Zoroastrians fire worshipers.

Zoroastrianism had never before and would never again permeate a society so thoroughly as it did the Sāsānian empire. According to the Sāsānian monarchy's official line, religion and the state are twins, inseparable and interdependent. The state patronized Zoroastrian priesthood and fire-temples, and the monarchs made free use of Zoroastrian symbols to support their legitimacy. In this symbiosis of religion and ruling authority the Zoroastrian empire was the mirror of the Byzantine empire and precursor to the Islamic.

Maintaining orthodoxy is a heavy responsibility, however, and as Kartīr's list indicates, religious challenges facing the Sāsānian empire were formidable. The most serious challenge was from Christianity, of which Kartīr lists two varieties, probably to distinguish Greek and Syriac-speaking Christians. He was writing before the Christological controversies of the fifth century, however, and by the sixth century, as we have seen, the Persian church was thoroughly dominated by Nestorians. Christians had a rocky relationship with their rulers, the degree of rockiness often depending on how much influence the likes of Kartīr wielded at court. The Zoroastrian priesthood's hostility to rival religions was balanced by the pragmatic needs of empire, and sometimes the influence of emperors' wives. In 562, Nestorians were granted official freedom, but proselytizing continued to be punishable by death.

Judaism

The Sāsānian empire was also home to important and historically influential Jewish communities. Jews had a presence in Mesopotamia from the eighth century BCE, but the most significant settlement of Jews took place after the Babylonian destruction of the Temple in Jerusalem in 586 BCE. Exiled Jews were concentrated around the canal system in central Babylon, where there were some villages made up entirely of Jews. A millennium later, Jewish

Figure 3.2 Rabbis studying Talmud. Photo: Israel images/Alamy

communities were still thriving in Sāsānian-ruled Iraq. Their lot was on the whole much better than that of the Jews in Palestine under Byzantine rule. In 614, when a Sāsānian general took Jerusalem, the Jews there treated the conquest as liberation. In Mesopotamia, out of the reach of heavy-handed Christian imperial authorities, Jews had freedom to think, to organize their own communities, to elaborate the law, and to debate among themselves and against Christians. The exercise of this freedom led to the most important formative development in Judaism after the exile: the compilation of the Babylonian Talmud and with it the creation of rabbinic Judaism.

The Talmud and the whole structure of rabbinic Judaism rested on a simple premise. Along with the written law, the Torah, which was revealed to Moses at Mount Sinai, God had at the same time given, in oral form, the Torah's authoritative interpretation and addendum. This oral Torah was no less authoritative than the written Torah, but its manner of transmission differed. Rather than coming down as written scripture, the oral Torah was transmitted from teacher to teacher, rabbi to rabbi, until it was finally recorded in the Mishna. In other words, the written scriptures could not stand alone, for God had also provided the authoritative commentary on those scriptures, and the rabbis owned the copyright. Consequently, the religious competition (read: Christians) was not free to read into the Hebrew scriptures whatever it liked. The Talmud was the culmination of this process and the ultimate commentary on the Mishna. Within a century after the Arab conquests the Muslim tradition had bought this rabbinic idea of dual revelation wholesale, applying exactly the same distinction between oral and written revelation to the Sunna of the Prophet and the Qur'ān. (We will have occasion to revisit the Muslim version of these ideas in chapter 6.)

Talmudic study, considered broadly, dealt with two kinds of material: commandments, called Halakha, and narratives, Aggada. It also dealt with two kinds of revelation, the orally transmitted Mishna Torah and the written Torah. The Talmud proper was a commentary on the Mishna and was originally referred to as Gemara, the completion of the Mishna. Writings elucidating the meaning of the written Torah were called Midrash and were gathered into separate collections. The talmudic and midrashic literature, taken together, forms a massive digest of Jewish tradition, encompassing legal and theological debates, ritual and liturgy, history, biography, folklore, philology, grammar, and exegesis.

This literature had an enormous shaping influence on Jewish identity, but it also had importance beyond the Jewish community. Here was a monotheistic community that preserved its independence in the face of the juggernaut of Christianity, that developed a sophisticated system of religiously sanctioned law, that held its own in polemical debates with Christians, and that preserved and transmitted a rich body of scripture and folklore. Jews criticized the doctrine of the Trinity, circulated stories of prophets, and handled scriptural texts with sophistication and subtlety. Such Jewish ideas were part of the religious atmosphere of the Near East and Muslims would readily make use of them.

Manichaeism

In addition to Christians and Jews, the Zoroastrian religious establishment had two major homegrown heresies to contend with: Manichaeism and Mazdakism. Manī, the founder of Manichaeism, was born in 216 in Mesopotamia and reared in Gnostic circles. When he was 12 he received his first revelation from an angelic "Twin." He was visited again at age 24 with a specific call: "Peace upon you, Manī, from me and from the Lord who sent me to you, and chose you to be an Apostle." Manī began preaching and gained the favor of Shāpur I, but when Bahrām I came to the throne Manī had to face the orthodox wrath of the very Kartīr we met with above. He died in prison in 276 CE (Widengren 1983: 967).

Manī presented himself as the end of a long line of prophets, beginning with Adam. He considered his most important predecessors to be the Buddha, Zoroaster, and Jesus, with whom he claimed a special affinity. Manī saw his message as the universal replacement for all earlier revelations – like them, but better. Manī's mythology was thoroughly Zoroastrian, built on the cosmic rivalry of Ohrmazd against Ahriman. His doctrine, however, was Gnostic: matter is evil, spirit is good; human beings are a mixture of light (spirit) and darkness (matter); and salvation involves freeing the soul from its enslavement to the material world. Consequently, serious Manichaeans – the "elect" – wanted as little as possible to do with sex, eating, drinking, possessions, or agricultural activity. Those who were caught up in such fleshly activities were condemned to a series of reincarnations, while those who had found the light were free to proceed to paradise (Widengren 1983: 972–84).

Manī and his followers were zealous missionaries and Manichaeism spread widely in Europe, where it was sometimes confusedly believed to be a sort of esoteric, "spiritual" version of Christianity. St. Augustine was associated with Manichaeans for several years, long enough to be equipped with the tools to become a devastating adversary of Manichaean doctrine later in life. Manichaeism also spread eastward, and Manichaean missionaries were particularly successful in central Asia, where the Uighur tribe was converted en masse and a Uighur ruler made Manī's doctrine the state religion. Eventually, Manichaean missionaries reached as far as the Chinese court. In Iran and Mesopotamia itself Manichaeism continued to thrive during the first century of Arab rule. After 750, however, followers of Manī, labeled zindīqs by the Muslims, were severely persecuted. Thus the movement was driven to extinction in Iraq by about 1000 CE (Widengren 1983: 989).

Mazdak

Two centuries after Manī, another Persian prophet, a sort of fifth-century communist named Mazdak, shook up the Sāsānian empire. A later Muslim scholar gives us a convenient summary of Mazdak's preaching:

> God placed the means of subsistence [arzāq] on earth so that people divide them among themselves equally, in a manner that no one of them could have more than his share; but people wronged one another and sought domination over one another; the strong defeated the weak and took exclusive possession of livelihood and property. It is absolutely necessary that one take from the rich for giving to the poor so that all become equal in wealth. Whoever possesses an excess of property, women or goods, he has no more right to it than another. (Yarshater 1968: 998)

This Robin Hood-style doctrine was, understandably, not particularly popular among those with an excess of property, women, or goods. Consequently, all sorts of propaganda was directed at the movement, and the Mazdakites were slandered for allegedly promoting communal marriage and thus encouraging promiscuity. In fact Mazdakism had more the character of a Zoroastrian reform movement that simply opposed gross inequities in wealth and privilege and made the mistake of trying to do something about it. Mazdak's program received some support from the Shāh Kavad, but was brutally repressed under Khusraw I.

The Mazdakites represent a rather extreme example of a deep and persistent preoccupation with social and economic justice in Iran and Mesopotamia. It was a preoccupation that did not escape the notice of Sāsānian rulers. A concern for the maintenance of justice became a pillar of Sāsānian political thought. Khusraw I, who destroyed Mazdak, nevertheless made justice the mainstay of his statecraft. He is credited with the first clear summary of what was to become an enduring political philosophy: "There is no ruler without men [read: soldiers], no men without wealth, no wealth without prosperity, and no prosperity without justice and good administration" (Morony 1984: 28). Such a philosophy of justice falls rather shy of altruism, but it at least tended to keep rulers alert to the concerns of their peasant subjects. In this "circle of justice," an idea which would be enthusiastically embraced by later Muslim political thinkers, the monarchy and peasant farmers are caught in a cycle of co-dependency. The result was a notion of justice quite different from Mazdak's Robin Hood way of thinking. For Mazdak, justice was a matter of conscience and morality; for Khusraw, it was just good policy. Seen together, however, the two represent differing forms of an enduring preoccupation with justice in Near Eastern civilization.

The Place of the Arabs in the Near East

What was the place of the Arabs amid this diverse mixture of creeds and cultures? During the sixth century Arabs were drawn into the political and religious life of the Near East in an increasingly tight orbit. By 530 both the Byzantines and the Sāsānians had found it useful to set up Arab proxy states on their southern frontiers. In that year the Emperor Justinian made one Hārith of the Banū Ghassān his appointed ruler of an Arab kingdom in southern Syria. For the next seventy years the Ghassānid kings were full participants in the intrigues of the empire. As converts to Monophysite Christianity they used what influence they had to intercede for their co-religionists elsewhere in the empire. The Ghassānid phylarch interceded with Justinian, and in 580 the Ghassānid King Mundhir II was an important participant in a Monophysite synod in Constantinople. The counterparts and rivals of the Banū Ghassān to the east were the tribe of the Banū Lakhm, who made their capital at Hīra in southern Iraq and had been entangled in Sāsānian politics since the early fifth century.

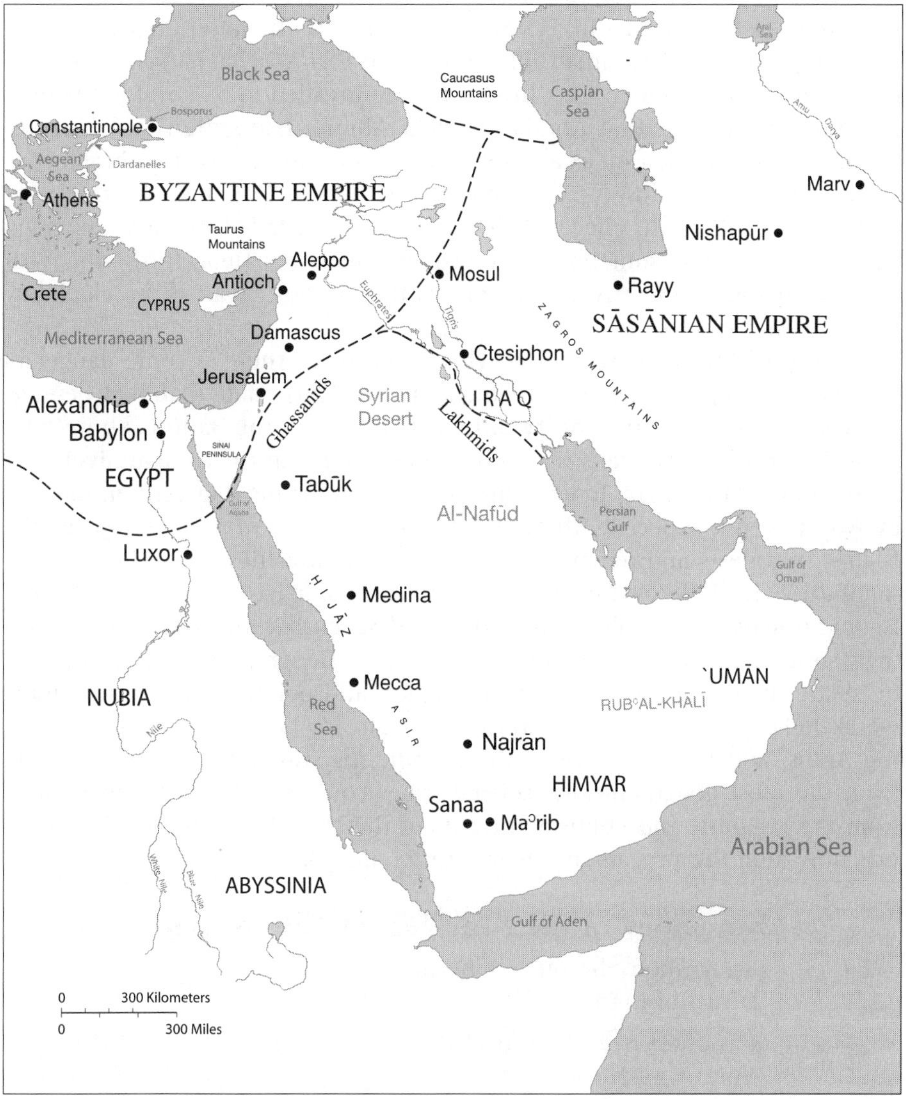

Map 4 The Near East in the early seventh century

South Arabia was also increasingly involved in the politics and religious life of the Near East. At the beginning of the sixth century South Arabia was still independent under the rule of Dhū Nuwās, last of the Ḥimyarite kings. Dhū Nuwās also happened to be Jewish. When the Monophysite Christian Abyssinians briefly invaded the Yemen in 513, Dhū Nuwās did not react kindly.

He invited the attention of the wider Christian world by attacking the Christian settlement of Najrān, first in 515 and again in 523. The latter attack involved a massacre, and the Abyssinian ruler, the Negus Ella Asbeha, had all the excuse he needed to take Yemen for Christianity. He invaded in 525 and left behind a deputy and the general Abraha. By 533 Abraha had gotten rid of Negus' deputy and set himself up as autonomous ruler of South Arabia. Abraha controlled Yemen for almost forty more years. He died in 570, the traditional year of Muhammad's birth, allegedly in the course of a failed military campaign against Mecca that somehow involved an elephant. Henceforth, the year 570 would stand out in Arab memory as the famous "year of the elephant" (see Qur'ān 105).

Because in hindsight we know what came next, there is some danger of giving more weight to these events among sixth-century Arabs than they deserve. As events of the seventh century unfolded, it was not the Banū Lakhm, Banū Ghassān, or South Arabians who took center stage, but the comparatively isolated Arabs of the Ḥijāz. Indeed, many of the Arabs most directly influenced by world events, especially those in Syria and Iraq, seem to have resisted the Islamic conquests and remained true to their old loyalties. There is a broader significance to these events, however, that does impact our understanding of Islamic origins. The Arabs of the sixth and seventh centuries were increasingly squeezed by the civilizations around them. Geography was not sufficient to isolate them from the currents of religion and politics in the surrounding world. Judaism and Christianity, in particular, already had a firm foothold among the Arabs, and the influence of these traditions was not likely to diminish. Even the most geographically isolated tribes could not long remain isolated from the religious and political currents of the Near East. The only question was how long the process of integration would take.

Chronology of the Near East of Late Antiquity	
269	St. Anthony becomes a hermit
277	Death of Manī
324	Conquest of Byzantium by Constantine
325	Council of Nicaea
410	Sack of Rome
431	Council of Ephesus
451	Council of Chalcedon
459	Death of Simeon Stylites
488–531	Persian monarch, Kavad I
513	Abyssinian invasion of Ḥimyar. An Abyssinian presence remains at Najrān
515	Jewish leader, Dhū Nuwās, attacks Najrān; massacres Christians there in 523

525	Abyssinian Negus Ella Asbeha invades Yemen; leaves his general, Abraha, behind
527–65	Reign of Justinian
530	Appointment of Hārith of Banū Ghassān as Byzantine phylarch launches Ghassānid/Byzantine alliance
531–79	Khusraw I Anūsharwān begins reign
532	Great Nika riot in Constantinople
533	Abraha autonomous in Yemen
540–62	Wars between Justinian and Anūsharwān
541–70	Plague
566	Justin II grants amnesty to Monophysites
570	Year of the elephant; Abraha, ally of the Byzantines, dies, allegedly in an abortive attack on Mecca which was thwarted by divine intervention
ca. 570	Sāsānians conquer Yemen
577	Mundhir torches Lakhmid capital of al-Hīra
580	Ghassānid Mundhir participates in Monophysite synod in Constantinople
582	Maurice accedes to the Byzantine throne; Ghassānid phylarchate dissolved
602	Emperor Maurice and his family murdered by Phocas
602	Khusraw I begins war with Byzantium
604	Lakhmid kingdom abolished by Khusraw II
610–41	Reign of Heraclius
613	Sāsānians take Antioch
614	Sāsānians capture Jerusalem
619	Sāsānians take Egypt
620	Sāsānians on outskirts of Constantinople
622	Heraclius sets out from Constantinople to attack Persians from rear
627–8	Heraclius advances through Iraq, sacks Ctesiphon
628	Khusraw II deposed
632	Traditional date for the death of Muhammad
636	Byzantines routed by Arabs at Yarmūk
637	Persian army defeated at al-Qādisiyya

Resources for Further Study

Peter Brown provides a beautifully written survey of the Near Eastern world in *The World of Late Antiquity* (1971). For much greater detail on the social and religious environment of the Byzantine empire, see A. H. M. Jones, *The Later Roman Empire, 284–602* (1986) and for the Christian background, W. H. C. Frend,

The Early Church (1982). A useful starting point for study of the Sāsānian empire is Ehsan Yarshater (ed.), *The Cambridge History of Iran*, vol. 3 (1968), which includes articles on all of the major religious movements discussed above. A handy collection of Zoroastrian texts in translation can be found in Mary Boyce, *Textual Sources for the Study of Zoroastrianism* (1990). For developments in Judaism during this period, see Jacob Neusner, *History of the Jews of Babylonia* (1968). Specific Jewish and Christian influences on Islam are documented by Richard Bell in *The Origin of Islam in its Christian Environment* (1926) and Abraham I. Katsh, *Judaism in Islam* (1954). For the history of Christian communities after the conquests, see M. Gervers and R. Bikhazi (eds.), *Conversion and Continuity: Indigenous Christian Communities in Islamic Lands, Eighth to Eighteenth Centuries* (1990).

4

THE LIFE OF MUHAMMAD

It is in sixth-century Arabia, when the Arabs of the Ḥijāz were just beginning to feel the encroachment of Near Eastern religion and civilization, that the Muslim tradition places the life of Muhammad. The story of Muhammad's life took its final form much later, however, through the work of Ibn Isḥāq, an other wise minor scholar of Medina who secured his place in history by compiling the first full biography, or sīra, of Muhammad. All accounts of Muhammad's life lead back to Ibn Isḥāq. His *Sīrat Rasūl Allāh,* written about a century after Muhammad's death, provides our first coherent outline of Muhammad's career. Sīra literature proliferated after Ibn Isḥāq, who died in 767 CE; other early biographers included al-Wāqidī (d. 822) and the prolific and learned Muhammad ibn Jarīr al-Ṭabarī (d. 923). Although these later scholars drew in additional information, no subsequent biography differs in basic structure from Ibn Isḥāq's *Sīra.* Dependence on Ibn Isḥāq has increased in modern works on Muhammad, which naturally favor earlier sources over later. Consequently, a student who browses a modern biography of Muhammad, like Montgomery Watt's two-volume *Muhammad at Mecca* (1953) and *Muhammad at Medina* (1956), is essentially reading Watt's commentary on Ibn Isḥāq. The same is true of most textbook treatments of Muhammad.

Rather than rely on these various commentaries on Ibn Isḥāq, whether ancient or modern, astute readers will wonder why they should not go back to the original for themselves. This is an excellent idea, and readers without knowledge of Arabic can do so quite readily by means of an English version of Ibn Isḥāq's biography, translated by Alfred Guillaume under the title, *The Life of Muhammad* (Ibn Isḥāq 1955). Those who have the inclination to read the 700 or so pages of Guillaume's translation for themselves can skip the remainder of this chapter, which is simply another severely edited version of the same. A word of warning is in order, however. Ibn Isḥāq's text comes to us through the work of a ninth-century scholar, Ibn Hishām, and Ibn Hishām is not ashamed to tell us that he heavily edited Ibn Isḥāq's work. Consequently, when we read Ibn Isḥāq, we are actually reading what Ibn Hishām thought should be preserved of Ibn Isḥāq's biography a century after Ibn Isḥāq wrote it. One further warning is in order. In the synopsis that follows I will defer the crucial question of where Ibn Isḥāq got his information and whether what he relates is historically accurate. Instead, I will approach Ibn Isḥāq's *Sīra* as a literary text from which we can expect to learn what an eighth-century scholar believed about Muhammad and what issues he thought important as he compiled his biography. Keeping these cautions in mind, what does Ibn Isḥāq have to tell us about Muhammad?

Prologue and Setting

Following good biblical precedent for sacred biography (see Matthew 1), Ibn Isḥāq begins his work with two genealogies. The first genealogy traces the ancestry of Muhammad son of ʿAbd Allāh through the line of Qusayy, the founder of Mecca, to Ismāʿīl, Ibrahīm, Shem, Noah, and finally back to Adam. A second genealogy gives a more detailed account of Ismāʿīl's descendants which explains various divisions among Arab tribes. (In an interesting side note to the genealogy we are informed that the inhabitants of Egypt have kinship with the Arabs because Hagar was Egyptian.) The major effect of the genealogy is to immediately establish a place for Muhammad and the Arabs in monotheist sacred history. Before we know anything else about him, we know that Muhammad is in the lineage of Noah and Abraham.

After this genealogical prologue, Ibn Isḥāq moves on to the immediate historical setting of his story in pre-Islamic Arabia. He begins with a South Arabian king, Rabīʿa ibn Naṣr, who, Nebuchadnezzar fashion, has a terrifying dream which he cannot understand or remember. Two Daniel-like soothsayers independently recount the dream and recognize it as foretelling the downfall of the kingdom of Ḥimyar, the invasion of the Abyssinians, and the rise of an Arab prophet, whose dominion will last to the end of time. In the following pages this prophecy gradually unfolds in history. Dhū Nuwās, a convert to Judaism, takes the throne of Ḥimyar; his massacre of Christians at Najrān leads directly to an Abyssinian invasion (and, according to Ibn Isḥāq, a citation in Sūra 85 verse 4 of the Qur'ān); and the Abyssinian general Abraha takes power. The account culminates in the famous year of the elephant, when Abraha foolishly sets out to destroy the Kaʿba in Mecca with a force led by an elephant named Maḥmūd. The expedition brings Abraha into direct encounter with Muhammad's grandfather, ʿAbd al-Muṭṭalib, the leader of the Quraysh. (ʿAbd al-Muṭṭalib is remembered for having rediscovered the sacred well of Zamzam in the sacred enclosure at Mecca, and Ibn Isḥāq uses this event as the excuse to recount the history of the sanctuary from Abraham onward.)

The Meccan expedition also brought about Abraha's downfall. Maḥmūd the elephant knelt down and refused to move whenever he faced Mecca; Abraha's army was smitten by birds carrying plague-producing stones; and Abraha himself suffered a gruesome death preceded by his fingers falling off one by one. Mecca was thus saved by divine intervention, and once again Ibn Isḥāq finds clear reference to these events in the Qur'ān, Sūra 105: "Hast thou not seen how thy Lord did with the Men of the Elephant? Did He not make their guile to go astray? And He loosed upon them birds in flights, hurling against them stones of baked clay and He made them like green blades devoured." In this auspicious year of Mecca's deliverance, 570 CE by modern reckoning, Muhammad was born.

Birth and Childhood

Muhammad's father ʿAbd Allāh died before his son was born. During her pregnancy, Muhammad's mother Āmina heard a voice saying, "You are pregnant with the Lord of this people." A light used to shine forth from her by which she could see the castles of Buṣrā in Syria. On the eve of his birth a Jew in Yathrib was overheard announcing to his fellow Jews: "Tonight has risen a star under which Aḥmad is to be born." The Prophet's mother reported that when he was born he put his hands on the ground and lifted his head toward heaven.

Further miraculous signs followed Muhammad's birth. According to Meccan custom he was given over to a Bedouin foster-mother to be nursed. From the time that she took him, his foster-mother's breasts were full, her ailing donkey perked up, her livestock began to produce great quantities of milk, and the family generally prospered. When he was somewhat older, Muhammad was tending sheep with his foster-brother (every prophet, he later said, had at one time been a shepherd) when two men dressed in white came upon him carrying a golden basin filled with snow. "Then they seized me," Muhammad later recounted to his companions, "and opened up my belly, extracted my heart and split it; then they extracted a black drop from it and threw it away; then they washed my heart and my belly with that snow until they had thoroughly cleaned them." On another occasion when Muhammad and his

Figure 4.1 Angels attending the birth of Muhammad (detail from a fourteenth-century illustrated life of the Prophet). Artistic depictions of Muhammad are anathema to modern Muslims, but this was not always the case. The image of Muhammad as an infant, while not shown here, appeared in the original painting. Photo: Topkapi Palace Museum, Istanbul, Turkey

playmates had removed their shirts an unseen figure slapped Muhammad and ordered him to put his shirt back on. In this way God protected the boy's purity and modesty in the midst of a pagan environment.

Christians and Jews especially tended to notice that there was something unique about the child Muhammad. A group of Abyssinian Christians, for example, wanted to take him back to their country, for, as they told his foster-mother, they knew all about him and saw that he was destined to have a great future. Later, when the boy accompanied his uncle Abū Ṭālib on a caravan to Syria, the hermit Baḥīra, who had never before paid any attention to Arab caravans, suddenly became uncharacteristically hospitable. He hosted the whole party for a feast, and when Muhammad was left outside to tend the camels, the monk insisted that he be brought in. Baḥīra knew from a book that he had diligently studied what the marks of prophethood were, and he recognized these marks in Muhammad. In particular, he saw the seal of prophethood between his shoulders. Baḥīra solemnly warned Abū Ṭālib to protect Muhammad from the Jews, who would be sure to harm him if they knew his true identity. Indeed, Ibn Isḥāq reports that a number of Jews predicted the coming of a prophet in Arabia, but later perversely refused to acknowledge Muhammad's claims.

When Muhammad was 6 years old his mother Āmina died, leaving him an orphan (see Qur'ān 93:6–8). He was cared for by his grandfather, ʿAbd al-Muṭṭalib, until the latter's death, when his uncle, Abū Ṭālib, became his guardian.

Early Adulthood

As an adult Muhammad was known for his integrity. "He grew up," Ibn Isḥāq tells us, "to be the finest of his people in manliness, the best in character, the most noble in lineage, the best neighbor, the most kind, truthful, reliable, the furthest removed from filthiness and corrupt morals, through loftiness and nobility, so that he was known among his people as 'The trustworthy.'" His stellar reputation attracted the attention of a wealthy business woman, the widow Khadījah, who hired him to trade for her in Syria. His first business trip was wildly successful, and Khadījah's son Maysara, who accompanied Muhammad, noticed that two angels shaded him as he traveled at the height of the day. Khadījah was duly impressed and proposed marriage. Her cousin Waraqa, a Christian who had been awaiting the coming of a prophet, confirmed the wisdom of her choice. "I knew," he told Khadījah, "that a prophet of this people was expected. His time has come."

Another incident further illustrates Muhammad's reputation. When Muhammad was 35, the Quraysh set out to demolish and rebuild the Kaʿba. The project began auspiciously. Timbers were gathered from the wreck of a Greek ship, an Egyptian carpenter was hired, and God sent a bird to remove a poisonous snake that stood in the way of the work. When the old building had been demolished to the foundations, a member of the Quraysh induced an earthquake when he tried to move a foundation stone; it was thought wise to leave the foundations alone. The rebuilding proved problematic. When the walls had been built up to the level of the famous black stone, the various clans of the Quraysh began to quarrel over the right to put the black stone in place. An elder of the Quraysh finally suggested that they make the next man to enter arbitrator. To the delight of all, this turned out to be Muhammad,

Figure 4.2 The Ka'aba and its surroundings in the early twentieth century. The cube-shaped building was a center of pilgrimage before the rise of Islam. It has been rebuilt numerous times since the time of Muhammad. The most distinctive feature of the site is a black stone built into the foundation of the building. Photo: Courtesy of the Fine Arts Library, Harvard College Library

the trustworthy, who proposed a solution worthy of Solomon. He ordered the black stone to be put on a cloak, and called on members of each tribe to lift the cloak together. Finally, Muhammad himself placed the stone in position with his own hand.

Muhammad's trustworthiness was accompanied by piety. He loved solitude, and one month of every year he spent at Mount Ḥīrā outside of Mecca. There, Ibn Isḥāq tells us, he practiced taḥannuth, a somewhat mysterious form of religious discipline. On his return he used to circumambulate the Ka'ba seven times before going home. During one of these stays at Mount Ḥīrā, in the month of Ramaḍān of his fortieth year, Muhammad was visited by the angel Gabriel (see Qur'ān 2:181).

The Beginning of Revelation

"He came to me," Muhammad later remembered,

> while I was asleep, with a coverlet of brocade whereon was some writing, and said, "Read!" I said, "What shall I read?" He pressed me with it again so that I thought it was death; then he let me go and said "Read!" I said, "What shall I read?" He pressed me with it the third time so that I thought it was death and said "Read!" I said, "What then shall I read?" – and this I said only to deliver myself from him, lest he should do the same to me again.

Whereupon, Gabriel gave Muhammad what would become the first verses of Sūra 96 of the Qur'ān:

> Recite: In the Name of thy Lord who created,
> created Man of a blood-clot.
> Recite: And thy Lord is the Most Generous,
> who taught by the Pen,
> taught Man that he knew not.

When Muhammad awoke the words were burned into his memory. As he set off down the mountain, he saw Gabriel standing on the horizon, a vision described at the beginning of Sūra 53:

> This is naught but a revelation revealed, taught him by one terrible in power, very strong; he stood poised, being on the higher horizon, then drew near and suspended hung, two bows'-length away, or nearer, then revealed to his servant that he revealed. His heart lies not of what he saw; what, will you dispute with him what he sees?

These first experiences of revelation terrified Muhammad, but he received immediate reassurance from Khadījah and from her Christian cousin Waraqa. Waraqa, in particular, was ecstatic at the news and assured Khadījah that Muhammad had been visited by the great Nāmūs, the very same being who had visited Moses, and that he would be the prophet of his people. Khadījah was less euphoric but more practical. She devised a careful test to determine whether the agent of revelation was good or evil. Once, when Gabriel came to Muhammad while they were together, Khadījah "disclosed her form and cast aside her veil." The angel immediately departed, thus demonstrating his modesty and thereby establishing his angelic credentials.

For three years Muhammad's message spread quietly and privately, and a group of followers formed around him. Khadījah was the first to accept Muhammad's message. The second Muslim, according to Ibn Isḥāq, was Muhammad's

10-year-old cousin, ʿAlī son of Abū Ṭālib, followed by Zayd b. Ḥāritha and Abū Bakr. Abū Bakr proved to be an effective missionary. Through his influence ʿUthmān b. ʿAffān, al-Zubayr b. al-ʿAwwām, ʿAbd al-Raḥmān b. ʿAwf, Saʿd b. Abū Waqqās, and Talḥa b. ʿUbayd Allāh – all prominent names in early Islamic history – became Muslims. After these Ibn Isḥāq gives a long list of other early converts.

Ritual worship – ṣalāt – was the first duty placed on this early community of Muslims. Gabriel himself taught Muhammad how to perform the ritual ablutions and the ṣalāt. On the first day of instruction Gabriel prayed at the following times:

> Noon prayer – when the sun declined
> Evening prayer – when his shadow equaled his own length
> Sunset prayer – when the sun set
> Night prayer – when the twilight had disappeared
> Morning prayer – when the dawn arose

On the second day of instruction, however, he varied the pattern as follows:

> Noon prayer – when his shadow equaled his height
> Evening prayer – when his shadow equaled the height of two men
> Sunset prayer – when the sun set
> Night prayer – when the first third of the night had passed
> Morning prayer – when it was clear but the sun was not yet shining

"O Muhammad," he declared when he was finished, "prayer is in what is between your prayer today and your prayer yesterday." (According to later scholars, Ibn Isḥāq incorrectly dated this report and the incident actually occurred much later.)

Opposition

After three years of quiet persuasion, God instructed Muhammad to go public with his message. "Proclaim what you have been ordered" (Qur'ān 15:94) came the revelation, and "Warn thy family, thy nearest relations" (26:214). Ibn Isḥāq is careful to forewarn us of what would follow. "Prophecy is a troublesome burden," he says. "Only strong, resolute messengers can bear it by God's help and grace, because of the opposition which they meet from men in conveying God's message. The apostle carried out God's orders in spite of the opposition and ill treatment which he met with."

The worst of the ill treatment came from Muhammad's tribal kinsmen. His uncle, Abū Lahab, was particularly troublesome, earning a rare personal condemnation from God in Sūra 111: "Perish the hands of Abū Lahab, and perish he! His wealth avails him not, neither what he has earned; he shall roast at a flaming fire and his wife, the carrier of the firewood, upon her neck a rope of palm-fiber." According to Ṭabarī's version of Ibn Isḥāq, Muhammad called together the leaders of the Quraysh, about forty men in all, to summon them to Islam. After Muhammad miraculously multiplied food and drink for them all, Abū Lahab rudely cut the meeting short before Muhammad could have his say. Muhammad called the same group together the next day, performed the same miracle, and called them to accept his message. Only 'Alī responded, and Muhammad's announcement – "This is my brother, my executor, and my successor among you. Hearken to him and obey him" – was met with scornful laughter.

The Qurayshī leaders' derision quickly grew into more serious opposition when Muhammad began to preach against their gods. From that point the leaders of the Quraysh began to plot his destruction. The Prophet's uncle and guardian, Abū Ṭālib, stood in the way, however, and although he never became a Muslim, he steadfastly defended Muhammad until his death. He also secured the support of Muhammad's immediate clansmen, the Banū Hāshim, with the exception of Abū Lahab. Muhammad's position was also reinforced by dramatic conversion of another uncle, Ḥamza, who was renowned for his physical strength and his prowess as a warrior and hunter.

Taking Ḥamza's conversion as a sign that their efforts at direct bullying had failed, Muhammad's opponents stooped to more conniving methods. They first bribed him with offers of wealth, honor, and power. When their generosity was spurned they promised to accept him if he would produce miraculous signs for them. Finally, they consulted some Jewish rabbis for tricky theological riddles. The rabbis came up with three: ask him, they suggested, about the young men who disappeared in ancient days; ask him about the mighty traveler who reached the confines of both East and West; and finally ask him what the spirit is. Muhammad accepted the challenge. He promised an answer the next day, but forgot to add, "if God wills." Consequently, God delayed his answer fifteen days to teach his Prophet a lesson about who was in charge of the process of revelation. In the end God vindicated Muhammad by sending Sūra 19, in which the rabbis' riddles are answered.

It was during this period of intense disputation that later biographers place the now infamous story of the satanic verses. Ibn Isḥāq himself makes no mention of the event, but Ṭabarī recounts traditions to the effect that Muhammad, under severe pressure to compromise, came up with verses which offered an accommodation with the Meccan pantheon. "Have you considered al-Lāt and al-'Uzzā, and Manāt, the third, the other?" he allegedly recited, "These are the swans exalted, whose intercession is to be hoped for." God quickly stepped in with a correction, which now appears in Sūra 53: "Have you considered al-Lāt and al-'Uzzā and Manāt, the third, the other? What, have you males, and He females? That were indeed an unjust division. They are naught but names yourselves have named, and your fathers." Muhammad was thus delivered from going soft on polytheism, to the continued frustration of his opponents.

Unable to get at Muhammad directly, his enemies targeted the weak among his followers. Slaves were especially vulnerable. The owner of a slave named Bilāl used to take him out at the hottest part of the day to torture him by placing a great rock on his chest, insisting that he renounce his faith. "One, one!" Bilāl gasped. One day Abū Bakr witnessed the torture and offered to trade a pagan slave for Bilāl, thus emancipating him. Another young convert, ʿAmmār b. Yāsir, used to be exposed to the sun in the heat of the day along with his parents; ʿAmmār's mother was finally killed in this way for refusing to abandon her faith. In contrast to such perseverance, another tradition passed on by Ibn Isḥāq allows that the persecution was so severe that apostasy was excusable. In the face of such suffering those being tortured would have willingly named a beetle their God if they were told to.

It was partly to escape this danger of apostasy, according to Ibn Isḥāq, that a band of Muslims fled to Abyssinia at the Prophet's urging. Eighty-three men, many accompanied by their families, emigrated and were hospitably welcomed by the Negus, the Abyssinian monarch. When the Qurayshī leaders learned of this, they sent a delegation to seek the extradition of the refugees. Quraysh designs failed, however, when the Negus and his bishops were moved to tears by a reading of Sūra 19, immediately recognizing how close the Muslims were to Christians in belief. The Muslim delegation also managed to persuade the Negus, with some clever apologetics, that their views of Jesus were close enough to be tolerated.

Meanwhile, back at Mecca, the conversion of ʿUmar b. al-Khaṭṭāb had dealt the Quraysh a further setback. As a polytheist ʿUmar had been a formidable opponent of the Muslims, and he was just as formidable a Muslim. This continued success of Muhammad's mission seemed to call for extreme measures, and Muhammad's opponents responded with a boycott of the Banū Hāshim and the Banū Muṭṭalib. The two clans were to be entirely cut off from buying and selling, marrying and being given in marriage. Under the boycott the Muslim community suffered extreme privation for two or three years until their sympathizers within the Quraysh finally united to annul the agreement.

The Night Journey and Ascent to Heaven

Sometime in this period (Ibn Isḥāq is unconcerned with the precise chronology) Muhammad made a miraculous one-night visit to Jerusalem, carried by

Figure 4.3 Bilāl sounding the call to prayer from the Kaʿba. Bilāl has become a symbol of racial tolerance in Islam, and an iconic figure for African and African American Muslims. Photo: Topkapi Palace Museum, Istanbul, Turkey/Bildarchiv Steffens/The Bridgeman Art Library

a winged steed, Burāq, and accompanied by Gabriel. Whether he traveled in body or in spirit, Ibn Isḥāq is not certain. He is confident, however, that the Prophet was back in his bed before dawn, and that Muhammad remembered sufficient details about various caravans he had passed to prove that – whether in body or spirit – the journey was real. In Jerusalem Muhammad met Abraham, Moses, and Jesus, and led a delegation of prophets in prayer.

He also passed an important test. Water, wine, and milk were offered to him, and he wisely chose the milk, ensuring that his community would remain rightly guided.

Before returning from Jerusalem to Mecca, Muhammad was given a view of hell and a full tour of heaven. Suffering in hell he saw those who had robbed orphans eating and excreting fire-like stones, he saw adulterers eating putrid meat, and he saw mothers of bastard children suspended by their breasts. Leaving these sobering scenes behind, Muhammad ascended through the seven heavens, meeting prophets in each: Adam in the first, Jesus and his cousin John in the second, Joseph in the third, Idrīs in the fourth, Aaron in the fifth, Moses in the sixth, and Abraham ("Never," Muhammad reported, "have I seen a man more like myself") in the seventh. In the seventh heaven God laid the requirement of fifty daily prayers on Muhammad and his community. Fortunately, Moses sent Muhammad back to negotiate a lower number, for "Prayer is a weighty matter and your people are weak." After shuttling several times between Moses and God, Muhammad came away with five obligatory prayers, because, as he said, "I had been back to my Lord and asked him to reduce the number until I was ashamed, and I would not do it again."

The honor he enjoyed among the prophets in heaven contrasted rather sharply with the mockery Muhammad continued to face on his return to earth, where the Muslims' situation continued to decline. The final blow came when Muhammad's two most important supporters, his wife Khadīja and his uncle and protector Abū Ṭālib, died in the same year. Without Abū Ṭālib to shield him from his Meccan opponents, Muhammad began actively looking for allies outside of Mecca. His first abortive attempt was among the Banū Thaqīf in the neighboring town of al-Ṭā'if. Muhammad traveled to al-Ṭā'if alone, where he was rudely rebuffed. On his return to Mecca, however, God gave him the consolation of converting seven jinn to Islam, an event alluded to in the Qur'ān (46:28–32 and 72:1).

Muhammad continued his search for supporters outside of Mecca, and his opening was not long in coming. In 621 a delegation of Muslims from the oasis at Yathrib met secretly with Muhammad at al-ʿAqaba to pledge their support. The next year they came back with a much larger delegation of converts to renew their pledge. But by the time of their second meeting, God had ordered a crucial shift in policy: the Muslims were allowed to fight. To this point Muhammad had been required to bear opposition patiently, but the time for patience was past. "Leave is given to those who fight," God revealed to Muhammad, "because they were wronged – surely God is able to help them – who were expelled from their habitations without right, except that they say 'Our Lord is God'" (Qur'ān 22:40–2). The Muslims of Yathrib, known as the Anṣār (the helpers), were now no longer just religious supporters of Muhammad, but also military allies. The year was 622 by modern reckoning, and the pieces were now in place – a new activism and new allies – for the crucial event of Islamic history and the turning point of Muhammad's career.

The Hijra

After the second pledge at al-ʿAqaba, Muhammad ordered his followers to relocate to Medina (Yathrib's new name), where they would come under the protection of the Anṣār. The Meccan Muslims left in small groups while Muhammad, ʿAlī, and Abū Bakr stayed behind awaiting permission from God to follow. At last, after narrowly escaping a murder plot, Muhammad and Abū Bakr fled to Medina, leaving only ʿAlī behind to discharge the Prophet's remaining obligations. The two hid in a cave for three days, miraculously protected from Qurayshī pursuers.

Once in Medina, Muhammad immediately demonstrated consummate political skills. His first need was a site for his headquarters – a delicate choice given the environment of tribal factionalism and his outsider status. Astute as ever, Muhammad delegated the decision to his camel and constructed his mosque at the site where his mount first sat down. The Prophet's mosque, a simple rectangular building, was to serve as a place for congregational prayer, as courtroom, and as military headquarters.

Having established his base of operations, Muhammad next set out to clarify his political position. Medina was torn by tribal and religious differences. The two dominant tribes, the Aws and the Khazraj, had been fighting for years. Medina also had three significant Jewish tribes, the Banū Qurayẓa, the Banū Qaynuqāʿ, and the Banū al-Naḍīr. The Meccan emigrants brought by Muhammad further complicated the religious and tribal mix. Into this context Ibn Isḥāq places the Constitution of Medina, a document which establishes a rudimentary political order. The basic features of this order were simple: Muslims were to act as a single community, or umma, regardless of tribe; Jews allied with the Muslims were to be treated as part of this umma; and Muhammad was to be accepted as arbitrator of all disputes.

This new political reality immediately produced a new problem that could never have been foreseen in Mecca. In Mecca, to be a Muslim had been neither fashionable nor advantageous. In Medina, Islam was in vogue, and Muhammad was ascendant. Consequently, Muhammad's biggest challenge was an entirely new class of troublemaker, the so-called munāfiqūn or hypocrites, who outwardly adhered to Islam but secretly sought to undermine the Prophet's mission at every opportunity. The munāfiqūn formed a sort of fifth column made up of a loose alliance of Jews, dissatisfied polytheists, and ambitious political types frustrated by Muhammad's ascendancy. The worst of these was one ʿAbd Allāh ibn Ubayy, whose ambitions to be ruler of Medina had been frustrated by the Prophet's arrival. The Qur'ān has a good deal to say about the hypocrites, and Ibn Isḥāq takes up a large chunk of his biography recounting encounters with the munāfiqūn and Jews that gave rise to particular Qur'ānic revelations.

While he battled hypocrites on the home front, Muhammad also opened new battle lines in the conflict with his Meccan enemies. About a year after the Hijra, Muhammad initiated a series of military expeditions and raiding parties. The first of these raids brought little bloodshed. This changed dramatically with a controversial raid in which a caravan of the Quraysh was ambushed by a party of Muslims at the end of the sacred month of Rajab, a month during which the shedding of blood or taking of booty was taboo. God relieved Muslims' anxieties about the violation of the sacred month with this reassurance: "They will ask you about the sacred month, and war in it. Say, war therein is a serious matter, but keeping people from the way of God and disbelieving in Him and in the sacred mosque and driving out His people there from is more serious with God" (Qur'ān 2:214). The raid at Nakhla was a foreshadowing of a much larger escalation of the conflict which would hand the Muslims their first great victory.

The Battle of Badr

Muhammad's opportunity came in the month of Ramaḍān, when news arrived of a large caravan from Syria, accompanied by thirty or forty men led by the Meccan leader Abū Sufyān. Muhammad called on the Muslims to attack the caravan, and a small force set out to meet it. Meanwhile, word reached Mecca of the Muslim threat, and a large force was organized to go out from Mecca to protect the caravan. Abū Sufyān rerouted the caravan and reached Mecca safely, but the two armies faced each other at a place called Badr, where there was water. The Muslims established their position first, and seized the water source, keeping the Meccans from it. After some preliminaries involving individual combat, full battle was joined on Friday morning, the seventeenth day of Ramaḍān.

Ibn Isḥāq's account of the Muslim victory at Badr is peppered with accounts of individual heroism, martyrdom, and revenge. One ʿUmayr was eating some dates when he heard the Prophet promise paradise to any who died in battle. He immediately flung the dates aside and threw himself into the battle saying, "Is there nothing between me and entering paradise save to be killed by these men?" Another Muslim, ʿĀṣim, asked Muhammad, "What makes the Lord laugh with joy at His servant?" Muhammad answered, "When he plunges into the midst of the enemy without mail." At this ʿĀṣim threw off his mail coat, plunged into the battle and was killed. When the former slave, Bilāl, saw his ex-master, who used to torture him, being led away as a prisoner, he cried out, "The arch-infidel Umayya ibn Khalaf! May I not live if he lives!" Umayya was hacked to death.

Several sources witnessed angels fighting alongside the Muslims at Badr in fulfillment of a promise of God: "I shall reinforce you with a thousand angels riding behind you" (Qur'ān 8:9). The angels wore white turbans, and at least one witness heard the voice of Gabriel. In one case a warrior was about to strike off the head of a polytheist, but an angel got to him first. (The Qur'ān, according to Ibn Isḥāq, has something to say about those who were killed by angels in Sūra 4, verse 99.) Badr was the only battle in which angels actually engaged in combat. In later battles they served as reinforcements but did not fight.

After the battle, the Muslims quarreled about the spoils, and the whole of Sūra 8 of the Qur'ān was revealed. The sūra serves as God's commentary on various aspects of the battle, but it also lays out a specific rule of some importance: the Prophet is in charge of the division of booty and one-fifth of the spoils of war goes to God and his Apostle.

Confrontation with the Jews of Medina

Emboldened by victory, Muhammad returned to confront the threat at home with renewed vigor. The Jews of the Banū Qaynuqāʿ repudiated their agreement with Muhammad, and Muhammad besieged them until they surrendered unconditionally. The hypocrite ʿAbd Allāh ibn Ubayy intervened on their behalf, and the Jews were handed over to him. Muhammad also incited the assassination of Kaʿb ibn al-Ashraf, a poet and a hardened opponent of Muhammad who showed his disgust at the success of the Muslims by composing elegies to the slain Quraysh and lewd verses about Muslim women. After Kaʿb's murder, Ibn Isḥāq tells us, there was no Jew in Medina who did not fear for his life, and the Prophet instructed his followers to "Kill any Jew who falls into your power." At least one of his followers, Muḥayyiṣa ibn Masʿūd, is celebrated for having zealously followed the Prophet's instructions by killing his Jewish business partner, an act of selflessness that so impressed Muḥayyiṣa's brother Ḥuwayyiṣa that the latter became a Muslim.

These events were accompanied by a major change in the religious practice of Muslims. Until this time Muslims, like Jews, had faced in the direction of Jerusalem for prayer. After Badr, as Muhammad was praying toward Jerusalem, he received a revelation directing him to turn toward Mecca. This change in the direction of prayer – the qibla – had huge symbolic importance, for it made an Arabian sanctuary the central focus of ritual, and it seemed to seal Muhammad's break with the Jews of Medina and to inaugurate a new, more independent, and more Arab monotheism.

The Battle of Uḥud

After Badr, victorious abroad and with their enemies on the run at home, the Muslims had every reason for confidence. That confidence was soon severely shaken. The Meccans, determined to avenge their defeat at Badr, organized a force to move against Medina. On hearing the news the Medinan defenders were divided over tactics. The Prophet at first suggested that they remain in Medina, and the hypocrite ʿAbd Allāh ibn Ubayy sided with him. Others urged him to go out to meet the enemy in the field. The latter prevailed, to the disgust of ʿAbd Allāh ibn Ubayy, who withdrew, taking about a third of the men with him. The Prophet went out with about 700 men, and the two armies met at a place called Uḥud. The Muslims both inflicted and suffered major losses. One of the worst losses was the death of the Prophet's uncle, Ḥamza, who was slain by the javelin-wielding slave Waḥshī, who had been promised his freedom in return for the deed. The Prophet himself came away with smashed teeth and an injured lip and at one point in the battle the rumor spread that he was dead. In the end the Meccans withdrew, claiming to have evened the score. To this ʿUmar made the famous reply: "We are not equal. Our dead are in paradise; your dead in hell."

Badr had taught the Muslims about victory; at Uḥud they learned fortitude in the face of defeat. Once again, God gave them a commentary on the battle to drive the lesson home. Uḥud, the Qur'ān assures the Muslims, was a test. How else could God know who were true believers, except by observing who persevered in the face of adversity (3:136)? And if Muhammad had died, what of it? "Muhammad is naught but a Messenger. Messengers have passed away before him. Why, if he should die or is slain, will you turn about on your heels?" (3:137).

Treachery followed on the heels of defeat. In the fourth year after the Hijra, when the Prophet visited the Jews of the Banū an-Naḍīr with a routine request, they plotted his assassination as he waited outside their walls. God revealed the plot to Muhammad, and the Prophet withdrew, raised a force against the tribe, burned their palm groves, confiscated their property, and expelled them from Medina. God affirmed this course of action with the revelation of the whole of Sūra 59, for "whosoever makes a breach with God, God is terrible in retribution."

The expulsion of the Banū an-Naḍīr was by no means the end of the Prophet's troubles with the Jews. A group of Jews made common cause with the Meccan leaders, forming an alliance against the Muslims. When word of Meccan designs came to Muhammad, he ordered the digging of a defensive ditch around the city. The work was long and difficult, but was eased by a number of miracles granted to Muhammad. When the workers came upon a particularly difficult rock the Prophet spat in some water, poured it on the rock, and it was pulverized. On another occasion he multiplied a handful of dates until there were enough to feed all of the workers. After the trench had been completed, the Quraysh and their allies arrived and laid siege to Medina. After a lengthy standoff during which the Medinans suffered severe privation, the alliance against Muhammad fractured and the Meccans withdrew.

After the withdrawal of the Quraysh, God ordered Muhammad to attack the treacherous Jews of the Banū Qurayẓa. He besieged them for twenty-five nights, until they surrendered. After the surrender, Muhammad appointed Saʿd ibn Muʿādh of the Aws, the tribal ally of the Banū Qurayẓa, to determine their fate. Saʿd ordered the men killed, their property seized and divided, and the women and children taken captive. The Prophet had trenches dug in Medina's marketplace and between 600 and 900 men of the Banū Qurayẓa were brought to him in batches and beheaded there.

The following year brought a number of minor raids. One in particular, the raid on the Banū al-Muṣṭaliq, stands out because of an embarrassing incident involving Muhammad's young second wife, ʿĀ'isha, whom we have not yet met because (in contrast to modern biographers) Ibn Isḥāq shows limited interest in the marriages or domestic life of the Prophet. ʿĀ'isha went along on the raid, and on the return journey was accidentally left behind while she was searching for a necklace she had dropped when she had gone off to relieve herself. Fortunately (or not), a young warrior who had fallen behind the main body of troops noticed her. Her rescuer placed her on his camel and set off to catch up with the army. A whole night passed before they were missed, and when ʿĀ'isha was finally led into camp on the camel of a young, handsome man, scandal swept through the ranks. It was a perfect opportunity for troublemakers, and once again ʿAbd Allāh ibn Ubayy was at the forefront, busily spreading malicious accusations against the Prophet's wife. ʿAlī offered a simple and practical solution: "Women are plentiful," he told the Prophet, "and you can easily change one for another." First, however, he advised Muhammad to interrogate his wife's slave girl. In spite of a beating the only accusation the girl could come up with was that ʿĀ'isha used to fall asleep when dough was rising, allowing her pet lamb to eat it. The scandal was only resolved, and ʿĀ'isha vindicated, by a special revelation which, incidentally, confirmed an important point in Islamic law: "Why, when you heard it, did the believing men and women not of their own account think good thoughts, and say, 'This is a manifest calumny'? Why did they not bring four witnesses against it? But since they did not bring the witnesses, in God's sight they are the liars" (Qur'ān 24:11). In the absence of four reliable eyewitnesses, ʿĀ'isha was vindicated and her accusers duly punished.

The Peace of al-Ḥudaybiyya and the Farewell Pilgrimage

In the sixth year after he entered Medina, Muhammad felt confident enough of his position to attempt a pilgrimage to Mecca. The Quraysh sent out a force to stop him, and the Prophet camped outside Mecca at a placed called al-Ḥudaybiyya, where the companions of the Prophet made a solemn pledge of loyalty to him. Prolonged negotiations with the Quraysh followed, which ended in a ten-year peace treaty. According to the terms of the agreement the Muslims were not to enter Mecca that year, but would be allowed to come for three nights to perform pilgrimage in future years. Fugitives from Mecca were to be returned by the Muslims. Although no blood was shed, in Ibn Isḥāq's view, "No previous victory in Islam was greater than this. There was nothing but battle when men met; but when there was an armistice and war was abolished and men met in safety and consulted together none talked about Islam intelligently without entering it. In those two years double as many or more than double entered Islam as ever before."

After the peace of al-Ḥudaybiyya, the Muslims went from victory to victory. In the seventh year after the Hijra, the oasis of Khaybar was taken. In the same year a large party of Muslims who had been exiled in Abyssinia returned. At the end of the year the Prophet entered Mecca for the first time since his flight to perform pilgrimage. Finally, two years later, some tribal allies of the Quraysh violated the terms of the peace of al-Ḥudaybiyya and Muhammad moved against Mecca. The Quraysh surrendered and the Prophet entered the city as victor less than eight years after he had left it as a fugitive. In the same year Muhammad subdued the important towns of al-Ṭā'if and Tabūk.

The following year, the ninth after the Hijra, is remembered as the year of deputations. Delegations came from throughout the Arabian peninsula to offer their submission to the Prophet. Muhammad also sent out his own representatives to call the Arabs to Islam. It was at the urging of his deputy, Khālid ibn Walīd, for example, that the Christians of Najrān became Muslims. One significant hold-out was a rival prophet, Musaylima, who wrote to the Prophet suggesting a power-sharing arrangement. Musaylima was not subdued until after Muhammad's death. One of Muhammad's last actions was to send letters to the rulers of surrounding nations, Arab and non-Arab, to call them to Islam.

In the tenth year after the Hijra Muhammad performed the pilgrimage for the last time, and delivered his most famous and most treasured speech. After giving specific instructions about the Ḥajj and some practical marriage counseling, he concluded with an exhortation to unity: "Know that every Muslim is a Muslim's brother," he said, "and that the Muslims are brethren." It was advice his followers would sorely need in the years to come.

Muhammad died in the quarters of his wife, 'Ā'isha, following a brief illness. After the Prophet's death, 'Umar was in a state of denial, but the more realistic and astute Abū Bakr announced to the Muslims, "O men, if anyone worships Muhammad, Muhammad is dead: if anyone worships God, God is alive, immortal!"

Evaluation

By any measure Ibn Isḥāq's biography of Muhammad makes fascinating reading. It also offers a plausible and widely accepted explanation for the rise of Islam in Arabia. According to this account Islam arose from the life and experience of a single, remarkable individual. And whether one takes a modern, secular viewpoint, labeling Muhammad a religious genius, or the Muslim viewpoint, calling it revelation, either way Islam starts with a solitary, sixth-century Arab prophet meditating in a cave. But how far should we trust this story of Muhammad's life? The question leads in two directions. First, and most obviously, what were Ibn Isḥāq's sources? How did he know what he knew, and how did he come to structure his account of Muhammad as he did? These questions lead us to an examination of the ḥadīth, Islamic tradition literature. We will return to that topic in chapter 6.

There is, however, another possible line of inquiry. Ibn Isḥāq lived more than a century after Muhammad. Do we have earlier records, especially records contemporary with Muhammad's life, by which we might evaluate Ibn Isḥāq's account? In other words, can we get behind Ibn Isḥāq? The obvious answer would seem to be an emphatic Yes. We have, after all, the chief product of Muhammad's religious mission, the Qur'ān. If the Qur'ān comes to us largely unchanged from the time of Muhammad then it will provide the surest and clearest evidence of Muhammad's religious vision.

Traditional Chronology of Muhammad's Life	
570	Year of the elephant. Mecca is delivered from Abraha's invasion and Muhammad is born
605	Rebuilding of the Ka'ba in which Muhammad acts as arbitrator
610	Muhammad is visited with his first revelations
613	The Prophet begins to proclaim Islam publicly, beginning a period of intense opposition. Emigration of Muslims to Abyssinia. Quraysh boycott of the Banū Hāshim and Banū Muṭṭalib
619	Khadīja, Muhammad's wife, and Abū Ṭālib, Muhammad's uncle and protector, die

622	The Hijra. Muhammad and his followers emigrate to Yathrib where Muhammad becomes ruler, marking the beginning of the Islamic era
624	Battle of Badr. Expulsion of the Banū Qaynuqāʿ. Change in qibla
625	Battle of Uḥud. Expulsion of the Banū an-Naḍīr
627	Battle of the Ditch. Massacre of the Banū Qurayẓa
628	Peace of al-Ḥudaybiyya
630	Muslims occupy Mecca
632	Muhammad dies after giving a farewell address in which he urges his followers to remain unified

Resources for Further Study

The best entry point for study of the life of Muhammad is Alfred Guillaume's *The Life of Muhammad: A Translation of Ibn Isḥāq's Sīrat Rasūl Allāh* (1955). For a literary analysis of the sīra see Uri Rubin, *The Eye of the Beholder: The Life of Muhammad as Viewed by the Early Muslims* (1995), and for a historical analysis of the sources see F. E. Peters, *Muhammad and the Origins of Islam* (1994b), especially the final chapter on the quest of the historical Muhammad. Michael Cook's attempt to write a biography of Muhammad based on the Qur'ān resulted in a very slim book, *Muhammad* (1983), which is not so much a biography as it is Cook's sometimes idiosyncratic take on the major themes of the Qur'ān. The most useful part of the book is chapter 7, where Cook offers a critique of the traditional sources. A great many modern biographies accept the essential reliability of the Muslim sources but put a modern spin on the interpretation of those sources. The most comprehensive of these is William Montgomery Watt, *Muhammad at Mecca* (1953) and *Muhammad at Medina* (1956). Watt also published an abbreviated version of his biography in *Muhammad: Prophet and Statesman* (1961). Others include Maxime Rodinson, *Muhammad* (1980) and Martin Lings, *Muhammad: His Life Based on the Earliest Sources* (1983). Among modern Muslims, biographies of the Prophet by the Egyptian Muhammad Ḥusayn Haykal (1995) and the Indian Muslim, Shiblī Nuʿmānī (1979), have been particularly influential.

5
THE QUR'ĀN

Approaches to the Qur'ān

The Qur'ān is no ordinary book. Its title, which means "recitations," reflects both the structure and function of the text. The Qur'ān should be thought of as a sort of anthology of discrete "recitations," and, like poetry, it is best recited aloud. There are other respects in which the Qur'ān is no ordinary book. When we think of a book, we are normally concerned primarily with what it has to say. In the case of the Qur'ān, however, the meaning of the text is often displaced by other concerns. Why this is so can be illustrated from the story of a major archeological find.

In 1972, in the course of a restoration project at an ancient mosque in Ṣan'ā', Yemen, a laborer unearthed an extensive deposit of soggy paper and parchment. The deposit turned out to be a repository of fragments from hundreds of ancient codices of the Qur'ān. (The codex – codices in the plural – was the forerunner of the modern book.) An official of the Yemeni Antiquities Authority noticed that some of the documents appeared to be very old and began to look for help in restoring and preserving them. In the following years the find generated a good bit of interest among scholars and excitement even bubbled over into the mainstream – in 1999 the *Atlantic Monthly* published a cover story under the banner, "What is the Koran?" which centered on the Ṣan'ā' find and hinted that it might be a catalyst for a revolution in Qur'ānic scholarship. Scholars speculated that these might be the oldest fragments of the Qur'ān ever found and a critical new piece of evidence about the earliest history of the Qur'ānic text (Lester 1999).

Regardless of how old the Ṣan'ā' fragments actually turn out to be, the event in itself illustrates two important approaches to the Qur'ān that are quite independent of any concern for the actual content of the book. According to the first approach, characteristic of Muslim piety, the Qur'ān is a sacred object. The reason that the fragments were preserved at all was that someone considered the *physical* copies and fragments of the Qur'ān to be sacred. As holy objects the paper and parchment could not be burned or disposed of in any ordinary way, but had to be given a proper burial to preserve them from defilement. What mattered to those who buried these scraps of paper was not primarily what they said, but what they were.

A second way of approaching the Qur'ān is to view it not as a sacred object, but as a historical artifact. It is a text with a history, and the chief interest of the scholar is to ferret out when and where it originated and how it evolved into its present form. It might be assumed that such an approach is primarily the domain of non-Muslim scholars, but in fact Muslim scholars have been centrally concerned with the history of the Qur'ānic text. The Ṣan'ā' find was a reminder of how little we know for sure about the origins and early history of the text of the Qur'ān. Scholars were excited at the possibility that some of the documents might prove to be the oldest fragments of the Qur'ān yet found, but even the most optimistic guesses place the most ancient of the documents in the mid-eighth century, more than a century after the conquests. (For the sake of comparison, our most ancient manuscript fragment of a New Testament document, part of the Gospel of John, has been dated to within forty years of the gospel's authorship.) That Qur'ān fragments penned more than a century after the conquests might be our very oldest documentary evidence of the text is a testimony to how little really firm evidence we have about how, when, and where the Qur'ān originated.

There is, of course, a third and rather obvious way of approaching the Qur'ān, and that is to focus on what it says. This tends to be the major interest of contemporary readers who suffer from the modern, secular habit of thinking of a book chiefly as a means of conveying a message. But this is not the primary way in which a great many Muslims have experienced the Qur'ān. One reason for this is quite simple: the majority of Muslims through most of history have not had direct access to the content of their scriptures, either because they have been illiterate, or because they do not understand Arabic. Consequently, they experience the Qur'ān as an object of devotion, a thing of beauty, and a nexus of spiritual power, but not necessarily or primarily for its discursive meaning. There are other, more complicated reasons why the Qur'ān is experienced for more than its message, but we must put off dealing with those for now.

These three ways of approaching the Qur'ān – as sacred object, as historical artifact, and as discursive text to be interpreted and understood – each raise different questions, all of them important to our understanding of Islam. We

(a)

(b)

Figure 5.1 Qur'ān manuscripts showing variations in calligraphic style and illumination. The first is from an early manuscript in Kufic calligraphy. The second is in Maghribi style. Photo: A. Private Collection/The Bridgeman Art Library; B. Musee Conde, Chantilly, France/The Bridgeman Art Library

will consider each in turn, and we begin with the question that has both historical and logical priority: where did the Qur'ān originate and how did it come to have its present form?

The History of the Text

A striking characteristic of the Qur'ān is the extraordinary uniformity of the Arabic text in all extant editions. (This assertion applies only to the consonants in the text, not the vowels.) Whether we compare modern printed editions or the oldest manuscripts, the basic Arabic text in any given Qur'ān is consistent with every other – so consistent, in fact, that when small anomalies are discovered they loom large. So, for example, slight differences in verse ordering in some of the Ṣan'ā' fragments have assumed a huge importance for scholars, and, similarly, a great deal has been made of small variances between the Dome of the Rock inscriptions and the canonical text of the Qur'ān. But such anomalies are so few and so minor that at first blush it might appear that the text of the Qur'ān has no history – or that its history is limited to changes in styles of Arabic calligraphy. For at least twelve centuries the text has proven remarkably immune to the forces of time.

This preservation of the uniformity and consistency of the text is in itself a remarkable achievement of Islamic civilization. Muslims have been justifiably proud that their scripture has remained so timeless and changeless. Indeed, the consistency of the text is sometimes offered as evidence to support Muslim claims that the Qur'ān is inimitable, unequaled among scriptures. There is some merit to the claim, and the Qur'ān itself supports it (17:88).

But this should not prevent us from asking, has the text of the Qur'ān *always* been so uniform? The answer given within Muslim tradition is a qualified Yes. Yes, the text has remained consistent, but only from the time that it was put in its present form by the order of the Caliph 'Uthmān in about 650. The Muslim tradition thus allows about forty years for the evolution of the Qur'ān from the beginning of Muhammad's revelations to the establishment of a canonical text. For the remaining fourteen centuries, however, the Qur'ān is believed to have remained unchanged. There is one other significant qualification to the Muslim affirmation that the Qur'ān has remained the same since 'Uthmān. The earliest manuscripts of the Qur'ān lack vowels and pointing, the dots that distinguish some Arabic consonants from each other. Without pointing a "t" might be indistinguishable from a "b". Hence actual recitations of the Qur'ān might vary according to which vowels are inserted and how the consonants are pointed, and seven differing systems of reciting the text are accepted as canonical. Rarely do these variations have real significance for understanding and interpreting the text, however. In practice, moreover, most modern editions of the Qur'ān will have uniform vowels as well as consonants because one particular way of reciting the Qur'ān has gained widespread acceptance in modern times.

Most contemporary scholars of the Qur'ān will agree with the Muslim tradition that the text has remained uniform for a very long time, but with an important qualification. The text has, indeed, remained uniform from the era of our earliest extant manuscripts, but our earliest manuscripts date from the ninth century. That leaves a gap of roughly 200 years between the life of the Prophet and our first indisputable evidence of a uniform, stabilized text of the Qur'ān. Thus the scholarly tradition can allow up to 200 years for the evolution of the Qur'ānic text – perhaps even more if some of the materials were circulating before the seventh century (Wansbrough 1977: 52).

The Muslim and the Western scholarly traditions thus share the conviction that the Qur'ānic text did have a prehistory, but they differ, sometimes sharply, about the length and nature of that prehistory. For Muslims, the process was simple, short, and linear: Muhammad began to receive revelations from God through the angel Jibrīl – Gabriel – in 610; the Prophet recited the revelations in the presence of his followers throughout his career; his followers dutifully memorized or wrote these revelations down on whatever materials they could find. After Muhammad's death some of his companions gathered and organized the revelations in written collections. Finally, around 650, 'Uthmān arranged for the collection and editing of an official version of the Qur'ān from the best sources, both written and oral, and ordered all deviant copies destroyed. Described in this way the process sounds rather orderly and tidy. Some Muslim sources preserved reports that suggest that in fact it may have been quite messy. Some traditions report that revelations were lost – according to 'Ā'isha one portion was eaten by a domestic animal – and that some legitimate revelations were excluded from the finalized text. Shī'ītes, for example, have remained convinced that verses clearly indicating the place of 'Alī as proper successor to Muhammad were edited out, and Islamic legal scholars were convinced that there was originally a Qur'ānic revelation to justify the stoning of adulterers. Such reports should not necessarily be taken at face value, since they reflect a later context when it was useful to be able to claim that God had more to say than merely what was included in the Qur'ān. They do, however, form a part of the traditional Muslim view of how the Qur'ān came to be and indicate that Muslims themselves do not deny that the Qur'ān went through a process of formation and molding before the text was finally stabilized. In the Muslim account, however, this process of formation was exceedingly swift, ending less than two decades after the death of Muhammad.

In one respect the character of the Qur'ān accords well with this traditional account of its swift formation. The text is hastily and lightly edited. This is often a source of frustration to the novice reader. The Qur'ān has no narrative framework, its sūras are ordered without any apparent concern about content, and even within each sūra topic and tone fluctuate abruptly and without warning. The editors of the final text, whether in ʿUthmān's time or later, were apparently not concerned to smooth out these rough edges. A closer look at a particular passage will reinforce this impression. Toward the beginning of Sūra 22, for example, we read:

> And among men there is such a one that disputes concerning God without knowledge and follows every rebel Satan, against whom it is written down that whosoever takes him for a friend, him he leads astray, and he guides him to the chastisement of the burning. O men, if you are in doubt as to the Uprising, surely We created you of dust then of a sperm-drop, then of a blood clot, then of a lump of flesh, formed and unformed that We may make clear to you. (22:3–5)

These verses exemplify a fairly common pattern in the Qur'ān. In one verse God will be talking about himself in the third person; in the next he will suddenly switch to the first person plural. It would be fair to conclude that the final editors of the Qur'ān did not feel the freedom or the inclination to iron out such wrinkles in the text. They took what they were given and compiled it as best they could, but they did not work with it.

Other features of the Qur'ān fit much less comfortably with the traditional account of its hasty compilation. Around the time of its canonization, for example, some words and passages in the Qur'ān were apparently unintelligible to its readers. In a number of passages the Qur'ān itself seems to acknowledge that its readers might have a hard time understanding its language by conveniently offering explanatory glosses. In twelve separate instances a difficult word is accompanied by the phrase "And what shall teach you what is the . . . ," which is then followed by an explanation. Sūra 101 provides a double example:

> In the Name of God, the Merciful, the Compassionate. The Clatterer! What is the Clatterer? And what shall teach thee what is the Clatterer? The day that men shall be likely scattered moths, and the mountains shall be like plucked wool tufts. Then he whose deeds weigh heavy in the Balance shall inherit a pleasing life, but he whose deeds weigh light in the Balance shall plunge in the womb of the Pit. And what shall teach thee what is the Pit? A blazing Fire!

Readers were simply not expected to know what the words translated here as "Clatterer" and "Pit" meant. Translators of the Qur'ān still do not know, and Arberry's (1955) translation given here is no more than an overconfident guess. The very earliest Muslim Qur'ān commentators also had to guess. They had little idea what to do with these and many other words in the Qur'ān. Hence their guesses are often wildly different from one another and simply show that no one really knew these words, and that a good part of the language of the Qur'ān was foreign to them. The traditional account of the formation of the Qur'ān cannot account for this gap in knowledge. If the Qur'ān was composed during Muhammad's lifetime and compiled within twenty years of his death, there is simply not enough time to allow for such widespread forgetfulness. The language of the Qur'ān should have been familiar to Muslims from the beginning, and that knowledge should have been passed on as it was recited, taught, and commented on. Apparently this was not the case.

It seems, then, that by the time of its canonization much of the material included in the Qur'ān was very old – old enough that the vocabulary was archaic and there was no one around who remembered what it originally meant. Two explanations seem possible. Either the tradition is correct and the Qur'ānic materials did originate in the early seventh century, but they were collected and canonized in the eighth or ninth; or, alternatively, the Qur'ān was canonized in the seventh century, but some of its content was already ancient by that time. These explanations do not exclude one another, but both possibilities do call the traditional account into question.

Perhaps the most serious reservations about the traditional account of the Qur'ān's origins arise from the question of context. Broadly speaking, the Qur'ān includes four overlapping kinds of material: oracular utterances (especially of judgment), polemical passages, narrative passages, and religious law. Little of this material, with the possible exception of the first category, fits well in the seventh-century Arabian context. The narrative passages, with some rare exceptions, draw on characters and themes from biblical literature. They tell stories about Adam, Noah, Abraham, Moses, Solomon, and Jesus, and the stories they tell are recognizable variants of biblical accounts. In some cases these variants are familiar to us from Jewish or Christian tradition. In particular, a number of Qur'ānic narratives have a very close resemblance to similar narratives preserved in the Talmud or in midrashic literature. Similarly, Qur'ānic accounts of Jesus closely resemble accounts found in non-canonical Christian sources.

The Qur'ān clearly deals in stories that were "in the air" among Christians and Jews in the Near East. If we place the Qur'ān in seventh-century Arabia, we can only make sense of its origins by importing significant Jewish and Christian influences into the Ḥijāz – influences for which there is very little convincing evidence. It would seem at least as plausible to suggest that perhaps Arabia is not the context for the origins of the Qur'ān and that the Islamic scriptures more probably came together in a Near Eastern environment – in Syria and Palestine – during the first 150 years after the Arab conquests.

The Qur'ān's polemics also fit better in a Syrian religious environment. The Qur'ān polemicizes against Christians, Jews, and idolaters. The idolaters have usually been identified as pagan Arabs, but Hawting (1999) has convincingly argued that polemics against idolatry are more probably directed at Jews and Christians. Polemics against Arabian Jews might make some sense; there were, apparently, significant Jewish communities in the Arabian peninsula. But where do the Qur'ān's anti-Christian polemics come from? A superficial reading of the book leaves the impression that God is exceedingly distressed at the manifest errors of Christians. One of the Qur'ān's most elegant and oft-quoted sūras is clearly anti-Trinitarian, and has always been understood as such:

> In the Name of God, the Merciful, the Compassionate. Say: "He is God, One, God, the Everlasting Refuge, who has not begotten, and has not been begotten, and equal to Him is not any one." (Sūra 112)

When the Qur'ān mentions Jesus it seldom neglects to remind us that he is not God's Son, that he never claimed to be God's Son, and that Christians blaspheme by saying so. All of this would suggest that the Qur'ān emerged from an environment dominated by Christianity. Yet the tradition records only a limited Christian presence in either Mecca or Medina. So who was there to argue with, and who was to care whether God had a son?

Jesus in the Qur'ān

The fact is that the Qur'ān has an astonishingly thorough Christology (Parrinder 1976; Robinson 1991). Muslims, of course, are not astonished because presumably God should be expected to know all that can be known about Jesus. But scholars or students who are concerned to match text with context should be startled. Jesus is a dominant prophetic figure in the Qur'ān and arguably its most fully developed character. We learn about his miraculous virgin birth, about miracles he performed as a child, about his disciples. We also have somewhat mysterious accounts. One of these seems connected with the Last Supper, another seems to deny the Crucifixion. Jesus is given standard Christological titles: Rūḥ Allāh, the Spirit of God, and Kalām Allāh, a Word from God. Yet against this apparent exaltation of Jesus, the Qur'ān repeatedly and emphatically denies that Jesus is the Son of God and insists that he is a messenger – a remarkable messenger, perhaps, but only a messenger.

In this tendency to exalt Jesus while keeping his feet firmly planted on earth, the Qur'ān shows a remarkable affinity with certain non-orthodox varieties of Christianity. We have already seen that the broad themes of Qur'ānic Christology were anticipated by Manichaeism. Like the Qur'ān, Manī had taught that the human Jesus was only a prophet, and that he did not, in fact, die on the cross. But perhaps the more direct resemblance is to a form of Jewish Christianity. This is not to suggest that there was a direct genetic relationship between any of these groups and Islam. But it seems reasonable to suggest that they show the effects of the same milieu – that the environment which produced the Manichaean and Jewish–Christian Christologies was a religious and intellectual environment very similar to that in which the Qur'ān was formed. Perhaps that environment was seventh-century Arabia, but if so Christianity in its many varieties must have penetrated the peninsula far more thoroughly than anyone has convincingly shown. Moreover, Muslim tradition must for some reason have chosen to suppress knowledge of such penetration. It seems much more likely that the context for the formation of the Qur'ān is not Arabia, but farther north, and not before the conquests, but after.

Alert readers will have noticed two apparently contradictory results of this survey. The language of the Qur'ān appears archaic and rooted in an Arab environment. By contrast, its thematic content fits snugly into the religious milieu of the Near East. Should this surprise us? Only if we insist on squeezing the formative period of the Qur'ān into the first five decades of the seventh century. In that case both features of the Qur'ān become inexplicable. But if we allow the possibility of a much longer period of formation it will not seem strange that later redactors (editors) of the Qur'ān preserved older traditions – some of which were opaque to them – in a way that was relevant to their own milieu. This is, after all, what redactors do.

The most thorough exploration of this hypothesis may be found in the work of John Wansbrough. In two seminal works, *Quranic Studies* (1977) and *The Sectarian Milieu* (1978), Wansbrough set out to apply methods developed in biblical studies to the Qur'ān. His hypothesis, that the Qur'ān was standardized about 200 years later than the Muslim tradition reports, has been challenged, but has yet to be convincingly refuted (Wansbrough 1977: 52). In fact, Wansbrough's arguments, given the state of the evidence, are substantially irrefutable. Unless firmly datable documentary evidence can be produced to show that the Qur'ānic text was stable in the seventh century, Wansbrough's hypothesis cannot be dismissed. Neither, however, can the hypothesis be firmly established, as Wansbrough's numerous critics have been quick to point out.

Consequently, students of Islam are faced with a set of contrasting paradigms for the formation of the Qur'ān. Proponents of one paradigm accept the traditional Muslim view, sometimes with superficial revision. The other paradigm places the canonization of the Qur'ān in a Near Eastern environment during the two centuries following the conquest. Neither paradigm can be definitively proven, both have weaknesses, and they are quite incompatible. My own sympathies have been expressed here with a degree of confidence that could be misleading. I have my doubts, and on many days the slightest bit of evidence could sway me.

The Qur'ān in Muslim Piety

Pious Muslims, of course, will be inured to such speculations about the origins of their scripture. From the perspective of Muslim piety and Muslim theology the Qur'ān comes from God and its sacred origins are the only origins that matter. Belief in the sanctity of the Qur'ān is reflected in a variety of pious practices. The concern for the proper disposal of Qur'ānic texts that motivated those who preserved the Ṣan'ā' repository is just one example of a whole complex of scruples governing the handling of the Qur'ān. A Qur'ān should never be carried below the waist, should never be placed beneath other books, and (according to some scholars) should not be touched by a ritually impure Muslim or by an unbeliever. The Qur'ān itself can be taken to justify these scruples: "It is surely a noble Qur'ān in a hidden book – none but the purified touch it – a sending down from the Lord of being" (56:77–80). Muslim scholars differed over how rigorously such regulations should be applied, but they agreed that a copy of the Qur'ān is a holy object and must in some way be protected from defilement. The practice of the majority of contemporary Muslims shows that they concur. A most efficient way to instigate a riot in most any Muslim city from Fez to Jakarta would be to publicly deface the Qur'ān.

What is noteworthy about these pious scruples is that they apply not just to the content of the Qur'ān, but to the Qur'ān as a physical object. Nor is it necessary to have a full copy. Any fragment of the Qur'ān is sacred and a focus of divine blessing and power. In the Pakistani context in which I was brought up, the use of Qur'ānic texts as amulets to ward off evil was pervasive, and I often observed copies of the Qur'ān placed on the doors of unguarded buildings for protection from thieves. Similar uses of the Qur'ān as a talisman against evil or a source of spiritual power and blessing can be observed throughout the Islamic world. It is not, in some contexts, surprising to see a pious Muslim kissing or rubbing his face against the pages of the Qur'ān.

Power and blessing also accompany the verbal recitation of the Qur'ān. Such recitation is central to all Muslim ritual observance and a pervasive influence in Muslim piety. Recitation is required in ritual prayers, and is ubiquitous at public occasions of almost every kind, including weddings, funerals, political events, social gatherings, and times of national emergency or mourning. Memorization of the entire Qur'ān is not uncommon and confers on those who are successful the designation ḥāfiẓ al-Qur'ān and special status within the community. Recitation is also a highly developed and valued art form. The spiritual value and power attributed to the recited Qur'ān is sometimes quite independent of the meaning of the text. Non-Arabic speaking Muslims often learn to recite the text of the Qur'ān fluently without understanding the discursive meaning of what they are reciting.

The Eternity of the Qur'ān

Westerners and modern-minded Muslims often concur in disparaging and dismissing pious practices surrounding the Qur'ān as vestiges of superstition. In fact, in light of traditional Muslim beliefs about the nature of revelation, pious scruples and rituals surrounding the Qur'ān make a great deal of sense. To see why, we can begin with the Muslim assertion that the Qur'ān is the Word of God. It is a deceptively simple claim, and might be taken as meaning no more than that the Qur'ānic message comes from God and that humans should therefore heed that message. It is possible that this was the sum of what Muslims at first believed about the Qur'ān. If so, they quickly learned more sophisticated ways of thinking. The idea of the Word – the Logos – had a long history in Greek thought, from whence it had made its way into both Jewish and Christian theology. The Word of God, for both Christians and Jews, had come to mean not just the content of God's communications, but a pre-existent emanation from God (see the Gospel of John 1:1–13).

The Qur'ān itself gave Muslims reason to start thinking along similar lines. The idea of a pre-existing Book, the archetype of the earthly book, is alluded to in several Qur'ānic statements: "No! I swear by the fallings of the stars (and that is indeed a mighty oath, did you but know it) it is surely a noble Koran in a hidden book none but the purified shall touch, a sending down from the Lord of all Being" (56:78; cf. 85:22). Once Muslims had begun to think of the Qur'ān as having a pre-existing form – as the divine Logos – they inherited a whole set of theological problems long familiar to Christians. Was the heavenly Qur'ān eternally pre-existent, or created? What was the relation of the heavenly Qur'ān to its earthly copies? And if the Word was eternally pre-existent, what was its relation to the divine essence?

These questions came to a head in 833 CE, during the reign of the 'Abbāsid Caliph Ma'mūn. If Ma'mūn had been a Christian we would immediately recognize him as a partisan of the Arian heresy. He, along with his successor Mu'taṣim and the religious establishment they patronized, sought to enforce as official doctrine the belief that the Qur'ān was created, and they did so for reasons that Arius might have found cheering. The opposing idea that the Qur'ān was eternal and uncreated had already set down deep roots, however, and was defended by a formidable scholar, Ibn Ḥanbal, who would not be dissuaded from his convictions by any amount of flogging. Ibn Ḥanbal and like-minded religious scholars were systematically persecuted by Ma'mūn and Mu'taṣim during the famous miḥna, a rare instance in Islamic history of an organized inquisition.

In the end the miḥna failed, and the Caliph Mutawwakil reversed the policy of his predecessors. The orthodox doctrine which triumphed bore a curious resemblance to orthodox Christian doctrine. The divine Word is uncreated, eternally existing with God, and this same eternal, uncreated Word is manifested on earth in the form of a book. Just as the Christians taught of the Word *incarnate* – the Word made flesh – so orthodox Muslim theologians, to use Henri Wolfson's imaginative phrase, came to believe that the Qur'ān was the Word *inlibrate* – the Word made Book (Wolfson 1976: 244–63).

For those who took the doctrine of the eternity of the Qur'ān most seriously, any and every manifestation of the Word of God was "uncreated." The most extreme of the creeds insist that the Qur'ān is God's uncreated Word in whatever form it is found (Wensinck 1932: 127). Thus the words of the Qur'ān qualify as what scholars of religion would call a theophany – the closest the believer can come to direct encounter with God. Seen in this light, a Muslim's scrupulous concern to protect the text from defilement is no more superstitious than a Roman Catholic believer's reverence for the elements of the Eucharist. Both practices are rooted in theology that is concerned with the earthly manifestation of the Divine Logos. And just as Christian theology has often been more preoccupied with what Jesus *was* than with what he *said*, so too with Islamic theology and the Qur'ān.

The Inimitability of the Qur'ān

A logical corollary of the doctrine that the Qur'ān is uncreated was belief in its inimitability. The Qur'ān itself challenges its critics to produce anything like it:

> This Koran could not have been forged apart from God; but it is a confirmation of what is before it, and a distinguishing of the Book, wherein is no doubt, from the Lord of all Being. Or do they say, "Why, he has forged it?" Say: "Then produce a sūra like it, and call on whom you can, apart from God, if you speak truly." (10:38–40)

> Say, "If men and jinn banded together to produce the like of this Koran, they would never produce its like, not though they backed one another." (17:88)

These claims came to be understood by Muslims as objective statements about the literary merits of the Qur'ān. It simply could not and would never be equaled in beauty or perfection.

Such doctrines about the nature of the Qur'ān fit rather uneasily with what Muslims remembered about the actual revelation of the Qur'ān in history. On the one hand, the Qur'ān was perfect and eternal; on the other hand, it had been revealed piecemeal over the course of twenty-two years in a particular historical context and collected in a very imperfect manner after Muhammad's death. Equally problematic was the question of how the Qur'ān could have existed from eternity when it so clearly reflected the immediate context of the life of the Prophet. According to the orthodox understanding of revelation, the Qur'ān was dictated to the Prophet. Muhammad himself had no part in its production except as a faithful (indeed, infallible) transmitter of the message. Yet, as we will see in the following section, Muslim interpreters of the Qur'ān insist that the Qur'ān must be interpreted in light of the events of Muhammad's life. This tension between the status of the Qur'ān as a sacred object and the practical problem of actually interpreting and applying its message continues to fuel discussion among Muslims.

Interpreting the Qur'ān

The best way to get at the meaning of the Qur'ān, one might think, would be to pick up a translation and read it for oneself. Inexpensive translations are accessible enough, after all, and why should one read a textbook synopsis when one can read the original, which happens to be rather more interesting? This is excellent advice for anyone who wishes to read the Qur'ān for personal edification. It turns out to be very poor advice for anyone concerned to understand how Muslims approach the content of the Qur'ān. A simple comparison will make this clear. Suppose that a student unfamiliar with the Bible, but knowing it to be Christian scripture, was to begin reading it to try to understand Christianity. She would likely begin at the beginning, in Genesis, and before she was a quarter of the way through she would not need to read any further to know that Christianity is a religion that condones child sacrifice, misogyny, and genocide. If our student had some vague impression of endemic violence, wife battering, and child abuse in Western societies she would immediately know where to place the blame. The dominant religious tradition of Western civilization is quite obviously a misogynistic and violent religion, as anyone who begins to read its scriptures can immediately see.

Unfortunately, this sort of attitude is increasingly evident in introductory religion courses, but any believing Christian or Jew will immediately see the error. Just as Christians and Jews read the Hebrew scriptures through the lens of an ancient and sophisticated interpretive tradition, and so do not feel bound to sacrifice their children, wipe out unbelievers, or even, in the case of Christians, keep kosher, so also Muslims and the Qur'ān. An instinct to completely bypass the interpretive tradition of the community and to read the scriptures idiosyncratically is largely a modern tendency, characteristic of scripturalist movements (sometimes mischaracterized as fundamentalist) – but that is to anticipate a topic which will be dealt with more fully in its proper place. My point here is simply to say that outsiders to a tradition often become unwitting scripturalists when they read someone else's Holy Book.

One antidote is to keep in mind what a traditional Muslim scholar would need to know before he ventured an interpretation of a particular passage of the Qur'ān. He would, of course, need to begin with a thorough knowledge of the Arabic vocabulary and grammar of the passage. A translation would certainly never do. Intricacies and uncertainties in the vocabulary would take him into the field of lexicography, and by extension he would have to become a student of the early Arabic literary tradition, and especially Arabic poetry. Naturally he would need a comprehensive grasp of the interpretations of all of the major Qur'ān commentators who preceded him. After mastering the language of the passage, and becoming aware of the different possible readings, he will move on to consider its context. For this purpose he will need to have a thorough knowledge of the life of Muhammad, and specific knowledge of the circumstances in which the particular passage was revealed. Is the audience of the passage general or specific? Is a particular command limited by particular circumstances, or meant for general application? To answer such questions our scholar will need to be familiar with the extensive literature which describes the "occasions of revelation," the asbāb al-nuzūl. Our scholar will further need to collate the passage with any other passages which are parallel or concerned with similar topics. He will need to determine whether there are other later Qur'ānic verses which replace, modify, or further explicate the passage. Finally, he will have to do the same with the ḥadīth literature, searching out traditions from the Prophet which limit the application or explain the intent of the passage. To sum up, authoritative interpretation of the Qur'ān ideally requires access to a substantial library, which would include material from all of the major branches of Muslim traditional knowledge. This should provide sufficient reason for newcomers to the text, particularly non-Muslims, to be circumspect about venturing casual opinions about what a particular passage means. The Qur'ān, in other words, is a book which cries out for interpretation.

Central Themes

The Qur'ān's need for interpretation does not spring from any confusion about the basic message of the book, however. The overall thrust of the Qur'ān is remarkably simple, and can be summarized in a paragraph. It begins, of course, with God. God is One, the Creator of all that is, including humankind. We humans owe God exclusive allegiance and worship, but we tend to allow our attention to wander and to associate created beings with God. Such association, called *shirk*, is the most basic of sins. God is merciful, however, and that mercy is most clearly manifested in the form of prophets and scriptures sent as reminders to call forgetful humans back to exclusive worship of God. Scriptures and prophets also give specific guidance for how God wants people who worship him to behave. The Qur'ān is the culmination of these "reminders." The stakes are high: those who reject God's reminders will burn in hell; those who follow his guidance will enjoy the delights of paradise. This message is consistent throughout the book, and is communicated in such a variety of different ways that it is hard to miss. Muslims themselves often take the first sūra of the Qur'ān as a convenient summary of its message.

Qur'ānic Narratives

While the overall thrust of the book may be clear, however, many of the details are bedeviling. The Qur'ān is, to adapt an old Puritan adage, a pool in which a gnat could swim and an elephant drown. This mix of an easily grasped message with puzzles that have kept centuries of scholars guessing is perhaps best illustrated from the narrative portions of the Qur'ān. The Qur'ān is particularly fond of stories about prophets, most of them familiar from the Hebrew scriptures and Christian scriptures. We read accounts of Adam, Noah, Abraham, Joseph, Moses, David, Solomon, and Jesus. We also read about less familiar figures such as the Arab prophet Ṣāliḥ. The names and the details of the stories differ, but the point is almost always the same: when God sends a prophet, woe to those who reject his message. The stories are told for a narrow didactic purpose, and we are seldom in doubt about what we are supposed to learn from them.

If we come at these narratives looking for a satisfying story, however, we will only be frustrated. One of the curious characteristics of many Qur'ānic narratives is their allusive quality. The Qur'ān seems to assume that we don't need to be told the whole story, presumably because we already know it. Consequently, although the overall point is usually clear enough, the significance of the details is often a mystery. A quick read of the Qur'ān's story of Joseph in Sūra 12, for example, leaves the reader mystified about the significance of many of the details. Why, for example, is Joseph thrown into prison immediately after he has been convincingly proven innocent? And what are we to make of the mysterious scene in which the prominent women of Egypt simultaneously cut themselves when they see Joseph?

We have already touched on the most likely explanation for this allusive quality of Qur'ānic narratives. The Qur'ānic stories are closely related to narratives familiar from Jewish and Christian tradition and they reflect an environment of competition with Jews and Christians in which these narratives were in the air. Once we acknowledge this environment we will not be surprised that elements, for example, of the Joseph narrative in Sūra 12 are strikingly similar to stories about Joseph in Jewish midrashic literature. The Qur'ān, in other words, is betraying one of its major functions as a polemical work formed in a polemical environment. This is an explanation which most Muslims will have no difficulty rejecting, but it does seem to make sense of the material. The more important point, from our perspective, is that there was plenty to keep commentators busy.

Along with stories of prophets the Qur'ān also has a good deal to say about previous scriptures. As with the prophets, there is little variation among scriptures apart from the names. Moses was given the Torah, David the Zabūr, Jesus the Injīl. These all contained essentially the same message as the Qur'ān. Since casual observation will show that extant versions of these scriptures do not match the Qur'ān, many Muslims have concluded that Jewish and Christian scriptures have been corrupted. Thus the major challenge for Muslim interpreters of these passages is to make sense of the relationship between Islam and previous dispensations.

Qur'ānic Law and the Problem of Abrogation

If the need for interpretation had been limited to filling in the details of narratives, interpretation of the Qur'ān might remain simply an interesting scholarly diversion. When the Qur'ān is approached as a source of practical guidance, however, the task of interpretation becomes urgent. God says a good deal in the Qur'ān about how he would like human beings to behave, but he does not always express himself with quite the degree of clarity that his most rigorous followers might wish. On the thorny issue of wine-drinking, for example, the Qur'ān has these varied statements:

> This is the similitude of Paradise which the god-fearing have been promised: therein are rivers of water unstaling, rivers of milk unchanging in flavor, and rivers of wine – a delight to the drinkers. (47:15)

> They will question thee concerning wine, and arrow-shuffling. Say: "In both is heinous sin, and uses for men, but the sin in them is more heinous than the usefulness." (2:217)

> O believers, draw not near to prayer when you are drunken until you know what you are saying. (4:46)

> O believers, wine and arrow-shuffling, idols and divining-arrows are an abomination, some of Satan's work; so avoid it; haply so you will prosper. Satan only desires to precipitate enmity and hatred between you in regard to wine and arrow-shuffling, and to bar you from the remembrance of God, and from prayer. (5:92)

Taking these passages together it is at first glance not easy to tell whether God is on the fence about wine, is mildly disapproving, or supports total prohibition.

Two solutions are possible. First, it is possible that God's opinion varies according to context. There are some situations in which drinking wine (or some kinds of wine?) might be tolerated, and others in which drinking it is absolutely prohibited. If this is the case the only way to know it will be to go outside the Qur'ān for information about the context. One must know to whom God was speaking, about what kind of wine, and in what circumstances. Only by doing so can one know how God's command is applicable to one's own circumstances. Discussions of wine in the commentaries encompass all of this information.

A second, more daring, solution is to hold that some of God's commands are marked for expiration. According to this view, God had from the start intended to replace some earlier commands with later ones. When his followers become aware of the change the earlier commands are thenceforth abrogated. This possibility that God may choose to revise his commands in this way is broached by the Qur'ān itself:

> And when We exchange a verse in the place of another verse – and God knows very well what He is sending down – they say, "Thou art a mere forger!" Nay, but the most of them have no knowledge. Say: "The Holy Spirit sent it down from thy Lord in truth, and to confirm those who believe, and to be a guidance and good tidings to those who surrender." (16:101)

The use of abrogation as a technique of interpretation became so widespread that one scholar confidently asserted that any Muslim scholar was a fraud who didn't have a full grasp of the science of abrogation (Burton 1990: 39). To fully grasp the science of abrogation, of course, one would need to have a correspondingly firm grasp of the context of revelation and know with some certainty the order in which particular verses of the Qur'ān were revealed.

Women and Gender in the Qur'ān

A final example of the complexity of interpreting the Qur'ān that has been of particular concern to modern Muslims is centered on Qur'ānic pronouncements related to women. The Qur'ān has a good deal to say about women, some of it potentially offensive to modern sensibilities. Women are assigned half the inheritance share of men. The legal testimony of one man is equated to that of two women. Men are permitted to marry up to four wives, while women must content themselves with a single husband. And, in a particularly controversial set of verses, men are declared the "maintainers" of women, and apparently given permission to beat their wives. On the other hand, as modern Muslim apologists have vigorously argued, the Qur'ān was well ahead of its time in granting independent property rights to women, assigning them legal agency, and generally improving their lot in comparison with both pre-Islamic Arabia and pre-Islamic Near Eastern civilizations.

So which is it to be? Does the Qur'ān severely constrain the rights of women and reinforce a patriarchal social order? Or does it sow the seeds of women's liberation? The answer is both, or neither, depending on the interpreter. Modern liberal interpreters have had no difficulty in asserting that the passages on women that are apparently restrictive must be contextualized to seventh-century Arabia. They have argued that the overall thrust of the Qur'ān leads to a message of equality.

Similarly, with regard to the question of whether women must be veiled outside the home, modern Muslim interpreters have diverged widely from one another. Some have argued that the Qur'ānic verses which seem to require Muslim women to seclude themselves are specifically directed to the Prophet's wives and to specific circumstances in which they needed to be protected. More traditional interpreters take these verses at face value as general instructions to all Muslims of all times.

The Problem of Context

What none of these interpreters can do without – no matter what the issue, no matter how divergent the conclusions – is context. The Qur'ān is largely inaccessible without the professional help of scholarly interpreters. Its narratives are allusive, its instructions devoid of context, and much of its vocabulary opaque. To properly understand any given passage of the Qur'ān we desperately need information about the context of its revelation. Context is something that the Qur'ān itself simply cannot provide. It is, however, exactly what the literature that grew up concerning the life of Muhammad – the sīra and ḥadīth literature – does best. The details of the Qur'ān are inexplicable apart from these traditions about Muhammad. In chapter 4 we have already surveyed the main outlines of the biography of Muhammad. In the following chapter we turn to the sources of Muhammad's biography and to the question of how the traditional story of Islamic origins came to be shaped.

Resources for Further Study

The most accessible starting points for study of the Qur'ān are Michael Cook, *The Koran: A Very Short Introduction* (2000) and, more weighty and less up to date, Richard Bell (revd. Montgomery Watt), *Introduction to the Qur'ān* (1970). For a modern Muslim scholar's take on the content of the Qur'ān, see Fazlur

Rahman's *Major Themes of the Qur'ān* (1980), and for a particularly sympathetic but explicitly Christian appreciation of the Qur'ān, see the many works of Kenneth Cragg, especially *The Event of the Qur'ān* (1971).

Among English translations of the Qur'ān, A. J. Arberry's translation, *The Koran Interpreted* (1955), has the greatest literary merit. The form of Arberry's translation is inconvenient for quick reference, however, and a better choice for everyday use is the ubiquitous Yūsuf 'Alī (1989) translation, which includes the Arabic text. The extensive notes in the Yūsuf 'Alī translation provide an interesting window onto how one modern Muslim views the Qur'ān, but they should be read with care as an idiosyncratic interpretation comparable, perhaps, to the notes in the Scofield Reference Bible. For a graceful translation of some shorter sūras along with a CD of professional Qur'ān recitations, see Michael Sells, *Approaching the Qur'ān* (1999). Various indexes and concordances of the Qur'ān are available, including Mustansir Mir, *Dictionary of Qur'ānic Terms and Concepts* (1987) and Hanna Kassis, *A Concordance of the Koran* (1983).

The most controversial contributions to modern critical scholarship of the Qur'ān are John Wansbrough's *Quranic Studies* (1977) and *The Sectarian Milieu* (1978). Wansbrough's work would be more controversial if it was easier to read. Students without a substantial background in the technical language of biblical criticism will find it rough going, and may wish to start with one of the many reviews or articles responding to Wansbrough's arguments.

For glimpses into the Muslim interpretive tradition, see the abridged translation of Ṭabarī's commentary in *Commentary on the Qur'ān* (1987), Helmut Gatje, *The Qur'ān and its Exegesis* (1976), and Mahmoud Ayoub, *The Qur'ān and its Interpreters* (1984). For trends in modern Muslim interpretation of the Qur'ān, see Kenneth Cragg, *The Pen and the Faith* (1985), J. M. S. Baljon, *Modern Muslim Koran Interpretation* (1961) and J. J. G. Jansen, *The Interpretation of the Koran in Modern Egypt* (1974).

Studies on specialized themes are abundant, and what follows is but a small selection: Barbara Freyer Stowasser, *Women in the Qur'ān: Traditions and Interpretation* (1994); Nicholas Awde, *Women in Islam: An Anthology from the Qur'ān and Hadīths* (2000); Jane Dammen McAuliffe, *Qur'ānic Christians: An Analysis of Classical and Modern Exegesis* (1991); Reuven Firestone, *Journeys in Holy Lands: The Evolution of the Abraham-Ishmael Legends in Islamic Exegesis* (1990); and Toshihiko Izutsu, *God and Man in the Koran* (1987) and *Ethico-Religious Concepts in the Qur'ān* (1966). For a Muslim feminist treatment of the Qur'ān see Amina Wadud, *Qur'ān and Woman: Rereading the Sacred Text from a Woman's Perspective* (New York: Oxford University Press, 1999).

6

THE TRADITION LITERATURE

The Qur'ān requires context. The life of Muhammad summarized in chapter 4 seems to provide that context. But what are our sources for the life of Muhammad? In other words, what did Ibn Isḥāq and scholars like him have to work with? And how reliable is his data? On the surface of it, the answer seems promising. Like other Muslim scholars of his time, Ibn Isḥāq regarded himself simply as a collector and transmitter of information. Unlike modern scholars he felt no pressure to be original, but claimed to merely transmit what he himself had received. When two contradictory reports had reached him, he is careful to record both. When he has doubts about the credibility of a report, he tells us so. Most importantly, he is zealous in documenting his sources. Ibn Isḥāq did not, of course, employ footnotes or the whole apparatus of modern scholarship, but he scrupulously adhered to the no less rigorous standards of Muslim scholarship, according to which each significant unit of information is traced back to its original source by means of a simple and elegant system of attribution. In his account of Muhammad's death, for example, Ibn Isḥāq relates the following:

> (1) Ibn Shihāb al-Zuhrī told me [i.e., Ibn Isḥāq] from 'Ubayd ibn 'Abd Allāh ibn 'Utba from 'Ā'isha
> (2) that she used to hear the apostle say, "God never takes a prophet to Himself without giving him the choice." When he was at the point of death the last word I heard the apostle saying was, "Nay, rather the Exalted Companion of paradise." I said (to myself), "Then by God he is not choosing us! And I knew that that was what he used to tell us, namely that a prophet does not die without being given the choice." (Ibn Isḥāq 1955: 680)

The first part of the report, which lists the chain of transmitters, is the isnād, the footnote of Islamic scholarship. The substance of the report given in the second part is the matn, or subject matter. Together, the isnād and the matn make a ḥadīth report, and collected ḥadīth reports are the foundation of historical writing. Hence Ibn Isḥāq's sīra and every traditional biography of the Prophet is essentially a collection of ḥadīth reports selected and arranged in such a way as to provide a roughly chronological account of Muhammad's life.

The Science of Ḥadīth

The importance of ḥadīth in the development of Islam cannot be overemphasized. The ḥadīth report was the basic unit of Islamic literature and scholarship and the primary means of preserving information from the past. Considered generically, ḥadīth reports were not necessarily connected with Muhammad; they simply provided a means of transmitting and documenting historical anecdotes. These anecdotes might concern the lives of Hebrew patriarchs, administrative decisions of the caliphs, or historical reports of just about any kind. By the time of Ibn Isḥāq, however, Muhammad had become the principal focus of ḥadīth collectors. The reasons are obvious. According to the belief of pious Muslims, Muhammad lived a virtually perfect life, the events of his life form the necessary context for understanding the Qur'ān, and his words and actions were one of the foundations of Islamic law. If there was any historical knowledge worth having, it was knowledge of what the Prophet had said or done. Consequently, ḥadīth *par excellence* was ḥadīth traced back to the Prophet Muhammad. To make this clear, scholars gave other historical reports a separate technical designation, calling them athār, so that the term "ḥadīth" could be reserved for prophetic traditions.

Reports about the Prophet could be sorted and filed in any number of ways. Compiling a sīra was one such way of organizing ḥadīth, but there were many others. Ḥadīth could, for example, be collected to provide a basis for legal decisions, and one of our earliest extant collections of ḥadīth is a digest of the legal opinions from the scholar Mālik ibn Anas entitled the *Muwaṭṭa'*. Ḥadīth could also be compiled to provide background to the Qur'ān, forming the sub-genre of asbāb al-nuzūl, or "occasions of revelation." Or ḥadīth collections could simply function as repositories of historical trivia. Collections of awā'il ḥadīth, for example, function as a sort of early Arab-Islamic *Guinness Book of World Records* by storing information about famous "firsts" – from the first Islamic martyr to the first to use a toothpick. Ibn Isḥāq himself has a fondness for such awā'il traditions and includes many in his sīra. Another significant category of ḥadīth is the so-called ḥadīth qudsī, a direct word from God which was revealed to Muhammad through Gabriel but did not find its way into the Qur'ān.

The whole towering edifice of traditional Islamic learning is built upon the building blocks of ḥadīth, and looming over the whole enterprise is a crucial question: how is one to know whether a particular report is authentic? Muslim specialists in the study of ḥadīth had a carefully crafted answer. To know whether a particular tradition is authentic one must study the record of its transmission, the isnād (literally, support). If each of the transmitters listed in the isnād was a trustworthy character, and so long as the chain of transmission is complete and continuous, then the report should be deemed reliable. The worth of a tradition, in other words, rests entirely on the quality of its transmission. Only traditions with near-perfect isnāds could be considered ṣaḥīḥ, or sound. Gaps or weaknesses in the chain of transmission, or accusations of forgetfulness (or worse) against one of the transmitters, will lower a tradition from the highest category of ṣaḥīḥ to one of four lesser categories: good, fair, doubtful, or forged.

To ḥadīth specialists of the tenth century and later, to make use of ḥadīth in a prophetic biography, a legal manual, or a Qur'ān commentary was presumptuous unless one had first accomplished the more fundamental task of sifting reliable from unreliable traditions. These scholars tended to accuse the likes of Ibn Isḥāq – just about everyone who was not a professional ḥadīth scholar, in fact – of laziness and carelessness.

Ḥadīth specialists themselves were anything but lazy or careless, of course, and they diligently transmitted ḥadīth reports about themselves to prove the point. The search for knowledge, ṭalab al-ʿilm, is glorified in the tradition literature itself, and the heroes of this process are the scholars who traveled ceaselessly in order to collect ḥadīth and to make good the promises enshrined in ḥadīth: "One who travels a road in search of knowledge, God will have him travel one of the roads of Paradise" (Ābū Dawūd, tradition 3641). The journey in search of ḥadīth became symbolic of the effort and sacrifice the muḥaddithūn, scholars of ḥadīth, were willing to put in for the sake of knowledge.

The signature activity of the great muḥaddithūn was not travel, however, but the much more sedentary activity of sifting and evaluating traditions. The process reached its zenith in the ninth century (about a century after Ibn Isḥāq) in the work of Muhammad ibn Ismāʿīl al-Bukhārī (d. 870) and Muslim ibn al-Ḥajjāj (d. 875). Bukhārī and Muslim each compiled collections of reliable or ṣaḥīḥ traditions which eventually gained an authoritative status only slightly below that of the Qur'ān in the Muslim community. Besides the collections of Bukhārī and Muslim, four other collections of ḥadīth have traditionally been assigned canonical status: those of Abū Dawūd, al-Tirmidhī, al-Nasā'ī, and Ibn Majā.

By the time Ibn Isḥāq compiled his biography the isnād system had taken root, and even if Ibn Isḥāq himself did not satisfy the rigorous standards of the later muḥaddithūn he nevertheless works from the same premise – that is, the way one measures the credibility of a tradition is by the quality of its isnād. If the witnesses are reliable, it must have happened. Many modern scholars seem to agree. Some even argue that scholars like Ibn Isḥāq were, in fact, making use of written sources and that by following the trail of isnāds we can reconstruct these earlier writings (e.g., Motzki 1991). When Ibn Isḥāq cites a tradition of al-Zuhrī, for example, he may have had access to al-Zuhrī's own written collection of traditions. If this is so, why should it not be possible to reconstruct early compilations of ḥadīth by extracting and recompiling traditions from later collections? In any case, if isnāds represent reality, then many of the reports do actually go back to the companions of the Prophet and the only problem is to determine which ones do and which do not. Some of these traditions were authentic, some forged, but optimistic scholars are confident that in most cases they can tell the difference by carefully scrutinizing the chain of transmitters of each tradition.

The whole system seems to fit together tightly, and while we may quibble about the accuracy of this or that fact or tradition, there seems no reason to doubt that what Ibn Isḥāq tells us is, in its broad outlines, a fairly reliable account of the Prophet's career. This, on the whole, has been the attitude that modern biographers of Muhammad have adopted. Biographers like Montgomery Watt, Maxime Rodinson, and Martin Lings may not place the same level of trust in the isnād as their Muslim predecessors, but they are still convinced that the tradition literature contains a core of authentic traditions and that a careful historian can identify those that ring true. Ibn Isḥāq's account may need some evaluation and revision around the edges and in the details, but the gist of it inspires confidence.

The Origins of Ḥadīth

As always, the devil is in the detail, however. When we move outside of Ibn Isḥāq's biography to compare the numerous parallel traditions which describe a particular incident our confidence is quickly shaken. For any given incident in Muhammad's life there are likely to be a dozen or couple of dozen differing traditions that recount the facts in varying and often incompatible ways. Examples are abundant both in the tradition literature itself and in modern scholarly treatments. I have abridged and paraphrased the example that follows from Patricia Crone's *Meccan Trade and the Rise of Islam* (1987a). Readers can have recourse to a full version of the argument in Crone's book (the same example is cited by Cook [1983] in his biography of Muhammad). I have tried to capture both the gist and the tone of Crone's argument here, although I have departed from the order of her presentation.

The case in question concerns a small but significant nugget of information about pre-Islamic Arab trade. In the course of describing the historical background to Muhammad's life, Ibn Isḥāq unpretentiously passes along a report that an ancestor of Muhammad, Hāshim, was "the first to institute the two caravan journeys of the Quraysh, summer and winter." This Hāshim was also the first to provide tharīd, a kind of broth in which bread is broken which, according to Ibn Isḥāq's sources, was a means of providing for hungry Meccans in lean years. To further document the facts, Ibn Isḥāq passes along part of a poem which confirms and celebrates Hāshim's philanthropy and foresight (Ibn Isḥāq 1955: 58).

Many modern biographers of Muhammad simply accept the facts of this tradition at face value: the Quraysh were traders, and they made two long-range caravan journeys each year, one in the summer, one in the winter. What possible motive, after all, could Ibn Isḥāq or his sources have to concoct such information? It seems like innocuous historical detail innocently recounted. Moreover, it is valuable information to the modern historian concerned with the role of trade in the rise of Islam. Modern historians would, in fact, be delighted to learn more about this important subject of caravan trade.

Fortunately for them, although Ibn Isḥāq is stingy with detail about the two journeys inaugurated by Hāshim, later Muslim scholars are more generous. Ibn al-Kalbī, for instance, whom we met previously as the author of *The Book of Idols*, turns out to know a great many more details about Quraysh trading patterns than Ibn Isḥāq. Meccan trade, he tells us, used to be purely local until Hāshim traveled to Syria. In Syria Hāshim cooked tharīd, and this culinary marvel won the attention of the Byzantine emperor. Thereafter Hāshim was able to use his standing at the Byzantine court to win permission to trade in Syria, and on his way back to Mecca he made agreements with various tribes along the route for safe passage. These agreements were called īlāf. Thereafter the Meccans traded regularly in Syria, making two journeys a year, one in summer and one in winter (Crone 1987a: 109–10).

The story is interesting and sounds plausible, but it raises some problems. Not only did Ibn al-Kalbī know many more details about Meccan trade than Ibn Isḥāq, he also knew differently than his own father, who had given exactly the opposite story. According to Kalbī, Hāshim was responsible not for inaugurating international trade but for ending it, thereby keeping the Quraysh close to home where they would have more time to worship (Crone 1987a: 110). Other scholars offer us further important details. The journeys, some tell us, were not to Syria but rather were the migrations of the Quraysh to al-Ṭā'if in the summer and their return in the winter. Or they were trading journeys to Syria and Yemen, or to Syria and Ethiopia, or to Syria, the Yemen, Ethiopia, and Iraq (ibid. 205). In any case, the effect of the inauguration of these journeys was that it brought food to Mecca, somehow easing hunger. This hunger was the result of a pre-Islamic famine in Hāshim's time, or a famine among the Quraysh in Muhammad's time, or it was the hunger of poor Meccans (ibid. 207). Then there is the matter of the īlāf. Ibn al-Kalbī tells us the īlāf were safe-passage agreements with tribes along the caravan routes. But other traditions interpret this unfamiliar word to mean "habit" (i.e., of going on journeys), "clinging to" (these journeys), "mutual love," "harmony," "blessing," "pacts," or "protection." Evidently no one had any idea what the word meant (ibid. 208–9).

The traditions thus disagree irreconcilably in many significant details: the nature of the journeys, their destination, and their results. This makes the key points of agreement all the more significant. All the reports agree that the journeys, whatever their nature, were performed by the Quraysh, that they were in summer and winter, that they had something to do with food and relieving hunger, and that they involved īlāf, whatever that might mean. It would seem reasonable to accept these areas of agreement as an authentic core of historical fact that was later embellished with colorful details as the tradition literature grew. After all, how could such a variety of different scholars who differ about everything else come up with these facts except from some common historical tradition (Crone 1987a: 211)?

As it turns out, we can make a fairly confident guess about where they came up with these core facts. Sūra 106 of the Qur'ān reads:

> In the Name of God, the Merciful, the Compassionate
> For the īlāf of the Quraysh,
> their īlāf of the winter and summer journey,
> So let them serve the Lord of this House
> Who has fed them against hunger,
> And secured them from fear.

The information that the variant traditions agree on is no more than what Sūra 106 gives us. This Qur'ānic passage, in other words, is the likely point of origin for all the different variations on the story of Hāshim and the two journeys. All of the other details found in Qur'ān commentaries, sīra literature, or other collections of ḥadīth amount to no more than guesses about what Sūra 106 is referring to. References to the winter and summer journeys, to the Quraysh, to hunger, and to the strange word īlāf appear in all the accounts simply because these are the items that need to be explained. It is clear that the earliest biographers and commentators on the Qur'ān had no idea what the actual background to the sūra was. Had they known, they would presumably have at least been able to agree on the meaning of īlāf (Crone 1987a: 203–31).

It turns out, then, that what appeared to be a simple historical fact, which we should have no reason to question, is more likely the result of creative efforts to understand the Qur'ān. As Crone concludes, what Muslim scholars were offering "is not their recollection of what Muhammad had in mind when he recited these verses, but, on the contrary, so many guesses based on the verses themselves. The original meaning of these verses was unknown to them. Either it had never been known to them or else there had been a gradual drift away from it" (Crone 1987a: 210). In principle, she concedes, one or another of the contradictory "facts" recounted in traditions could be correct, but it is equally probable than none of them are, and, in any case, we have no way of telling. Arguments similar to Crone's about the two journeys could be made about many other details of the prophetic biography. For example, many details of the battle of Badr recounted in chapter 4 – stories about the participation of angels, for instance – are best understood as exegetically derived.

So far, then, we can identify the following general characteristics of the ḥadīth literature that give us reason to be skeptical about its value as a historical source for the life of Muhammad. First, the literature is massive, diverse, and filled with contradictory traditions. For any given fact or event, we can usually find numerous variant traditions, often incompatible with one another. We might choose to believe some of these accounts, but we clearly cannot accept them all or even most. Second, traditions manifestly grew in specificity and detail over time: later sources know much more about the Prophet than earlier ones, and they are more certain of their knowledge. Third, a great deal of the tradition literature is directly connected to the Qur'ān. This applies not only to traditions which appear in specific works of Qur'ān commentary, but also traditions in historical and legal works. Ibn Isḥāq's sīra, as we will have occasion to note below, is packed with traditions which are suspiciously helpful in understanding the Qur'ān. Finally, it turns out that isnāds are no help in identifying authentic traditions for the simple reason that isnāds could be invented just as easily as the text of a tradition.

In Quest of the Historical Muhammad

Readers whose prior knowledge of the origins of Islam comes from popular writings are likely to be taken aback by the suggestion that much of what they were taught as history is not history but exegesis. The sort of skepticism about the ḥadīth literature expressed here is hardly revolutionary, however. The arguments of scholars like Crone, Cook, Hawting, and others are only the most recent fruit of a century and a half of growing skepticism among Western scholars about the reliability of our sources for the life of Muhammad. Among the first skeptics were two scholars working in India, Alois Sprenger and William Muir. Both suspected that much of what was accepted as authentic in Muslim tradition was in fact forged, and they each expressed their skepticism in writings on Muhammad published during the 1850s. Both were also optimistic, however, that a core of authentic traditions could somehow be sifted out of the mass of forgeries and they did not hesitate to write full-fledged biographies of Muhammad based on those traditions they trusted.

Such optimism was severely challenged by the work of the great Hungarian Islamicist, Ignaz Goldziher. In 1890 Goldziher published *Muhammedanische Studien* in German (translated into English in 1973 as *Muslim Studies*), a book which remains a classic in the study of early Islam. Studying the ḥadīth literature against the background of the first two centuries of Islam, Goldziher became convinced that the tradition literature had grown up in the years after the Arab conquests – that ḥadīth did not reflect the life of the Prophet, but rather the beliefs, conflicts, and controversies of the first generations of Muslims. In Goldziher's own words, "The ḥadīth will not serve as a document of the infancy of Islam, but rather as a reflection of the tendencies which appeared in the community during the more mature stages of its development" (Goldziher 1973, 2: 18). Ḥadīth reflects historical reality, to be sure, but it is the historical reality of the Umayyad and early ʿAbbāsid empires, not seventh-century Arabia. There were limits, however, to Goldziher's skepticism. He reserved his major criticism for the ḥadīth collections proper, and remained much more optimistic about the authenticity of traditions that appeared in historical reports. The wider application of his skepticism to historical accounts like Ibn Isḥāq's sīra was left to later scholars.

A half a century after Goldziher, Joseph Schacht applied Goldziher's method to the development of early Islamic law. Schacht's most useful insight was, in retrospect, no more than common sense: isnāds, he argued, tend to grow backwards over time. In its first incarnation a tradition might be traced to an eighth-century scholar. The next time we meet it, it will have an isnād going back to one of the early caliphs. After the ninth century, the same tradition will be graced with an isnād which goes back to the Prophet himself. Schacht's conclusions turn the logic of the Muslim ḥadīth scholarship on its head: the traditions with the very worst isnāds are likely to be early, and those with near-perfect records of transmission betray their late development. By carefully comparing isnāds of parallel traditions Schacht thought that he could date when particular traditions originated, thereby developing a rough chronology for the early growth of Islamic law. He concluded that Islamic law began with the administrative practice of the Umayyads, who were eclectic and pragmatic, adopting legal ideas from whatever convenient sources were at hand. Over time these legal rules were enshrined in ḥadīth and projected back to the life of the Prophet in order to give them an Islamic justification (Schacht 1950: 165).

Both Goldziher and Schacht maintained that the ḥadīth literature reflected historical reality and that an industrious scholar could mine the literature for information about the early growth of Islam. More recent scholars, while sharing their predecessors' skepticism, have looked in a different direction for the origins of ḥadīth. Once again, the seminal arguments are found in the work of John Wansbrough. In *Quranic Studies* (1977) Wansbrough argued that the ḥadīth literature is largely exegetical in origin; that is, that the bulk of the tradition literature is closely tied to the interpretation of the Qur'ān. Ḥadīth originated not out of actual historical events, but out of the propensity of early Muslims to tell stories related to the Qur'ān. Early storytellers who entertained audiences with pious stories gave way to Qur'ān commentators who supplied them with respectable isnāds and used them to interpret the Qur'ān (Juynboll 1983: 11–14).

More recently John Burton has taken up a variation on Wansbrough's position, arguing that Goldziher and Schacht take ḥadīth too seriously as rooted in real life. The only reality that ḥadīth reflects, according to Burton, is a literary reality. The whole mass of Muslim tradition is, in his words, "the documentary precipitation of . . . an 'academic exercise,' a paper war whose raw materials had been supplied by the exegesis of a document, the Holy Qur'ān" (Burton 1994: xxiii). The origins of ḥadīth, he claims, had nothing to do with real life and everything to do with the problem of interpreting scripture (ibid. xv). Virtually all of the topics and themes of the ḥadīth and sīra literature can be traced to the Qur'ān.

The implications are startling. If the skeptics are right, the story of Muhammad's life told in the last chapter cannot confidently be read as history. The tradition literature may have grown out of late seventh- and early eighth-century political and theological squabbles, as Goldziher argued, or out of early legal debates, as Schacht claimed, or simply out of the need to interpret the Qur'ān, as Burton suggests, but it cannot be confidently traced to any real events of the Prophet's lifetime. Consequently, Ibn Isḥāq's sīra (along with the whole corpus of ḥadīth literature) may be of limited use for discovering what Muhammad himself said, did, or believed.

The Sīra and the Shaping of an Islamic Worldview

But even if the story of Muhammad cannot confidently be read as history, it can still tell us a great deal about the origins of Islam. Without the biography of Muhammad there would be no Islam that we would recognize as such. We may be able to imagine a form of Arab monotheism that existed before the story of Muhammad was coherently formulated, but, if so, what we are imagining is not Islam. It follows that those who first formulated the story of Muhammad in a coherent way were, in some sense, the originators of Islam. It further follows that the best way to understand how Islam came into being is to understand the class of scholars – the 'ulamā' – who were responsible for the growth of the ḥadīth literature and the formulation of the story of

Muhammad. A careful reading of the biography of Muhammad can reveal a great deal about the concerns, values, and pressures that shaped the worldview of these scholars. In particular, the biography of Muhammad reflects several shared scholarly preoccupations that had a shaping effect on Islam.

Scholars were, first of all, preoccupied with interpreting the Qur'ān. As we have seen, the Qur'ān is dependent upon the story of Muhammad and the ḥadīth literature for its interpretation, and a large part of Ibn Isḥāq's sīra is clearly intended to help us to understand particular passages of the Qur'ān. For example, if we come cold to Sūra 8 (The Spoils) a number of questions will inevitably arise: what are "the spoils" after which the sūra is named, and what does it mean that they belong to God and the Messenger? Who are the "two parties" mentioned in verse 7? What is the significance of the angels mentioned in several places in the sūra? Is there a single context for the whole sūra? What is the nature of the victory the sūra seems to allude to rather vaguely, and why does God warn Muslims not to turn their backs on their enemies? If we confined ourselves to the Qur'ān, we would remain clueless. Fortunately, Ibn Isḥāq comes to the rescue with his account of the battle of Badr which is perfectly constructed to answer each of these questions. The same can be said about his account of the battle of Uḥud.

Much of what Ibn Isḥāq passes on, in other words, is what Jewish scholars would call Midrash, stories which are meant to help us understand scripture. To label the sīra literature Midrash is not so controversial as it might seem. As we have already seen, traditional Muslim scholars acknowledged that the prophetic biography functioned as a commentary on the Qur'ān, and they used it as such. Their assumption, however, was that the story of the Prophet's life could explain scripture because it described what actually happened. As we have seen, however, many of the traditions which find their way into the sīra can be shown to have *originated* out of efforts to understand obscure passages of the Qur'ān. In other words, the nature of the Qur'ān and the need to understand it comprised a potent shaping force on the development of the biography of Muhammad.

Another shaping force on the prophetic biography was the need to establish Muhammad's prophetic credentials, an impulse especially evident in miracle stories. As we have seen, Ibn Isḥāq describes a number of miracles surrounding Muhammad's life, and he is by no means unique among Muslim scholars in emphasizing the miraculous. A whole genre of the tradition literature is devoted to miraculous "proofs" of prophecy, dalā'il al-nubuwwa. A palm tree sighs as the Prophet passes, a cluster of dates jumps off the tree at his command, the moon is split down the middle, and on several occasions the Prophet feeds crowds with small amounts of food. The pervasiveness of miracles in early biographies comes as a surprise to anyone reared on modern accounts of the Prophet, where such miracles are systematically expunged in sensitivity to modern discomfiture with the supernatural. For many modern people, miracles are simply a vestige of superstition, and for many modern Muslims there are also theological reasons to want the miracle accounts to disappear, for the Qur'ān strongly implies that Muhammad wrought no miracles. The Qur'ān records criticism by Muhammad's opponents, in fact, for failing to come up with any supernatural signs other than the Qur'ān itself. As a matter of dogma, then, many modern Muslims and non-Muslims agree that Muhammad could not possibly have performed miracles.

Ibn Isḥāq and his sources clearly did not suffer from any such modern hang-ups about the supernatural. Nor are the miracle accounts in Muhammad's biography superfluous. To the contrary, accounts of the miraculous are central to several key themes of the sīra: the uniqueness and purity of the Prophet, the recognition of Muhammad's prophethood by Christians and Jews, and the abundant blessing or baraka that flowed from his person. For example, when two angels approached Muhammad, removed his heart, and cleansed it, they were establishing a basis for the doctrine of the purity (ʿiṣma) of the Prophet according to which Muhammad was impeccable (maʿṣūm), divinely shielded from major error or impurity. Similarly, when the young Muhammad is divinely warned to put his shirt back on, God is protecting the modesty and purity of his messenger. A number of miraculous occurrences cluster around the theme of the marks of prophethood. Pious Christians, like Baḥīra, were especially prone to notice signs of his prophetic office – angels shading him, for instance. In a number of cases miraculous signs were granted to vindicate the Prophet in the face of Jewish or Christian criticism.

The largest single category of miracles, however, supports a major theme in popular Islamic piety; that is, the Prophet as a source of grace or blessing: Muhammad's wet nurse (and her donkey) flow with milk, Muhammad miraculously feeds the leaders of the Quraysh when he announces his prophethood, and he miraculously supplies food to workers before the battle of the Ditch.

These miracle accounts fit within well-established patterns in Near Eastern religious life. Christians were used to treating the miracles of Jesus as attestations of his divinity, and Christian saints were commonly miracle-workers. In such an environment to follow a prophet who performed no miracles was a distinct disadvantage. The similarity of Muhammad's food miracles to well-established patterns of miracle stories in Near Eastern religion reflects the environment in which the sīra was shaped. Perhaps even more significantly, Muslim society had by this time already begun to produce its own miracle-working holy men, and if Muslim saints were able to perform miracles it would seem rather cheap to deny them to the Prophet.

The point to be emphasized here is that the ḥadīth and sīra literature grew up in an environment of powerful stereotypes about what a holy man or prophet should be like, and these stereotypes had a strong shaping effect on the biography of Muhammad. The stereotyping can be observed in the chronological structure of the sīra itself. Muhammad received the first revelations at age 40; his birth, death, and the Hijra to Medina all took place on the same day of the same month; every year has one major event; and every major battle is followed by a confrontation with the Jews (Crone 1987a).

A third shaping influence on the story of the Prophet was an intense preoccupation with the articulation and legitimation of Islamic norms of behavior. When Ibn Isḥāq recounts how Gabriel taught Muhammad to pray, for example, the account is explicitly prescriptive and the reader is meant to come away knowing the precise time periods within which each of the five prayers must be performed. Such model behavior is called Sunna. The idea behind prophetic Sunna is simple: since Muhammad was God's messenger, he knew better than anyone else how to put God's will into practice. Therefore the Prophet's words and behavior are the best commentary on the Qur'ān and an authoritative model for Muslims. When the idea of Sunna was fully developed, the Sunna came to be considered just as authoritative as the Qur'ān, and the major ḥadīth collections contain traditions which describe how Gabriel revealed the Sunna to Muhammad along with the Qur'ān. This idea of dual revelation, as we noted in chapter 3, was almost identical with the rabbinic idea of the dual Torah. Just as Moses received both an oral and a written Torah at Mount Sinai, so Gabriel brought two kinds of revelation (waḥī) to Muhammad: revelation meant to be recited, that is, the Qur'ān, and unrecited revelation, the Sunna. The difference between the two was of form not of substance; both forms of revelation contained God's revealed will for humanity.

The practical result of the idea of Sunna was to place an enormous weight of significance on every aspect of the Prophet's life. His every word and action was potential law for Muslims. Conversely, there was enormous pressure to justify every rule of behavior from the Prophet's example. Consequently, a large section of the ḥadīth literature, particularly in legal compendiums, can be shown to have grown out of the idea of Sunna. There is even a ḥadīth acknowledging this pressure: if any action is praiseworthy then surely the Prophet must have done it. (For a full discussion of this tradition, see Rahman 1965: 73.)

Finally, the religious scholars of Islam were preoccupied with claims to legitimacy, prestige, and lineage among later Muslims. It is no accident, for instance, that Ibn Isḥāq makes ʿAlī the first convert to Islam, or that other sources put Abū Bakr first. Ibn Isḥāq is alleged to have had Shīʿite sympathies and the Shīʿītes believed that ʿAlī should have been caliph from the start. The prestige of being the first to convert was thus closely tied to arguments over the succession to Muhammad. Similarly, Ibn Isḥāq's long lists of early converts are of more than academic interest, for after the conquests prestige (and sometimes income) were dependent on how early an individual (or his ancestors) had become a Muslim. The same could be said about the many other lists in the sīra: those who participated in the battle of Badr, those who led expeditions, those who died as martyrs. The question of who had played a part in the Prophet's life, what part they had played, and whether they were a hero or villain was an enormously important question for later Muslims. Status within the community and political legitimacy were staked on genealogical claims. Affiliation with the Quraysh, early conversion, or any other close tie to the Prophet were an enormous source of prestige for later generations of Muslims, and the sīra literature was shaped in part by such claims.

The result of this shaping process was a story that powerfully and persuasively explained where the community had come from, why things were as they were (or how they should be different), how Muslims should behave, and why they were right and Christians and Jews were wrong. The story of Muhammad and the origins of Islam functioned, in other words, as the central narrative in Islamic salvation history, a story to which Muslims of the eighth century and after could look to understand who they were and to learn what they should be.

The story of the life of Muhammad formed only one part of the Islamic tradition, of course, but it was the critical piece without which nothing else could make sense. If we imagine the Islamic tradition as an interlocking jigsaw puzzle, the Qur'ān forms the central piece. But as we have seen, like the first piece of any puzzle, it is difficult to make sense of in isolation. The events of the life of Muhammad fit around the Qur'ān, providing us with the context which allows us to make sense of it. The story of Muhammad's life did not grow up in isolation, however. It was shaped simultaneously with the formation of Islamic law, Islamic theology, ṣūfī piety, and Islamic political thought and it reflects the concerns of all of these. In other words, the Islamic tradition did not enter the world fully formed. Rather it grew, took root, and flourished over the course of several turbulent centuries. In the following section we turn back to the historical processes that lay behind the formation of Islam, beginning with the Islamic conquests.

Resources for Further Study

General introductions to ḥadīth and the science of ḥadīth criticism include Alfred Guillaume, *The Traditions of Islam* (1980), John Burton, *An Introduction to the Hadīth* (1994), and Muhammad Zubayr Siddiqi, *Hadīth Literature* (1993). The seminal contributions to modern debate on the origins and authenticity of ḥadīth are volume 2 of Ignaz Goldziher's *Muslim Studies* (1973) and Joseph Schacht, *The Origins of Muhammadan Jurisprudence* (1950). For more recent contributions to this debate, see G. H. A. Juynboll's *Muslim Tradition* (1983), William Graham's *Divine Word and Prophetic Word in Early Islam* (1977), and John Burton's response to Goldziher and Schacht in his *Introduction to the Hadīth* (1994).

A number of Muslim scholars have responded critically and creatively to the ideas of Goldziher and Schacht, among them Fazlur Rahman in *Islamic Methodology in History* (1965) and M. M. Aʿzamī in *Studies in Early Hadīth Literature* (1992). Modern debates about Sunna and ḥadīth among Muslims are described in G. H. A. Juynboll, *The Authenticity of the Tradition Literature* (1969) and Daniel Brown, *Rethinking Tradition in Modern Islamic Thought* (1996).

My extended illustration of the exegetical origins of ḥadīth was based on Patricia Crone's argument in *Meccan Trade and the Rise of Islam* (1987a). Crone has been the most eloquent skeptic about the value of historical traditions more generally, a theme which recurs in most of her several books. Michael Cook, *Muhammad* (1983), gives a concise summary of the major issues surrounding the sources for the life of Muhammad. F. E. Peters, "The Quest of the Historical Muhammad" (1991), offers a more detailed analysis of these sources and compares sources on the life of Jesus and sources on the life of Muhammad. Peters's article is reproduced in his *Muhammad and the Origins of Islam* (1994b). Contrasting conclusions about the reliability of early historical traditions are reached by Albrecht Noth, *The Early Arabic Historical Tradition* (1994) and Fred Donner, *Narratives of Islamic Origins* (1998).

PART TWO

THE EXPANSION OF ISLAM

7
THE CONQUESTS

It took the Arabs only thirty years to conquer the Near Eastern world, and to those they conquered it must have seemed that they came from nowhere. The Near Eastern imperial system, which had held together the diverse cultures and religions of the Near East for half a millennium, disintegrated at a stunning pace. In 602 the Byzantine Emperor Maurice was brutally murdered by the pretender, Phocas. Ostensibly to avenge this murder of his ally, the Persian emperor Khusraw II Aparwēz went to war against the Byzantines. For twenty years Khusraw had his enemies on the run and Persian dreams of recreating the ancient Achaemenid Persian empire – the empire of Cyrus and Darius – seemed within grasp. In 613 Antioch fell to the Persians, followed by Jerusalem in 614. In 619 Egypt was taken, and in 620 Sāsānian forces were on the outskirts of Constantinople. But in the meantime a new emperor had seized the throne in Constantinople. Heraclius proved to be a military genius. In 622 he set out with a small force from Constantinople to attack Khusraw from the rear. In 628, after a brilliant campaign through Iraq, Heraclius took Ctesiphon. Khusraw was deposed, and in the next four years the Sāsānian empire had ten different kings, ending with unfortunate Yazdagard III, last of the Sāsānian monarchs.

By 632, when Arab armies entered the scene, both empires were exhausted. War, plague, and internal political conflicts had left them spent. Heraclius regained the Byzantine provinces of Syria and Egypt, which had been lost to Khusraw, but the fortifications and military infrastructure of those provinces had been destroyed. The Sāsānian imperial government was in utter disarray. Heraclius had, in a stroke of uncharacteristic political ineptitude, resurrected

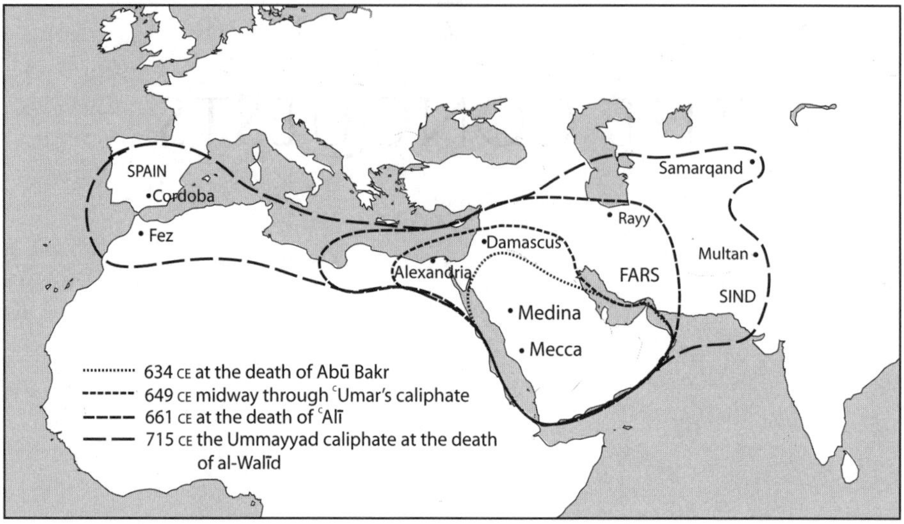

Map 5 The expansion of Islamic rule, seventh and early eighth centuries

old conflicts with the Monophysites in Syria and Egypt. Most ominously of all, both the Byzantines and the Sāsānians had ditched their old Arab allies, the Banū Ghassān and Banū Lakhm. Consequently, when Arab armies entered Syria and Iraq, they stumbled upon a political and military vacuum.

Once begun, the Arab campaign was stunningly swift. In 636 CE an Arab army decisively defeated Byzantine forces at the battle of Yarmūk, near the Jordan river, signaling the end of nearly seven centuries of Roman rule in Syria. The contest at Yarmūk was a concerted effort by the Roman army in Syria to counter the Arab threat, which had begun three years earlier when the first Arab forces arrived. The Byzantine Emperor Heraclius sent his top generals, Vahan and Theodore Trithurios, to oppose the Arabs with a sizeable army (anywhere from 15,000 to 30,000 men). The Byzantine army was routed, and both generals were allegedly killed, along with the emperor's brother. In the aftermath of the battle, the victors systematically laid siege to and occupied all of the major cities of Syria: Damascus in the same year, Jerusalem in 638, and the final holdout, Caesarea, in 640. With all of Syria and Palestine taken, the road to Roman-ruled Egypt was open. A permanent Arab garrison was established at Fusṭāṭ, site of present-day Cairo, in 641. Alexandria was taken in 642, briefly lost, then permanently occupied in 646.

Within three years of the victory at Yarmūk another Arab army destroyed the Sāsānian imperial army at the battle of al-Qādisiyya in southern Iraq. Incursions into Persian-ruled Iraq had begun under the command of the Arab military genius, Khālid ibn Walīd, in 633. In this initial phase of expansion the Arabs occupied several towns along the Euphrates, most importantly al-Hīra, but after Khālid's departure for Syria Persian forces decisively defeated an Arab army at the battle of the Bridge. Another Arab force was dispatched, and met with a large Persian army not far from al-Hīra. The result was a decisive victory for the Arabs, which dealt a fatal blow to the Sāsānian empire. For all its significance, there is uncertainty about the details of the battle of al-Qādisiyya – later chroniclers disagreed over whether the contest took place in 635, 636, or 637 – but the outcome was clear enough. By the early 640s all of Iraq was under Arab control and Persian imperial power was destroyed. Within another twenty years, by 661, the Arab conquerors ruled from the borders of central Asia to North Africa and from Yemen to northern Syria. By 750 the political reach of the Islamic empire stretched from Spain to India, and from Sub-Saharan Africa to central Asia.

Chronology of the Arab Conquests

630	Traditional date of Muhammad's conquest of Mecca
633	Incursions into Iraq begin. City of al-Hīra taken
634	Arabs defeat small Byzantine force in southern Syria
636	Byzantine army decisively defeated by Arab forces at the battle of Yarmūk in Syria. Damascus occupied
637	Sāsānian imperial army routed at al-Qādisiyya. Sāsānian capital, Ctesiphon, taken
638	Jerusalem surrenders
640	Caesarea taken
642	Alexandria taken. It would later be lost, then retaken for good in 646
647	First Arab raids in North Africa
649–50	Persepolis, ancient Persian capital, taken
651	Most of Iran conquered
655	Byzantine navy destroyed by Muslim fleet
657	Battle of Ṣiffīn and the period of internal strife that follows distracts from further conquests
673–8	Arabs besiege Constantinople
705–15	Arab general Qutayba captures Bukhārā and Samarqand and establishes Muslim supremacy in central Asia
710	Completion of conquest of North Africa
711	Arab army of 6,000 under Muhammad b. Qāsim takes Sindh, extending Arab rule to the Indian subcontinent. Invasion of Spain
732	Battle of Tours; Franks halt Arab advance
751	Battle on the Talas; Arabs defeat Chinese army in central Asia
827	Arabs begin conquest of Sicily
831	Capture of Palermo; raid in southern Italy

Psychological Impact

The speed of the Arab expansion is staggering, and it is not surprising that the descendants of victors and vanquished alike portray the conquests as cataclysmic. Later chroniclers saw the Arab defeat of the Byzantine and Sāsānian empires as a complete upheaval of the political, social, and religious culture of the Near East – a realignment that left the world changed forever.

From the perspective of the defeated Byzantines, the conquests were disastrous, crippling the empire and wrenching away centers of Greek culture – Damascus, Alexandria, and Carthage – the religious treasures of Jerusalem, and the breadbasket of the empire, the Nile valley. Only apocalyptic language would do to depict such a nightmare, as the following excerpts, taken from Walter Kaegi's translations, show. Sophronius, Patriarch of Jerusalem at the time of the conquests, described how the Arabs had "risen up unexpectedly against us because of our sins and ravaged everything with violent and beastly impulse and with impious and ungodly boldness" (Kaegi 1992: 210–11). The anonymous writer of the Doctrina Iaocobi (ca. 634) describes the empire as "humiliated," "diminished and torn asunder," and "fallen down and plundered" (Kaegi 1992: 211). The late seventh-century Armenian historian Sebeos turned to the Old Testament prophecies of Daniel to make sense of what had happened:

> But who would be able to tell the horror of the invasion of the Ishmaelites, which embraced land and sea? The fortunate Daniel foresaw and prophesied evils similar to those which were to take place on earth. By four beasts he symbolized the four kingdoms which must arise on the earth . . . "And the fourth beast, terrible, dreadful, his teeth of iron, his claws of bronze; he ate and crunched and trampled the rest underfoot" . . . This fourth kingdom, which rises from the south, is the kingdom of Ishmael. As the archangel explained it, "The beast of the fourth kingdom will arise, will be more powerful than all the kingdoms and will eat the whole world. His ten horns are the ten kings who will arise, and after them will arise another who will surpass in evil all of the preceding ones." (Kaegi 1992: 213–14)

For centuries European chroniclers continued to describe the conquests in similar tone. The psychological impact was felt far away from the conquered lands. To the Venerable Bede (673–735) the Arabs were "a terrible plague" which "ravaged Gaul with cruel bloodshed" (Bede 1969: 557; Rodinson 1991: 4).

Christian historians were at least around to record their side of the story. The Sāsānians left no heirs to represent them. Sāsānian political power was entirely supplanted by the Arabs, and Sāsānian political, religious, and social structures were absorbed into the new regime and took on an Islamic cast.

Muslim chroniclers of the ninth and tenth centuries also portrayed the conquests as a complete break with the past. The historian al-Ṭabarī portrays the conquests as no less than a reshaping of civilization – the Arabs' gift to the world. In negotiations with Rustam, the Persian general, al-Ṭabarī reports that the Arab commander offered the following challenge:

> God has sent us and has brought us here so that we may extricate those who so desire from servitude to the people [here on earth] and make them servants of God; that we may transform their poverty in this world into affluence, and that we may free them from the inequity of the religions and bestow on them the justice of Islam. He has sent us to bring His religion to His creatures and to call them to Islam. Whoever accepts it from us, we shall be content. We shall leave him on his land to rule it with us; but whoever refuses, we shall fight him, until we fulfill the promise of God. (Ṭabarī 1992, 12: 67)

Seen through later Muslim eyes the Arab conquests were the victory and vindication of a new faith, the inevitable triumph of true religion, which could only be explained as an act of God. Ṭabarī repeatedly emphasizes the enormous odds against the Muslims. At al-Qādisiyya, for instance, he alleges that the Muslims numbered 12,000 and defeated a Persian army ten times that large (Ṭabarī 1992, 12: 56, 60).

Muslim and Byzantine chroniclers agree that the Arab conquests marked a decisive historical watershed that in the space of thirty years left the political, social, cultural, and religious landscape of the world permanently altered. It is easy to sympathize with their viewpoint. A lightning-quick series of military conquests; the replacement of a ruling elite; the birth of a new religion – together these factors seem to mark the conquests as a radical turning point in history.

Archeological Data: The "Invisible" Conquests

Archeological data tell a somewhat different tale. If we look for evidence of the burning, looting, or destruction described by Bishop Sophronius in 635, we find none. No systematic sacking of cities took place, and no destruction of agricultural land occurred. The conquests brought little immediate change to the patterns of religious and communal life. There were no mass or forced conversions. Christian, Jewish, or Zoroastrian communities in Syria and Iraq may have felt threatened, but they continued to thrive. New synagogues, churches, and monasteries were still being built into the eighth century, and churches or synagogues were not converted to mosques on any noticeable scale. The first urban mosques were not built until after 690, and the urban landscape of the Near East remained largely unaffected by the conquests (Pentz 1992). There was certainly change, but in the same directions and at the same pace as before the conquests (Morony 1984: 507–26). Two key measures offer telling evidence that the conquests brought little immediate disruption to the patterns of religious and social life in Syria and Iraq: production of wine (forbidden in Islamic law) continued unchanged, and pigs (considered unclean by Muslims) continued to be raised and slaughtered in increasing numbers (Pentz 1992).

Neither do we find evidence of dramatic change in the law or political institutions of the conquered territories in the years immediately following the conquests. What did change was the ruling class. The new rulers spoke Arabic, represented a different ethnicity, and kept aloof from their conquered subjects. But for all the differences change came slowly even at the highest levels of political affairs. The new rulers continued to use Greek and Persian in administrative documents. They continued to mint Byzantine-style coins complete with the image of the emperor holding a cross, and Sāsānian-style coins bearing Zoroastrian symbols and Sāsānian dates (Morony 1984: 38–51). They were dependent on the old Persian and Greek bureaucrats and institutions. Major reform of the language of administration or of coinage did not take place until 695 – sixty years into Arab rule. Earlier attempts at reform reportedly failed in the face of stiff popular resistance. The Arab rulers also continued the same patterns of taxation. The conquests replaced the top rung of the Byzantine and Sāsānian ruling classes with Arabs, but they did not immediately or violently alter the administrative, religious, economic, or cultural landscape of the Near East.

While the conquests did increase Arab migration and settlement in Syria and Iraq, even this was the continuation and acceleration of a pattern already under way. Inscriptions show that substantial populations of Arabs lived in Syria, that settled Arabs had become well integrated in Syrian-Byzantine society, and that the Arab population and influence in some towns grew rapidly in the century preceding the conquests. We see something similar in Iraq. Since Arabs were already well integrated into the societies of Iraq and southern Syria well before the conquest, a good many of the "conquered" peoples were culturally and linguistically more akin to their new rulers than they had been to their old (Pentz 1992). This did not necessarily mean that Iraqi or Syrian Arabs welcomed the conquerors. Many did not, and much of the fiercest resistance in both Iraq and Syria came from Arabs. Arab forces allied with the Byzantines played a significant role in the battle of Yarmūk. What it did mean was that the Arab conquerors were not dealing with a culturally or linguistically alien population and that they were by no means the initiators of the Arabization of the Near East. Rather, they were part of a process that had begun long before and would continue long after. (For a much more detailed treatment of this process, see Morony 1984: 507–26.)

Even for many non-Arab populations of the Near East, the conquests were a welcome change. The majority population of Iraq was Aramaic-speaking peasants, and patterns of life for such Aramean or Egyptian peasants continued much as before. Christians continued to be Christians and Jews continued to be Jews. The old Persian or Byzantine ruling classes were displaced, and the destination of tax revenues changed, but for most there was little reason to prefer the old rulers of Constantinople to the new ones in Medina or Damascus. Monophysite Christians in Egypt, for instance, were less liable to harassment by Arabs, who cared little about their Christological peculiarities, than by the Byzantine establishment that had branded them heretics. It is easy to believe the reports that Egyptian Christians and Jews aided the Arab armies by rising in revolt against their erstwhile rulers.

So which will it be? Were the conquests a decisive turning point, or more of the same? A historical watershed or just the culmination of forces long at work? The best answer is both. The conquests brought decisive and enduring change because they put Arabs in the position of rulers. They became rulers, moreover, who stayed on and who retained their Arab identity and language. But the societies they ruled over were not immediately transformed. The Arabs manifestly did not enter a cultural or religious vacuum. While at the level of political and military affairs the Arab conquests brought immediate and drastic change, at the level of cultural and social history the conquests had little immediate effect. The religious and social life of the Near East was not suddenly altered. Enduring change would come, but gradually over the course of more than a century. Meanwhile, Christians continued to argue over theology and seek out relics, wild-looking holy men continued to roam Syria, and rabbis to discuss Halakha. Manichaeans did not suddenly lose their missionary zeal, or Mazdakites their passion for justice.

The Arab conquerors inherited this whole hodgepodge of Near Eastern cultures and religions. What would they do with it? They were new to the task of ruling the world. How would they go about it? If we were to look to the precedent of other similar conquerors – Vandals, Goths, Slavs, and much later, Turks and Mongols – we might have expected the Arabs to quickly embrace the ideology – including the religious ideology – of their predecessors. We might, quite plausibly, have expected the Arabs to rule as Christians, to adopt Greek as their language, and to claim the mantle of Rome. Alternatively, we might, somewhat less plausibly, have expected them to embrace Zoroastrianism and claim the throne of the King of Kings. In the end they did neither. Rather, thrust into the role of world rulers, the Arabs interacted with the environment into which they came and forged a completely new cultural synthesis – Arab roots and Arab language melded with Near Eastern patterns of civilization and religious life. The conquests are significant because they enabled this fusion by putting the ingredients together in the same crucible. How Arab identity combined with Near Eastern patterns of religious life to form something completely new is one of the fascinating riddles of early Islamic history and the focus of the next chapter.

Resources for Further Study

Fred Donner provides an excellent introduction to the topic of the conquests as a whole in *The Early Islamic Conquests* (1981). While Donner is primarily concerned with the Arab side of the story, more specialized studies by Michael Morony (1984) and Walter Kaegi (1992) help us to see the conquests and their effects from the vantage point of the conquered territories of Byzantine Syria and Sāsānid Iraq. One of our most important historical sources, not just for the conquests but the whole sweep of early Islamic history, is Ṭabarī's monumental history, *Tārīkh al-rusul wa-al-mulūk*, now available in a 40-volume translation; accounts of the conquests themselves are concentrated in *The Challenge to the Empires* (1993) and *The Battle of al-Qādisiyyah and the Conquest of Syria and Palestine* (1992). Irfan Shahīd's multi-volume *Byzantium and the Arabs* (1984, 1989, 1995) is the definitive work on pre-Islamic Arab populations outside of the Arabian peninsula. For a more general survey of pre-Islamic Arab history see Jan Retsö, *The Arabs in Antiquity: Their History from the Assyrians to the Umayyads* (2003). For a useful survey of the archeological data bearing on the conquests see Peter Pentz, *The Invisible Conquests* (1992).

8
RELIGION OF EMPIRE

Arab leaders seem to have shared our expectation that it would be the most natural thing in the world for the Arabs to assimilate into Near Eastern cultural and religious milieux – for the conquerors to be conquered by their new environment. From the start the conquests were administered in such a way as to avert this most predictable of outcomes. A seventh-century Iraqi Jew or Egyptian Christian curious to learn more about his new rulers might initially have found the task rather frustrating. The Arabs kept to themselves. They did not come to settle, or to assimilate, but to rule, and their leaders did what they could to prevent their troops from going native.

Arab Colonial Policy

The outlines of a system of colonial administration are attributed to the Caliph ʿUmar (r. 634–44), who led the Muslims during the most dramatic and crucial phases of the Arab conquests. ʿUmar discouraged assimilation in several ways. In Iraq and Egypt he confined the Arabs to garrison cities, called amṣār (sing. miṣr). The most important of these eventually developed into some of the empire's most influential cities: Kūfa and Baṣra in Iraq, and Fusṭāṭ (later Cairo) in Egypt. These cities were placed in such a way as to dominate major population centers without being absorbed into them. Moreover, as a matter of military policy, they were located on the desert side of existing settlements, giving the Arab armies easy means of communication and reinforcement. In Syria, where Arabs were already a significant part of the population before the conquests, this policy was modified and Arab quarters were established in major cities.

'Umar also reportedly discouraged the Arabs from abandoning the rigorous life of the nomad warrior for the comfortable life of the agrarian landlord. 'Umar's predecessor, Abū Bakr, allegedly experimented with the distribution of expropriated land. The continuation of such a policy would have been disastrous to both tax and military policy, however, by removing land from the tax rolls and distracting soldiers from their martial duties. Consequently, 'Umar revised the policy to allow subject populations to retain title to their land. Expropriated lands became the common property of the conquerors, and proceeds from such lands were systematically distributed among the Arabs on the basis of how long they had been adherents of Islam. The names and salaries of those eligible for this massive entitlement program were put down in an official register called a dīwān. A participant in the early conquests might, for example, receive 3,000 dirhams per month, while an Arab who had joined the Islamic venture at a later time received a tenth as much (Morony 1984: 56, 58–9). Predictably, the dīwān system planted seeds of economic disparity which would later grow to bear bitter fruit. But the more immediate consequence, presumably intended, was that the Arabs did not simply step into the shoes of the settled agrarian classes. Rather, they remained an occupation force and a mobile military aristocracy, enriched by the proceeds of the land, but not tied to it.

The early Arab rulers' concern to avert assimilation is also reflected in the sanctions placed on his non-Muslim (read: non-Arab) subjects. 'Umar allegedly accepted the surrender of the Syrian Christians on the basis of the following commitments:

> We shall not build, in our cities or in their neighborhood, new monasteries, churches, convents, or monks' cells, nor shall we repair, by day or by night, such of them as fall in ruins or are situated in the quarters of the Muslims.
>
> We shall keep our gates wide open for passersby and travelers. We shall give board and lodging to all Muslims who pass our way for three days.
>
> We shall not give shelter in our churches or in our dwellings to any spy, nor hide him from the Muslims.
>
> We shall not teach the Qur'ān to our children.
>
> We shall not manifest our religion publicly nor convert anyone to it. We shall not prevent any of our kin from entering Islam if they wish it.
>
> We shall show respect toward the Muslims, and we shall rise from our seats when they wish to sit.
>
> We shall not seek to resemble the Muslims by imitating any of their garments, the *qalansuwa*, the turban, footwear, or the parting of the hair. We shall not speak as they do, nor shall we adopt their *kunyas*.
>
> We shall not mount on saddles, nor shall we gird swords nor bear any kind of arms nor carry them on our persons.

We shall not engrave Arabic inscriptions on our seals.
We shall not build houses overtopping the houses of the Muslims. (Lewis 1987: 217–19)

This document is almost certainly a later forgery, but its provisions nevertheless reflect the spirit of early Arab administration. Many of these regulations, like the prohibition on the bearing of arms, are simply standard-issue colonial policy designed to keep the subject population in its place. Other provisions are more surprising: non-Muslims were not to dress like Arabs, take Arab names, use Arabic, or teach the Qur'ān. The very strangeness of these provisions in light of the later development of Islam suggests that they are early. (The prohibition on teaching the Qur'ān might be explained by concern to prevent the sacred from being defiled by infidels, but if so the language of prohibition is surprisingly narrow; we would expect any handling of the Qur'ān to be included.) Taken together, these regulations seem to suggest that Arabness, including language, dress, and religion, was something that the Arabs did not intend to allow their subjects to corrupt by imitation. The cumulative effect of these policies was to establish the Arabs as a superior and dominant military aristocracy.

What is important for our purposes is that religion was part of this mix. The Arab conquerors apparently understood their religion to be a peculiar possession of the Arabs – a sort of national religion akin to the religion of the Hebrews. The Hebrew scriptures tell of the Hebrew tribes entering Canaan to subdue the land, not to convert its inhabitants. The Arab conquests seem to have followed a similar paradigm, albeit with less bloodshed.

Conversion to Islam

When non-Arabs did convert to Islam, it came as something of a surprise and led to some confusion. It seems apparent that the Arabs had not foreseen this situation and had very little idea of what to do with non-Arab converts. Consequently, the only way to convert at this early stage was to become a sort of honorary Arab. In particular, non-Arab converts had to be assimilated into the Arab tribal system by affiliating with an Arab patron. As we have already seen, they were not called converts but "clients" or mawālī (sing. mawla) in Arabic. These mawālī took on the tribal affiliation of their patrons, and their legal status was defined according to this affiliation.

The confusion created by conversion is reflected in early tax policies. As long as there was a clear line of distinction between Arab rulers and non-Arab subjects taxation was, in theory, a fairly simple affair. Non-Arabs were generally assessed two taxes, a land tax (kharāj) and a head tax (jizya). The administration of these taxes varied from region to region, reflecting variations in tax policy in various provinces of the Byzantine and Persian empires, and the overall tax burden was roughly equivalent to that under the preceding empires. Arabs were also taxed, but on a different basis. This simple division was threatened by conversion. Should tax status change on conversion? For the first eighty years or so of Arab rule the answer was generally no. The Arab aristocracy refused to sacrifice the cash cow that paid for the continuing expansion of the empire.

At one level, then, Islam in its earliest form functioned as an Arab imperial ideology. It was a religion of Arabs, for Arabs. If others wanted in, they had to adopt Arab ways, becoming part of the Arab imperial system. This Arab-centered worldview overwhelms later Muslim accounts of the early empire. We know of course that Arab rule encompassed the whole, brilliant spectrum of Near Eastern cultural and religious life described in the previous chapter, but in later Muslim accounts of the early empire this whole colorful world of Near Eastern society vanishes. Following a common pattern in conquest narratives, the story is told as though the world the Arabs entered was empty, as though the conquests erased all that came before. In this story the only significant characters are Arabs. Arab rulers fight with Arab armies to expand Arab rule. They form Arab tribal alliances to quell Arab rebellions. Non-Arabs enter the story from time to time to sign documents of surrender. They also continue to play a significant supporting role insofar as they provide the tax base by which the Arab rulers and Arab armies are funded, and we begin to hear more and more about ambitious Arab "clients" who are drawn into the conflicts and intrigues of the Arabs. But the political and religious history of the early empire can be read, and often is written, as though the Arabs were living in a bubble, isolated from the cultural and religious forces of the conquered lands.

Leadership

Within this Arab-centered worldview, the theme that looms largest is leadership. Muslims remember uncertainties about leadership from the very beginnings of their history. The early political history of the Arab empire was extraordinarily turbulent, filled with intrigue and conflict. When the Prophet Muhammad died, later reports tell us, he left no instructions about succession. His followers were left to fend for themselves, and they were not at all sure of what to do. Only the quick thinking of two of Muhammad's close companions, Abū Bakr and ʻUmar, kept the community of Muslims from fragmenting. In the course of a raucous tribal meeting, ʻUmar carried the crowd with him when he declared his allegiance to Abū Bakr. Abū Bakr became leader of the community – the first caliph – by general acclamation.

Most of Abū Bakr's two years as caliph was spent asserting and defending his authority as the leader of a unitary Arab state by quelling rebellious tribes, and subduing rival "prophets" in what historians remember as the Ridda (apostasy) wars. Abū Bakr thus established by precedent the principle that there could be only one legitimate leader of the Muslims at one time. Before Abū Bakr died he appointed ʿUmar as his successor, apparently in an effort to avoid a repeat of the confusion that had followed Muhammad's death.

The sources record no serious challenges to ʿUmar's leadership of the community. ʿUmar's ten-year rule was the era of the most dramatic Arab conquests, but his caliphate ended abruptly when he was murdered by a slave, apparently without political motive. After his death things were never quite the same. According to ʿUmar's instructions, his successor was to be chosen by committee. Six prominent Muslims were sequestered and instructed to choose a leader from among themselves. The results were predictable. The next caliph, ʿUthmān, was a disaster. In 656 unhappy tribesmen murdered him in his house in Medina, a story that has been vividly preserved in Muslim tradition. ʿUthmān's murder precipitated a crisis in the Muslim community and led directly to fitna – civil war.

The First Civil War

ʿUthmān's murder was followed by thirty-five years of intermittent conflict resulting in permanent schism. Historians have usually divided the period into two civil wars. The first fitna, or schism, began with a conflict over succession to the caliphate which pitted Muhammad's son-in-law ʿAlī against an alliance of the Prophet's widow, ʿĀ'isha, and two close companions of the Prophet, Ṭalḥa and Zubayr. ʿAlī won handily in a battle made famous by the somewhat scandalous memory of ʿĀ'isha herself participating from atop a camel.

Victory at the "Battle of the Camel" did little to solve ʿAlī's problems, for he still had the murdered caliph's angry relatives to deal with. Taught by their tribal mores to demand a life for a life, ʿUthmān's kin among the Banū Umayya felt they had no choice but to seek vengeance for their kinsman's death. On the other hand, ʿAlī, ʿUthmān's would-be successor as caliph and the Prophet Muhammad's son-in-law, had more than a little sympathy for ʿUthmān's killers. The dead caliph's supporters, led by the infamous Muʿāwiya, the Umayyad governor of Syria, refused to accept ʿAlī's caliphate. There was no choice but to fight it out, and the two met to do just that in the momentous battle of Ṣiffīn.

The military conflict at Ṣiffīn seems to have been indecisive, but Muʿāwiya's Syrians proved the more adept at psychological warfare. At a key point in the conflict the Syrians are reported to have raised portions or copies of the Qur'ān on their spears in an appeal for arbitration. ʿAlī apparently felt honor-bound to agree to the Syrian proposal, a fateful decision that was to be his undoing. ʿAlī's Iraqi supporters were split over the morality of the decision, and the more rigorous among them withdrew their support from him. By so doing they earned the blame (or credit) for founding a complex of volatile political-theological movements which shared the designation Khawārij (anglicized: Khārijites) because they went out (kharaja) from ʿAlī. A chief distinction of the more extreme Khārijites was a readiness to do away with any leader who failed to live up to rigorous moral standards. ʿAlī was an early victim of this principle; a Khārijite assassinated him in 661. After ʿAlī's death, opposition to Muʿāwiya melted away, went underground, or was bought off. Muʿāwiya was acknowledged caliph without serious rival and the capital of the empire shifted north to Damascus.

Toward the end of a fairly lengthy and politically successful reign, Muʿāwiya designated his son Yazīd to succeed him, a move that aroused his opponents' anger for two reasons. They were angry, first, because dynastic succession was positively un-Arab and, second, because Yazīd was reputed to be over-fond of worldly pleasures. Thus, when Muʿāwiya died in 680, the opposition he had subdued emerged from underground in a second outbreak of civil war. This opposition crystallized around the children of the first fitna: ʿAbd Allāh son of al-Zubayr and Ḥusayn son of ʿAlī.

The Martyrdom of Ḥusayn

Ḥusayn's threat was short-lived. In October of 680 he led a small force from Medina to Kūfa in response to a desperate plea for aid from Kūfans who had been loyal to his father. His small expedition, which included women and children, was met by a vastly superior Syrian force at Karbalāʾ in Iraq. He was killed there on the tenth day of the month of Muḥarram. Ḥusayn's martyrdom continues to be remembered and re-enacted on that day by Shīʿite Muslims. Shīʿite celebrations of Ḥusayn's martyrdom at Karbalāʾ have had an enduring and shaping effect on Shīʿite piety and politics, a theme we will return to in chapter 9.

While Ḥusayn's martyrdom had a long-term impact, Ibn al-Zubayr proved the more immediate threat to Umayyad claims. He established himself as caliph in Medina, and at one time controlled more territory than the Syrian caliphate. Meanwhile, however, a new branch of the Umayyad family, the Marwānids, had risen to power in Syria after Yazīd's death. The turning point came when Marwānid forces decisively defeated the supporters of Ibn al-Zubayr at the battle of Marj Rāhiṭ. Ibn al-Zubayr held out in Medina until 692, when he was killed in the course of an attack on Mecca by the Umayyad governor of Iraq, Ḥajjāj ibn Yūsuf, who went on to build a reputation for efficient and brutal loyalty to the Umayyad cause.

Ḥusayn and Ibn al-Zubayr present an ironic contrast. Ibn al-Zubayr had a fair amount of political and military success and at one time ruled a vast expanse of the empire; today, only the specialists in Islamic history know his name. Ḥusayn, on the other hand, was an abject political and military failure; yet his martyrdom altered history and his passion is re-enacted yearly by millions of Shīʿī Muslims. With the death of Ibn al-Zubayr no serious rivals to the power of the Umayyads remained and the Marwānid Caliph ʿAbd al-Malik established his control from Spain to central Asia.

What is the point of all of this detail, and what does early Islamic political history tell us about the worldview of the earliest Muslims? It tells us, at the minimum, that the Arabs were inordinately passionate about leadership. Conflicts over the caliphate reveal a deep-rooted and widespread consensus that there could only be one legitimate caliph at a time, and that it was extraordinarily important that the right one be chosen. Leadership, in other words, was invested with deep moral and religious import.

The Deputy of God

To understand why leadership was invested with such significance, we can begin with the title that leaders of the empire claimed: Khalīfat Allāh, the Deputy of God (the title is often abbreviated simply to Khalīfa from which it is anglicized as caliph). Later Muslim scholars portray the use of this title as an aberration. The proper title for the leader of the Muslim community, they argue, was Khalīfat Rasūl Allāh, Successor to the Prophet, not Khalīfat Allāh. The difference is hugely significant. The title Khalīfat Rasūl Allāh implies that the caliph is simply a steward of Muhammad's legacy, a mere trustee of the prophetic estate; by contrast, Khalīfat Allāh implies that the leader of the Muslims is the very voice of God on earth, invested with divine authority. In reality every Muslim claimant to the caliphate from ʿUthmān onward explicitly claimed the status of Khalīfat Allāh (Crone and Hinds 1986: 19). Thus, when ʿAlī fought Muʿāwiya and when Ibn al-Zubayr fought ʿAbd al-Malik, they were not fighting for a secular office. Each leader argued, and their followers passionately believed, that they spoke for God and dispensed the law of God. To reject God's chosen leader was to reject divine authority. Thus, from the point of view of his supporters, Ḥusayn's murder was an act of apostasy. Conversely, from the Umayyad perspective, dissenters were not just political rebels, but rebels against the rule and order established by God. The picture will seem very familiar when we consider Shīʿīte Islam. Indeed, a convincing argument has been made that the Shīʿīte community's distinctive emphasis on charismatic leadership reflects a very early phase in the development of Islam (ibid. 97–110). At this early stage, submission to God implied first of all submission to the human representative of God, the caliph.

Who was this God that aspirants to the caliphate fought to represent? He was, first of all, One. By the time of the conquests the Arabs had taken to the idea of monotheism with zeal. Moreover, the One God worshipped by the Arab conquerors had a proper name, Allāh, and particular historical and geographical associations with Arabia. Finally this One God, Allāh, was on the side of the Arabs and approved of Arab domination. Like the ancient Hebrews, the Arabs had a mission from God, and that mission involved conquest. Allāh clearly approved of the Arab conquests, and was behind their success. No matter how much they might fight among themselves about who among them was the true representative of Allāh, the early history of the empire leaves no doubt that this job belonged to an Arab. The Arabs, in other words, had a mandate from God – a manifest destiny – to subdue and dominate the world, and to enjoy the fruits of that domination. The policies of the early Arab rulers make it clear that the Arab conquerors believed themselves to be the rightful beneficiaries of the power and riches that come with conquest. This was not a regime dedicated to altruism. It was a frankly colonial regime in which the main function of the conquered populations was to support the Arab state and its continued expansion. The early Arab state was no more egregious in exploiting the resources of its subjects than the empires that preceded it, but exploit it did.

Personal Piety

But surely there was more to the religious vision of the Arabs than this passion for divinely guided leadership? Indeed there was, and we can catch a glimpse of a more personal side to the religion of the Arab conquerors in some of the oldest Islamic grave inscriptions:

> In the name of God, the Merciful, the Compassionate: This grave is for ʿAbd al-Raḥmān ibn Khayr al-Ḥurjī. O God, grant him forgiveness and make him enter Thy mercy, and we with him. When you read this inscription, ask for his forgiveness, and say "Amen." This inscription was written in Jumāda II of the year 31 [= 652 CE].

> In the name of God, the Merciful, the Compassionate: God is most great. Much praise be to God in the morning, and in the late afternoon, and in the long night. O God, Lord of Gabriel and Michael and Isrāfīl, grant forgiveness to Thābit ibn Yazīd al-Ashʿarī for his past and future sins, and to whosoever says "Amen, Amen, Amen, Lord of the Worlds." This inscription was written in Shawwāl of the year 64 [= 684 CE].

> May God grant forgiveness to Ḥakīm ibn ʿAmr, alive and well. Amen, Lord of the Worlds, Lord of all People. Written in the beginning of Dhū l-Ḥijja in the year 85 [= 704 CE]. May He make him enter paradise . . . (Donner 1998: 86–7)

These privately funded inscriptions reflect a deep personal piety expressed in reverence for and dependence upon God, certainty of an unseen world inhabited by angels, firm belief in heaven and hell, and pious angst about one's personal destiny in the afterlife. The same piety is also reflected in our earliest official inscription which dates from the reign of Muʿāwiya:

> This dam belongs to the servant of God Muʿāwiya, commander of the believers [Amīr al-mu'minīn]. The servant of God in Ṣakhr built it with God's permission in the year 58 [= 677/678 CE]. O God, grant forgiveness to the servant of God Muʿāwiya, commander of the Believers, make him firm and assist him, and let him reap the benefit of it. ʿAmr ibn Janāb[?] wrote [this]. (Donner 1998: 87)

Such inscriptions give us scant details about the content of Muslim belief. They make no mention of Muhammad, prophets, or the Qur'ān. But they nevertheless speak volumes about the religious ethos of the earliest Muslims, who were marked by deep concern for obedience to God and personal destiny.

To summarize: the religion of the Arab conquerors reflected a deep monotheistic piety, it was unabashedly political, and it was decidedly Arabocentric. The chief duty of man was submission to the One God, Allāh, and the way to submit to Allāh was to align oneself with his representative on earth, the caliph. This much we can say with confidence. But is this all? Working from later Muslim accounts of the early history of Islamic empire we would ordinarily say much more about the content of early Muslim belief. We would need to say a good deal, for example, about prophets in general and about the life of the Prophet Muhammad in particular. We would also have a good deal to say about Islamic scripture, the Qur'ān, and about God's specific requirements in the way of law and ritual practice. Looking back through the eyes of later Muslims, the religion of the Arab conquerors was a faith with a law-centered religion, a specific founder-Prophet, a fully formed and canonical scripture, and a well-defined system of worship. The main responsibility of the Muslims was to understand and apply the divine will revealed in the Qur'ān and put into practice by the Prophet Muhammad.

We would have little reason to question this picture, but for the simple fact that it cannot be firmly documented from contemporary sources. The name of Muhammad, for example, is absent from the kind of early religious inscriptions quoted above. We know that the worship of Allāh was widespread, but Muhammad's name is conspicuously absent until the reign of ʿAbd al-Malik, when its use is suddenly widespread. This is no proof that the early Muslims had no place for Muhammad, but it does raise the suspicion that his importance and centrality increased over time. As for the Qur'ān, we have no documentary evidence for a complete, canonical text before the ninth century. While much of the material in the Qur'ān is evidently very old – a point we explored in chapter 5 – there is no firm evidence that it was accepted as a canonical scripture at this early period. Again, this does not prove that the Qur'ān was not circulated in its final form at an earlier stage, but it does raise the suspicion that it had not yet achieved the universal acceptance and importance that it was later to gain. Exactly when the materials of scripture were collected and when they came to be widely accepted as a closed canon we simply cannot say with any degree of confidence.

The Arabs, then, were pious monotheists and believed that they had a mandate to conquer and to rule. But this in itself was not enough to establish a new religion. Jews and Christians who populated the Near East had a good deal more experience with monotheism than the Arabs. What was to keep the Arabs from simply becoming absorbed into one of the existing monotheistic traditions? Nothing in the early inscriptions quoted above says anything that a pious Jew or Christian might not have said. Yet the Arabs did resist assimilation. How did they achieve this ideological independence? And what was their relationship with the monotheists they came to rule over? The answers to these questions are critical to our understanding of the development of a distinctive Islamic identity.

The Dome of the Rock

Some of our most important clues about the relationship of early Islam to Christianity and Judaism come from the first great Islamic architectural achievement, the Dome of the Rock. The Caliph ʿAbd al-Malik commissioned the building in 692, sixty years after the beginning of the Arab conquests, and the structure has physically dominated Jerusalem ever since. The Dome rests on a high platform atop Mount Moriah, the traditional site of Abraham's sacrifice of his son and of the Jewish Temple. It towers 30 meters above the level of the platform, and is centered on a massive outcropping of rock from which it derives its English name.

Just as the Dome of the Rock towers over the Jerusalem skyline, it also juts like a massive rock out of the fog of early Islamic history – the earliest work of Islamic architecture still standing in more or less its original form. Mosaic inscriptions in the Dome of the Rock include the earliest written fragments of the text of the Qur'ān. These inscriptions also give us a very rare early mention, perhaps our very first, of the Prophet Muhammad. Thus the Dome provides us with our first physical documentation of the existence of a belief system that is recognizably Islamic. By contrast, the earliest Islamic historical or literary texts, while they tell of earlier times, were not actually put into writing for almost a century after the construction of the Dome.

If we set out to "read" the Dome of the Rock as a text, what might we conclude from it about the beliefs of ʿAbd al-Malik and the Arab ruling classes of the late seventh century? We would likely conclude, first of all, that Jerusalem was of particular importance to these early Muslims and that within Jerusalem the Temple Mount was of special significance. The Dome of the Rock was not an inexpensive venture, nor was it hastily planned or constructed. A building of such magnitude and expense was not haphazardly placed, and we have every reason to think that ʿAbd al-Malik had good reason for locating the greatest monument to his reign in Jerusalem rather than in Damascus, his capital, or in any other place in the empire. He must also have had good reason for choosing its particular location in the city.

Later Muslim tradition suggests two quite different reasons why ʿAbd al-Malik may have had the Dome built where and when he did. First, this is the place, according to tradition, where God transported Muhammad on his miraculous "night journey," and the rock within the Dome is the rock from which he was taken into heaven. This rock, in fact, still has, to the eyes of pious Muslims, the visible mark of Muhammad's footprint. If this was the building's original purpose, however, the builders left no evidence in the inscriptions or decoration. There is no hint in these of any events of Muhammad's life, miraculous or mundane.

Muslim historians suggest another possible reason for the construction of the Dome. The empire was in the midst of a civil war, Mecca was in the hands of his rival, Ibn al-Zubayr, and ʿAbd al-Malik needed an alternative place of pilgrimage. The Dome of the Rock was built, according to this explanation, to divert pilgrims from Mecca to Jerusalem (Elad 1992). This story is historically plausible. The Dome clearly was built to function as a place of pilgrimage, as a cursory glance at the architectural plan will show. Unlike an ordinary mosque, the Dome is not physically oriented toward Mecca. It is built for pilgrims to circle the rock around which it is centered, and like the Kaʿba in Mecca, it conveys a clear message: this is the center of the spiritual world, the hub of the cosmos.

But once again, the Dome itself offers little evidence that the war between ʿAbd al-Malik and Ibn al-Zubayr was the driving force behind its construction. The extensive inscriptions give no hint of inter-Muslim conflict or rivalry. Instead, pilgrims read the following as they walk around the outer ambulatory of the shrine (Grabar 1996: 56–61):

> In the name of God, the Compassionate, the Merciful, there is no god but God, One, without associate. Say he is God, alone, God the eternal, He does not beget nor is he begotten and there is no one like him (Sūra 112). Muhammad is the envoy of God, may God bless him . . . Praise to God who begets no son and who

> has no associate in power and who has no surrogate for [protection from] humiliation and magnify his greatness. (Qur'ān 17:111)

As they proceed into the inner ambulatory, the same message is amplified:

> O people of the book, do not go beyond the bounds of your religions and do not say about God except the truth. Indeed the Messiah Jesus son of Mary was an envoy of God and his word he bestowed on her as well as a spirit from Him. So believe in God and in His envoys and do not say "three"; Desist, it is better for you. For indeed God is one God, glory be to Him that He should have a Son. To him belong what is in heaven and what is on earth and it is sufficient for Him to be a guardian. The Messiah does not disdain to be a servant of God, nor do the angels nearest [to him]. Those who disdain serving him and who are arrogant, he will gather all to himself. Bless your envoy and your servant Jesus son of Mary and Peace be on Him on the day of birth and on the day of death and on the day he is raised up again. This is Jesus son of Mary. It is a word of truth in which they doubt. It is not for God to take a son. Glory be to him when he decrees a thing He only says "Be" and it is. Indeed God is my Lord and your Lord, therefore serve Him; this is the straight path. (Qur'ān 19:30–3)

Judging by these inscriptions the Dome of the Rock is an architectural rejoinder to Christianity. ʿAbd al-Malik may have had reason to be concerned about his rival in Medina, Ibn al-Zubayr, but the inscriptions in the Dome of the Rock are concerned with another more immediate challenge. The majority of the subjects of the new empire were Christians, and Jerusalem was a city dominated by Christian monuments. In this environment the Dome of the Rock performed two functions. First, it provided a striking reminder of who was in charge. The Dome was built along Byzantine lines, by Byzantine-trained craftsmen, and it was calculated to show that the Muslim rulers could outmatch the glory of the Byzantine emperors on their own terms. Moreover, the placement of the structure ensured that the Christian population of the city would never forget who their new rulers were. A Christian pilgrim leaving the Church of the Holy Sepulcher would be faced with the Dome towering against the horizon, its magnificence easily surpassing any Christian structure in the city.

Second, the Dome reminded visitors that whatever else the Arab rulers might be, they were quite emphatically not Christians. The message of the inscriptions is categorical and polemical: Jesus is no more than a messenger and servant of God; Christian Trinitarian belief is misguided; to suggest that God could beget a son is idolatrous. The message of the Dome of the Rock and its inscriptions is overwhelming and clear: Muslims are dominant and they are distinct. The Muslims are conquerors, destined to rule, and they are not to be confused with Christians.

The message of the Dome is amplified when we place its construction in a larger context. The Dome was but one piece, admittedly the most majestic,

Figure 8.1 The Dome of the Rock. Photo: Photo © Mordechai Meiri/Shutterstock

of a larger program of ʻAbd al-Malik's that marks his reign as a milestone in the early articulation of Islamic identity. He initiated an extensive building program in Syria that involved the construction of roads around Jerusalem and Damascus, as well as the revitalization of the Temple Mount. More significantly, he completely reformed the empire's currency. Early coins issued by Arab rulers had simply been imitations or reissues of Byzantine or Sāsānian coins. In the same year that he commissioned the Dome of the Rock, ʻAbd al-Mālik began a series of reforms that culminated in a revolutionary new currency design. Earlier coins were adaptations of Byzantine designs featuring a standing figure of the caliph, dressed in Arab clothing and holding a sword, encircled by a profession of faith in Arabic: "There is no God but God alone, and Muhammad is the Messenger of God." Beginning in the late 690s, ʻAbd al-Malik began to mint coins unlike any that had come before. Figural images were removed completely and replaced by texts. An enlarged profession of faith was inscribed on one side, and the polemical, anti-Trinitarian words of Sūra 112 of the Qur'ān appeared on the reverse: "Say, He is God, alone, God the eternal, He does not beget nor is He begotten and there is no one like Him." Together, these reforms reinforce the impression left by the Dome that ʻAbd al-Malik's reign saw the emergence of a newly assertive Arab religious identity that was geographically centered on Syria and Palestine and competitive with Christianity.

That the Dome is a rejection of Christianity is clear enough. What is not so clear is what it can tell us about the early Muslim attitude toward Judaism. Anti-Jewish polemics are entirely absent from the building's texts. This comes as something of a surprise given the prominence of anti-Christian polemics in the inscriptions. But what are we to make of the Dome's placement on Mount Moriah, Judaism's most sacred site? Was it built specifically to identify with the Jewish tradition, or to compete with it (Elad 1992)? Once again, the Dome itself is silent.

The Constitution of Medina

There is other evidence, however, that early Muslims felt a strong kinship with the Jews. A document from the early years of Islam, the so-called Constitution of Medina, portrays the relationship of Muslims and Jews as a cordial partnership. The document is included in one of the earliest biographies of Muhammad, and describes the organization of the Muslim community, the umma:

> In the name of God the Compassionate, the Merciful. This is a document from Muhammad the prophet [governing the relations] between the believers and Muslims of Quraysh and Yathrib, and those who followed them and joined them and labored with them. They are one community [umma] to the exclusion of all men. (Ibn Isḥāq 1955: 231)

After this unexceptional beginning, the document becomes more detailed about how various kinds of conflicts and disputes are to be settled within the community, culminating with a call to refer all disputes to God and to Muhammad. Then comes a surprise:

> The Jews shall contribute to the cost of war so long as they are fighting alongside the believers. The Jews of the B. ʿAwf are one community [umma] with the believers [the Jews have their religion and the Muslims have theirs], their freedmen and their persons except those who behave unjustly and sinfully, for they hurt but themselves and their families. The same applies to the Jews of the B. al-Najjār, B. al-Ḥārith, B. Sāʿida, B. Jusham, B. al-Shuṭayba. Loyalty is a protection against treachery. The freedmen of the Thaʿlaba are as themselves. The close friends of the Jews are as themselves. (Ibn Isḥāq 1955: 232–3)

The surprise is that the Jews and Muslims are defined as part of a single umma. As such, they will act together in war and peace, and they will all acknowledge the authority of the Prophet:

> The contracting parties are bound to help one another against any attack on Yathrib. If they are called to make peace and maintain it they must do so; and if they make a similar demand on the Muslims it must be carried out except in the case of a holy war. Every one shall have his portion from the side to which he belongs; the Jews of al-Aus, their freedmen and themselves have the same standing with the people of this document in pure loyalty from the people of this document. (Ibn Isḥāq 1955: 233)

A traditional understanding of the Constitution of Medina situates the document during a brief period in the career of Muhammad in Medina (see, for example, Hamidullah 1968). According to that picture, this close partnership with the Jews was fleeting and ended long before the conquests. But is it possible that Arabs and Jews continued to feel a very close kinship well after the conquests? There are hints of such a relationship in non-Muslim sources. Two modern scholars, Patricia Crone and Michael Cook, in their controversial book *Hagarism* (1977), used these sources to experiment with the hypothesis that Jews and Arabs were partners in conquest. If we open the door to this possibility, the Dome of the Rock and its inscriptions may appear in a new light. In the Dome we have a magnificent building on a Jewish holy site that specifically rejects Christian claims about Jesus. Could early Islam have had the character of a Jewish–Christian hybrid, combining a Judaic monotheism and law with a characteristically Christian preoccupation with Jesus?

Such arguments are highly speculative and based on circumstantial or disputed evidence. The most that we can say for sure is that early Islam displays a close symbolic relationship with Judaism, and the Dome of the Rock hints at this relationship. Whether or not the ties between early Muslims and Jews were close at the time of its building, the Dome uses a site with specifically Jewish symbolism to express a dominance over Christianity. Seen more broadly, the Dome reflects many of the chief features of early Arab Islam: a preoccupation with political leadership, a close symbolic relationship with Judaism, and a competitive relationship with Christianity.

But the Dome also points to the future. It reflects what Islam would soon become: a religion no longer centered on caliphal authority, but on a text, the Qur'ān, and on a Prophet, Muhammad. The living authority of the caliph was to be replaced by a community of scholars. The Dome, along with other evidence from the reign of ʿAbd al-Malik, indicates a religious community in flux – in the process of defining itself. Islam as we know it in the Qur'ān, the life of the Prophet, and the tradition literature was the culmination of this process of self-definition, and in these sources we see evidence of the process of negotiating an Islamic identity. Even after the fundamental elements of Islamic tradition had taken shape and become well established as the agreed-upon core of Islamic belief, however, the process of negotiating identity continued. The context for this process was the period of the great caliphal empires, and it is in this context that the basic Muslim political and theological options – Shī'īte, Khārijite, Ismā'īlī and Sunnī Islam – took shape.

Resources for Further Study

Gerald Hawting, in *The First Dynasty of Islam* (2000), provides an accessible introduction to the Umayyads. For a primary source on the early political history of the caliphate, see BalāDhūrī, *The Origins of the Islamic State* (1916, 1924). For a thoughtful and balanced evaluation of the historical sources for this period, see Fred Donner's *Narratives of Islamic Origins* (1998). The religious significance of the early caliphate is discussed in Patricia Crone and Martin Hinds, *God's Caliph* (1986).

On the sectarian environment and particularly Muslim–Christian polemics in the early period, see Daniel J. Sahas, *John of Damascus on Islam* (1972), David Thomas, *Anti-Christian Polemic in Early Islam* (1992), and J. W. Sweetman, *Islam and Christian Theology* (1947). Hawting, in *The Idea of Idolatry and the Emergence of Islam* (1999), argues that Qur'ānic polemics against idolatry were in fact directed at rival monotheists rather than Arab pagans.

The boldest assertion of a Jewish–Muslim alliance during the period of the conquests is Crone and Cook's *Hagarism* (1977). For a rather more conservative account of Jews in Arabia, see Gordon Newby, *A History of the Jews of Arabia* (1988), and for a broad overview of Jewish–Arab relations see Solomon D. Goitein, *Jews and Arabs* (1955).

On the Dome of the Rock, see Oleg Grabar, *The Shape of the Holy* (1996), which looks like a coffee-table book but goes well beyond the normal confines of that genre with its stunning illustrations, computer-aided simulations, translations of the Dome's inscriptions, and incisive text. Julian Raby and Jeremy Johns, in *Bayt al-Maqdis: 'Abd al-Malik's Jerusalem* (1992), bring together some of the best and most controversial scholarship on the Dome.

9

THE CALIPHATE

Ibn al-Muqaffaʿ

Some fifty years after ʿAbd al-Malik commissioned the Dome of the Rock, and around the same time that Ibn Isḥāq was compiling his biography of Muhammad, a young and talented assistant to the governor of Baṣra, Ibn al-Muqaffaʿ (d. 756), wrote a treatise offering political advice to the ʿAbbāsid Caliph al-Manṣūr. The ʿAbbāsids were new to the business of ruling, and Manṣūr was only the second in the dynasty, so presumably he could use advice. Ibn al-Muqaffaʿ, the son of a Persian tax collector who had been tortured for mishandling tax revenues (hence the nickname "al-Muqaffaʿ," the cripple), was happy to oblige. He advised his ruler on how to prudently handle his army and bureaucracy, and how to choose his closest advisers with the overall aim of retaining the allegiance of his subjects. His most pointed advice, however, had to do with religious policy, an area that Ibn al-Muqaffaʿ felt called for firm leadership. In particular, he thought that the caliph should put an end to the inconsistencies and contradictions among the various schools of Islamic law by enforcing his own inspired opinions and compiling a single, consistent code of justice (Pellat 1976).

We have no idea how Manṣūr received this advice, but we do know where the counsel came from. Ibn al-Muqaffaʿ was an aficionado of Persian literature and an unabashed transmitter and promoter of Persian ideas. He is best known, in fact, as a translator from Persian to Arabic. His most famous translation was the famous Kalīla and Dimna stories, a collection of folktales which originated in India. He also translated Persian political works, and among these was the so-called "Testament of Ardashīr," in which the Persian monarch Ardashīr declares, "Religion and kingship are two brothers, and neither can dispense with the other. Religion is the foundation of kingship, and kingship protects religion. For whatever lacks a foundation must perish, and whatever lacks a protector disappears" (Duchesne-Guillemin 1983: 877). This notion of the intertwined fortunes of religion and state is an idea we have already met in the Sāsānian empire, and it was to become an oft-repeated refrain in Islamic political thought.

Ibn al-Muqaffaʿ did not last long. He had a falling out with the caliph and was brutally tortured and killed at age 36. His political ideas outlived him, however, for two reasons. First, they are part of a larger trend, reflecting the growing impact of Persian ideas in Islamic political thought. Second, they raise the perennial question of Islamic political theory; that is, what exactly are the religious duties and prerogatives of the caliph? From as far back as we can tell, Muslims were remarkably united on the centrality of the caliphate to the political (and religious) order of the Islamic empire. They agreed, in other words, that there must be a single (male) caliph who embodies the political unity of the Muslims. They disagreed, however, on just about every other point: the qualifications of the caliph, the manner and means of his appointment, the nature and extent of his authority, and the grounds for his removal. The issue boiled down to a single fundamental question: was the caliph, like an Arab tribal shaykh (or a modern president), merely an ordinary human being elected to an extraordinary position, or was the post open only to extraordinary men, like the Prophet, especially chosen and gifted by God. Prophet or president? Fount of divine guidance or ordinary servant of God charged with implementation of His law?

Faced with this question, Ibn al-Muqaffaʿ outlined two extremes to be avoided. According to one view, the caliph was an infallible source of religious guidance possessing intrinsic authority to which his followers were thus bound to submit. At the other extreme were those who held that the caliph was intrinsically no different from any other believer. His authority rested purely on his faithfulness to Islamic law, and if he erred he could and should be removed and replaced. Ibn al-Muqaffaʿ sought a middle ground. The caliph's authority was not infallible or absolute, but it was unique. He alone possessed the right and the responsibility to exercise authority as the chief arbiter of Islamic law, ensuring the unity of the believers (Pellat 1976). The general direction of Ibn al-Muqaffaʿ's ideas is clear: the caliph was neither prophet-like nor a glorified tribal shaykh, but something in between – in other words, a king.

These three alternative job descriptions for the caliph – infallible religious guide, tribal shaykh, or king – represent the extremes of Islamic political theory; it was in response to and reaction to these extremes that orthodox Sunnī political theory eventually took shape. Consequently, to understand "orthodox" political thought, we need first to understand the alternatives.

The Shīʿite Vision

The Shīʿite political vision goes back to the memory of an event toward the end of Muhammad's life. As Muhammad was returning from his farewell pilgrimage – his last before he died – he stopped with his followers near a pool called Ghādir Khumm. There he gathered his companions together and asked them whether he was not closer to them than they were to themselves. After they replied enthusiastically that it was so, Muhammad dropped his bombshell. He took ʿAlī by the hand and said, "He of whom I am the patron, of him ʿAlī is also the patron." By these words, Muhammad designated ʿAlī as his chosen successor (Vaglieri 1993).

The choice, from the point of view of ʿAlī's supporters, was a natural one. ʿAlī was Muhammad's closest male relative, by marriage and by birth, and the Qur'ān itself seems to give a special place to the family of the Prophet. Shīʿī Muslims also came to believe that ʿAlī's succession had already been divinely revealed to Muhammad during the Prophet's miraculous ascent into heaven. The failure of the early leaders of the community to recognize the claims of ʿAlī or to accord special status to the family of the Prophet after Muhammad's death was at best a grievous error, at worst apostasy.

Those who championed the claims of ʿAlī became known as the party of ʿAlī or Shīʿat ʿAlī. Shīʿī political thinking was thus based on the conviction that legitimate leadership of the community was reserved for a man who was God-ordained and who possessed extraordinary God-given qualities – qualities that happened to be exclusive to members of the household of the Prophet, the ahl al-bayt. Leadership in the community thus properly belonged only to a member of the Prophet's family who received the inspired designation (naṣṣ) of his predecessor. (The Prophet, for instance, designated ʿAlī, who in turn designated his son al-Ḥasan, who designated his brother Ḥusayn, and so on.) Those so designated were called imāms, the only legitimate leaders of the community.

The theory didn't work out well in practice, and the development of Shīʿism was shaped by a series of political and military failures. When ʿAlī finally did become caliph, his rule was immediately contested. After ʿAlī's death his son Ḥasan turned out to have no stomach for fighting, and abandoned his claims to the caliphate in favor of Muʿāwiya, who had him poisoned in any case, just to be safe. After Ḥasan's death, Ḥusayn made himself a martyr at Karbalā', and Ḥusayn's son, ʿAlī Zayn al-ʿĀbidīn, perhaps having learned from his father's example, refused to be drawn into the contest for leadership. The supporters of the family of the Prophet were forced to look elsewhere for a candidate. In 685, Mukhtār, a formidable insurrectionist, raised a rebellion in the name of another son of ʿAlī, Muhammad ibn al-Ḥanafiyya, the stepbrother of Ḥasan and Ḥusayn. Mukhtār won Kūfa for a time, but his rebellion was

Figure 9.1 Iraqi children with poster of the twelve imāms beginning with ʿAli, pictured at right. The Twelfth Imām appears at lower left with face blanked. Photo: Andrew Stern

crushed in 687. After the death of Mukhtār there were no major Shīʿite rebellions until the rise of the ʿAbbāsids some sixty years later.

Thus the early experience of the Shīʿites is a story of political failure, and this experience of failure took the Shīʿī Muslims in two quite different directions. The majority of Shīʿites, following the leadership of Ḥusayn's grandson, Muhammad al-Bāqir, and al-Bāqir's son, Jaʿfar al-Ṣādiq, abandoned their political ambitions and became quietists. The new quietism was made possible by a remarkable and ingenious turn of doctrine. Al-Bāqir and Jaʿfar taught that the true imāms possessed special knowledge – ʿilm – which was hidden from ordinary mortals and which gave them understanding of the hidden meanings of the Qur'ān. As the protectors of this esoteric knowledge, the imāms performed an essential spiritual function which was far more important than their political function. Thus, whether they hold power or not, the imāms are essential to the very existence of the world and to the spiritual well-being of their followers. Consequently, it is wrong to put them at risk by unwisely rising in rebellion. In fact, it is the obligation of followers of the imām to engage in taqiyya, the concealment of one's true beliefs, in order to preserve the Shīʿī community in the face of a hostile environment. The practice of taqiyya became a crucial element of Shīʿī political doctrine, allowing mainline Shīʿī Muslims to reconcile political idealism with a de facto acceptance of the status quo.

Figure 9.2 Shīʿite pilgrims in Karbalā commemorating the martyrdom of Ḥusayn (d. 680 CE). Photo: © Antoine Gyori/AGP/Corbis

Not all Shīʿī Muslims were willing to go the quietist route, however. While Jaʿfar al-Ṣādiq was following in his father's footsteps and making Shīʿīsm safe for scholars, Jaʿfar's uncle Zayd ibn ʿAlī, was busy keeping the old spirit of rebellion alive. In 740, Zayd led a rebellion in Kūfa that, like previous rebellions, was soon crushed. His followers were not to be deterred, however. The supporters of Zayd formed their own branch of Shīʿīsm, the Zaydīs, distinguished by its militant political philosophy. In contrast to the Imāmī followers of Jaʿfar al-Ṣādiq, the Zaydīs insisted that the only real imāms were those who were willing to actually fight for leadership of the community. Thus there had been no imām between Ḥusayn and Zayd, and when a true imām did emerge it was a religious obligation to fight on his behalf.

The ʿAbbāsids

Other branches of the ahl al-bayt were also keeping the militant spirit alive. In the first half of the eighth century the ambitions of two such movements coincided in a dramatic turnover of power, the ʿAbbāsid revolution. In the early part of the eighth century, Abū Hāshim, the son of Muhammad ibn al-Ḥanafiyya, had built up a support base in the Iranian province of Khurāsān by forming a secret propaganda network. After Abū Hāshim died in 718, members of the ʿAbbāsid family, descendants of the Prophet's uncle, al-ʿAbbās, took over his movement. The ʿAbbāsid leader, Muhammad ibn ʿAlī, claimed to be the designated successor to Abū Hāshim. From their base in Kūfa the ʿAbbāsids sent missionaries to Khurāsān, where they proclaimed the imminent coming of "the preferred one from the house of Muhammad." The phrase was a brilliant piece of propaganda aimed at attracting as wide a range of Shīʿī sympathizers as possible to the ʿAbbāsid cause while simultaneously obscuring the identity of the ʿAbbāsid leadership. In 750 the ʿAbbāsids swept the Umayyads out of power on a wave of Shīʿī enthusiasm.

The ʿAbbāsid charade could not last. Once in power, Shīʿī enthusiasm for the descendants of ʿAlī threatened the legitimacy of the ʿAbbāsids. Consequently the new rulers dispensed with the fiction of Shīʿī sympathy, and brutally repressed their erstwhile allies. They had their main Shīʿī supporters murdered, including the leading propagandist of the movement, Abū Muslim. About seventy years later, Caliph Ma'mūn (r. 813–33) made a bid to recapture Shīʿī sympathies and return the ʿAbbāsids to their roots by naming the grandson of Jaʿfar al-Ṣādiq, the imām ʿAlī al-Riḍa, as his political successor. ʿAlī al-Riḍa died before the plan could be tested, however, and the ʿAbbāsids had to continue to derive their political legitimacy from other sources.

After the rise of the ʿAbbāsids the Shīʿī political ideal remained very much alive, in both quietist and militant forms. Jaʿfar al-Ṣādiq, who had witnessed the ʿAbbāsid rise to power, preached a politically quiescent Shīʿīsm, and during his lifetime the majority of Shīʿī Muslims seem to have been united behind his imāmate. Jaʿfar's teachings on the imāmate were perfectly suited to help Shīʿī Muslims make sense of their situation after their betrayal by the ʿAbbāsids. Acknowledgment of the true imām was a religious obligation, but it was not necessary to get oneself killed trying to get him into power. Shīʿī Muslims could even cooperate with the enemy and accept a position under an illegitimate ruler so long as the aim was to promote justice. In the end God would restore the true imāms to their rightful place, and the best that believers can do is wait for Him to act. This was clearly a philosophy that privileged survival over unrestrained idealism.

Twelvers

After Jaʿfar's death the Shīʿī community once again split. The majority of Shīʿī Muslims accepted Jaʿfar's son Mūsā al-Kāẓim as the seventh imām and continued to follow the quietist teaching of Jaʿfar. This group, called Twelvers, acknowledged five imāms after Mūsā, ending with the imāmate of the once and future twelfth imām, Muhammad al-Mahdī. In 874, according to Twelver teaching, the twelfth imām was taken into concealment (ghayba) by God, who wished to safeguard him from his enemies. For several decades the twelfth imām continued to communicate with his followers through official representatives called Bābs, but in 941 he entered what Twelvers call the greater ghayba and since that time he has remained incommunicado. In spite of his silence, however, Twelvers believe that the imām remains alive, and they await his emergence from ghayba when he will be revealed as Mahdī, "the guided one," ushering in the end of time.

Meanwhile, the absence of the infallible imām left a gap in religious authority which Shīʿī scholars have been happy to fill. The logic is simple. In the absence of the imām, those who transmit the authoritative teachings of the imāms are the surest source of guidance. It is the fuqahā', therefore, the transmitters and interpreters of ḥadīth from the imāms, who stand in the place of the imām and act as his agents. Thus religious guidance and the administration of Islamic law are the rightful domain of the Shīʿī scholars.

Political authority, however, is another matter. A logical corollary of Twelver doctrine was that no regime could claim genuine political legitimacy unless it was headed by the imām, for the imām alone was the legitimate sovereign. In the absence of the imām, it made little difference whether the pretenders were Sunnī or Shīʿīte; in either case their rule was illegitimate. Thus some Shīʿī scholars even argued that participation in Friday prayers was illegal under the ghayba because a legitimate ruler is a prerequisite to convening the congregational prayer. Naturally the more cautious Shīʿī scholars were somewhat reluctant to appear to be seizing the prerogatives of the imām for themselves, and they generally resisted the idea that they could step into the imām's shoes in a political sense. This attitude changed only in the twentieth century, when the belief that scholars may represent the imām in the political sphere came to be widely discussed among Twelvers.

Ismāʿīlīs

Twelver quietism contrasts sharply with the tendency to militancy in the other main branch of Shīʿī Islam, the Ismāʿīlīs. On the surface the split between the two groups was over succession. Where the Twelvers contend that the imāmate passed from Jaʿfar al-Ṣādiq to his younger son Mūsā, the Ismāʿīlīs argue that Jaʿfar's elder son Ismāʿīl was his designated successor. At a deeper level the Ismāʿīlīs came to differ radically from the Twelvers over the political role of the imāmate and over political strategy and organization. In particular the Ismāʿīlīs engaged in energetic and highly organized missionary activity on behalf of the imām. Their missionary dāʿīs traveled from India to North Africa, establishing clandestine groups of Ismāʿīlī loyalists under the direction of a well-organized central leadership.

For about a century Ismāʿīlī activity remained underground and obscure, but in the late ninth and early tenth centuries the movement came dramatically into the open. First, a branch of Ismāʿīlīs called Qarmaṭīs (Carmathians) established states in southern Syria and in parts of Arabia. By 905 most of Yemen was under Ismāʿīlī control. Then, in 909, the imām made his move. By this time the movement had grown strong enough in North Africa for the imām to emerge from hiding and to take power there. The new rulers called themselves Fāṭimids, reflecting their claim to descent from the Prophet's daughter, and the state grew into one of the great Islamic empires, encompassing at its height North Africa, Sicily, Egypt, Syria, and much of Arabia, including Mecca and Medina. The Fāṭimids ruled from Egypt for two centuries until Salāḥ al-dīn al-Ayyūbī, the Saladin of Crusader lore, formally abolished the dynasty in 1171.

Nizārī "Assassins"

About eighty years before the final demise of the Fāṭimid state, Ismāʿīlī rule spread in another spectacular form in Persia and Syria. Beginning in 1090, a formidable Ismāʿīlī leader named Ḥasan-i Ṣabbah began to build a state made up of a widely dispersed network of mountain fortresses in Syria and Persia. The most important of these strongholds, Ḥasan-i Ṣabbah's headquarters, was Alamūt, a virtually impregnable castle perched atop a huge rock deep in the Elburz mountains on the southern end of the Caspian Sea. Although Ḥasan-i Ṣabbah's state began as a nominal extension of the Fāṭimid empire, it soon broke away. In 1094 a division over the succession to the Fāṭimid imāmate split the Ismāʿīlīs, and Ḥasan-i Ṣabbah and his followers put their support behind Nizār, the losing candidate for imām. The breakaway Nizārī state, based at Alamūt, continued until 1256, when it was finally vanquished by invading Mongols.

From Alamūt, which he allegedly never left after he conquered it in 1090, Ḥasan-i Ṣabbah became the terror of the Mediterranean. He and his successors dispatched Ismāʿīlī dāʿīs throughout the Near East to win new devotees for their imām and to expand the territory under Ismāʿīlī control. They were a secret society, often acting clandestinely and infiltrating the major centers of power. When opposed, the followers of Ḥasan responded by terrorizing their political enemies by means of targeted assassinations. Their first major victim was Niẓām al-Mulk, the powerful wazīr of the Saljūq rulers, who was stabbed to death in 1092 by an Ismāʿīlī assassin disguised as a ṣūfī. Other victims included

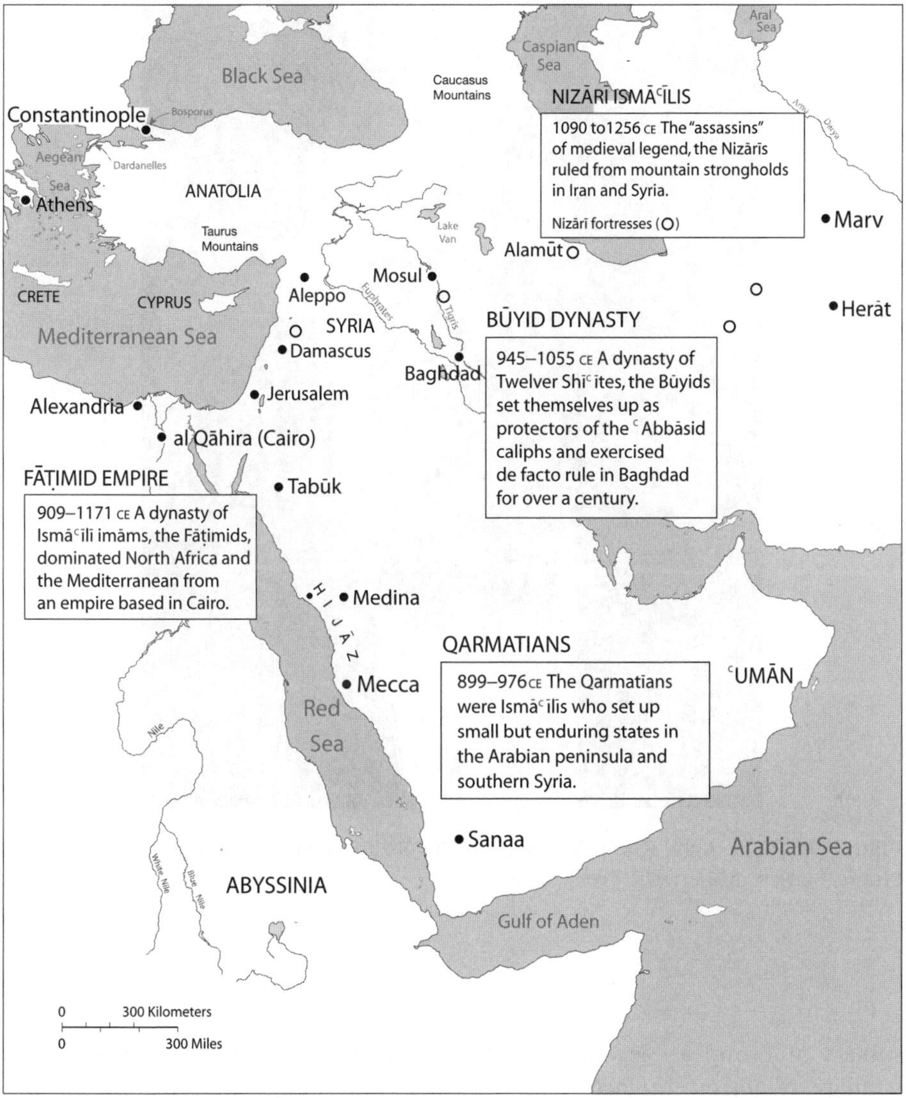

Map 6 Shīᶜīte bids for political ascendancy, tenth and eleventh centuries

the ruler of Homs in 1103, the Saljūq governor of Mosul in 1113, the wazīr of Aleppo in 1177, and the Crusader king of Jerusalem in 1192.

Terrifying legends about the Nizārīs spread to Europe through the Crusaders, leading to a long-standing, sometimes inordinate fascination in the West. The Syrian leader of the Nizārīs, the "Old Man of the Mountain," became the

Figure 9.3 The Agha Khan IV, imām of the Nizārī Ismāʿīlī community since 1957. Photo: Mark Cuthbert/UK Press/PA Photos

subject of European legend. The Nizārīs were so closely identified with a strategy of terror, in fact, that a local Syrian designation for the group, Hashīshiyyīn, made its way into European languages and became the origin of the English "assassin." (Why they were called Hashīshiyyīn to begin with is unclear, although theories and opinions abound.)

What is clear is that the Nizārīs (and the Fāṭimids before them) offered a compelling political and religious alternative for many Muslims. In the face of the rather obviously fallible and often patently unjust rule of caliphs and sultans, the utopian ideal of a perfect and infallible ruler who could unlock the mysteries of the cosmos had an obvious appeal. Many early observers of the Nizārīs were struck by the absolute devotion enjoyed by their leaders.

Khārijites

At the other end of the political spectrum from the Ismāʿīlī Shīʿītes, Khārijite leaders could hope for no such unqualified devotion from their followers. Tradition traces the origin of the Khārijites to a battle between ʿAlī and Muʿāwīya at Ṣiffīn in 657. When ʿAlī, faced with a military stalemate, agreed to submit the dispute to arbitration, some of his party withdrew their support from him. "Judgment belongs to God alone" (lā ḥukm illā li-llāhi) became the slogan of these secessionists. They also called themselves al-shurāt, "vendors," to reflect their willingness to sell their lives in martyrdom (Lewinstein 2002).

These original Khārijites opposed both ʿAlī and Muʿāwīya, and appointed their own leaders. They were decisively defeated by ʿAlī, who was in turn assassinated by a Khārijite. Khārijites engaged in guerrilla warfare against the Umayyads, but only became a movement to be reckoned with during the second civil war when they at one point controlled more territory than any of their rivals. Khārijites were, in fact, one of the major threats to Ibn al-Zubayr's bid for the caliphate; during his time they controlled Yamāma and most of southern Arabia and captured the oasis town of al-Ṭāʾif.

The most extreme faction of Khārijites was that of the Azāriqa, who condemned all other Muslims as apostates. The Azāriqa controlled parts of western Iran under the Umayyads until they were finally put down in 699. The more moderate Ibāḍī Khārijites were longer-lived, continuing to wield political power in North and East Africa and in eastern Arabia during the ʿAbbāsid period. The Ibāḍīs are the only Khārijite group to survive into modern times.

Because of their readiness to declare any opponent an apostate, the extreme Khārijites tended to fragment into small groups. One of the few points that the various Khārijite splinter groups held in common was their view of the caliphate, which differed from other Muslim theories on two points. First, they were principled egalitarians, holding that any pious Muslim ("even an Ethiopian slave") can become caliph and that family or tribal affiliation is inconsequential. The only requirements for leadership are piety and the acceptance of the community. Second, they agreed that it is the duty of the believers to depose any leader who falls into error. This second principle had profound implications for Khārijite theology, which we will take up in the following chapter. Applying these ideas to the early history of the caliphate, Khārijites only accept Abū Bakr and ʿUmar as legitimate caliphs. Of ʿUthmān's caliphate they recognize only the first six years as legitimate, and they reject ʿAlī altogether.

By the time that Ibn al-Muqaffaʿ wrote his political treatise early in the ʿAbbāsid period, the Khārijites were no longer a significant political threat, at least in the Islamic heartlands. The memory of the menace they had posed to Muslim unity and of the moral challenge generated by their pious idealism still weighed heavily on Muslim political and religious thought, however. Even if the Khārijites could no longer threaten, their ghosts still had to be answered.

The Sāsānian Revival

For the early ʿAbbāsid rulers neither the Shīʿīte nor the Khārijite model would do, for the new rulers boasted neither proper credentials nor outstanding piety. The Khārijite model had long since been discredited and, in any case, it required an idealistic brand of piety that was completely foreign to the new rulers. The Shīʿīte model might seem a natural choice; the ʿAbbāsids had, after all, come to power on a wave of Shīʿīte enthusiasm. But winning Shīʿīte Muslims over had required some cunning use of language, and once all was out in the open it was clear the ʿAbbāsid pedigree was insufficient to satisfy the majority of Shīʿītes. In the absence of an irrefutable claim to direct descent from ʿAlī, the legitimacy of the ʿAbbāsid rulers would be continually under threat. Al-Manṣūr showed that he understood the problem when he murdered every prominent Shīʿīte he could get his hands on.

As Ibn al-Muqaffaʿ knew, however, there was a venerable alternative. The Near Eastern pattern of absolute monarchy had been virtually perfected in the Sāsānian empire. The Sāsānian emperors based their legitimacy neither on religious pedigree nor on personal piety but on an aura of unassailable majesty and absolute power. The Sāsānian court was an Oz-like theatre calculated to make all ordinary mortals feel small and weak in the face of the unapproachable magnificence of the King of Kings.

The ʿAbbāsid caliphs embraced the Persian model of absolute monarchy with enthusiasm. They set up their court within a few miles of the former Persian capital, the caliph's courtiers called him the "Shadow of God on Earth," and the aura of the ruler was protected by layers of bureaucracy and an elaborate court protocol. Petitioners bowed and kissed the ground before the caliph's throne, and an executioner stood ready at his side to summarily put to death any courtier who fell out of the monarch's favor. Like the great Persian monarchs, the caliphs became the embodiment of justice, the ultimate protector of the weak against the strong. Ideally, no one was so strong as to defy him: his eye ranged everywhere, and no one in the kingdom was beyond the reach of his long arm.

In fact, the caliph's reach was not so long as Ibn al-Muqaffaʿ would have liked. The religious scholars, the ʿulamāʾ, who had emerged in pious opposition to the Umayyads, had developed an independent spirit. Ibn al-Muqaffaʿ's suggestion that the caliph take the articulation and administration of Islamic law into his own hands was clearly an effort to remove one of the main obstacles to making ʿAbbāsid absolutism absolute. Whether they wanted to take Ibn al-Muqaffaʿ's advice or not, the ʿAbbāsid rulers never did succeed in fully absorbing the religious scholars into their bureaucracy, however (that feat would only be accomplished much later by the Ottomans). The one serious ʿAbbāsid attempt to control the religious scholars, Maʾmūn's inquisition, seriously backfired. In virtually every other way, however, the Persian model of absolute monarchy dominated the political thinking of the rulers and their chief advisers.

The Islamic incarnation of Persian political thought reached its zenith with Niẓām al-Mulk (d. 1092), a leading figure in the rise of the Saljūq Turks to political and military dominance in the Islamic world. He was appointed wazīr by Alp Arslan, the founder of the Saljūq dynasty, and when Alp Arslan was assassinated Niẓām al-Mulk ensured the succession of his son, Mālik Shāh. Niẓām al-Mulk continued to serve Mālik Shāh until he was stabbed by a Nizārī assassin in 1092. He was 86 when he died.

Not long before his death, Niẓām al-Mulk recorded his advice to rulers in his celebrated Book of Government, the *Siyāsat nāma*. Writing in Persian, the experienced statesman began with a summary of his political theory:

> In every age and time God (be He exalted) chooses one member of the human race and, having adorned and endowed him with kingly virtues, entrusts him with the interests of the world and the well-being of his servants; He charges that person to close the doors of corruption, confusion and discord, and He imparts to him such dignity and majesty in the eyes and hearts of men, that under his just rule they may live their lives in constant security and ever wish for his reign to continue. (Niẓām al-Mulk 1978: 9)

The great overarching theme of Niẓām al-Mulk's treatise is justice. Heroic rulers go out of their way to make justice available to their subjects. What Niẓām al-Mulk gives us, in fact, is an elaboration of Khusraw I Anūsharwān's circle of justice that we met in chapter 3: "The monarchy depends on the army, the army on money; money comes from the land-tax; the land-tax comes from agriculture. Agriculture depends on justice, justice on the integrity of officials, and integrity and reliability on the ever-watchfulness of the King." The heroes of the account are just such ever-watchful rulers. One Ismāʿīl ibn Aḥmad, for example, used to go out to hold court even in the midst of a blizzard just on the off chance that a petitioner would come seeking justice. Tax collectors in particular must be kept honest, lest the peasants suffer distress, and unjust tax collectors must be removed (Niẓām al-Mulk 1978: 49–62).

The emphasis on justice is reinforced by a recurring political metaphor: the people are a flock, the ruler a shepherd. The shepherd's prosperity depends on the health of his flock, and the health of the flock depends on the wisdom and justice of his officials, especially his wazīr. Thus Niẓām al-Mulk tells the story of how one pre-Islamic Persian king came upon the odd sight of a shepherd who had just executed his sheepdog on a gibbet for the crime of consorting with wolves. The king immediately caught the lesson and went back to do the same to his evil prime minister (ibid. 24–32). As this example illustrates, the great heroes of Niẓām al-Mulk's work are not Islamic rulers, although such do appear, but rather Persian kings, especially Anūsharwān, "the just," who exemplifies the impartial administration of justice without regard to wealth or position (ibid. 34–43).

Niẓām al-Mulk has little to say about religion, but he finds occasion to repeat the well-worn maxim, "kingship and religion are like two brothers" (ibid. 63). For this reason he thinks it a good idea for the ruler to patronize religious types and to learn as much as he can about the Qur'ān, the traditions, and the law. It is clear, however, that in his mind sound religion is instrumental to good government: heresy is one more source of political disorder and thus a danger to the position of the ruler. In fact, heresy and rebellion are virtually the same. The root of all heresy and the archetypical rebel in Niẓām al-Mulk's book was the pre-Islamic religious revolutionary, Mazdak, and he tended to see in every major heresy of his time clear echoes of the Mazdakite threat (ibid. 195–211).

Clearly Niẓām al-Mulk was living in the past. The precedents that matter to him are pre-Islamic Persian precedents, and when he looks back he sees no major break between the Sāsānian monarchy and his own time, only continuity. The rules for good government are the same, the problems they face are the same, only the names have changed.

Al-Māwardī and the Sunnī Compromise

While Niẓām al-Mulk was trying to remake his Saljūq pupils into Persian monarchs by educating them in the niceties of Sāsānian political lore, Islamic legal scholars had already put the finishing touches to their own political theory. About fifty years before Niẓām al-Mulk wrote his advice to rulers, a gifted legal scholar with close ties to the 'Abbāsid caliphs, Abū'l Ḥasan al-Māwardī (d. 1058), completed his own treatise on political theory, *The Rules of Governance*, with the aim of outlining a constitutional theory for the caliphate. Māwardī's work, in other words, is a work of Islamic law and as in any work on Islamic law his purpose is to differentiate between what is obligatory, what is permissible, and what is forbidden in the structure and administration of the state.

The raw material that al-Māwardī had available to him in shaping a theory of the caliphate was, first of all, the ḥadīth literature. The Prophet, as it turned out, had a good deal to say to his companions about the caliphate by way of forewarning them of difficulties ahead. In particular, political ḥadīth weigh in heavily against both the Khārijites and the Shīʿī Muslims and in favor of quietism. Khārijite-style rebellion against a ruler is anathema, for, as the Prophet said, "He who obeys me, obeys God; he who disobeys me, disobeys God. He who obeys the ruler, obeys me; he who disobeys the ruler, disobeys me." And if the ruler was evil and unjust? "You will hear and obey the prince, even if he beats your back and steals your property. Hear and obey," and "They [the rulers] will be judged for what they do, and you will be judged for what you do." To defy the governing authority by withdrawing from the community as the Khārijites had done amounted to apostasy: "Whoever abandons the ruling power and separates from the general body of believers, then dies, dies a pagan" (Burton 1994: 48).

Shīʿī Muslims fare little better than Khārijites in the main body of political ḥadīth. On the sensitive question of who among Muhammad's companions was best qualified to succeed him, ḥadīth scholars reported that when asked by his son, "Which is the best Muslim after Muhammad?" ʿAlī replied, "Abū Bakr." To the further question, "Then who?" ʿAlī replied, "ʿUmar." Fearing to ask the next question, lest his father mention ʿUthmān, the son suggested, "Then yourself?" To which ʿAlī humbly replied, "No. I'm just another ordinary Muslim" (Burton 1994: 43).

As these traditions indicate, mainline Islamic political theory emerged, in the first instance, as a reaction against the extreme positions of the Khārijites and the Shīʿītes, and in favor of maintaining the unity of the community, even if this meant compromising on ideals. The idealism of the Khārijites and the Shīʿītes threatened to tear the Muslims apart, and the main body of religious scholars would have nothing to do with it. If the Khārijites insisted that the ruler must be absolutely righteous to be obeyed, the traditionists answered that the ruler must be absolutely obeyed whether righteous or not. In answer to the Shīʿī claim that particular individuals were intrinsically fit to rule, the traditionists insisted that the intrinsic authority was vested not in an individual, but in the community. Whoever the community agreed upon, so long as he met minimum qualifications, could be the ruler. But when the Khārijites contended that there were no limitations other than piety on who could hold the office of caliph, the mainline religious scholars firmly insisted that only a member of the Quraysh could qualify. Just about every element of Sunnī political theory, as it is reflected in the tradition literature, grew up as a reaction to the danger of schism.

The religious scholars had no great love for the Umayyad rulers, and there is therefore a strong anti-Umayyad tendency in the ḥadīth. This is why, when the "rightly guided" caliphs are listed, the Umayyads (with one exception) are omitted. Muhammad is reported to have precisely predicted how long righteous rule would last. The apostolic succession would last only thirty years, according to one tradition, after which God would grant authority to whom He pleased. The rightly guided caliphs are only Abū Bakr, ʿUmar, ʿUthmān,

'Alī, and one lonely Umayyad, 'Umar b. 'Abd al-Azīz, who gained a reputation for piety. But, evil or not, it is better to put up with a tyrannical ruler than to endure chaos. The scholars who shaped the tradition were appalled by tyranny, but they were scared to death of anarchy.

When al-Māwardī came to write his *Rules of Governance*, then, certain points were already clearly established. There must be only one caliph; the caliph must be of the Quraysh; the caliph must be obeyed; the caliph must meet certain minimal standards of mental and physical fitness. But beyond these absolutes one cannot help but be struck by al-Māwardī's flexibility. The caliph, for example, is to be selected by qualified "electors" from among the Muslims. These electors are to judge among the qualified candidates and choose the best, a precedent set by the nomination of Abū Bakr by a group of companions led by 'Umar and by the selection of 'Uthmān by a committee. But what if a committee of electors is unavailable? In that case one elector will do. It is also fine for a caliph to name his own successor, as Abū Bakr did when he selected 'Umar. In other words, it doesn't matter much how the caliph is selected. Just about any method will do (Māwardī 1996: 3–14).

Al-Māwardī's flexibility reflects, in part, the plasticity of the tradition in the face of the legitimist claims of Shī'ītes. The differences in the manner of selection for each of the first three caliphs – Abū Bakr by nomination and spontaneous affirmation, 'Umar by his predecessor's appointment, 'Uthmān by a closed committee of electors – are calculated to justify a range of political options and to answer the inflexibility of Shī'ī claims. These traditions suggest that there is no one "right" way to select a caliph, and therefore no easy way to challenge the legitimacy of a particular caliph's selection. Whether such traditions are authentic or not, there was no better way to combat Shī'ī claims.

Al-Māwardī had other reasons for his flexibility, however. He lived during a time when the caliphate seemed to be rapidly fading into irrelevance. Five years before his birth the Fāṭimids had taken Egypt. Twenty-five years before that the 'Abbāsid caliphate had come under the control of a family of Persian Shī'ī warlords, the Būyids. The caliphs had long since dispensed with the fiction of direct rule in the provinces of the empire, where real power was taken over first by dynasties founded by 'Abbāsid governors, then by Turkish warlords.

Al-Māwardī was determined not to let changing reality undermine the relevance of the law, and his work is, at one level, a shrewd attempt to argue for the continuing indispensability of the idea of the caliphate even when the caliph was reduced to a figurehead. We see this especially in a curious passage in which al-Māwardī raises the question of what to do with a governor who seizes power for himself – a question of perennial relevance for the caliphs ever since the governor of Egypt, Ibn Ṭūlūn, had founded his own dynasty two centuries earlier in 868. In such a situation, al-Māwardī argues, the caliph should recognize the de facto power as soon as possible:

> Governorship by usurpation is coercion in the sense that its holder acquires by force certain districts over which the caliph gives him a decree of appointment, assigning him their management and the maintenance of public order therein. By seizing power, the governor becomes an independent and exclusive controller of political matters and administration, while the caliph, by his permission, becomes the implementer of the dictates of religion, thus transforming unlawfulness into legality, and the forbidden into the legitimate. (Māwardī 1996: 36)

And even if the usurper is a bad apple, it is still better to recognize his power, for

> It is up to the caliph to sanction his appointment as a means of winning him over and putting an end to his disobedience and intransigence, or to make the enforcement of his administrative decisions conditional upon the appointment of a duly qualified deputy by the caliph, so that the qualifications of the deputy may compensate for the shortcomings of the governor. (Māwardī 1996: 37)

What al-Māwardī is most concerned about, in other words, is not that the caliph hold real power, but that the principle of the caliphate continue to be acknowledged. Al-Māwardī knew, it seems, that it was not the caliph who maintained the unity of the Islamic world in the face of its apparent political disintegration. The real source of unity was the broad agreement of the community on certain ideals and principles – ideals and principles that found their finest expression in the institutions of Islamic law. The caliph as it turned out, was not the most important protector of the Prophet's legacy; rather, as the tradition so eloquently testifies, "The scholars are the heirs of the Prophet." The main work of the scholars was the elaboration of Islamic law.

Resources for Further Study

Hugh Kennedy, *The Prophet and the Age of the Caliphs* (1986), is an excellent starting point for a historical overview of the early caliphate. For the evolution of Muslim political thought more generally, see A. K. S. Lambton, *State and Government in Medieval Islam* (1981), and Antony Black, *The History of Islamic Political Thought* (2001). See also Muhammad Hamidullah, *Muslim Conduct of State* (1977). Primary texts referred to in this chapter include Māwardī, *The Ordinances of Government* (1996) and Niẓām al-Mulk, *The Book of Government* (1978).

For a general overview of Twelver Shīʿīsm, see Heinz Halm, *Shi'ism* (1991), Moojan Momen, *An Introduction to Shi'i Islam* (1985), Etan Kohlberg, *Belief and Law in Imami Shi'ism* (1991), Muhammad Ḥusayn Ṭabāṭabā'ī, *Shi'ite Islam* (1975), and William Chittick, *A Shi'ite Anthology* (1980). Studies of the imāmate include

S. A. Arjoman, *The Shadow of God and the Hidden Imām* (1984), Abdulaziz Abdulhussein Sachedina, *Islamic Messianism: The Idea of the Mahdi in Twelver Shi'ism* (1981) and *The Just Ruler in Shi'ite Islam: The Comprehensive Authority of the Jurist in Imamite Jurisprudence* (1988), and J. M. Hussain, *The Occultation of the Twelfth Imam* (1982). For more specialized topics in the study of Shīʿīsm, see J. R. Cole and N. Keddie, *Shi'ism and Social Protest* (1986), P. J. Chelkowski (ed.), *Ta'ziyeh: Ritual and Drama in Iran* (1979), and Shahla Haeri, *Law of Desire: Temporary Marriage in Shi'i Iran* (1989).

Farhad Daftary's *The Ismāʿīlīs: Their History and Doctrines* (1990) provides an excellent survey of the movement as a whole. Specific studies of the Nizārī Ismāʾīlīs include Marshall Hodgson's *The Order of the Assassins* (1955) and at a more popular level Bernard Lewis, *The Assassins* (1967).

PART THREE

ISLAMIC INSTITUTIONS

10
ISLAMIC LAW

The Coffee Debate

We can begin to gain a sense of the logic and workings of Islamic law by fast-forwarding several centuries to sixteenth-century Mecca. For sixteenth-century Meccans, coffee was all the rage. The same was true in Cairo, Istanbul, and Aleppo. Coffee houses punctuated the urban landscape of Middle Eastern cities like oases, as they still do. But in the sixteenth century, unlike the twenty-first, coffee and coffee shops were something new, an innovation only recently imported from Yemen. Arabic accounts of the earliest uses of coffee agree that the first to drink the brew were late fifteenth-century Yemeni ṣūfīs, Muslim mystics, who found the effects of caffeine enlivening to their late-night devotional exercises. Some ṣūfīs even seem to have made coffee-drinking part of their ritual practice of dhikr, the remembrance of God. Yemenis carried their coffee habit with them to the major cities of the Middle East. It was in this way that coffee was reportedly first introduced to Cairo through the Yemeni quarters of the great Islamic seminary of Al-Azhar during the first decade of the sixteenth century. The habit quickly spread. (On the various theories and debates about the origins of coffee, see Hattox 1988: 12ff.)

By the end of the first decade of the sixteenth century coffee and coffee houses had become popular enough to spark serious controversy. (These controversies are colorfully described by Ralph Hattox in *Coffee and Coffeehouses*, and I am indebted to his book for many of the facts recounted here.) In 1511 Khā'ir Beg, the muḥtasib or marketplace inspector in Mecca and a minor official of the Cairo-based Mamlūk sultanate, became alarmed at the spread of

Figure 10.1 A coffee house in Cairo. Coffee was first spread in the Middle East by sixteenth-century Yemeni ṣūfīs. Photo: Robert Harding Picture Library Ltd/Alamy

coffee and coffee houses and convened an assembly of legal experts to consider the matter. The assembled scholars faced two questions which would continue to be debated for over a century. First, was the consumption of coffee in itself permissible or prohibited? Second, regardless of the permissibility of the drink itself, were the social gatherings and activities that had come to be associated with the drinking of coffee permissible? On the second question the Meccan jurists quickly agreed; given what they knew of coffee-inspired gatherings, such gatherings were unedifying and should be suppressed by the authorities. On the first question, however, the legal experts waffled, arguing, first, that coffee should be considered permissible until proven otherwise, but covering their tracks by suggesting that if coffee could be proven to produce intoxication (or other harmful effects) it might be declared a prohibited substance. On the latter point the legal scholars deferred to expert medical witnesses. These were duly called by the prosecution and, all too predictably, testified to the harmful effects of coffee. Consequent to this expert testimony, the assembled jurists agreed that coffee was proscribed, and Khā'ir Beg banned the sale or consumption of coffee in Mecca, burned stores of coffee, and had those involved in the illicit activity flogged (Hattox 1988: 30–7).

The local Meccan decision did not stick, and in the following decades the fortunes of coffee and coffee-drinking oscillated. When the question was referred to Cairo, the official Mamlūk religious establishment refused to endorse absolute prohibition, and Meccans enthusiastically returned to their coffee-drinking ways. Fourteen years later, in 1525, another jurist, one Ibn al-ʿArrāq, once again ordered all of the coffee houses of Mecca shut down, not because he considered coffee prohibited, but on the basis of the reprehensible activities associated with coffee establishments. Ibn al-ʿArrāq died the next year and the coffee houses reopened. In 1534 an anti-coffee activist in Cairo preached against coffee and instigated a riot in which coffee houses were attacked, and rival pro- and anti-coffee mobs had at each other. The conflict was only resolved when a leading judge decided in favor of the pro-coffee faction (Hattox 1988: 39). Finally, in 1544 an Ottoman decree reportedly prohibited coffee, but without lasting effect (Hattox 1988: 38). By mid-century it was clear that the anti-coffee faction had lost the battle.

For our purposes, the outcome is less important than what the controversy illustrates of the logic of Islamic legal thinking. When the jurists of Mecca were faced with a new behavior or custom, they immediately knew their duty, and that duty was to determine, as best they could, God's estimation of that behavior. For this purpose they had inherited from the tradition of Islamic legal thinking a convenient five-point scale against which any human action can be measured. According to this scheme, the drinking of coffee and every other action must fall into one of five categories: obligatory (wājib), recommended (mandūb), neutral (mubāḥ), discouraged (makrūh), or prohibited (ḥarām) The basic task of Islamic jurists is to make determinations about where particular actions fall on this five-point scale, and this is what the Meccan ʿulamāʾ set out to do in the case of coffee-drinking.

Revelation and Reason

The problem, then, was theoretically a simple question of discovering what God had to say about coffee. For this purpose scholars had at their disposal two sources of revelation, the very Word of God, the Qur'ān, and the normative example of the Prophet, the Sunna. As we have seen, Muslim dogma about revelation gave these sources equal authority as sources of guidance. Both the Qur'ān and the Sunna were waḥī, revealed to Muhammad by Gabriel, and they differed only in form, not in authority. Of the two sources, the Sunna was in practice the more useful since the Prophet had expressed himself on such a vast array of practical topics. The Sunna was also challenging to work with, however, since it did not come pre-packaged, but could only be mined from the ḥadīth, and the ḥadīth literature was rather rich in forgeries, contradictions, and uncertainties. Still, if either the Qur'ān or the ḥadīth had anything to say about coffee, the sixteenth-century Meccan 'ulamā' would certainly have found themselves on familiar ground, and they would have set about exegeting the texts, sorting out contradictions, and weighing the reliability of various reports.

The obvious difficulty was that God had issued his final opinions about human behavior some 900 years earlier, in the pre-coffee era, and the majority opinion on revelation discouraged any expectation of an update. Exactly how to proceed in such circumstances is one of the oldest and most persistent questions in Islamic legal theory, and the waffling of the Meccan 'ulamā' nicely illustrates the two major options. According to the reports, the first instinct of the council was to apply the principle of basic permissibility according to which a substance is considered permissible until proven otherwise. God in his omniscience can be presumed to have been able to foresee the introduction of coffee, and he presumably would have warned against it if he thought it harmful. In the absence of such an explicit prohibition, one must presume permissibility. To this way of thinking, revelation is taken to be complete and comprehensive, and definitive answers to moral and legal questions can only be known from the Qur'ān and the Sunna. The most extreme representatives of this way of thinking, called Ẓāhirīs because they confined the law to what was ẓāhir or externally obvious in revelation, had thrived in the tenth and eleventh centuries. By the time of the coffee controversy Ẓāhirīs were long extinct as an organized movement, but the powerful logic of their position still carried weight.

There was another possibility. What if God had never intended his revelation to cover all eventualities, but rather expected human beings to use their minds to extrapolate beyond the revealed sources? This option required a certain degree of confidence in the ability of human reason to handle fundamental moral questions, and consequently it was somewhat daring. Early in the development of Islamic law – a period we will consider in detail below – debate between exponents of reason and the partisans of tradition raged fiercely. The debates were both theoretical and practical. The underlying theoretical issue with which theologians had to grapple was whether human reason in any form could be trusted to make moral judgments about right and wrong. But from a juristic viewpoint the question was narrower and more practical: to what extent could reason be considered a legitimate tool for the elaboration of Islamic law, and what were the limits on its use? By the sixteenth century these issues had been largely settled, but with conflicting answers to the theoretical and practical questions. In theory Muslim legal scholars were, after the eleventh century, almost unanimously pessimistic about the efficacy of human reason. Human beings are helpless to make moral decisions without revelation. But in practice all of the major legal schools found ways to permit the application of reason at least in limited ways.

Qiyās

Discussion of the practical application of reason centered on one particular method that Islamic scholars called qiyās or analogical reasoning. The logic of qiyās rested on the presumption that God had his reasons for commanding or forbidding particular activities, and that a clever scholar could discover these reasons and apply them to new situations. God, for instance, was widely known to have prohibited wine, or, to be more precise, a beverage which the Qur'ān calls khamr, the definition of which was a matter of disagreement. If the reason for the divine proscription on khamr was found to be its intoxicating properties, then the prohibition might be extended, by application of qiyās, to other intoxicants. This was exactly the approach that some jurists took, arguing that any intoxicant was forbidden by analogy with khamr.

The jurists gathered in Mecca in 1511 were apparently open to such an argument: if coffee could be shown to be intoxicating, it must be forbidden. They were aided by a linguistic peculiarity. The word *qahwa*, used for coffee, was also one of the words used for wine (Hattox 1988: 18). In the end their final decision did not rest on a systematic argument linking coffee and wine. There were others willing to take up just such a position, however. The argument for prohibition of coffee by analogy with wine must have had proponents, since defenders of coffee offered vigorous refutations. The reasoning adopted by the Meccan council of 'ulamā' turned out to be more pallid. Coffee was prohibited simply because it is vaguely harmful to one's well-being.

Although the assembled jurists of Mecca had reached their verdict, however, that was hardly the end of the matter. Anti-coffee jurists very soon had to face the inconvenient fact that other jurists, and as it turned out, more influential ones, disagreed with their decision. What the Meccan jurists had arrived at, in other words, was not God's law in an objective sense, but simply their own best understanding of God's law. No Muslim jurist would doubt that God had an opinion about coffee, but most of them shared a healthy sense of their own fallibility in understanding his opinions. They could only do their best, and their best might not be enough. This process of seeking to understand God's law the legal scholars called fiqh – understanding. Scholars who engaged in this process were fuqahā'. Fiqh and the rulings that resulted from it were, at best, an approximation of the true law of God, and the pro-coffee lobby was free to argue that the assembled Meccan 'ulamā' had gotten it quite wrong.

Fiqh, in other words, is not the same as Sharī'a. Sharī'a is the sum of all God's rulings on human actions, and if the Sharī'a as a whole was precisely spelled out, we would have no doubt about whether coffee is permissible and, if so, in precisely what circumstances it might become impermissible. God has not spelled out his will at this level of precision, however. Rather, he has left that task to human beings, as a test of our devotion. Consequently, no matter how hard we toil, there will always be a gap between God's perfect will – the Sharīʿa – and our limited and fallible understanding of it, reflected in fiqh.

The Schools of Law

Disagreements over the law of God are thus to be expected. Some disagreements, however, are bigger than others. An observer of intellectuals in any field is likely to be struck by their contentiousness; but while any two given scholars may be expected to find something to disagree about, if they can discover a common intellectual enemy they will be well on their way to forming a "school." It is roughly in these terms that we can understand the relationship among different Islamic "schools" of law, or madhhabs. Madhhabs, in other words, might be thought of as groupings of scholars who disagreed with one another less, or on less important points, than they disagreed with the scholars of another madhhab.

At the time of the coffee controversy the number of these major groupings of Sunnī legal scholars had settled out at four – the Ḥanafī, the Mālikī, the Shāfiʿī, and the Ḥanbalī schools – the same four madhhabs, in fact, that still survive among contemporary Sunnī Muslims.

Sunnī schools of Islamic law and their founders

Ḥanafī (Abū Ḥanīfa, d. 767). Associated with the city of Kūfa and known for allowing, in theory, a higher degree of juristic flexibility than other schools through the application of personal judgment (ra'y) and juristic preference (istiḥsān). The earliest Ḥanafī works are those of Abū Yūsuf (d. 798) and al-Shaybānī (d. 805). In modern times Ḥanafīs predominate in central Asia, Turkey, Cairo and the Nile delta in Egypt, and the Indian subcontinent.

Mālikī (Mālik ibn Anas, d. 796). Characterized by acceptance of the practice of the people of Medina as a source of precedent and an indication of Sunna. Early works include the *Muwaṭṭa'*, attributed to Mālik, and the *Mudawwana* of Saḥnūn. Mālikīs make up the majority in North Africa and Upper Egypt.

Shāfiʿī (Muhammad ibn Idrīs al-Shāfiʿī, d. 822). Named for the greatest early systematizer of Islamic legal theory, but in substance similar to Mālikī law. Shāfiʿīs are most numerous in Malaysia, Indonesia, southern Arabia, East Africa, and parts of Upper Egypt.

Ḥanbalī (Aḥmad ibn Ḥanbal, d. 855). Known for emphasis on ḥadīth and sometimes considered a grouping of traditionists rather than a school of law. Ḥanbalī scholars, especially Ibn Taymiyya (d. 1328), have had an enormous influence on later developments in Islamic law by virtue of their opposition to taqlīd and insistence on going back to the sources, the Qur'ān and Sunna, for themselves. Ḥanbalīsm is the official and dominant madhhab in modern Sa'ūdī Arabia.

Ẓāhirī (Dāwūd ibn Khalaf, d. 884). Now extinct, but nevertheless influential by virtue of a consistent refusal to go beyond the plain meaning of revelation in applying the law.

The madhhabs differed not just on particular legal points, but also on questions of method and theory. On the matter of intoxicants, for example, the Ḥanafīs differed from the other schools of law in holding that the Qur'ān did not prohibit all intoxicants as a class, but only beverages which fit within the strict definition of khamr. In other words, they resisted the application of qiyās to extend the prohibition on khamr to other intoxicants. For Ḥanafī jurists, khamr was limited to (1) fermented raw grape juice; (2) cooked grape juice of which more than one-third of the original volume remains; (3) intoxicants made from dates; (4) intoxicants made from raisins. According to Ḥanafī "understanding" or fiqh, then, alcohol content was not, in itself, the central issue. Drunkenness is still forbidden, but beverages containing alcohol that are made from honey, wheat, or barley are not, in themselves, prohibited. These may be forbidden in certain circumstances, when taken with the unlawful intention of making oneself drunk, for example, but the *potential* for intoxication is not, in itself, reason enough for prohibition.

From a Ḥanafī perspective, then, any effort to prohibit coffee by analogy with khamr, or because its effects were somehow seen to resemble intoxication, was out of the question. This did not mean, however, that coffee-related activities were necessarily licit; an otherwise permissible substance might well be used for illicit ends or in illicit circumstances. Consequently, Ḥanafī authorities seem to have been more amenable to closing down coffee shops than to prohibiting coffee.

Leadership of the hardcore anti-coffee faction fell to Shāfi'ī 'ulamā', who had fewer reservations about prohibiting coffee outright. Theirs was an uphill battle, however, for two reasons, one practical and the other theoretical. The practical obstacle for the anti-coffee jurists was the simple fact that the political influence of the Ḥanafī 'ulamā' was on the rise. The rulers of the Ottoman empire made the Ḥanafī school the official madhhab of the empire, and Ḥanafī 'ulamā' became a part of the official bureaucracy, their fortunes intertwined with the interests of the Ottoman state. In 1517 the Mamlūk state was absorbed into the Ottoman empire, and Ḥanafī law was thereafter ascendant throughout the central Islamic lands.

Islamic Law and the State

Although the Ottomans succeeded in absorbing the ʿulamāʾ into the state apparatus to a greater extent than any previous Muslim state (a point to be developed in chapter 14), some level of interdependence between rulers and religious scholars was nothing new. The office of qāḍī, or judge, was by its very nature tied to the political establishment, and government appointed qāḍīs were handing down legal decisions from the early Umayyad period onward. The ʿulamāʾ as an identifiable class emerged in opposition to the ruling establishment, however, and the tradition literature reflects a deep awareness among scholars of the dangers of becoming too embroiled in politics. Abū Ḥanīfa, for instance, reportedly refused on principle to take a position as qāḍī. The earliest great legal scholars prided themselves on their independence, and their work was, like most scholarship, an idealistic rather than a pragmatic enterprise. God's law was God's law, whether anyone ever chose to enforce it or not.

In any case, implementation of the law on earth was not the main object of Islamic law. The question of ultimate importance for any pious scholar was not the judgment of men, but of God, and the ultimate aim of the enterprise was to guide human beings to paradise. This meant that even if a ruler chose to ignore his rulings, the pious legal scholar still had a job to do, and the godlessness of a given regime did not excuse believers from discovering and obeying the Sharīʿa for themselves. The judgment of God awaited, and paradise was at stake. For this reason it will come as no surprise that the concerns of Islamic law cover areas that could not conceivably be adjudicated in a courtroom, and that no government would care to touch. The most obvious example is all of those acts which fall into the categories of recommended (mandūb) or discouraged (makrūh). God will certainly take these acts into account in the distribution of rewards at the Judgment, and Islamic scholars thus must be concerned with them, but they fall completely outside the purview of the state. Even where absolute obligations and prohibitions are at stake, there are huge areas of Islamic law that do not belong in a courtroom, particularly the detailed requirements of religious ritual. In practice human courts are limited to adjudicating disputes between human beings and must leave disputes between human beings and God to a higher court. It was incumbent upon the fuqahāʾ, however, to take into account the whole of God's law.

This is not to say that Islamic legal scholars were unconcerned about the earthly enforcement of whatever could be enforced of God's law. The majority insisted, in fact, that it was the duty of the state to apply the Sharīʿa, and they were quite willing to tell the ruler how to go about it. Rulers, in turn, hired legal scholars as qāḍīs to adjudicate court cases, and as muftīs, to issue fatwas, or legal rulings, on practical questions. In the coffee controversy the Ḥanafīs thus had a decisive advantage by virtue of the official patronage of the state. Shāfiʿī firebrands could rant and rave and whip up mobs, but they could not suppress the coffee culture on their own. For that, the coercive power of the state was needed, and that, in the Ottoman empire at any rate, was fast becoming a Ḥanafī monopoly.

Ijmāʿ

Besides facing a political establishment lukewarm to their views, anti-coffee jurists had to contend with a theoretical obstacle arising from the internal logic of Islamic legal thinking. Simply put, the legal opinion of an individual was not worth much. Fiqh was not an individual but a collective enterprise. A particular ruling carried weight only to the extent that it was affirmed by other scholars and adopted by the community. Pro-coffee advocates were thus able to argue that the consensus, or ijmāʿ, of the community was decisively in their favor. Coffee had, after all, been consumed on the premises of the great mosque in Mecca by even the most pious of Muslims for some years. The opponents of coffee could invoke no such consensus.

The doctrine of ijmāʿ, consensus, was not just one of the deciding factors in the coffee controversy, but a crucial principle of Sunnī legal theory. Although there were differences among the madhhabs about the rules for its application, the idea of ijmāʿ was based on the simple premise that the Muslims (or Muslim scholars) could not all be wrong at the same time. An individual opinion or ruling on a point of Islamic law could only be considered tentative, or ẓannī, because of the fallibility of the interpreter. But a tentative ruling could be moved into the realm of certainty by the agreement of the community because that consensus was, by definition, infallible. The Prophet himself had affirmed that "my community will never agree upon an error," and the Qur'ān warned, "And whoso opposes the Messenger after the guidance had been manifested unto him, and follows other than the believers' way, We appoint for him that unto which he himself had turned, and expose him unto Hell – hapless journey's end!" (4:115).

At least one pro-coffee jurist explicitly invoked the principle of ijmāʿ to establish the permissibility of coffee. Coffee had been consumed for some time, he argued, and if it was indeed an intoxicant, pious Muslims would certainly have taken steps to forbid it, yet pious Muslims consumed coffee without compunction (Hattox 1988: 59). Thus the consensus of the Muslims was established and the permissibility of coffee can be considered certain. In the end, then, it was the umma's enthusiastic reception of coffee that was decisive in resolving the question of whether God approved of it or not.

The Uṣūl al-Fiqh

When assembled in a tidy package, the system of legal reasoning applied in the coffee controversy nicely illustrates the four-source theory of Islamic law that dominated Islamic legal thinking from the ninth century on. According to the broad outlines of this theory the two scriptural sources of Islamic law, the Qur'ān and the Sunna, were extrapolated and applied to new situations by means of qiyās, and qiyās was, in turn, given certainty by ijmā'. There was disagreement around the edges, and especially about some supplementary principles of law (see below), but on the whole Muslim jurists from the ninth to the nineteenth century showed remarkable agreement on the basic four-source framework. The theory itself became the focus of an entire branch of scholarship, the study of the "roots of jurisprudence" or uṣūl al-fiqh.

Sources and principles of Islamic law

The Qur'ān. The basic source for knowledge of divine commands, but not to be interpreted or applied apart from its elaboration in the example of the Prophet. About 600 verses of the Qur'ān have relevance to Islamic law, most of these dealing with religious duties ('ibādāt). About eighty verses have legal relevance in the narrower sense of law that Westerners are used to.

The Sunna. The most important material source of law. The words and actions of the Prophet Muhammad are both an authoritative commentary on the Qur'ān and a source of authoritative precedent in their own right. The Sunna of the Prophet is contained and transmitted in the ḥadīth literature. Shī'ī jurists include within the Sunna the rulings of the Shī'ī imāms, since the precedents set by the imāms are considered authoritative.

Qiyās. A means of applying a known command from the Qur'ān or Sunna to a new circumstance by means of analogical reasoning. When the rationale ('illa) of a command is known, other similar cases can be judged according to the same rationale.

Ijmā'. The consensus of Muslims on a point of law. The majority of Sunnī jurists consider consensus to be infallible, giving rise to certain knowledge. They differ, however, on what constitutes authoritative consensus and how to arrive at it.

Ijtihād. The toil or effort exerted by a scholar in seeking to discover the intent of the Lawgiver on a given point of law. Ijtihād is not a source of law, properly speaking, but a reference to the process by which the law is elaborated. The terms *ijtihād* and *qiyās* are sometimes used interchangeably.

A jurist qualified to exercise ijtihād is called a mujtahid. From the fifteenth century onward Muslim scholars argued about whether there were any mujtahids left and thus whether ijtihād could still operate.

Taqlīd. Adherence to authoritative precedent. A jurist not qualified to exercise ijtihād must limit himself to the application of established rulings. In modern times taqlīd has developed a bad reputation, and is often interpreted to mean blind and dogmatic adherence to past decisions. In premodern usage it might be better seen as a simple acknowledgment that not everyone is a genius.

Istiḥsān. The application of a jurist's personal judgment allowing him to depart from the strict application of qiyās. The method is defended by Ḥanafī jurists, but criticized by al-Shāfiʿī as arbitrary.

Istiṣlāḥ. The overruling of the strict application of a legal rule on the basis of considerations of the public good (maṣlaḥa).

Ẓarūra. The principle of necessity according to which an established rule of law is suspended in dire circumstances.

Not all Muslims bought into this system. The four-source theory of Islamic law illustrated by the coffee controversy is specifically Sunnī, especially in granting such a decisive role to consensus. The largest of the Shīʿī communities, the Twelvers, for instance, follow a distinct legal tradition called the Jaʿfarī school, traced to the sixth Shīʿī leader, Jaʿfar al-Ṣādiq. Jaʿfarī fiqh does not differ markedly from the major Sunnī schools on most points of substance, although there are significant exceptions. For example, Shīʿī jurists allow a form of temporary marriage called mutʿa, require more stringent procedures for divorce, and differ significantly from Sunnīs on the rules of inheritance. More importantly, the Twelvers diverge from the Sunnīs on two key points of legal theory. First, they held that the Sunna encompasses the teachings of the Shīʿī imāms in addition to those of the Prophet. Second, the doctrine of consensus has less relevance for Shīʿītes since, ideally, authority vests in the living representatives of God, the imāms. Moreover, from a Shīʿī point of view the majority of the community, that is the Sunnīs, patently did agree upon a rather egregious error by failing to recognize the unique claims of ʿAlī and his descendants. Consequently, the infallibility of the community is a hard sell among the Shīʿa.

The Substance of the Law

The sixteenth-century coffee controversy, while useful for illustrating the theory and internal logic of Islamic law, is in certain respects misleading. In particular, it may leave us with the impression that Islamic law was an infinitely flexible, malleable, and evolving system and that Muslims were constantly going back to the Qur'ān and Sunna and happily exercising qiyās, ijtihād, and ijmā' in an unceasing quest to discover anew for themselves the will of the divine lawgiver in the midst of changing circumstances. This is exactly what a number of modern Muslim thinkers would like Islamic law to be, and some have worked hard to make it so. In fact, however, the theory of Islamic law did not shape the law so much as it justified what was already in place. The substance of the law was well established before the theory of the sources of Islamic law was fully articulated, and the articulation of the four-source theory of the law did not lead to the revaluation of the substance of the law – it merely provided justification for rulings previously established.

Another respect in which the coffee example may mislead is by giving the impression that the concerns of Islamic law are very much like those of the modern undergraduate. The world of coffee and coffee shops feels comfortably familiar to many moderns, and we can happily cheer on the jurists who rose in defense of the universal right to a coffee high. (That ṣūfīs were at the heart of the coffee culture is bound to heighten sympathy.) In reality the major concerns of Islamic legal scholars are so utterly alien to the normal concerns of many modern non-Muslims as to almost defy translation. In manuals of Islamic law, which follow a fairly stable structure after the ninth century, more than half of the attention is directed to the duties that humans owe to their creator. Moreover, these religious duties or 'ibādāt are not reducible to the sort of formless notions of piety or good behavior which the modern Methodist churchgoer might feel warm toward. God, it turns out, has specific and demanding ideas about how his servants must show their respect.

Ritual Purity

One must not, for instance, attempt any act of worship – including touching a copy of the Qur'ān – without first attending to matters of ritual purity. Consequently, manuals of Islamic law begin by outlining in detail the rules for purification, or ṭahāra. These begin with wuḍū', the minor ablutions required before the five ritual prayers. For an act of prayer to have any meaning the worshiper must first wash his face, his hands up to the elbows, his head, and his feet up to the ankles in accordance with the command of God in Qur'ān 5:6. On the face of it this might seem a simple enough requirement, but the jurists know better. They differed over whether it was obligatory or merely recommended to rinse one's mouth and nostrils as well. They argued over whether the area between the beard and the ears constitutes the face, and whether the whole beard must also be washed. They disagreed about whether elbows were included with arms, how much of the head needed to

Figure 10.2 Worshipers in New Delhi, India, performing ritual ablutions. Photo: Grant Rooney/Alamy

be wiped, and whether one could keep one's turban on through the process. They discussed whether the feet must be washed, or could just be wiped, or whether it made no difference (Ibn Rushd 1994, 21: 3–20).

These arguments involve the minor ablutions. If, however, one has fallen into a state of major impurity, a full bath (ghusl) is required before religious duties can be performed. Occurrences that bring on a state of major impurity include sexual intercourse, wet dreams, menstruation, and postnatal bleeding. External objects could also be a source of pollution or najāsa, among them alcohol, pigs, dogs, and carrion. Jurists disagreed over whether someone in a state of major impurity could enter a mosque, some prohibiting it absolutely, others permitting it conditionally. Most jurists proscribed recitation of the Qur'ān in such a state of impurity (Ibn Rushd 1994, 21: 3–50).

These requirements are stringent, but not inflexible. Adjustments were made in particular for travelers and the sick. Nor should these requirements be interpreted as a way of putting substance to a conviction that cleanliness is next to godliness. The issue was not cleanliness, but obedience to God's specific requirements. Thus a substantial section of law deals with tayammum, the use of clean earth to satisfy the requirements of ritual purity when water is not available (Ibn Rushd 1994, 21: 67–79).

Acts of Worship

When the requirements for ritual purity are met and the believer sets out to perform a required act of worship, God's first concern is with attitude. "An act," according to a well-known saying of the Prophet, "is valued according to its intentions" (Ibn Rushd 1994, 1: 3). Going through the motions will not do; without proper intention the duty to God is not fulfilled, and the act of worship invalidated. Moreover, the statement of intention must be specific to the particular act of worship. If the worshiper sets out to perform the maghrib prayer, for example, he must state his intention to fulfill that specific obligation and to perform the required three units of prayer.

As the table below indicates, the prayers are divided into units (rakʿa), each ending in prostration; the number of units differs depending on the particular time of prayer. The precise limits on the times of the prayers were a matter of some discussion, but the table reflects general practice.

Prayer	Units	Earliest start	End
Fajr	2	Dawn	Sunrise
Ẓuhr	4	Sun at its zenith	An object's shadow equals its length
ʿAṣr	4	End of the ẓuhr	Immediately before sunset
Maghrib	3	After sunset	The disappearance of twilight
ʿIshāʾ	4	End of maghrib	Dawn

The actual manner of performing the prayers turns out to be only a small part of the concern of jurists. One of the more sobering questions that kept them alert was whether a Muslim who acknowledges the obligation to perform the prayer, but intentionally refuses to do so, should be executed, or merely imprisoned until he mends his ways. Only a small minority favored execution (Ibn Rushd 1994, 1: 98). Other considerations were more commonplace, but no less important. One of the requirements of prayer, for example, is to face Mecca, and a necessary prerequisite of prayer is thus establishing the qibla. This is simple enough in a mosque, where the work has been done for you, but what if the worshiper is alone in unfamiliar territory at prayer time and happens to have a faulty sense of direction? Most jurists agreed that it was sufficient to give it one's best effort, even if the direction ended up being off. But what if, after praying, the worshiper discovers that he was wrong? Al-Shāfiʿī held that the prayer was invalidated and had to be repeated. Mālik and Abū Ḥanīfa thought that repeating the prayer was unnecessary because they held that the effort in itself fulfilled the obligation (ibid. 121–5). Mālik did think it a good idea to repeat the prayer, however, if there was sufficient time. Any number of other errors could invalidate prayer. These included immodest dress and speaking or laughing during prayer. Interrupting prayer to kill a scorpion or snake is generally thought to be permissible, however (ibid. 130).

The five obligatory prayers were but the start. There were special rules to be outlined for Friday congregational prayers, for prayer while on a journey, for prayers during wartime, and prayers for the sick. Then there were bonus prayers, not obligatory, but a source of merit, and special prayers for rain, special prayers during the month of Ramaḍān, and special prayers for the two major ʿīd festivals. All of these were set topics that every teacher of Islamic law had to deal with, and every manual of Islamic law discussed in detail.

Beyond prayer, all the other major religious obligations called for equally detailed attention. Consequently, four of the so-called "five pillars" – the confession of faith, ṣalāt, almsgiving, pilgrimage, fasting – take up a huge amount of space in manuals of Islamic law. These are not alone, however, and there is a sense in which they are inseparable from a variety of other obligations listed below.

Islamic religious duties (ʿibādāt) in Islamic legal texts

Ṭahāra. Requirements for ritual purity, discussed above.

Ṣalāt. Ritual worship performed five times each day at prescribed times, and in the prescribed manner.

Funeral obligations. Requirements for the bathing of the dead (except battlefield martyrs, who are buried unwashed), funeral shrouds, prayers over the dead, and burial.

Zakāt. Poor-tax, usually administered by the state, for the support of eight categories of people named in Qur'ān 9:61: "Zakāt is for the poor and needy, and those who collect zakāt, and those whose hearts are to be reconciled, and to free captives and the debtors, and for the cause of Allāh, and for the wayfarers; a duty imposed by Allāh. Allāh is Knower, Wise." Zakāt is levied on certain categories of wealth above a certain defined threshold called the niṣāb. For holdings of gold and silver, the tax rate is 2.5 percent; for camels, cows, and sheep the formulas are rather more complicated.

Ṣiyām. Fasting, including obligatory and bonus fasts. The major obligatory fast involves abstention from food, drink, and sexual intercourse from dawn to sunset during the month of Ramaḍān.

Iʿtikāf. The practice of secluding oneself, usually in a mosque and often during Ramaḍān, for a set period of time. Iʿtikāf is voluntary, but rendered obligatory in fulfillment of a vow.

Ḥajj. The once-in-a-lifetime obligation, contingent upon physical and financial ability, to perform the ritual pilgrimage in Mecca. The jurists are particularly preoccupied with outlining the complex requirements for the valid completion of each stage of the pilgrimage.

Jihād. The obligation to make war against polytheists. The majority of jurists defined the duty as a collective rather than an individual duty; so long as some within the community fulfilled the duty, the requirement was fulfilled for all. Jurists discussed specific rules regarding allowable means, treatment of prisoners, conditions for the declaration of war, and the making of truces. Jurists also discuss, in detail, the rules for division of the spoils of war.

Additional topics included in most legal texts. Oaths and vows; sacrifices; slaughtered animals; hunting; sacrifice on behalf of newborns; foods and beverages; use of prohibited substances under duress.

So far the Western-trained lawyer will have found little that she will recognize as law, properly speaking. When jurists move on from discussion of obligations to God (ʿibādāt) to consider human obligations to one another (muʿāmalāt), however, the issues seem familiar. Here we enter the more recognizable world of marriage and divorce, contracts, property law, inheritance, and criminal penalties. Such issues clearly belong in the courtroom. The impression of crossing some great divide from religious concerns to real law is misleading, however. The kinds of concerns and the style of legal reasoning are much the same whether a jurist is dealing with prayer or marriage.

Marriage and Divorce

Discussions of marriage in Islamic legal texts place it squarely in the category of civil contracts. A marriage is a contract entered into by the groom and the bride or a male guardian of the bride, the walī, usually her father. The first topic in discussions of marriage is the question of whether marriage is an obligation, and, if so, who is subject to that obligation. Only the Ẓāhirī school held marriage to be an obligation, although some Mālikīs held it to be obligatory on some, depending on how liable the individual is to fall into evil. The validity of a marriage contract depended, first of all, on the consent of the contracting parties. There was a good deal of discussion, however, about whose consent was required and in what circumstances. Jurists distinguished between those who had reached puberty and those who had not, between virgins and non-virgins, and between slave and free. Jurists generally agreed that minor sons and daughters could be married without their permission. Jurists disagreed about whether a walī was a requirement in all cases for a valid marriage contract, and they discussed at length exactly who qualified as a guardian.

A second major requirement of a valid marriage contract was the payment of dowry, in accordance with the command of the Qur'ān, "And give unto the women, (whom you marry) free gift of their marriage portions" (4:4). Jurists disagreed over whether there was an absolute minimum for the dowry. Those who argued for such a minimum often considered the dowry a form of compensation paid to the woman, and drew an analogy to laws relating to theft. They agreed that there was no maximum for the dowry, and that the dowry remained the property of the woman.

Jurists discussed at length the various impediments to marriage, and they divided these impediments into two categories: perpetual and temporary. Perpetual impediments are established by lineage or marriage. Marriage to mothers, daughters, sisters, paternal aunts, maternal aunts, and nieces is prohibited by virtue of lineage. Marriage to mothers-in-law or daughters-in-law is prohibited because of the relationship established through the prior marriage. Foster relationships and wet-nursing also establish permanent impediments like those established by lineage. A foster-son is prohibited from marrying his foster-mother or foster-sister. Among temporary impediments, a man may marry no more than four women at the same time, two sisters may not be married to the same man, and marriage to an idolater or idolatress is prohibited (although marriage to one of the "people of the book" is permitted).

A woman, once married, has the right to food and clothing from her husband. Jurists disagreed, however, about whether this right should be seen as a form of compensation for sex. Jurists agreed that in the case of a polygamous marriage, a wife also has the right to justice among the wives in regard to sexual relations.

Islamic jurists treat slavery matter-of-factly, as an ordinary facet of life, and discussions of marriage therefore encompass questions about marriage between slaves, whether marriage of a free man to a slave woman or a free woman to a slave man is permissible, and whether a slave can be compelled to marry. These discussions also touch on concubinage, that is, the right of male slave-owners to sexual relationship with female slaves, although more detailed discussion of these issues is taken up in chapters on slavery.

A major preoccupation of jurists with regard to divorce (ṭalāq) was what constituted an irrevocable divorce. The general rule established by the Qur'ān (2:229–30) is that a third declaration of divorce gives the divorce permanent effect, and that until that point the husband is free to think again. The tricky question was whether a threefold declaration pronounced at a single place and time constituted irrevocable divorce, or whether it just counted as a single declaration. Whether revocable or irrevocable, the declaration of divorce initiates a waiting period ('idda) to establish whether the wife is pregnant. In the case of a revocable divorce, the husband has the unilateral right to take the wife back with or without her consent during the waiting period. The waiting period will vary in length depending on whether the wife menstruates or is pregnant. In the case of an irrevocable divorce remarriage is only possible if the divorced wife is first married to and divorced from another man.

All of this is likely to come across as rather medieval to the modern reader. The reason is simple. It is. One should hardly expect twelfth-century legal preoccupations to match twenty-first-century expectations. The problem this raises is obvious. How are modern Muslims to respond to this voluminous, brilliant body of legal literature which purports to elucidate the eternal, unchanging law of God when so much of it seems anachronistic? What is of unchanging value here, and what is liable to revision? As we will see in the chapters 16 and 17, this has been one of the great challenges and preoccupations of modern Muslim reformers.

The Origins of Islamic Law

The resulting system of law, composed of jurisprudential theory and substantive law, is one of the great achievements of Islamic civilization. The intricacies and puzzles of fiqh engaged the greatest Muslim minds, and the resulting literature is monumental. The elaboration of the law, in fact, is rightly portrayed as a signature achievement of Islamic civilization, for, according to one of the most widely distributed maxims in modern surveys of Islamic law, law is the very "core and kernel of Islam" (Schacht 1964: 1). This magnificent system was fully formed by the tenth century. This is not to say that no development took place after that (to the contrary, some of the most creative and controversial legal minds – al-Ghazālī and Ibn Taymiyya – made their contributions in later centuries), but the basic material of Islamic law had been worked out by this time. The question naturally arises for Muslims and non-Muslim scholars alike: where did it all come from?

The question of the origins of Islamic law has two parts. First, when and how did the theory of Islamic law (marked especially by the dual authority of the Qur'ān and prophetic Sunna) take hold? Second, where did the material of Islamic law – the substantive rules and practices that the jurists inherited and worked with – come from? Of the two questions the first is the easier to answer.

Al-Shāfiʿī and Islamic Legal Theory

Something resembling the four-source theory of law first shows up in the writings of the brilliant jurist Muhammad ibn Idrīs al-Shāfiʿī, who died about two centuries after Muhammad in 822. Al-Shāfiʿī's introduction to legal theory, his *Risāla,* is a dazzling piece of work and historians of Islamic law should be excused for having credited al-Shāfiʿī with having almost single-handedly shaped Islamic jurisprudence. As it turns out, no one paid much attention to al-Shāfiʿī's work for more than a century, and in more recent scholarship he has therefore been lowered from founder of Islamic jurisprudence to eccentric genius whose ideas were well ahead of their time and would only be appreciated much later (Hallaq 1993: 587–605). Be that as it may, the career of al-Shāfiʿī in the early ninth century represents the earliest possible date for the coming together of the four-source theory of Islamic jurisprudence. The theory of Islamic law may have come into general acceptance only much later, but it could hardly have been earlier. We know this because it is clear from al-Shāfiʿī's writings that the views of the law that he had to contend with were quite different from those that would become orthodox legal theory.

The main issue centered on the idea of prophetic Sunna. For al-Shāfiʿī and later mainstream jurists, Sunna meant the Sunna of the Prophet, and the Sunna of the Prophet could only be known from ḥadīth reports. In other words, a reliable ḥadīth report from the Prophet trumped all other sources of precedent. Shāfiʿī's logic was simple and compelling: who better than the Prophet to explain the meaning and practical application of revelation? If we know what the Prophet did or said on a particular occasion, it must reflect God's will, for it is unthinkable that God's chosen messenger would have departed from revelation. This elevation of prophetic Sunna and identification of Sunna with authentic ḥadīth reports is the chief mark of Islamic legal theory in its mature form.

Compelling or not, the trouble with al-Shāfiʿī's program was that Muslim jurists already had in place a body of law to protect. Circles of legal scholars in Kūfa, Medina, and Syria had been busily shaping their legal traditions without any special emphasis on prophetic ḥadīth. They were not about to sacrifice all of their hard work to satisfy the demands of al-Shāfiʿī's theory, no matter how compelling. So they put up a fight, and the late eighth and early ninth centuries became a period of intense controversy centered on the uṣūl al-fiqh, and especially the meaning and status of Sunna.

For al-Shāfiʿī's rivals and predecessors, Sunna was a flexible concept. Certainly, one could appeal to the Sunna of the Prophet, but one could also talk about the Sunna of Abū Bakr or the Sunna of ʿUmar in the same breath. Thus there were many "sunnas" and many sources of authority to draw from. Moreover, even if the Sunna of the Prophet deserved special respect, al-Shāfiʿī's rivals were not convinced that ḥadīth was the most reliable source for that Sunna. A convincing argument could be made (and has been revived in modern times) that the best indicator of the Prophet's Sunna is the living practice of the community. Thus the Medinan jurists relied heavily on the practice of the people of Medina in the argument that the people of Medina

Figure 10.3 Mausoleum of al-Shāfiʿī in Cairo. Photo: © Creswell Archive, Ashmolean Museum, Oxford. neg. EA.CA.4394. Image courtesy of Fine Arts Library, Harvard College Library

had faithfully continued the practice of the Prophet. Consequently, Islamic legal literature before al-Shāfiʿī was remarkably light on ḥadīth.

After al-Shāfiʿī the logic of the partisans of ḥadīth became overwhelming, and the "schools" of law in Kūfa, Medina, and Syria were put on the defensive. They were left with only one alternative, and that was to come up with ḥadīth to justify their positions. It was not necessary, however, to draw reports out of thin air. All that was necessary was to find ways of attributing existing reports to the Prophet. The result was that laws that in the eighth century were attributed to a caliph were traced back to the Prophet in the ninth, and the ḥadīth literature ballooned in size and in diversity as rival schools of law sought to justify their legal theory by couching it in ḥadīth.

In summary, we can divide the evolution of Islamic legal theory into four periods:

1 For the first hundred years or so after the conquest, the caliphs were at center stage in legal developments and if there was any theory at work, it centered on the authority of the caliph as a source of Sunna and thus of law.
2 During the eighth century legal circles in opposition to the caliphs developed in regional centers, formulating independent legal ideas and traditions. The most important of these centers were Medina and Kūfa.
3 From the late eighth century the flexible and ad hoc style of legal reasoning in the regional schools of law came under challenge from a growing traditionist movement. Partisans of ḥadīth, most eloquently represented by al-Shāfiʿī, argued that all substantive law must be traced to the Qur'ān or ḥadīth traced to the Prophet. The result was a period of polemics and controversy over the sources of Islamic law.
4 By the beginning of the tenth century the traditionist thesis had won the day, and the four-source theory of Islamic law was widely accepted.

The origins of the substance of Islamic law are much harder to trace. If the Qur'ān is placed in a seventh-century Arabian context, then it is clear that certain rudimentary elements of Islamic law grew up in response to scripture. The basic religious duties, laws of inheritance and marriage regulations, for example, are articulated in embryonic form in the Qur'ān. Consequently, tracing the origins of these foundational elements of Islamic law amounts to the same problem as tracing the origins of the Qur'ān itself, and many scholars are satisfied to simply attribute the origins of Islamic law to Muslim concern to apply the Qur'ān. This apparently reasonable hypothesis will fail, however, if a later date for the canonization of the Islamic scripture is accepted. If the Qur'ān originated in seventh-century Arabia, then some basic elements of Islamic law also originated there. If, on the other hand, the Qur'ān was canonized after the Arab conquests, then it may be taken to reflect the early formative period of Islamic law rather than shaping it.

Regardless of which way we go on this debate, however, Islamic law contains much that cannot be explained simply as a response to the Qur'ān. The question here is whether the Arabs brought all of this with them from Arabia, or simply picked up what they found after the conquests. The evidence is heavily in favor of the latter. As we have seen, the ḥadīth literature – our main documentation for the growth of Islamic law – clearly reflects the concerns of the Near Eastern environment within which Islam came to maturity. The question of where each particular element of Islamic law came from is not all that important, however. The reality is, that regardless of where particular legal ideas or practices came from, Muslim jurists "islamized" the law by fitting it into a coherent and all-embracing system. Whatever the genetic origin of a particular legal idea, it is the system of Islamic jurisprudence which we discussed above that makes the law Islamic.

Thus we will get an accurate sense of the nature of Islamic law, not by trying to trace the origins of its minutiae, but by stepping back and taking stock of its broader place within the structure of Islamic life and thought. Islamic law is arguably the foundation of this structure. It is the means of practical guidance for daily life, the medium for discussion of political institutions, and the essential grounding for the spiritual life. Law is the hub of the wheel that connects to every aspect of Islamic belief and practice. The most important reality of the universe is that God cares how humans act, and that they defy his will at their peril. We have seen a system like this before. In granting this place of primacy to the law, Islam clearly belongs in the same family as rabbinic Judaism. Both systems grew up independent of prevailing political structures. Where rabbis drew on Torah and Mishna, the ʿulamāʾ had their Qurʾān and Sunna. While the rabbis issued responsa, muftīs wrote fatwas. Islamic law is the rabbinic ideal universalized.

Resources for Further Study

The best general introduction to the field of Islamic law is Noel J. Coulson, *A History of Islamic Law* (1964). Other introductions include Asaf A. A. Fyzee, *Outlines of Muhammadan Law* (1949), Ignaz Goldziher, *Introduction to Islamic Theology and Law* (1980), and Joseph Schacht, *An Introduction to Islamic Law* (1964). My source for the extended illustration which begins the chapter is Ralph Hattox, *Coffee and Coffeehouses: The Origins of a Social Beverage in the Medieval Near East* (1988).

Important Islamic legal texts in translation include Muhammad ibn Idrīs al-Shāfiʿī, *Islamic Jurisprudence: Shāfiʿī's Risāla* (1961), Ibn Rushd, *The Distinguished Jurist's Primer* (1994), and Ahmad ibn Naqīb al-Misrī, *Reliance of the Traveler* (1994). Bernard Weiss provides a detailed summary and analysis (though not a translation) of another important work in *The Search for God's Law: Islamic Jurisprudence in the Writings of Sayf al-Dīn al-Āmidī* (1992).

On Islamic legal theory and the debate over the origins of Islamic law, see Joseph Schacht, *The Origins of Muhammadan Jurisprudence* (1950), Yasin Dutton, *The Origins of Islamic Law* (1999), John Burton, *The Sources of Islamic Law: Islamic Theories of Abrogation* (1990), Ahmad Hasan, *The Early Development of Islamic Jurisprudence* (1970), and Wael Hallaq, *A History of Islamic Legal Theories: An Introduction to Sunnī uṣūl al-fiqh* (1997).

More specialized studies in Islamic law include Abraham Udovitch, *Partnership and Profit in Medieval Islam* (1970), Baber Johansen, *The Islamic Law on Land and Rent* (1988), David Powers, *Studies in Qur'an and Hadith: The Formation of the Islamic Law of Inheritance* (1986), Franz Rosenthal, *Gambling in Islam* (1975), Jamal J. Nasir, *The Islamic Law of Personal Status* (1986), Jeanette Wakin, *The Function of Documents in Islamic Law* (1972), John Kelsay and James Turner Johnson (eds.), *Just War and Jihad: Historical and Theoretical Perspectives on War and Peace in Western and Islamic Traditions* (1991), Majid Khadduri, *The Islamic Law of Nations: Shaybani's Siyar* (1955), and Patricia Crone, *Roman, Provincial and Islamic Law: The Origins of the Islamic Patronate* (1987b).

11

ISLAMIC THEOLOGY AND PHILOSOPHY

Compared with Islamic law, which had the lofty ambition of guiding believers to paradise, the goals of Islamic theology were modest. Islamic theologians had little expectation that theologizing would lead anyone to paradise, and they applied themselves instead to the limited project of fortifying believers against error. By identifying heresy, however, they also mapped out the boundaries of an Islamic orthodoxy.

The mention of orthodoxy will raise eyebrows, for it has become dogma among scholars of Islam to assert that Islam has no orthodoxy, only orthopraxy, right practice. While this assertion correctly emphasizes the primacy of Islamic law over Islamic theology, the claim seriously misleads by seeming to suggest that the Islamic tradition has encouraged a casual attitude toward doctrine. In reality the prolific production of creeds, commentaries on creeds, and refutations of heresy by Muslim scholars indicates that issues of doctrine were rather urgent for them. It is true enough that Muslims never developed a central institution, a papacy or an ecclesiastical body, whereby authoritative doctrine could be defined and established, but the same is true in the field of Islamic law. Muslim scholars were just as keenly and urgently aware of the need to distinguish truth from error as they were of the need to define right behavior.

One of the stock literary products in the effort to establish true doctrine was the heresiography, a sort of guidebook to theological error. Most of what we know, or think we know, about the earliest development of Islamic theology comes from such encyclopedias of heresy – the *Maqālāt al-Islamiyyīn* of al-Ashʿarī (d. 935), *al-Farq bayn al-Firāq* by al-Baghdādī (d. 1037), and the *Kitāb al-Milāl wa'l Niḥāl* of al-Shāhrastānī (d. 1153) are the best known. These guides to heresy provide an excellent starting point for a survey of the theological issues with which Islamic theologians of the tenth century and after were most preoccupied.

The basic unit of the heresiography is the sect. Sects are often named after the person who is blamed for originating the particular error, and there are seventy-three of them, of which only one is rightly guided. Muslim heresiographers were free to split hairs about the precise identification of the seventy-two ways of going astray, but they knew there must be precisely seventy-two because the Prophet had said so. "The Jews are divided into seventy-one sects and the Christians into seventy-two," the Prophet had assured his companions, "but my community will be divided into seventy-three sects." Why excelling in divisiveness should be a matter of pride is a puzzle, but those who quoted the tradition were apparently not troubled by that question. The Prophet was more specific in another report: "My community will be divided into seventy-three sects but only one of these will be saved, the others will perish" (Shāhrastānī 1984: 10). We must leave aside the crucial question of identifying the one sect that will be saved, focusing for now on the other seventy-two.

Some important heresies

Among the most important of these seventy-two ways of getting it wrong were the following:

The Mu'tazilites. Known as the people of justice and unity, and condemned as "Zoroastrians of the community" by their critics, the Muʿtazilites dominated ʿAbbāsid court circles under the caliphs Ma'mūn and Muʿtaṣim. Their doctrine has been encapsulated in a handy summary, the five points of Muʿtazilism:

1. Unity (tawḥīd). God's oneness is absolute. Nothing else, including God's attributes or God's speech, the Qur'ān, is eternal, and God does not resemble his creation in any way.
2. Justice (ʿadl). God is obligated to act justly, giving out rewards and punishments in strict accordance with each person's performance.
3. "The promise and the threat." When God makes a promise, or issues a threat, he is bound to carry through with it.
4. The intermediate position. A grave sinner (fāsiq) can be considered neither a believer nor an unbeliever.
5. Commanding the right and forbidding the wrong. It is a duty to oppose injustice (e.g., rebel against an evil ruler) if one has the ability.

Qadariyya. Forerunners of the Muʿtazilites in championing human freedom. The origins of the Qadariyya have been particularly associated with al-Ḥasan al-Basrī, to whom is attributed a famous epistle to the Caliph ʿAbd al-Malik in defense of human freedom.

Jabriyya. The opposite of the Qadariyya.

Khārijites. Those who "went out" from ʿAlī because he had failed to obey the book of God. The Khārijites insisted that to be Muslim one must act like a Muslim, and if one does not act like a Muslim one is an unbeliever and an apostate.

Murji'a. Those who postpone judgment about the ultimate fate of grave sinners, leaving the decision to God. The general tendency of ḥadīth tends to be Murji'ite, and in its extreme form Murji'ism holds that someone who has said the creed will reach paradise, "even if he commits adultery and theft." The Murji'a have been stereotyped as politically passive.

Zanādiqa. Something of a catch-all category to be applied to any apparent resurgence of Iranian religion.

Shīʿites. See chapter 9. A wide range of movements connected by the elevation of ʿAlī and the family of the Prophet in general.

A full listing of all seventy-two would be cumbersome. Fortunately there were other more manageable ways of categorizing heresy. Al-Shāhrastānī, for example, classifies Muslim sects roughly according to the theological issue which seems to be their distinctive concern. It turns out that the issues on which Muslims are divided can be grouped under four main headings: (1) the freedom of the will, (2) the attributes of God, (3) faith and works, and (4) the leadership of the community. Al-Shāhrastānī begins with the most serious threat to orthodoxy, the Muʿtazilites, and the issue which earned them the soubriquet "the Zoroastrians of the community," the freedom of the will.

Freedom and Determinism

The ḥadīth literature reflects a strikingly deterministic mood, summed up in the tradition, "Everyone is guided to that for which he was created." According to another tradition, every forty-two-day-old embryo is assigned the exact date of its death. Before creation God decreed and wrote down the exact course of events for his creation, with practical implications that are lucidly summed up in the words of an early creed: "What reaches you could not possibly have missed you; and what misses you could not possibly have reached you" (Wensinck 1932: 103).

The logical end of such an attitude was reached by a group of sects that al-Shāhrastānī calls the Jabriyya, who deny to human beings any power to act on their own. God produces each human deed as surely as he causes every movement of an inanimate object. A human being is in reality no different from an inanimate object when it comes to agency; he is absolutely powerless, and deeds can only be attributed to him in a metaphorical sense, so that to say "So and so did such and such" is similar to saying "The sun rose." Rewards and punishments for deeds are likewise determined and are in no way contingent upon human action (Shāhrastānī 1984: 72–6).

The ethical problem raised by determinism is obvious. If the final score (and perhaps not just the final score, but each play) has already been fixed in advance, why should the players put any effort into the game? There is also a moral problem. Strict determinism puts God in the position of rewarding and punishing people for the very deeds that he himself made them perform. This seems to make a mockery of the Qur'ān, which so clearly calls people to moral action and promises reward for good deeds and punishment for wickedness. It is also difficult to see how any notion of God's justice can survive such determinism.

The various opponents of determinism are labeled *qadariyya* by the heresiographers. The name makes little sense, since *qadar* is a reference to divine power, and the Qadariyya should logically be those who emphasize God's power over against human freedom. Nevertheless, and against the objections of the partisans of free will themselves, the name stuck. Heresiographers preserve bits of information about the alleged founders of the doctrine, among them Ḥasan al-Baṣrī, a famous eighth-century mystic and theologian. An early document in the controversy, an epistle attributed to Ḥasan, was supposedly written in response to a query from the Caliph ʿAbd al-Malik. The epistle argues on the basis of the Qur'ān that humans have real freedom to act, and that evil acts in particular cannot be attributed to God. One of the curious features of the letter is the absence of any references to ḥadīth, a feature which has been cited in support of its authenticity and early date. There is a more obvious explanation for the absence of ḥadīth: there were none available. The ḥadīth literature is completely devoid of traditions defending free will, so that even if the epistle is a later forgery (a possibility that cannot be discounted), the author simply had no pro-qadarite ḥadīth to draw on. The complete absence of pro-qadarite traditions in the ḥadīth literature is an indication that the doctrine of free will was a fairly late development among Muslims and that some form of determinism was the default setting for the earliest Muslims.

It was, in fact, not until the tenth century that Muʿtazilite theologians, the theological successors to the Qadariyya, took up the defense of free will in a much more systematic way. The argument was simple enough to make. The Qur'ān declares that humans will be rewarded or punished according to their deeds. If our deeds are not our own, however, then God is unjust to punish or reward. Belief in the justice of God therefore requires a corresponding belief in human freedom, for if humans are not free, God is not just. On the basis of this vigorous advocacy of divine justice, the Muʿtazilites called themselves the People of Justice and Unity (Ahl al-ʿAdl wa'l Tawḥīd). As this self-designation indicates, however, the Muʿtazilites were not a single-issue movement. Their most original contribution to Islamic theology, in fact, was the development of the second plank of their program, the unity of God.

God's Attributes

Muslim theologians agree that God is One, and that this is his most important quality. They also know from the Qur'ān that he has certain other qualities. It is safe to say, for example, that God is knowing, living, powerful, and generous. It is also safe to say that he speaks. But what is the relationship between God's oneness and his various other qualities? For instance, is the One God still God if he is stripped of knowledge? The answer would seem obvious. It is inconceivable that God, in the Islamic sense, would still be God without knowledge. But if God is not God apart from his knowledge, then God must be forever knowing, ergo God's knowledge must be eternal.

It was roughly in these terms that Muslim theologians discussed the attributes of God and their relation to his essence. Two choices seemed possible. On the one hand, some theologians rallied around God's oneness by sharply distinguishing the divine attributes from the divine essence. The essence of God is his eternal oneness, and all of his other qualities are subordinate. Their opponents accused such theologians of taʿtīl, "stripping" God of his attributes, thus replacing the God of revelation with a faceless philosophical construct. At the other extreme were others – al-Shāhrastānī calls them Ṣifātiyya – who insisted that the attributes of God were real beings that eternally subsist in God. God's knowledge is an eternal being, and so too is his power, his life, and his speech. The attributes are not the same as God, and they are not to be called God, but they are nevertheless real, eternal beings, and we are thus left with multiplicity within the being of God. The choice was not a happy one: a bland, faceless, philosopher's God, stripped of personality, or a God of multiple, eternal aspects disconcertingly reminiscent of the three-in-one godhead of the Christians.

The peculiar status of one of God's attributes added a twist to the problem. Among God's attributes is the attribute of speech, which is simply to say that God is known to communicate with his creatures. Unlike his other attributes, however, God's speech is uniquely manifested in a tangible form, the Qur'ān. True, the earthly form of the Qur'ān is simply a copy of the original, heavenly version, but the problem still arises: what is the relation of God's speech, encapsulated in the Qur'ān, to the essence of God? At one level this problem is simply a subset of the general problem of attributes and the answers fall out along the same lines: either God's speech is created by God and subordinate

Figure 11.1 Men studying the Qur'ān at the Sultan's school, Oman. Photo: Robin Laurance/Impact-Photos

to him, or it is an eternal, uncreated attribute of God. But in this case the debate had serious practical implications. If the heavenly Qur'ān was, indeed, eternal and uncreated, then the book that Muslims held in their hands was, in some sense, a manifestation of an eternal aspect of God. Accordingly, some theologians went so far as to argue that every syllable, sound, and written character of the Qur'ān is pre-existing and eternal. If, on the other hand, God's speech was a created thing, might the Qur'ān not be seen as a mere book, subject to the limiting and shaping effects of time and environment? Once again the choice was fraught with danger: ordinary book with an extraordinary message or physical manifestation of the eternal Word of God?

During the eighth century, conflict over the status of the Qur'ān turned both nasty and political. The Caliph al-Ma'mūn, in a bid to assert control over religious scholars and to establish Mu'tazilite theology as state creed, tried to force the 'ulamā' to affirm the createdness of the Qur'ān. His inquisition, the famous miḥna, was a short-term success – the majority of religious scholars caved in – but it was a failure in the longer term. Ma'mūn's successor, Mu'taṣim, continued the policy, but persecution made a hero of the most vigorous opponent of Mu'tazilite doctrine, Aḥmad ibn Ḥanbal, who refused to recant in the face of torture and imprisonment, and in the end the tradition-minded 'ulamā' emerged stronger and more independent than ever.

The Caliph Mutawwakil reversed course and embraced the viewpoint of the more traditional religious scholars.

Anthropomorphism

Another issue connected with the problem of attributes was also of deep importance for Islamic piety, that is, the problem of what language could be used to describe God. When God is said to speak, for example, what exactly does that mean? When we say that God hears or sees, does it imply that he must have ears and eyes? Does God actually sit on a physical throne? And at a more serious level, when God is said to be good or generous, do those descriptions apply to God in exactly the same way they would apply to a human being? Again, al-Shāhrastānī describes the extremes. On the one hand are the anthropomorphists who insist that God has an actual body with members and limbs, hands and feet, head and tongue, two eyes and two ears. He also has long, black, curly hair. It is true that God's body is unlike other bodies, and his flesh unlike other flesh, for he does not resemble any other creature, but the difference is a matter of degree. His body is real and humans can theoretically touch him, shake his hand, and see him. Thus the Prophet is reported to have said, "God met me, shook hands with me and put his hand between my shoulders, until I felt the coldness of his fingers" (Shāhrastānī 1984: 90). At the other extreme are theologians so shy of attributing human characteristics to God that they insist on highly metaphorical readings of the Qur'ān: God's throne is a metaphor for his sovereignty, God's face indicates his essence, and his hands stand for his grace.

The problem of anthropomorphism came to be especially focused on a single question: is it possible for a human to see God? According to a tradition from the Prophet, when the believers have entered paradise, "Allāh will remove the veil and the vision of their Lord will be the most precious gift lavished upon them" (Wensinck 1932: 65). Anthropomorphists had no problem with this: the believers would see God's physical form with physical eyes. The Muʿtazilites, however, argued that to speak of seeing God in a physical sense was absurd, and any such vision must at best be metaphorical: to see God meant to "see" him with one's heart, that is, to know him.

Faith and Works

The question of exactly what it will mean to see God is rather less urgent, of course, than the question of who will be so lucky. The problem of exactly who is a Muslim and how one can know became a central concern of theologians. The path to becoming a Muslim is rather straightforward, involving assent to a simple statement of faith – There is no God but God and Muhammad is the Messenger of God – along with submission to the duties that followed from that confession. Consequently, the problem was not how to get into the community of believers, which was simple enough, but defining what it would take to be thrown out. The debate focused on the status of a Muslim guilty of a grave sin. Did such a sinner remain a Muslim, or did his sin make him an apostate? Since an apostate was liable to death, the question carried some weight.

The issue was also politically charged. The killers of ʿUthmān allegedly justified their deed on the basis of his sin, and the first Khārijites reportedly withdrew their support from ʿAlī because he had sinned in submitting to human arbitration rather than the command of God. At the battle of Ṣiffīn the Khārijites had rejected the leadership of both Muʿāwīya and ʿAlī, on the grounds that both had fallen into grave error. Their withdrawal was a political act, but based on a theological premise. ʿAlī had sinned by agreeing to arbitration and abandoning the principle that judgment belongs to God alone. Thus he had disqualified himself from leadership, for a grave sinner who failed to repent could not be considered a Muslim, much less allowed to be the leader of the community of Muslims. Thus the Khārijites established themselves at one extreme on the question of who could be considered a Muslim. A true Muslim will be recognized first and foremost by his deeds.

The reaction to the Khārijite movement was associated with the position of the Murji'a, whose basic argument was that the judgment about whether an individual was a believer or not must be postponed, that is, deferred to God. (The name of the sect is derived from the Arabic *irjā'*, postponement.) An anti-Khārijite tradition attributed to a pious companion of the Prophet, Abū Dharr al-Ghifārī, captures the gist of the Murji'a viewpoint: "I came to the Prophet and found him sleeping in a white garment," Abū Dharr reported. "I came a second time and found him still sleeping. The third time I found him awake. When I sat down near him, he said to me: 'Whoever says, There is no God but Allāh and dies in that belief will enter Paradise.' I replied, 'Even if he commits fornication and theft?' He answered: 'Even if he has fornicated and stolen.'" Abū Dharr repeated his question three times. After the fourth, Muhammad added, "Even though Abu Dharr should turn up his nose" (Wensinck 1932: 46). In another group of anti-Khārijite traditions, a gaunt and austere looking Bedouin comes up to the Prophet and charges him to act justly (or to fear God). When one of the companions of the Prophet offers to strike off the stranger's head for his insolence, the Prophet tells him to let the man go, for "I am not ordered to split open the hearts of men." He warned, however, that "from the descendants of this man there will arise people who fluently read the book of Allāh, but it will not pass beyond their throats. They will pass through religion as an arrow passes through a hunted animal" (Muslim 1994: tradition number 148). The tradition is an apt depiction of the Khārijite ethos: pious, ascetic, and devastating to the unity of the community.

The theological questions raised by the Khārijites and the Murji'ites came to be focused on the distinction between *islam*, submission, and *īmān*, faith. Although the Qur'ān does not differentiate islam and īmān, it does implicitly recognize the possibility of outward conformity without inner conviction by denouncing hypocrites, the munāfiqūn, who declared their allegiance to the Prophet while seeking to undermine his authority. The ḥadīth literature systematizes the distinction between faith and submission. On one occasion a man reportedly came to the Prophet, and asked: "O Apostle of Allāh, what is faith?" He answered, "Believing in Allāh, His angels, His book, His meeting, His Apostles, and the final resurrection." Thereupon the man asked, "O Apostle of Allāh, what is Islam?" Muhammad answered, "Islam is serving God without associating anything with Him, performing the ordered ṣalāt, paying over the obligatory zakāt, and fasting during Ramaḍān." Then the man asked, "O Apostle of Allāh, what is righteousness [Ihṣān]?" He answered, "Serving Allāh as if He were before your eyes. For though you do not see Him, He sees you." According to another tradition the Prophet said, "Islam is external, faith belongs to the heart" (Wensinck 1932: 23).

It was clearly possible, then, to be Muslim and to perform the outward works identified with Islam without the inner conviction of faith, but was it also possible to have faith apart from works? The Khārijites, of course, vehemently rejected the possibility. At the other extreme, the Murji'a, along with Abū Ḥanīfa and his followers, held that faith was unaffected by works. An early Ḥanafī creed asserts that no one can be declared an infidel, nor can a person's faith be denied, on the basis of sin. A somewhat later creed states the case more starkly: "Works are distinct from faith, and faith is distinct from works, as is proved by the fact that often the Faithful is exempted from works, whereas it is not possible to say that he is exempted from faith." Deeds are excluded from the formal definition of faith, which consists of "confessing with the tongue, believing with the mind, and knowing with the heart" (Wensinck 1932: 125). This definition allows even a grave sinner to possess faith, and it would thus be wrong to declare such a person an infidel. The Murji'a, moreover, considered faith to be an invariable quantity which could neither increase nor decrease; either you have it or you don't, and how you act is not a reliable diagnostic tool.

Uncomfortable with the Khārijite and Murji'ite extremes, the Mu'tazilites tried a compromise position, incorporating works in their definition of faith, which, they argued, consists of three elements: conviction of the truth, confession with the tongue, and confirmation with deeds. If one does not confess with the tongue, one is an unbeliever (kāfir); if one does not believe in the heart, one is a hypocrite (munāfiq); and if one does both but commits a grave sin, one is a sinner (fāsiq). The grave sinner is neither a believer nor an infidel, but occupies an intermediate no man's land between the two. For now the sinner should be treated as a member of the community, but if he dies unrepentant he will be condemned to hell. Some Mu'tazilites, in an effort to be fair, assigned such sinners a higher grade in hell than complete infidels. The Mu'tazilite compromise, as we will see, came close to the eventual "orthodox" solution to the problem of faith and works.

Leadership

The final opportunity for schism, the question of the leadership of the community, was sketched out in chapter 8 and need not detain us long here. In al-Shāhrastānī's view, the extremes are two. On the one hand he condemns as Khārijite any group that rebels against a legitimate imām, or that holds that the leadership in the community is not limited to a member of the Quraysh. At the other extreme are the many branches of the Shī'ītes, whose common error he succinctly summarizes:

> The Shī'ī Muslims are those who follow 'Alī. They hold that 'Alī's caliphate and imāmate were based on designation and appointment, either open or hidden. They maintain also that the imāmate must remain in 'Alī's family; if it were ever to go outside of it, this would be either because of a wrong on the part of another, or because of dissimulation on the part of the rightful imām. According to them the imāmate is not a civil matter, validly settled by the will of the people appointing an imām of their own choosing: it is a fundamental matter and a basic element of religion. Messengers of God may not ignore and disregard it, nor leave it to the choice of the common people. (Shāhrastānī 1984: 125)

Al-Shāhrastānī ends with an account of the Ismā'īlī Shī'a, making it clear that their insistence on the necessity of absolute submission to an authoritative, rightly guided imām is dangerous precisely because it is so attractive, a sentiment shared by the famous theologian al-Ghazālī.

The Sunnī Consensus

Faced with so many opportunities to stray from the truth, how is one to identify the one sect whose fortunate followers will reach paradise? Al-Shāhrastānī's answer, couched in a tradition of the Prophet, goes to the very heart of the self-definition of Sunnī Islam. When the Prophet was asked which of the sects would lead to salvation, he replied, "Those who follow the Sunna and the agreement of the community." When he was further asked, "What is the Sunna and the agreement of the community?" he replied, "That which I and my companions practice." The Prophet is also reported to have said, "In my community there will always be some who till the day of judgment will possess truth." Again, he said, "My community will not agree on an error." In other words, orthodoxy is defined by the broad consensus of the community. It is the middle way, the path that avoids extremes, and which has been well trodden and marked out by the pious ancestors of the community, preserved by scholars in the Sunna of the Prophet and confirmed by the consensus, the ijmāʿ, of the community (Shāhrastānī 1984: 10).

Sunnī theologians did not see their position as having evolved or developed in history, but as the original and authentic Islam. Theirs is simply the unadulterated Islam of the Prophet's Sunna and the pious ancestors, a broad, clear stream, flowing directly from the time of the Prophet; the various sects are like rivulets which have branched off into error to the right or to the left. Thus the root and definition of heresy is innovation, bidʿa, and every heretic is an innovator, succumbing to the temptation to wander away from the assured doctrine of the ancestors into the field of speculation. In accordance with this claim to represent the broadly catholic middle way, the *via media* of Islam, Sunnī scholars used heresy as a foil. To be Sunnī was to be neither a qadarite advocate of free will nor a jabrite determinist, neither a Khārijite nor a Murji'ite, neither a stripper of God's attributes nor an anthropomorphist. The major importance of these movements from a Sunnī theological perspective, in other words, is that they represent what true Islam is not.

The moderating tendency of Sunnī Islam is clearly reflected in the main body of the ḥadīth literature, and thus can be considered to have deep roots in Islamic thinking. It was during the early ʿAbbāsid caliphate, however, that Sunnī orthodoxy began to be clearly articulated and systematized. Two people are celebrated by later Muslims as the outstanding figures in this process, the great champion of tradition, Aḥmad ibn Ḥanbal, and an ex-Muʿtazilite theologian Abū'l Ḥasan al-Ashʿarī. The lives of both are steeped in legend, but the legends simply serve to highlight their symbolic status as quintessential defenders of orthodoxy.

Aḥmad ibn Ḥanbal

Ibn Ḥanbal is remembered as the exemplary defender of ḥadīth. He not only collected and memorized a prodigious number of traditions, he also sought to embody the spirit of ḥadīth, scrupulously avoiding any practice which he could not justify by reference to the prophetic Sunna. Reports of his life honor his exemplary character – he is reported to have forgiven al-Muʿtaṣim for persecuting him in simple obedience to the Qur'ān – as much as they do his scholarly accomplishments. He is most famous for heroically enduring torture and imprisonment during the Muʿtazilite inquisition under Ma'mūn and Muʿtaṣim. The record of his interrogations before Muʿtaṣim stands out as a monument among human struggles of conscience.

The principle of conscience for which Ibn Ḥanbal endured torture was straightforward loyalty to the Qur'ān as the uncreated Word of God and adherence to the plain sense of the Qur'ān and the Sunna. He particularly opposed metaphorical interpretation; what the Qur'ān and Sunna assert is simply to be accepted as reality without engaging in any hermeneutical gymnastics. Eschatological images, for example – punishment in the tomb, the basin of Muhammad, the bridge, the balance, the trumpet, the guarded tablet – are not to be reduced to metaphor, but accepted as realities. Heaven and hell are not metaphorical, but real. Similarly, anthropomorphic language in the Qur'ān and the ḥadīth – God's throne, his hands, and his eyes – is simply to be accepted, "without asking how." Thus he roundly condemns the use of analogical reasoning as a theological method.

A refusal to go beyond what is written is the consistent emphasis of Ibn Ḥanbal's theology. Consequently he will not be confined by systematic categories. He is clearly not Khārijite, for he refuses to condemn any individual to hell unless there is a specific tradition to that effect – but neither can the Murji'a claim him, for he refuses to exclude works from the definition of faith, and holds that faith can increase or decrease. On the question of qadar he is a strict determinist: everything is from God, including adultery, theft, and murder – yet he does not hesitate to baldly assert that God is just. In politics he is a quietist. Friday prayers, jihād, the pilgrimage, and taxes remain obligatory whether the ruler is just or unjust, and Muslims should distance themselves from any schism in the community; yet his resistance to caliphal authority is legendary.

Al-Ashʿarī

As a conscientious objector when it came to applying systematic reasoning to theology, Ibn Ḥanbal could only defend his position by appeal to the Qur'ān or Sunna. Abū'l Ḥasan al-Ashʿarī felt under no such restraint. Where Ibn Ḥanbal stood stalwartly by the content of orthodox tradition, al-Ashʿarī drew the sword of reason to fight in its defense. According to the story of his conversion, al-Ashʿarī began as a talented Muʿtazilite theologian, groomed to take over from his teacher, the great Muʿtazilite, al-Jubbāʾī. Then he experienced a series of life-transforming dreams. In his first dream the Prophet appeared to him and instructed him to defend the doctrines related in the ḥadīth. Consequently, al-Ashʿarī did exactly what we would expect from a newly converted follower of Aḥmad ibn Ḥanbal. He dropped everything to study ḥadīth and repudiated all things Muʿtazilite. At this the Prophet was forced to return in another dream in which he angrily informed al-Ashʿarī that his instructions had not been to give up theology, but to defend the traditions by means of it (Ashʿarī 1940: 27–8). Thus, to the minds of later Muslim historians at least, al-Ashʿarī's conversion is symbolic of the fusing of ḥadīth-based orthodoxy with the methods of dialectical theology pioneered by the Muʿtazilites.

Another story traces al-Ashʿarī's dissatisfaction with Muʿtazilite theology to a dialogue with his master, al-Jubbāʾī, in which al-Ashʿarī proposed a hypothetical problem. Suppose, he suggested, we imagine three brothers. One dies an unbeliever, the second a believer, and the third dies as an infant. What is their status? Al-Jubbāʾī answered that the believer would be glorified, the unbeliever damned, and the infant will be in limbo, safe from damnation, but not on the level of the believer. Al-Ashʿarī had a follow-up question: can the infant do anything to rise to the same level as the believer? No, replied al-Jubbāʾī, for the reward of the believer was earned by obedience, and the infant has done nothing to earn a reward. What then, asked al-Ashʿarī, if the infant complains to God, "The fault is not mine. If you had allowed me to live, I would have been obedient"? To this al-Jubbāʾī replied, "God will say to him, 'I knew that if you survived you would surely be disobedient and incur punishment. Therefore I considered what was best for you and brought death upon you before you reached the age of responsibility.'" By now it is clear that al-Jubbāʾī is in the trap, and it is only left for al-Ashʿarī to spring it. How then, he demands, will God reply to those in hell who will cry out, "O my Lord, you knew his condition as you know mine. Why did you not consider what was best for me?" At this al-Jubbāʾī was left tongue-tied (Ashʿarī 1940: 27).

Kalām

Such use of reasoned argument to beat the heretics at their own game became the trademark of Ashʿarīte theology. It was by fully embracing this method of kalām, the dialectical approach to theology, that al-Ashʿarī came to represent a symbolic turning point in the development of Islamic theology.

In the content of his theology al-Ashʿarī portrays himself as no more than a devotee of tradition and a loyal follower of Aḥmad ibn Ḥanbal:

> The belief we hold and the religion we follow are holding fast to the Book of our Lord, to the Sunna of our Prophet, and to the traditions related on the authority of the Companions and the Successors and the imāms of the ḥadīth; to that

> we hold firmly, professing what Abū ʿAbd Allāh Aḥmad ibn Muhammad ibn Ḥanbal professed, and avoiding him who dissents from his belief, because he is the excellent imām and the perfect leader, through whom God declared truth, removed error, manifested modes of action, and overcame the innovations of the innovators, the deviation of the deviators, and the skepticism of the skeptics. (Ashʿarī 1940: 49)

In reality, this claim to be a foot soldier in the army of Imām Aḥmad is disingenuous. The content of al-Ashʿarī's theology turns out to be far more nuanced than that of Ibn Ḥanbal, and he shows the consistent effort to chart the middle course between extremes which is the hallmark of Sunnī theology and which leads him to depart from Ibn Ḥanbal on key points.

Al-Ashʿarī is as unyielding a determinist as Ibn Ḥanbal, for instance, but he is much more sensitive to both the ethical and the moral challenges raised by the qadarites and Muʿtazilites. His solution had already been pioneered by his predecessors among the Muʿtazilites: although God is the creator of every act, human beings nevertheless "acquire" those actions. God creates the act, and he creates in humans the power to perform the act, but the act still belongs to the human agent. This doctrine of acquisition (kasb), whereby ultimate agency remains with God while responsibility is nevertheless assigned to the creature, became the characteristic solution in Ashʿarīte theology to the problem of divine determinism.

On the problem of anthropomorphism al-Ashʿarī systematically opposed the metaphorical interpretation of the Muʿtazilites, but he also denied any resemblance between God and his creatures. The danger of associating God with creation was so serious, in fact, that it would be sinful to even move one's hand while reading a passage concerning the hand of God. It is wrong to seek out metaphorical explanations, thus denying the plain sense of scripture; it is equally wrong to attribute human characteristics to God. Thus the language of the Qur'ān and the tradition is simply to be accepted, *bilā kayfa*, without knowing how: "God is upon His throne, as He has said, 'The Merciful is seated on The Throne.' He has two hands, *bilā kayfa*, as He said, 'I have created with My two hands' . . . and He has two eyes, *bilā kayfa*, as He has said, 'Under Our eyes it floated on.'"

On the question of faith, al-Ashʿarī follows Ibn Ḥanbal. Works are an element in faith, therefore faith can increase and decrease, and sin impairs faith. Following the Murji'a, however, orthodox theologians were unwilling to declare Muslims apostates on the basis of sin. The following summary of the distinctive tenets of Ashʿarīte theology shows this consistent tendency to straddle extremes:

1 Divine determinism. Every action is created independently by God simultaneous with its occurrence.

2 The doctrine of acquisition (kasb). Humans are responsible for their actions by virtue of their acquisition of acts created by God.
3 The eternity of God's attributes. God's attributes are eternal and are "neither God nor other than God."
4 The eternity of the Qur'ān. The Qur'ān is the eternal, uncreated Word of God. Discussion of whether the sounds or letters of earthly copies are eternal is an innovation and Muslims should not indulge in such speculations.
5 Faith includes works. Faith consists of belief, knowledge, and works, hence faith can increase and decrease, and sin impairs it.
6 Sinners are not to be declared unbelievers, or consigned to hell.
7 The intercession of the Prophet. Muhammad will intercede for his community on the Day of Judgment, just as tradition says he will, whether the Mu'tazilites like it or not.
8 Descriptions of God in revealed sources are to be accepted *bilā kayfa*, without knowing how; that is, without recourse either to rationalistic speculation or indulgence in anthropomorphism.

Jewish and Christian Influences

To this point I have portrayed Islamic theology largely as an intra-Islamic affair, and this accords with the impression left by Muslim heresiographers. Each heresy appears to arise from a concern that is uniquely Islamic. The Khārijites seem to come up with the problem of works and faith entirely in response to early political events. The Murji'a position arises purely in reaction to the Khārijites. The Qadariyya seem to be similarly motivated by simple concerns of piety. One heresy flows logically into another. The heresy of the Khārijites leads directly to the heresy of the Qadarites, which in turn sows the seeds of the more sophisticated and dangerous errors of the Mu'tazilites. On the other side, the Murji'a are the forerunners of the anthropomorphists. Moreover, virtually every item in the major creeds of Islam can be understood as the response to some schism, reinforcing the impression that Islamic theology is purely Islamic, and that all the issues branch from the trunk of a single tree rooted in the early history of Islam. Every so often we find a hint of awareness that Islam inhabits a wider theological world. The tradition literature itself acknowledges, by way of blame anyway, the close resemblance of certain Islamic heresies to the errors of other religious communities. The Prophet is reported to have said, "The Qadarites are the Zoroastrians of the community, the anthropomorphists are the Jews of the community, and the Rāfidites [Shī'ī extremists] are its Christians" (Shāhrastānī 1984: 16). But on the whole Islamic theology is usually depicted as having arisen directly from purely Muslim concerns – conflicts within the community and the struggle to understand the Qur'ān.

There is a problem with this picture. When we step back and look at the range of issues that Muslim theologians discussed and the terms they used it should all look strangely familiar. In fact the theological issues, problems, and terms of debate for Muslim theologians correspond almost precisely to issues and problems that had been discussed for centuries by other religious communities in the Near East. Discussions of free will initiated by the Qadariyya reflect similar discussions among Christians. Muslim discussions of the attributes of God adopt the ideas and sometimes the specific language of Christian discussions of the Trinity. The doctrine of the uncreated Qur'ān raises many of the same problems as the incarnation of Jesus. The question of faith and works was a perennial Christian theological problem. And the doctrine of prophetic intercession mirrors the intercession of Christ. To assert that these resemblances were merely coincidental and that Muslims came up with these issues entirely on their own is a serious challenge to common sense. It is true that, given the difficulty of the source material for early Islamic history, tracing specific lines of influence is often challenging. But there are sufficient clear cases of influence, along with an overwhelming body of circumstantial evidence, to continue to motivate the search for such connections. And even if we remain cautious in asserting direct "influence" we can at least say that Islamic theology shows the general effects of a theological environment saturated by discussions of the Trinity, the Incarnation, freedom of the will, and faith.

Islamic theology should be seen as a contribution to a continuing dialogue within the various traditions of Near Eastern monotheism – a new contribution to a wide-ranging and ongoing theological conversation. There were major and minor participants in this dialogue. Many of them were introduced in chapter 3: Nestorian and Jacobite Christians, Manichaeans, rabbinic Jews, and Jewish Christians were among the most important. The major topics of that conversation had already been set before the Muslims came on the scene, and having joined a dialogue already in progress, Muslim theologians were obliged to accept the basic rules of the game. Moreover, to talk of Muslims joining a theological dialogue is no mere metaphor. Early Muslims were drawn directly into real theological debates with Christians, and accounts of those debates clearly show that Christians and Muslims were very much on the same wavelength.

This is not to say that Muslims brought nothing new to the table. To the contrary, viewing Islamic theology against the backdrop of the wider spectrum of Near Eastern monotheist theology makes the distinctives of Islamic belief stand out more clearly. It allows us to see in particular that the theological dogma that sets Islam apart most clearly, and that comes to be the foundation of Ash'arīte theology, is the overwhelming and all-encompassing power of God. It was against this great rock of divine determinism that the Qadariyya and the Mu'tazilites threw their energy. This was also a point that the Christian theologian and critic of Islam, John of Damascus, fastened on as unique to Islam (Sahas 1972: 103–5).

Even where these traditions differed markedly, however, they shared a common approach. The kalām method, marked by the question and answer format, provided a common medium for theological expression. The theological method did not go unchallenged, however, and the most serious challenge came from a small club of participants in the theological dialogue of the Near East that we have so far ignored: the philosophers.

The Challenge of Philosophy

By contrast with the modesty of the theologians, who hoped only to defend the truth handed down to them, philosophers had a rather exaggerated view of their own work. Where theology sought only to preserve and protect the products of revelation, philosophers aimed to clear the deck and start from scratch. In reality, they started not from scratch, but from Aristotle. Islamic philosophy is a direct import from Greek philosophy, and the Islamic philosophers saw themselves as simply building on the work of Plato, Aristotle, and Plotinus. The Arabic designation for this intellectual tradition, *falsafah*, is a direct borrowing from the Greek *philo sophia*, the love of wisdom.

The Greek philosophical tradition was transmitted to the Arabs primarily by two means. First, after 813, during the reign of Ma'mūn, there was a flurry of translation activity whereby Greek texts were rendered into Arabic. Second, a classical medical tradition, closely allied to philosophy, flourished in the Near East both before and after the Arab conquests. The pioneer of the Arab philosophical tradition, the first to deserve to be called a philosopher, was al-Kindī, a ninth-century Christian (d. 870). It was in the tenth century, however, that the tradition truly flourished.

The philosophers began with an Aristotelian understanding of God as pure form, perfect and eternally contemplating himself. Aristotle's God creates problems for religious types, however. To begin with, he is not a creator in the ordinary sense. To the contrary, the world is eternal, and souls are eternal. This renders God entirely self-sufficient and independent of matter, solving a problem for the philosophers, but creating a whole host of problems for believers of most any stripe. Fortunately, a ready-made solution was at hand. Plotinus, the founder of Neoplatonism, had worked out a system that made the Aristotelian construction of God much more palatable, allowing God to remain self-sufficient while still assigning him credit for bringing into existence a world full of other beings. God does not exactly create the world, according to Plotinus. Rather, it emerges as the final stage in a series of emanations from God. Thus Islamic philosophy adopts an Aristotelian foundation and a Neoplatonic framework.

Prophecy and Revelation in Islamic Philosophy

The Neoplatonic system led to other problems for Muslims. For one thing, one would not expect an Aristotelian prime mover to be the sort of God who is given to revealing himself through prophets. Moreover, the problem of creation still rankles, since in this system the world, while an emanation and thus rather dependent on God for existence, is still an *eternal* emanation. Creation *ex nihilo*, out of nothing, seemed absurd to many philosophers. In the tenth century the philosopher Abū Naṣr al-Fārābī took up the problem of figuring out how the Islamic idea of prophetic revelation could be fitted into this system, and his solution provided a blueprint for later philosophers. The following discussion is based largely on Richard Walzer's translation of one of al-Fārābī's works (Fārābī 1985).

Al-Fārābī raises a perennial problem: how do we know things? For example, how do we know that the whole is greater than the part, or that things equal in size to one thing are equal to one another? His answer: we have built-in "faculties" which render us capable of acquiring knowledge. To be specific, humans have three such faculties: the faculty of sense, the faculty of reason, and the faculty of representation. To actually know something, however, our faculties must "connect" with a source of knowledge, the "active intellect." The relationship between the faculty and the active intellect is like that between the eye and the sun:

Figure 11.2 Al-Fārābī's image on a banknote from Kazakhstan. Photo: Private Collection

> For eyesight is a faculty and a disposition in matter and is, before it sees, potentially sight, and the colors are potentially seeable and visible before they are seen. But neither is the faculty of sight in the eye itself sufficiently qualified to become actually sight nor are the colors themselves sufficiently qualified to become actually seen and viewed. It is the sun which gives light to the sight of the eye, joining the two, and which gives light to the colors, joining it to them. Thus sight becomes through the light which it acquires from the sun actually seeing and actually sight, and the colors become through that light actually seen and viewed after having been potentially seeable and visible. (Fārābī 1985: 201)

In the normal operation of our reason, our minds absorb "intelligibles" from the active intellect just as our eyes absorb the reflected light of the sun.

Interesting, but what does any of this have to do with Islam? A great deal, as it turns out. Reason is not the only faculty which can connect with the active intelligence. Humans also possess a faculty of "representation" which can receive knowledge apart from rational deliberation. This knowledge can come through visions, sometimes in sleep, sometimes in waking life. Such visions in waking life are rare, but

> when the faculty of representation is extremely powerful in a man and developed to perfection . . . the man who has that sight comes to enjoy overwhelming and wonderful pleasure, and he sees wonderful things which can in no way whatever be found in other existents . . . This man will obtain through the particulars which he receives "prophecy" [supernatural awareness] of present and future events, and through the intelligibles which he receives prophesy of things divine. (Fārābī 1985: 225)

Prophets, in other words, have a highly developed faculty of representation which allows them to get at the same source of truth as the philosophers, but without so much effort. Prophecy is thus defined as a sort of special ability, and revelation is something that takes place in the prophet himself.

The implications are rather startling. Prophets are really not that different from philosophers. Prophets might be thought of as philosophers for the masses, in fact, because they are able to communicate truth in metaphors that ordinary people can handle. (Philosophers, of course, can see through the metaphors to the substance.) Since philosophers are not very good at making themselves understood, prophets are necessary, but they hardly have a monopoly on truth. To the contrary, the philosophers, including the Greek masters, are also recipients of "revelation," but through a different and more painstaking method.

The philosophers themselves might have been satisfied with this solution, but to outsiders to that small club it looked a lot like heresy. The classical orthodox critique of philosophy is al-Ghazālī's "Refutation of the Philosophers," in which he attempts to refute, point by point, twenty errors of falsafah, using its own methods against it. The three most crucial objects of his refutation are the philosophical ideas of the eternity of the world, the denial of bodily resurrection, and the idea that God's knowledge does not encompass particulars but only universals (Ghazālī 1997). Al-Ghazālī, ironically, paved the way for the absorption of the methods of philosophy into the mainstream. He rejected the conclusions of the philosophers, but he argued like them, and after him metaphysics became a significant branch of Islamic theology.

Philosophy and Mysticism

The greatest flowering of philosophy was in another direction, however – a direction that can best be illustrated by a famous philosophical parable, Ibn Ṭufayl's *Ḥayy ibn Yaqẓān*. The story begins with the unfortunate Ḥayy as an infant, marooned on a desert island. He is suckled and nurtured by a doe, and as he grows he has to learn everything from scratch. The real action begins when his surrogate mother dies. Ḥayy takes the death rather badly, and, not understanding what has happened, he dissects her body to try to bring her back to life. This process sets Ḥayy on the path to philosophical enlightenment. He learns that his real mother is no longer in her body, and concludes that her real being must be spirit and non-material. From here he launches on a path of reflection: the world consists of a chain of causation, but that chain of causation must have a beginning, a first cause. This first cause must be the creator. Ḥayy has become a monotheist. Not only that. Knowledge of the existence of God leads to contemplation and worship, and Ḥayy has developed into a philosopher-mystic (Ibn Ṭufayl 1972).

Meanwhile, on a nearby island, lives a tribe governed by revelation. Within the tribe is a young man who is not content with external conformity. He seeks inner spiritual meaning, a direct experience of the Divine. Since no one on the island can understand him, he retreats into seclusion on a deserted island. Or it would be deserted if Ḥayy had not gotten there first. The two get along splendidly. They discover that they have a great deal in common, and both realize that they have arrived at the same truth from different directions. After an abortive attempt to share their enlightenment with the legalistic islanders, the two return to the deserted island to live out their lives as mystical philosophers (Ibn Ṭufayl 1972: 165).

Among the lessons of the parable: philosophy and mysticism are a natural fit. The Neoplatonic ideas of the philosophers were perfectly suited to the speculations of the mystics, and it was in the mystical tradition that philosophical ideas had their most enduring impact.

Resources for Further Study

Several overlapping works by W. Montgomery Watt provide a useful overview of the main issues in Islamic theology. These include his *Islamic Philosophy and Theology* (1962), *The Formative Period of Islamic Thought* (1973), and *Free Will and Predestination in Early Islam* (1948). The classic introduction to the earliest development of Islamic theology is A. J. Wensinck, *The Muslim Creed* (1932). Other surveys include Duncan B. MacDonald, *The Development of Muslim Theology, Jurisprudence, and Constitutional Theory* (1903), and G. E. von Grunebaum, *Theology and Law in Islam* (1971).

On Muslim sects and heresies, see two works by Wilfred Madelung: *Religious Schools and Sects in Medieval Islam* (1985) and *Religious Trends in Early Islamic Iran* (1982). Shāhrastānī's work, referenced above, has been translated in part in *Muslim Sects and Divisions* (1984). For the early development of kalām and debates about the authenticity and attribution of early sources, see the works of Josef van Ess in German and a response to van Ess in Michael Cook, *Early Muslim Dogma: A Source-Critical Study* (1981).

On issues raised by the Muʿtazilites, see George Hourani, *Reason and Tradition in Islamic Ethics* (1985), Binyamin Abrahamov, *Islamic Theology: Traditionalism and Rationalism* (1998), J. R. T. M. Peters, *God's Created Speech* (1976), H. A. Wolfson, *The Philosophy of the Kalam* (1976), and Richard Frank, *Beings and their Attributes* (1978).

On Ashʿarīte theology and al-Ghazālī see *The Theology of al-Ashʿarī* (Ashʿarī 1953) and *Freedom and Fulfillment: An Annotated Translation of al-Ghazālī's Munqidh min al-Dalāl and Other Relevant Works of al-Ghazālī* (Ghazālī 1980), both translated by Richard J. McCarthy. See also the translation of al-Ghazālī's autobiography by Montgomery Watt in *The Faith and Practice of al-Ghazālī* (Ghazālī 1953), and Eric Ormsby, *Theodicy in Islamic Thought: The Dispute over al-Ghazālī's "Best of All Possible Worlds"* (1984).

On Islamic philosophy, see Fazlur Rahman, *Prophecy in Islam* (1958), Henry Corbin, *History of Islamic Philosophy* (1993), F. Shehadi, *Metaphysics in Islamic Philosophy* (1983), Michael E. Marmura, *Islamic Theology and Philosophy* (1984), Muhsin Mahdi, *Medieval Political Philosophy* (1963), P. Morewedge, *Islamic Philosophical Theology* (1979), Richard Walzer, "Islamic Philosophy" (1953), and Soheil M. Afnan, *Avicenna: His Life and Works* (1958). Philosophical works in translation referenced above include *Ibn Tufayl's Haqq ibn-Yaqzan* (1972) and Abū Naṣr al-Fārābī, *Al-Farabi on the Perfect State* (1985).

12
ṢŪFĪSM

The Parliament of Birds

The most straightforward introduction to ṣūfism is by means of ṣūfī parables, and among the most celebrated and treasured of these is the thirteenth-century Persian poet ʿAṭṭār's *Parliament of Birds*. ʿAṭṭār's story begins with a gathering of birds of all kinds who are troubled because they have no king. Guided and urged on by the excitable Hoopoe bird, who has impeccable mystical credentials based on a cameo appearance in the Qur'ān, the birds set out together in search of their ruler. The Hoopoe offers good news at the start. The birds can be assured that they do, indeed, have a king. His title is the *Sīmurgh* and he is the epitome of wisdom, beauty, and perfection – the only worthy object of love, in fact. He once dropped a feather in China and ever since he has been an object of intense longing to birds throughout the world (ʿAṭṭār 1993: 11–13).

But there is also bad news. The Sīmurgh's dwelling is inaccessible, no one knows how to get there, and no one has the capacity to find him. Despite this sobering warning the birds are overcome by longing to find their king, and they determine to set out together on the journey, with the indomitable Hoopoe as their guide. Before they depart the Hoopoe warns that the journey will be long and difficult, passing through seven valleys: the valleys of the quest, of love, of understanding, of detachment, of pure unity, of astonishment, and finally the valley of poverty and nothingness. At this distressing report a number of birds succumb to despair and die on the spot. Those who survive the shock set out on the arduous quest.

For years they travel. Many die of starvation, thirst, and fatigue along the way, so that in the end only thirty birds, a sadly torn and tattered band, complete the journey and arrive on the threshold of the Sīmurgh's dwelling. There they are crushed by despair. They realize at last that their quest has been futile, for the majesty of the Sīmurgh is too great to endure. (They are further discouraged by the Sīmurgh's gruff chamberlain.) These deterrents turn out only to be tests, however, and the birds pass the examination, resolving, like moths around a candle, to suffer annihilation rather than abandon the object of their desire. Finally, ushered into the dwelling of the Sīmurgh, they come to the end of their quest. "And perceiving both at once, themselves and Him," ʿAṭṭār recounts, "they realized that they and the Sīmurgh were one and the same being. No one in the world has ever heard of anything equal to it" (ʿAṭṭār 1993: 132). The Sīmurgh then reveals to them the secret of the unity and plurality of all beings. "The sun of my majesty is a mirror," he tells them. "He who sees himself therein sees his soul and his body, and sees them completely. Since you have come as thirty birds, *sī-murgh*, you will see thirty birds in this mirror. If forty or fifty were to come, it would be the same" (ibid.). The birds then pass away, surrendering themselves completely to contemplation of the Sīmurgh.

What ʿAṭṭār gives us here, in effect, is Neoplatonism made simple. An essential feature of the Neoplatonic system inaugurated by Plotinus in the third century was the pattern of emanation and return. The source of all being is the unknowable and unnameable One, a being defined by absolute unity and transcendence. From this ineffable One emanate successive spheres of being, mirroring the qualities of the One and characterized by increasing degrees of multiplicity, descending, finally, to the sphere of the material world. Just as all being emanates from the source of being, however, so also all is drawn back to that source. The cosmos is characterized by a cycle of emanation and return and the basic human quest is to accomplish this return; to free the soul from captivity to the illusions of the material world, thus achieving interior knowledge, *gnosis*, of the soul's unity with the One. As Christians had already discovered, Neoplatonism was the perfect philosophy for mystics.

Stages on the Path

Ṣūfīsm, then, aims to map out the spiritual journey of the soul on its return to the One. And because the ṣūfīs themselves were preoccupied with the interior life, we will begin not with their life in the world (that is, the historical development of ṣūfīsm), but with their world of ideas. Ṣūfī writers agreed, first of all, that the journey of the soul could be broken down into identifiable stages. ʿAṭṭār's seven valleys present an abridged version; most ṣūfī masters break the journey into many more stages. Many also distinguish between stations

Figure 12.1 Ṣūfī disciples in ecstasy, dancing and collapsing before six shaykhs (opaque watercolor, 1650/5). Photo: British Library, London, UK/© British Library Board. All Rights Reserved/The Bridgeman Art Library

(maqāmāt), which the ṣūfī arrives at through discipline and effort, and states (aḥwāl), which are a pure gift of God's grace and cannot be manufactured by human effort.

One of the few points of near-unanimity among those who map out the mystic quest is that the first stage is repentance. The agreement is not limited to Muslims – the seventh-century Nestorian Christian mystic Isaac of Nineveh concurs (Baldick 1989: 17). Repentance in this case does not mean merely turning from sin, however, but also turning away from the life of the material world in order to wholeheartedly pursue the spiritual path. After the ṣūfī has turned from the world and entered on the mystic path, the eleventh-century ṣūfī systematizer, al-Qushayrī (d. 1074), enumerates a total of forty-two subsequent stations and states. Among the most interesting are the following:

Mujāhada (struggle, a variation on jihād). A tradition of the Prophet distinguished between the greater jihād, the struggle of the soul, and the lesser jihād, physical warfare. For ṣūfīs, the greater jihād was striving in the spiritual quest: "Striving is essentially weaning the soul of its habitual practices and compelling it to oppose its passions at all times" (Qushayrī 1990: 14).

Zuhd (ascetic renunciation). The spiritual pilgrim must put aside even permissible pleasures in order to pursue the path single-mindedly.

Samt (silence). The mystic must learn to control his tongue in a literal sense and also metaphorically, to silently accept God's will: "There are two types of silence: outer silence and silence of the heart and mind. The heart of one who trusts completely in God is silent, not demanding any means for living. The gnostic's heart is silent in the face of the divine decree through the attribute of harmony" (Qushayrī 1990: 49).

Tawakkul (trust). Absolute contentment with what God provides and serenity in the face of privation: "[Tawakkul] is that anxious desire for the things of the world should not appear to you, despite the severity of your need for them, and that you should always remain truly content with God, despite your dependence on those things" (Qushayrī 1990: 116).

'Ubūdīya (servanthood). The first of the "states," in which the ṣūfī experiences a sense of complete subjection to his Lord: "Servitude is abandoning personal choice in the face of divine fate." It is intermediate between worship and adoration: "One who does not begrudge God his soul is in the state of worship, one who does not begrudge God his heart is in the state of servitude, and one who does not begrudge God his spirit is in the state of adoration" (Qushayrī 1990: 170).

Irāda (desire). Personal desire is overwhelmed and replaced by desire for God: "The murīd never slackens in his desire, day or night. He strives outwardly, while inwardly he suffers." According to an early ṣūfī, "Desire is painful rapture in the inner heart, a sting in the heart, a violent passion in the senses, an anxious desire in the inward being, fires burning in the hearts" (Qushayrī 1990: 177).

Dhikr (remembrance). The experience of constant awareness of God. "[Dhikr] is the very foundation of this path. No one reaches God save by continual remembrance of Him. There are two kinds of remembrance: that of the tongue and that of the heart. The servant attains perpetual remembrance of the heart by making vocal remembrance" (Qushayrī 1990: 207).

Wilāya (friendship with God; sainthood). The ṣūfī who has given himself entirely over to God and is granted protection by God from major sins and the performance of miraculous deeds (Qushayrī 1990: 268–74).

Maʿrifa (mystic knowledge). Knowledge which enters the heart directly from God. "[Maʿrifa is] the attribute of one who knows God (may he be exalted) by His names and attributes and is truthful toward God by his deeds, who then purifies himself of base qualities and defects, who stands long at the door, and who withdraws his heart continually (from worldly matters). Then he enjoys a goodly nearness to God, who verifies him as true in all his states. The temptations of his soul cease, and he does not incline his heart to any thought that would incite him to other-than-God" (Qushayrī 1990: 316–17).

Maḥabba (love). The response of the mystic to the love of God: "[Maḥabba is a] state experienced in the heart, too subtle for words. This state brings him to glorify God and to try to gain His pleasure. He has little patience in separation from Him, feels an urgent longing for Him, finds no comfort in anything other than Him, and experiences intimacy in his heart by making continual remembrance of Him" (Qushayrī 1990: 327–8).

Shawq (yearning; passionate longing). "Longing is the state of commotion in the heart hoping for meeting the Beloved" (Qushayrī 1990: 343).

As this list demonstrates, the purpose of the enumeration of stations and states is partly didactic, prescribing a path of discipline for the novice ṣūfī, and partly descriptive of the psychology of mysticism. The great ṣūfī writers excel in the field of spiritual psychology, in fact, and they stand among the great masters in the field. Not surprisingly the results are rather subjective and the lists vary. What is perhaps more worth noting is that they do agree on a surprising number of points, demonstrating that ṣūfīs were working within an established mystical tradition and not working from scratch. All agree, for instance, that the ṣūfī must pass through a number of difficult stages, finally reaching, at the culmination of the quest, the experiences of friendship with God, spiritual knowledge (maʿrifa or gnosis), and passionate yearning (shawq). We will return to the thorny problem of describing the destination of the quest, but first a more practical question: how is one to advance along the path?

The Spiritual Master

The first requirement for spiritual progress is a spiritual guide, along the lines of the Hoopoe bird in ʿAṭṭār's parable. There is some disagreement among ṣūfī teachers about whether a human guide is indispensable. Qushayrī, on the one hand, is clearly afraid of amateurs getting out of hand and is therefore adamant that each initiate must have a qualified guide. The great ṣūfī adepts, on the other hand, often claim to be beyond the need of human guidance. Ibn al-ʿArabī, for instance, claims to have been initiated into the spiritual path by Khidr, a mysterious Qur'ānic personality. To make such a claim requires a rather high view of one's spiritual prowess, however, and merely confirms the normal expectation that the ordinary ṣūfī needs a teacher. There was some flexibility to the pattern. The relationship between guide and disciple can, for instance, be mediated through visions. The aspiring ṣūfī may be led to a particular shaykh through a dream, and in many cases will claim to receive guidance through visions. (This pattern of master–disciple communication through dreams is not just a thing of the past; such patterns have been well documented in modern ṣūfī practice.) This, of course, allows for a wide range of long-distance educational opportunities for ṣūfī students, and even allows them the benefit of consulting long-dead ṣūfī masters.

The prevailing pattern was for the ṣūfī to attach himself to a living teacher in such a way that the relationship of master (pīr) and disciple (murīd) becomes a microcosm of the spiritual quest. Thus the disciple gives absolute obedience to the shaykh or pīr, who stands in the place of the Prophet, and ultimately the place of God. The expectation of obedience can extend even to apparently irrational or unlawful activities. According to a story told by al-Qushayrī, a young man was once instructed by a famous shaykh to violate his fast by joining with the shaykh in a meal. The man refused, and he subsequently fell out of God's favor and ended up a thief (Hoffman 1995: 142–3). The lesson is clear. The shaykh, given his superior knowledge, knows what is best, and disobedience to a master is dangerous. It is not uncommon for the shaykh to command his disciples with regard to employment or marriage.

Besides obedience, the disciple should also cultivate love for the shaykh, for the human love of the disciple for his guide becomes a practice ground for the cultivation of love for the Lord. The end result of the relationship is described as "passing away" into the shaykh (fanāʿ fī'l-shaykh), a state in which the disciple develops such an attachment to his master that he loses all sense of independent identity. Such absolute devotion to a master is essential for spiritual progress.

Ṣūfī Brotherhoods

The justification for the absolute authority of the shaykh is simple. Each guide–disciple relationship is but one link in a long chain of spiritual authority that is anchored in the Prophet Muhammad. Just as a chain of reliable scholars passed along exoteric knowledge by means of ḥadīth reports, so also the hidden wisdom of the ṣūfī path is passed on in an unbroken chain (silsila) or, rather, numerous different unbroken chains. Each ṣūfī has a spiritual lineage, traced first of all to the founder of his or her particular "path" (ṭarīqa) of ṣūfīsm, and then through that founder back to Muhammad. This means that Muhammad is the ultimate source of ṣūfī wisdom, and the definitive model of ṣūfī practice. Muhammad's ascent into heaven served as a particularly rich model for ṣūfīs, who saw in it a parable of their own mystical journey.

The idea of spiritual lineages also provides a convenient framework within which to place the growth of ṭarīqas or "brotherhoods." We will discuss the historical growth of these institutions below, but here it is important to note that ṣūfī institutions were not somehow a corruption of pure mysticism, but fit perfectly within the logic of the larger ṣūfī system. The members of each brotherhood saw themselves as bound to the authority of a particular founding figure. The ṭarīqas are therefore named after their founders, and initiates see themselves as preserving and transmitting their master's teachings. While the lineages might be suspect from a historian's perspective (many of the putative founders of ṭarīqas didn't found much of anything), the silsila provides a chain with which to link the members of a ṭarīqa together in allegiance to a common body of teaching and practice – a chain which ultimately reaches back to the Prophet himself.

Ṣūfī Ritual

Allegiance to the ṭarīqa is focused in particular on distinctive ritual practices. The basic discipline required of the ṣūfī disciple is the performance of wird (pl. awrād), set recitations which include prayers of penitence, prayers of blessing on the Prophet, and, most importantly, formulas for dhikr, the remembrance of God. For al-Qushayrī, dhikr is the pillar of ṣūfism. Justification for the practice of dhikr is found in the Qur'ān, which instructs believers to "remember God often" (33:40) and assures them that "the remembrance of God makes the heart calm" (13:28). For ṣūfīs, obedience to this Qur'ānic mandate became highly structured and disciplined, requiring the initiation and guidance of a shaykh. Al-Hujwīrī gives the following account of one ṣūfī's training in dhikr:

> Sahl [al-Tustarī] said to one of his disciples: Strive to say continuously for one day: "O Allāh! O Allāh! O Allāh!" and do the same the next day and the day after that – until he became habituated to saying those words. Then he bade him to repeat them at night also until they became so familiar that he uttered them even during his sleep. Then he said: "Do not repeat them any more, but let all your faculties be engrossed in remembering God!" The disciple did this, until he became absorbed in the thought of God. One day, when he was in his house, a piece of wood fell on his head and broke it. The drops of blood which trickled to the ground bore the legend, "Allāh! Allāh! Allāh!" (Nicholson 1959: 195)

As this description illustrates, dhikr can be performed aloud or in silence, although many ṣūfī teachers consider silent dhikr the superior form. The aim is that the remembrance of God should permeate the whole being so that all but God is forgotten, even the dhikr itself. Dhikr also often incorporates particular patterns of breath control and bodily movement.

Ideally, dhikr is unceasing and thus necessarily an individual practice, but it can also be performed with others in small groups or in large public gatherings. Group dhikr naturally requires more defined liturgical and ritual forms than individual dhikr, including a particular progression of recitations, the use of chanting techniques, stylized body movements, and a leader. One justification for group dhikr is that the synchronization of recitations and movement expresses a unity among the participants that points toward the unity of all souls in God. The particular bodily movements used in dhikr vary widely from order to order, but often provide a serious physical workout, leaving participants exhausted. The "whirling dervishes" of the Mevlevī order, for example, gyrate in a highly choreographed dance centered on the shaykh – a dance which depicts Mevlevī cosmology. Some Naqshbandīs whip their heads from side to side in time with the chanting of the two syllables of the name of God, "Al-lāh." Many dhikr performances culminate with some participants entering a trance in which they abandon ordinary bodily control. As a result of the popularity and accompanying commoditization of ṣūfīsm in the West, opportunities to observe dhikr performances have become abundant. Readers who wish to observe dhikr for themselves should keep their eyes open for commercial performances in their area, or ask their librarian about a film version. A particularly useful documentary, *I am a Sufi, I am a Muslim,* provides stunning visual images of dhikr ceremonies in Pakistan, Turkey, and Macedonia.

Ṣūfīs have differed over whether music should be allowed or encouraged as an aid to dhikr. The debate over samāʿ, "listening," is closely connected with the question of the general permissibility of singing in Islamic law. Although anti-music voices have been strong and persistent, the overall result of the long debate has been tolerance of music. One significant exception is the Naqshbandiyya order, one of the most widespread of the ṭarīqas and one of the most scrupulously "sober," which prohibits music. In many ṣūfī orders, however, music has become inseparable from dhikr. Consequently, indigenous musical traditions in many parts of the Islamic world, notably the Qawwālī tradition in the Indian subcontinent, are closely tied in with ṣūfīsm.

The question of the permissibility of music is intimately tied to questions about the unrestrained ecstasy that dhikr may bring on. Simply put, the problem is that "states" of mystical experience are supposed to be entirely the work of God, so that theoretically the ṣūfī can do nothing to manufacture such experiences. Group dhikr, however, particularly in its use of music and dance, seems calculated to encourage such states because participants will feel pressure to perform. More cautious ṣūfīs have therefore argued that it is wrong even to consciously will to move one's body in dhikr. The only allowable movement is compelled by a "state" given by God. Others disagree, countering that

Figure 12.2 The Friday dhikr of the Sammāniyya ṣūfī ṭarīqa in Omdurman, Sudan. Photo: © Michael Freeman/Corbis

imitating ecstasy is a fine way to bring on real ecstasy, and should therefore not be frowned upon. Either way, the danger of encouraging fraudulent experiences seemed very real to the more cautious among ṣūfī writers. The emotional effect of music in dhikr, and the conformity encouraged by bodily movement, make it difficult to tell who among the participants is experiencing advanced stages of mystic ecstasy and who is simply enjoying some strenuous aerobic exercise.

In addition to a particular system of dhikr, each order preserves a body of teaching. Much of this teaching is communicated anecdotally, and stories of earlier ṣūfīs form a significant part of ṣūfī literature. These stories function, in effect, as a supplement to the systematic exposition of ṣūfī doctrine, and they are exemplary and didactic in purpose. In fact the stories of early saints are similar in function to ṣūfī parables. They serve to illustrate and elucidate various stages of the mystic path, and they are calculated to motivate and inspire readers to greater devotion. Partly for this reason it may be a mistake to approach the stories of the early ṣūfīs like Ḥasan al-Basrī, Rābiʿa, or Dhū'l Nūn for what they can tell us about the historical development of ṣūfīsm, a topic we will have more to say about below. These stories have much more to tell us about what the authors of the later manuals in which they were included thought important.

A spiritual guide, a well-trodden path, and a system of ritual – these are the ṣūfī's chief means of help in advancing through the difficult valleys of the mystic quest. In practice, of course, such means are prone to become their own ends. A sociological analysis of ṣūfī practice could end here, for the structure of authority, community, and ritual in ṣūfī ṭarīqas offers the individual a coherent sense of purpose and place in the cosmos. Ṣūfī theory, however, seems to promise a spiritual and transcendent goal in relation to which the guide–disciple relationship, the practice of dhikr, and the various disciplines are merely instrumental.

The Destination

The goal of the mystic path is not easily described. Three overlapping concepts usually come into play in discussions of the highest levels of mystical experience: mystic knowledge, love, and "passing away." Together, these three interlocking ideas seem to encompass the major goals of the ṣūfī quest. The first, maʿrifa, or gnosis, is an apprehension of the divine unity in such a way that awareness of self is lost in awareness of God. According to al-Qushayrī, the mystic has reached a state of maʿrifa when "the temptations of his soul stop, and he does not incline his heart to any thought that would incite him to other-than-God . . . when he is sure in every glance of Him of his return to Him, and when God inspires him by making him aware of His secrets concerning his destiny" (Qushayrī 1990: 317). In a state of maʿrifa, the ṣūfī knows nothing but God, and is estranged from self. Maʿrifa is the ṣūfī counterpart to ordinary knowledge, ʿilm, but is far superior to it because it involves apprehension of reality in its totality. "Maʿrifa," according to a Sūfī saying, "is the gnostic's mirror. When he gazes in it, his Master is shown" (ibid. 319).

Love is the emotive counterpart to maʿrifa, reflecting the heart's desire for continued and increasing experience of God. In a state of love, according to al-Qushayrī, the mystic "has little patience in separation from Him, feels an urgent longing for Him, finds no comfort in anything other than Him, and experiences intimacy in his heart by making continual remembrance of Him" (Qushayrī 1990: 328). Some mystics separate out a further manifestation of love, shawq, or intense longing, "a state of commotion in the heart hoping for meeting the Beloved," in which the ṣūfī longs with all his being for God. This is a state in which, in words attributed to the early Egyptian Ṣūfī, Dhū'l Nūn, "fear of Hell fire, in comparison with the fear of being parted from the beloved, is like a drop of water cast into the mightiest ocean" (Schimmel 1975: 131).

The endpoint of both ma'rifa and love, encompassing them both, is fanā', the complete dissolution of the individual ego in God. Fanā' is a dying before death, a "passing away" of the individual self and a complete identification with the Divine Unity. It is not usually classified among the "states," but is in a sense a step beyond them, the final goal of the spiritual journey. Disturbed by the implications of this "passing away," and perhaps faced with the uncomfortable reality that those who claimed to have passed away seemed not to have gone very far, some sober ṣūfīs added a further stage, baqā', in which the mystic, having been annihilated and thus transformed, returns to ordinary existence to "continue" in God.

The attainment of these mountaintops of mystic experience is naturally marked by a certain euphoria, and this euphoria is, in turn, usually associated with the performance of dhikr. Thus the "ecstasy" of dhikr and the highest stages of the mystic quest come together. It is at this point that the most advanced ṣūfīs are most likely to be misunderstood by ordinary folk and most prone to find themselves in trouble with the law. In particular, the ṣūfī adept's complete identification with the One Reality of the universe may lead him or her to say or do things which, to the ordinary believer, may appear heretical or blasphemous. Ṣūfī poets aptly associate this state with drunkenness, and according to some, the God-intoxicated mystic cannot be held responsible for his words and actions because whatever he does or says in his "drunken" state does not proceed from his own will. Statements made in this state are called shaṭḥ, and the most famous are those that seem to claim divinity. The ṣūfī Abū Yazīd al-Bisṭamī's cry of "Glory be to Me!" and the martyr al-Ḥallāj's "I am the Truth!" are the most famous examples. From the perspective of ṣūfī apologists such statements are not blasphemous, but reflect the apprehension of a deeper level of reality than the ordinary believer has the capacity to comprehend. Thus when the ṣūfī al-Ḥallāj uttered apparent blasphemies, he was, according to one apologist, like a pearl diver "drowned in the limitless ocean of eternity, pure ecstasy overcame him. He entered into that sea with the quality of creaturehood, and he departed with the character of lordship. From the depth of that ocean he brought forth the pearls of everlastingness." It is easy enough to sympathize with these ṣūfī claims from the safety of distance, but perhaps we can also appreciate how the claim to be above the law, especially the law of God, was bound to chafe. The conflict came to a head in the famous trial and execution of the great mystic, al-Ḥallāj, which we will return to below.

Ṣūfī Cosmology

So far we have been describing the spiritual quest from the perspective of existential experience, adopting the perspective of the pilgrim on the ground.

There were plenty of ṣūfī writers, however, who made an effort to take a bird's-eye view, placing the spiritual quest in the context of a larger plan of the cosmos. Ṣūfī cosmology was treated most elaborately by a thirteenth-century genius, Ibn al-ʿArabī (d. 1240), whose ideas dominated ṣūfī cosmology after him, and who brought together the main intellectual currents of ṣūfism before him. I will use his system as the basis for my outline here, with an obligatory caution. His system is inordinately complex, and even those who have spent their lives studying his writings seldom claim to understand him. What follows will therefore be no more than an oversimplified caricature of his ideas.

Neoplatonism provided the basic framework for Ibn al-ʿArabī's cosmology. The system begins, of course, with God: Divinity in its essence is absolute Unity, unchanging, utterly transcendent. The world, by contrast, is characterized by multiplicity and constant change. The problem, then, is to understand the relation of God and the world, the One and the many. The generic Neoplatonic solution was to posit a series of "emanations," usually given the label "intellects," by which the divine essence was manifested. The emanations derive from the divine essence and their qualities are implicit in the essence of God. They are, in fact, God's own self-disclosure – mirrors in which God contemplates himself. Thus God and the world, the One and the many, are two sides to the same coin.

Into this Neoplatonic structure, Ibn al-ʿArabī placed Muhammad, but not the Muhammad of seventh-century Arabia, or even Muhammad the model mystic and ultimate initiator of the ṣūfī path whom we met above. Ibn al-ʿArabī's Muhammad is cosmic and pre-existent, the point of connection between the absolute and unknowable One and creation. Ibn al-ʿArabī thus identified Muhammad with the active intellect of Neoplatonism, an eternal emanation of God, and the mediator of all subsequent creation. Muhammad is the means by which the inaccessible God can be known, in accordance with a famous tradition: "I was a hidden treasure and I wanted to be known; therefore I created the world." As the agent of all later creation Muhammad occupied a place akin to that of the pre-existent Logos in the New Testament. Three titles sum up the place of Muhammad in Ibn al-ʿArabī's thought: he is the ultimate reality (haqīqat al-haqā'iq), the membrane (barzakh) between the creator and the creation, and the Perfect Man (al-insān al-kāmil).

Ṣūfīs developed these ideas with rich and colorful imagery, focused especially on the theme of light. The idea of the "light of Muhammad" was developed before Ibn al-ʿArabī, especially in the thought of Sahl al-Tustarī (d. 896). Even earlier Muslims had seen references to Muhammad in the famous "light verse" of the Qur'ān:

> God is the Light of the heavens and the earth; the likeness of His light is as a niche wherein is a lamp – the lamp in a glass, the glass as if it were a glittering star – kindled from a Blessed Tree, an olive tree that is neither of the East nor

> of the West, whose oil well nigh would shine, even if no fire touched it: Light upon light; God guides to His Light whom He will. (24:35)

The earliest Qur'ān commentators saw the lamp in this verse as Muhammad, through whom the light was manifested in the world. Al-Tustarī and Ibn al-ʿArabī took this idea and combined it with the idea of the pre-existent universal intellect so that, according to al-Tustarī, "When God willed to create Muhammad, he made appear a light from His light. When it reached the veil of the Majesty it bowed in prostration before God. God created from its prostration a mighty column like crystal glass of light that was outwardly and inwardly translucent" (Bowering 1980: 49–50).

In the work of poets inspired by such ideas Muhammad becomes the primordial light of lights, embodiment of the light of God, the manifestation of God, the "pupil in the eye of the world," the first principle of creation. This poetic record of praise for the Prophet has been brought together and brilliantly summarized by Annemarie Schimmel in *And Muhammad is His Messenger* (1985). The tradition culminates in ʿAbd al-Karīm al-Jīlī, the fourteenth-century interpreter of Ibn al-ʿArabī, and the following is Reynold Nicholson's translation of al-Jīlī's ode to the Prophet.

> O Center of the compass! O inmost ground of the truth!
> O pivot of necessity and contingency!
> O eye of the entire circle of existence! O point of the
> Koran and the Furqān!
> O perfect one, and perfecter of the most perfect, who
> has been beautified by the majesty of God the Merciful!
> Thou art the Pole [Quṭb] of the most wondrous things.
> The sphere of perfection in its solitude turns on thee.
> Thou art transcendent, nay thou art immanent, nay thine is
> all that is known and unknown, everlasting and perishable.
> Thine in reality is Being and not-being; nadir and
> zenith are thy two garments.
> Thou art both the light and its opposite, nay but thou
> art only darkness to a Gnostic that is dazed.
>
> (Nicholson 1921: 86–7)

Such elevation of Muhammad to the level of the "Perfect Man" by Ibn al-ʿArabī, al-Jīlī, and subsequent ṣūfīs was not limited to a small band of extreme mystics. Rather, these ideas came to be generally accepted and had an enormous impact on Islamic piety, reflected especially in poetic and devotional expressions of veneration of the Prophet, as Schimmel (1985) has shown. This image of the cosmic Muhammad dominated Muslim attitudes toward the Prophet from the thirteenth century on.

As it turned out, however, the historical Muhammad was not the only manifestation of the Perfect Man. The cosmic Muhammad may be the archetype, the ultimate reality by which God was manifested, but it is quite possible for others to share in that reality. Al-Jīlī's expression of the idea is rather jolting in its directness:

> The Perfect Man is the Quṭb [axis] on which the spheres of existence revolve from first to last, and since things came into being he is One for ever and ever. He has various guises and appears in diverse bodily tabernacles: in respect of some of these his name is given to him, while in respect of others it is not given to him. His own original name is Mohammed, his name of honor Abū'l Qāsim, his description Abdullah, and his title, Shamsu'ddīn. In every age he bears a name suitable to his guise [libās] in that age. I once met him in the form of my Shaykh, Sharafu'ddīn Ismā'īl al-Jabartī, but I did not know that he [the Shaykh] was the Prophet, although I knew that he [the Prophet] was the Shaykh . . . The real meaning of this matter is that the Prophet has the power of assuming every form . . . Thus, when he appeared in the form of Shiblī, Shiblī said to his disciple, "Bear witness that I am the Apostle of God"; and the disciple, being one of the illuminated, recognized the Prophet and said, "I bear witness that thou art the Apostle of God." No objection can be taken to this: it is like what happens when a dreamer sees someone in the form of another . . . if you perceive mystically that the ḥaqīqa of Mohammed is displayed in any human form, you must bestow upon the ḥaqīqa of Mohammed the name of that form and regard its owner with no less reverence than you would show to our Lord Mohammed. (Nicholson 1921: 105)

The earthly manifestation of the "idea" of Muhammad is thus the saint, or friend of God (walī; pl. awliyā'), and the cosmic Muhammad can, therefore, be seen as having had numerous expressions – in the prophets, in the saints, and, of course, in the physical Muhammad himself.

The axis of ṣūfī cosmology thus turns out to be the ṣūfīs themselves. In fact, the highest of the saints claim for themselves exactly that title, Quṭb, axis. The Quṭb (there is only one at any given time) is the head of a hierarchy of saints. Because he has experienced oneness with God he is, in effect, infallible, and he is the mediator between the world of humanity and the divine. The Quṭb is thus the axis around which the world turns, and as the self-manifestation of God, he is the very reason that the world came into being. In practical terms, because he is the barzakh, the interface between God and the world, the Quṭb's knowledge is limitless. Ibn al-ʿArabī had no doubt that he occupied this position. He went a step further, in fact, claiming to be the "Seal of the Saints" just as Muhammad was the "Seal of the Prophets" (Chodkiewicz 1993). It has not been lost on Ibn al-ʿArabī's detractors that this idea makes him superior to the Prophet in one respect.

The place of saints in ṣūfī cosmology helps to make sense of some of the more surprising claims of ṣūfīs. It is not at all uncommon, for example, for ṣūfī saints to perform miracles, called karāmāt (signs or graces). Many of these involve claims to supernatural knowledge – knowledge of people's hearts, knowledge of distant events, knowledge of the future, knowledge of languages they have not studied, or knowledge of books they have not read. The logic of such claims is simple. If the saint has truly identified with the ultimate revelation of God, the reality of Muhammad, then he can comprehend the whole universe, and there are no limits to his vision. Other common ṣūfī miracles include healing, banishing evil spirits, and flying (Hoffman 1995: 98–101). Thus the ṣūfī saint becomes a mediator between the ordinary and supernatural worlds, dispensing knowledge and power to his followers. In this way the ṣūfī saint has a foothold in two worlds. It is not always a comfortable position, as the historical experience of ṣūfīs will illustrate.

Ṣūfīsm in History: The Case of al-Ḥallāj

To grasp the major themes and problems in the historical development of ṣūfīsm we can begin with one of the best-known stories from that history, the martyrdom of al-Ḥallāj. Al-Ḥusayn ibn Manṣūr al-Ḥallāj was one of the dominant religious personalities of the early tenth century. In his early years he came under the influence of the great ṣūfī master, Sahl al-Tustarī. Then, after traveling extensively and performing the pilgrimage three times, he finally settled down in Baghdad, where he became famous for his enigmatic statements and bizarre behavior. On one occasion he was observed in the marketplace weeping bitterly and crying out, "Hide me from God, you people! Hide me from God! Hide me from God! He took me from myself and has not given me back" (Kritzeck 1975: 96). His most famously controversial statement is recorded in one of his writings: "If you do not recognize God, at least recognize His signs. I am that sign, I am the Truth [anā'l Ḥaqq], because through the Truth I am truth eternally." On another occasion, when he was interrupted in his devotions by one of his admirers, he said, "I hear people are going about saying I am a saint, and others saying that I am impious. I prefer those who call me impious; and so does God." When his visitor asked why, he replied, "They call me a saint because they respect me; but the others call me impious out of zeal for their religion. A man who is zealous for his religion is dearer to me, and dearer to God also, than a man who venerates a creature" (ibid. 97–8). On other occasions he spoke enigmatically about the inevitability of his execution: "No task is more urgent for the Muslims at this moment than my execution. Realize this, that my death will preserve the sanctions of the Law; he who has offended must undergo them" (ibid. 99).

In 904 the ʿAbbāsid chief qāḍī, Abū ʿUmar, himself a Mālikī, solicited opinions from other jurists about whether al-Ḥallāj's ideas were heretical, with mixed results. The Ẓāhirī Ibn Dāwūd gave his opinion that he should be put to death, but the Shāfiʿī judge, Ibn Surayj, wasn't so sure, for the man's outward piety was clear. Possibly because of Ibn Surayj's caution it was not for another seven years that official action was taken. In 911 a group of al-Ḥallāj's disciples were rounded up on the charge of following someone who claimed divinity. Al-Ḥallāj himself apparently went into hiding, but was captured and carried into Baghdad fastened to the back of a camel while a crier announced his heresy. Strangely enough, the public charge was association with extremist Shīʿī ideas (Ernst 1985: 107). No formal trial took place, but al-Ḥallāj remained locked up in the palace, where he continued to write, for another eleven years.

In 922 opponents of al-Ḥallāj again moved against him, and a formal investigation and trial began. While his enemies searched al-Ḥallāj's writings for evidence of blasphemy, his supporters roused mobs of sympathizers in the streets. The evidence was inconclusive and the charges of blasphemy easily evaded. His enemies were determined, however, and in the end al-Ḥallāj was convicted on the basis of his published views on the pilgrimage:

> If a man wants to go on Pilgrimage and cannot, let him set apart in his house some square construction, to be touched by no unclean thing, and let no one have access to it. When the day of the Pilgrimage rites comes, let him make his circuit round it, and perform all the same ceremonies as he would perform at Mecca . . . This will be a substitute for the Pilgrimage. (Kritzeck 1975: 100)

It made thin evidence, but was sufficient for al-Ḥallāj's nemesis, the Wazīr Ḥāmid, to bully a conviction out of the judge (Ernst 1985: 106–7).

The trial was of dubious legitimacy. Shāfiʿī, Ḥanbalī, and Ḥanafī jurists refused to have any part in it and it was left to the Mālikī qāḍī, Abū ʿUmar, to sign al-Ḥallāj's death warrant under heavy pressure from the Wazīr Ḥāmid. The ʿAbbāsid Caliph al-Muqtadir himself had second thoughts, and when he was suddenly taken with a fever he ordered the execution delayed. The caliph's mother had fallen under al-Ḥallāj's influence and was frantic about the verdict. The Wazīr Ḥāmid was resolute, however; he finally had his way, and the order was given for the execution (Ernst 1985: 107).

The account of al-Ḥallāj's execution is both gruesome and laden with symbolism. The night before his death was filled with passionate prayer, recorded by his disciples:

> Ḥallāj stood up and performed the ordinary Prayer of two bows. After that he fell to repeating the word illusion, illusion, illusion . . . to himself, and so continued till the night was more than half spent. Then for a long while he remained silent. Suddenly he gave a cry: Truth! Truth! And sprang to his feet. He bound his turban, donned his cloak, stretched out his arms, and facing the *qibla*, fell into ecstasy and talked with God. (Kritzeck 1975: 97)

In the morning he is reported to have approached the scaffold laughing. After performing ṣalāt, he prayed:

> These servants who are gathered to slay me, in zeal for Thy religion, longing to win Thy favor, forgive them, Lord, have mercy on them. Surely, if Thou hadst shown them what Thou has shown me, they would never have done what they have done; and hadst Thou kept from me what Thou has kept from them, I should not have suffered this tribulation. Whatsoever Thou wilt do, I praise Thee! Whatsoever Thou dost will, I praise Thee! (Kritzeck 1975: 103)

He was scourged to near-death, his hand was amputated, then his foot. He was then fastened to a scaffold, where he remained, still alive, until nightfall. At that point the caliph gave permission for his beheading, but the executioner considered it too late and left the deed till morning. In the morning he was dragged off the scaffold to be beheaded and uttered his final words: "All who have known ecstasy long for this . . . the loneliness of the Only One . . . alone with the Alone" (Kritzeck 1975: 104).

The great modern scholar of al-Ḥallāj, Louis Massignon, has seen in al-Ḥallāj's death a passion like that of Jesus, and it is easy to see why. The story exudes symbolism, and much of it seems to be deliberately modeled after the Gospel account. But what, exactly, is the lesson that al-Ḥallāj's death is supposed to teach us? The story has often been read as a cautionary tale, illustrating the dangers of the "drunken" ṣūfīsm espoused by al-Ḥallāj and foreshadowing the taming of ṣūfīsm which is often attributed to Abū Ḥāmid al-Ghazālī. Seen this way, the martyrdom of al-Ḥallāj is a watershed event in the ongoing struggle to balance the external demands of Islam with the extremes of ṣūfīsm. Al-Ḥallāj had to die in order to protect the Islamic community from the dangers of unrestrained antinomianism – something that he himself seemed to acknowledge when he called for his own death. After all, what would happen if Muslims were all allowed to perform the pilgrimage in their own homes? How could the Islamic community survive if every man could seek the true interpretation of the law in his own experience? Thus al-Ḥallāj's death seems to symbolize a deep rift between the law and spiritual life, between external and internal, between exoteric and esoteric – a rift that would need to be healed if ṣūfīsm was to find a lasting place in Islam.

This interpretation is not to be lightly dismissed, but it represents not so much a theme in the history of ṣūfīsm as a theme in the mythical construction of that history. In reality there has been no period in history when the institutions of Islamic law and ṣūfīsm have been wholly opposed to one another, except perhaps in the Wahhābī-dominated Saʿūdī state where the best effort was made to erase all traces of ṣūfī influence. Even in the case of al-Ḥallāj himself it is clear that most contemporary Islamic legal scholars were inclined to tolerate his ideas, and there is good reason to believe that he was actually convicted more for political reasons and the suspicion of extremist Shīʿī associations than for his mystical teachings. If al-Ḥallāj's death somehow illustrates the dangers inherent in ṣūfīsm, it is apparent that Muslims failed to learn the lesson. The teachings of Ibn al-ʿArabī and al-Jīlī, described above, are no less extreme than those of al-Ḥallāj, yet they became mainstream.

The theme that al-Ḥallāj's martyrdom best illustrates is not the conflict between Islamic law and the mystical impulse, but rather the self-perceived position of ṣūfīs as the conscience of Islam, forcing self-examination and challenging a religion of externals in sometimes audacious ways. Al-Ḥallāj is, in fact, a sort of living parable of the ṣūfī idea of malāma, deliberately seeking blame in order to challenge conventional morality and force deeper examination (Ernst 1985: 69–70). In the eyes of his interpreters, and perhaps even in his own eyes, al-Ḥallāj was acting a part.

Beginnings to the Tenth Century

Accounts of the early history of ṣūfīsm are filled with such living parables. We read, for example, about how the famous woman mystic of Baṣra, Rābiʿa, refused a marriage proposal from Ḥasan al-Baṣrī because "the tie of marriage applies to those who have being, but here being has disappeared, for myself has been negated and I exist only through Him . . . You must ask my hand of Him, not of me." On another occasion she refused an invitation to go outside on a beautiful spring day because "The contemplation of the Maker preoccupies me, so that I do not care to look upon what He has made." The life of a real woman may or may not be behind such anecdotes, but what we can be certain of is that we are being taught a lesson about a particular stage on the mystic path. Similarly, when we read anecdotes or statements from Abū Yazīd al-Bisṭāmī or Dhū'l Nūn we are reading, in large part, didactic illustrations put to use in ṣūfī manuals.

Consequently, it is difficult to say a lot about the early development of ṣūfīsm with much certainty. The etymology of the term "ṣūfī" itself gives us our best clue about the roots of the movement. "Ṣūf" is an Arabic word for wool, and in Nestorian Christianity wool was associated with asceticism and deliberate poverty. The most convincing explanation of the origin of the term is that the early Islamic mystics were seen as part of this older tradition of "wool wearers." (An intriguing but less plausible suggestion is that "ṣūfī" is a derivation of the Greek *sophos*, "wise," an indication of the Neoplatonic cast of Near Eastern mystical thought; an even more intriguing idea is that the term is a deliberate pun on the two words.) In any case, Christian ascetic connections are clear in other ṣūfī terms and practices, and the connection with the wool clothing of Christian monks therefore seems the most probable origin of the term (Baldick 1989: 15–24).

We can also see hints of a connection with Syrian Christian mysticism in some of the basic ideas and vocabulary of ṣūfīsm. Julian Baldick's iconoclastic book *Mystical Islam* (1989) offers a convenient summary of the evidence, much of it inferential. The remembrance of God, dhikr Allāh, which is the core of ṣūfī ritual practice is a familiar motif in Syrian Christianity, where the practice is especially connected with the repetition of the Jesus prayer. Calling down blame on oneself, inviting ridicule by socially unacceptable behavior, by acting mad or pretending to engage in immoral behavior, is another motif shared with Christian asceticism. The stages on the journey to spiritual fulfillment are anticipated in the teachings of the seventh-century Nestorian mystic Isaac of Nineveh, whose description of the path follows a familiar ṣūfī pattern, beginning with the stage of repentance and ending with the experience of special "graces" or gifts from God. The association of mysticism with poverty is again a common motif in Near Eastern Christianity (Baldick 1989: 15–24). We need not go so far as Baldick in reducing early ṣūfīsm to a branch of Christian asceticism in order to see in these patterns the shared effects of a common religious environment.

There is no reason to doubt that many of the early "founders" of ṣūfīsm, listed below, made significant contributions to the transmission and growth of mystical ideas among Muslims. It is equally clear that these ideas did not bear fruit in any systematic development of thought that could be called ṣūfīsm by later standards.

Early ascetics and mystics

Abū Dharr al-Ghifārī (d. 653). A companion of the Prophet credited in the tradition with ascetic tendencies, and considered by later ṣūfīs to be the model of the faqīr, embracing poverty to earn the riches of God.

Ḥasan al-Baṣrī (d. 728). A theologian and ṣūfī who preached fear of God and renunciation of the world in preparation for the terrible Day of Judgment. Also credited with upholding a doctrine of free will. Legends of his life are intertwined with stories of Rābiʿa, who often gets the better of him in their exchanges, thus demonstrating the superiority of love over renunciation and fear in the stations of ṣūfīsm.

Rābiʿa al-ʿAdawiyya (d. 801). A famous woman ṣūfī and converted prostitute. Alleged to have introduced an emphasis on love into ṣūfīsm in contrast to Ḥasan al-Baṣri's morose fear. She refused offers of marriage from Ḥasan and engaged in witty exchanges with other ṣūfīs.

Ibrāhīm ibn Adham (d. 776 or 790). A legendary early ascetic with a conversion story suspiciously like that of the Buddha. He left a royal life at Balkh to adopt the ascetic life and found enlightenment.

Al-Ḥārith ibn Asad al-Muḥāsibī (d. 857). A Baghdad theologian who emphasized fear of God and careful observance of religious duties, but opposed ostentatious piety. He developed the Christian mystical theme of sickness of heart.

Dhū'l Nūn al-Miṣrī (d. 859 or 861?). An Egyptian ṣūfī and alchemist, he figures in legends of miracles and magic. He is alleged to have originated the notion of maʿrifa, mystic knowledge.

Abū Yazīd al-Bisṭāmī (d. 874). Credited with numerous "drunken" sayings (shaṭḥ), especially his exclamation, "Glory be to me!" Scholars disagree about the possibility of direct Indian influence on his ideas.

Classical Manuals and the Growth of Ṭarīqas

Only from the late tenth century can we begin to talk with confidence of a coherent tradition of ṣūfīsm. It was from this time that ṣūfī writers began to gather the various ideas and practices among earlier ascetics and mystics into a coherent system. This early ṣūfī literature was marked by the first methodical delineation of "stages" in the mystic quest, and by the systematic collection and organization of ṣūfī "traditions," including both traditions of the Prophet and the sayings of earlier ṣūfīs. One of the earliest manuals is that of Kalābādhī (d. 990 or 995). Among the most influential was that of Qushayrī (d. 1074), on whom I relied heavily in my discussion of the "stations" above. Another famous contemporary of Qushayrī, al-Hujwīrī (d. 1075), also wrote a widely distributed manual of ṣūfīsm.

In the twelfth century we meet the figures who would be credited as the first founders of ṣūfī ṭarīqas, ʿAbd al-Qādir Gīlānī (d. 1166) and ʿAbd al-Qāhir al-Suhrawardī (d. 1168). The brotherhoods that bear their names, with a coherent body of teaching and a consciousness of spiritual genealogy, were not actually formed until the thirteenth century. The logic of the ṭarīqas, centered on the master–disciple relationship, was discussed above. But in addition to the personal tie of master to disciple, the brotherhoods quickly developed institutional manifestations that enabled the transformation of ṣūfīsm into a mass movement. The most important and visible of these institutional manifestations of ṣūfīsm was the ṣūfī "lodge" (*khānqāh* in Persian; *ribāṭ* in Arabic; *tekke* in Turkish). The earliest of these lodges were simply places of hospitality in which travelers and the poor could find food and lodging, and in this embryonic form khānqāhs may have existed as early as the tenth century. With the growth of widespread ṣūfī ṭarīqas, however, the khānqāh became a center of ṣūfī organization and activity.

Major Ṣūfī ṭarīqas

Qādiriyya. Named for ʿAbd al-Qādir al-Gīlanī and widely distributed from Indonesia to North Africa. ʿAbd al-Qādir's tomb in Baghdad is a major

Figure 12.3 Devotees at the shrine of Data Ganj Baksh, the tomb of the ṣūfī saint al-Hujwīrī, in Lahore, Pakistan. Photo: Mike Goldwater/Alamy

place of pilgrimage. In the twentieth century the Qādiriyya became involved in Algerian resistance to French imperial rule.

Suhrawardiyya. Named for ʿAbd al-Qāhir al-Suhrawardī, a disciple of Aḥmad al-Ghazālī. The Suhrawardīs became firmly established in India (now southern Pakistan), especially in the city of Multan, and they continue to be important in contemporary Pakistan. The order is known for strict control of master over disciple and for appreciation of poetry and poetic symbols.

Rifāʿiyya. Named for Aḥmad al-Rifāʿī (d. 1182), and known as the "howling dervishes" after the sound of their dhikr. The order is famous for a variety of strange practices like the eating of snakes, putting heated iron into their mouths, and body-piercing.

Naqshbandiyya. Founded by Bahāʾ al-Dīn Naqshband (d. 1389) of Bukhārā, the Naqshbandī ṭarīqa quickly spread and has become one of the largest and geographically most widely distributed orders, especially in central Asia, the Indian subcontinent, and Turkey. The Naqshbandīs are noted for encouraging silent dhikr, insisting on strict observance of Sharīʿa, and encouraging engagement in the world and in political life. A particularly influential branch of the brotherhood, the reformist "mujaddidī"

Figure 12.4 Rembrandt's depiction of the founders of four great ṣūfī orders, the Qādirī, Suhrawardī, Chishtī, and Naqshbandī orders. Photo: © The Trustees of the British Museum

Naqshbandīs, was founded by an important sixteenth-century Indian ṣūfī, Shaykh Aḥmad Sirhindī, whom we will encounter again in chapter 14.

Mevleviyya. Named for the title Mevlānā (Turkish for "our master"; the Arabic equivalent is Mawlānā) applied to the celebrated Turkish ṣūfī and poet Jalāl al-Dīn Rūmī (d. 1273). The Mevlevīs became famous in the West as the "whirling dervishes" because of their distinctive performance of dhikr. The order also became influential in the Ottoman empire's inner circles of power.

Bektashiyya. Founded around 1300 and closely associated with the professional army of the Ottoman empire, the Janissaries. The Bektashīs
practiced secret dhikr, and seem to display marked Christian and Shī'ī
influences and a number of unusual beliefs and rituals, like the sharing
of a sacramental meal of bread and wine. Modern Bektashīs have
monasteries very similar to their Christian counterparts in the Balkans.

Chishtiyya. Named for a village in Iran, the order was founded in the
thirteenth century and flourished in India where it appealed especially
at a popular level. It became the most important order in the subcontinent, but is virtually unknown elsewhere. A significant movement
of conversion to Islam among Indians is attributed to the work of Chishtī
saints of the thirteenth century who eschewed involvement with politics
and adopted the image of the Indian holy man.

The Pervasiveness of Ṣūfīsm

From the thirteenth through the nineteenth centuries the ṣūfī order and the
ṣūfī lodge were ubiquitous throughout the Islamic world. In the sixteenth
and seventeenth centuries it is not uncommon to find noted theologians and
scholars of Islamic law who have also been initiated into two or three different
ṣūfī orders. The most important legal and theological debates of later medieval
Islam are concerned with issues raised by ṣūfī teaching and practice. This pervasive influence of ṣūfī ideas and institutions in the lives of Muslims would
not be seriously challenged until the eighteenth century, and there would be
no real serious diminution of the role of ṣūfīsm until the modern period,
when Muslim reformers, anxious for a scapegoat for the apparent weakness of
Islam vis-à-vis the West, focused on ṣūfīsm as the root of passivity and conservatism in Muslim religious culture.

Resources for Further Study

The best general introduction to Islamic mysticism is Annemarie Schimmel's
Mystical Dimensions of Islam (1975). For a recent update, see Alexander Knysh,
Islamic Mysticism: A Short History (2000). Julian Baldick offers an iconoclastic
(and refreshing) rejoinder to the fawning appreciation which characterizes many
other treatments of ṣūfīsm in his *Mystical Islam* (1989). Older surveys still worth
a look include Arthur J. Arberry, *Sufism* (1950), Duncan B. MacDonald,
The Religious Attitude and Life in Islam (1909), and Reynold A. Nicholson, *The
Mystics of Islam* (1914). For an introduction to the ṣūfī orders, see J. Spencer
Trimingham, *The Sufi Orders in Islam* (1971).

Translations of classical ṣūfī manuals and hagiographies include R. A. Nicholson's (1970) translation of Hujwīrī, *The Kashf al-Mahjūb*, al-Qushayrī's *Principles of Sufism* (1990), and Farīd al-Dīn ʿAṭṭār, *Muslim Saints and Mystics* (1966). The indispensable source on al-Ḥallāj is Louis Massignon, *The Passion of al-Ḥallāj: Mystic and Martyr of Islam* (1994). For a penetrating study of "drunken" ṣūfīs, including al-Ḥallāj, see Carl Ernst, *Words of Ecstasy in Sufism* (1985).

A number of scholars have made valiant attempts to make sense of Ibn al-ʿArabī and his legacy. For a translation of one of his better-known works, see Ibn al-ʿArabī, *The Bezels of Wisdom* (1980), and for an ambitious attempt to disentangle his ideas, see William Chittick, *The Self-Disclosure of God* (1998). On his doctrine of sainthood, see Michel Chodkiewicz, *Seal of the Saints* (1993), and for the development of the idea of the Perfect Man after him, see R. A. Nicholson, *Studies in Islamic Mysticism* (1921), which includes a study of al-Jīlī's development of the idea. Other works on Ibn al-ʿArabī include Claude Addas, *Quest for the Red Sulphur* (1993) and S. Hirenstein and M. Tiernan, *Muhyiddin Ibn Arabi* (1993). On the wide Neoplatonist influence on Islamic thought, see P. Morewedge, *Neoplatonism and Islamic Thought* (1992), I. R. Netton, *Muslim Neoplatonists* (1982), and Franz Rosenthal, *Greek Philosophy in the Arab World* (1990).

Translations of ṣūfī poetry, especially that of Rumī, are now widely available. Other primary sources in translation include Margaret Smith, *Readings from the Mystics of Islam* (1959) and Michael Sells, *Early Islamic Mysticism: Sufī, Qur'ān, Miraj, Poetic and Theological Writing* (1996). For a survey of the ṣūfī poetic tradition, see Annemarie Schimmel, *As Through a Veil: Mystical Poetry in Islam* (1982).

An important study of contemporary ṣūfīsm which also sheds light on its development is Valerie J. Hoffmann, *Sufism, Mystics, and Saints in Modern Egypt* (1995). On the Naqshbandīs of the subcontinent see Arthur Buehler, *Sufi Heirs of the Prophet* (1998). The impact of modernity on ṣūfī institutions is dealt with in the several articles on ṣūfīsm in Nikkie Keddie, *Scholars, Saints and Sufis* (1972b). Finally, E. H. Waugh, *The Munshidin of Egypt* (1989), introduces one ṣūfī-inspired musical tradition.

PART FOUR

CRISIS AND RENEWAL IN ISLAMIC HISTORY

13

TURKS, CRUSADERS, AND MONGOLS

The Saljūqs

In 1055 the leader of a clan of Turkish nomads, Ṭoghril Beg, marched into Baghdad, delivered the caliph from the clutches of the Shīʿī Būyid family who had controlled the caliphate for a century, and announced himself as the new protector of the caliphate and the savior of Sunnī Islam. During the next century Ṭoghril Beg's clansmen, the Saljūq Turks, acting in the name of the caliph, built and ruled the largest Islamic empire since the high point of the unified ʿAbbāsid caliphate. Alp Arslan, nephew of Ṭoghril Beg, succeeded his uncle and ruled for a decade, 1063–73, and he in turn was succeeded by his son Mālikshāh, who ruled for twenty years, 1073–92. Throughout their combined thirty-year reign the mastermind behind Saljūq policy was the brilliant wazīr, Niẓām al-Mulk, whom we already met in chapter 9 as an enthusiast for Persian political ideas.

The Saljūqs were unlikely world rulers. They originated as a clan from the larger grouping of Oghuz Turks, part of a general movement of Turkish warrior nomads eastward from central Asia. The Saljūqs first entered Iran as mercenaries, hired out to the Sāmānid governors of western Iran. When the Sāmānid dynasty collapsed after 999, the Saljūqs quickly stepped in to fill the gap. In 1040 they decisively defeated their main Turkish rivals, the Ghaznavids, who were driven west into Afghanistan and northern India, where they enriched their own empire by plundering the Punjab. Victory over the Ghaznavids left Khurāsān to the Saljūqs, who based themselves in the city of Nīshāpūr. After their 1055 conquest of Baghdad, the Saljūq empire expanded to include all of the former Būyid territory.

Although the unified Saljūq empire lasted a relatively short time, the Saljūqs' brief period of ascendancy signaled two trends in Islamic history that long outlasted them: the ascendancy of Sunnī Islam and Turkish domination of the political and military order. We will examine each of these trends in turn, beginning with the first.

Al-Ghazālī and the Sunnī Revival

The revival of a Sunnī caliphate and Saljūq patronage of the 'ulamā' sparked a resurgence of Sunnī intellectual life and institutions. The spirit of this Sunnī renaissance is exemplified in the work of the theologian turned mystic Abū Ḥāmid al-Ghazālī (d. 1111) whose autobiography, *Deliverance from Error*, records an exemplary (and schematized) Muslim spiritual and intellectual journey. Al-Ghazālī's journey began with a state of profound doubt and skepticism, a spiritual and intellectual sickness which demanded an urgent search for a cure. He subsequently explores every medicine for doubt that the Islamic intellectual tradition of his time could offer: theology, philosophy, Ismāʿīlī Shīʿīsm, and ṣūfīsm. Theology, he finds, is useful for confirming and reinforcing one's beliefs, but only if one does not question its premises. For those whose doubts are more profound, philosophy promises a method of examining the very foundations of belief, but that promise also turns out to be illusory. The philosophical method can yield impressive results at the level of mathematics or natural science, but when extended to the realm of metaphysics it sinks to the level of speculation. Ismāʿīlī Shīʿīsm offers a tempting way out: since we are patently unable to arrive at any level of certainty through the exercise of reason, it is clear that we need external guidance. Humans, in other words, cannot arrive at the truth without the help of an authoritative teacher, an imām. But how, asks al-Ghazālī, are we to recognize such a teacher? In the end al-Ghazālī finds assurance and satisfaction only in ṣūfīsm (Ghazālī 1953).

Al-Ghazālī's autobiography has often been read as the inspiring spiritual odyssey of a unique and gifted individual. It may be truer to al-Ghazālī's purpose to see it as the reflection of a broader religious consensus – not the journey of an individual, but of an intellectual culture which had tried Muʿtazilite theology, Greek philosophy, and Shīʿīsm, found them all wanting, and finally found its solace in a synthesis of Islamic law, Ashʿarīte dogma, and ṣūfī spirituality.

In any case, al-Ghazālī's efforts to bring the different strands of mainline Muslim intellectual culture together into a coherent whole were not isolated. The Saljūq period was also the age of al-Qushayrī (d. 1074), the author of the most influential of all ṣūfī manuals whom we met in the last chapter, who sought to give ṣūfism a solid grounding in tradition. The career of al-Māwardī (d. 1058), shaper of a mature Sunnī theory of the caliphate, extended into the Saljūq period. Of more long-term significance than such individual achievements, however, was the growth of Islamic institutions. The Saljūq period initiated the age of the madrasa – the Islamic college – as the chief institutional means for the preservation and transmission of knowledge (Makdisi 1981). During this period important madrasas were founded for every major school of law under the patronage of Saljūq rulers and their officials. The most famous of these were the Niẓāmiyya madrasas founded by Niẓām al-Mulk which reflected his Shāfiʿī sympathies. The growth of the madrasa system reflected the establishment of the Sunnī consensus in the broader culture of Islam. The Nizārī Shīʿites continued their violent protest for two centuries more, but the serious Shīʿī bid for political supremacy was over in the central Islamic lands, and from now on Shīʿī Muslims had to accommodate themselves to an environment shaped by Sunnī dominance.

Sunnī dominance came in a package with Turkish military and political dominance, a phenomenon that had begun before the Saljūqs, and that would continue almost uninterrupted until the decline of the Ottoman empire in modern times. Ṭoghril Beg, Alp Arslan, and Mālikshāh were not entirely unique. To the east their Ghaznavid rivals were also Turkish. To the west the Saljūq conquests, particularly the defeat of the Byzantine army at Malazgirt in 1071, had opened the way into Anatolia for Turkmen tribes, leading to the gradual Turkification and Islamization of Asia Minor. A member of the Saljūq family, Sulaymān, founded a principality in Anatolia with its capital at Nicaea, and established a new dynasty, the so-called Saljūqs of Rūm. Consequently, a Saljūq Turkish army was the first military obstacle that the Crusaders met on their march out of Constantinople in 1097. Almost everywhere one looked after the eleventh century, Turks seemed to dominate the military and political order of the Islamic world.

Slave Soldiers

The growth of Turkish power and influence did not come only through conquests. In fact the Saljūqs – who were free Turks – were the exception rather than the rule. The more common paradigm for Turkish rise to power was through the institution of the slave soldier, the ghulām (or specifically in the Egyptian context, the Mamlūk).

The first use of slave soldiers on a large scale seems to have been by the ʿAbbāsid Caliph al-Muʿtaṣim, who bought 3,000 Turkish slaves as the nucleus of a new army. In 836 he also built a new capital, Sāmarrā, to quarter his slave troops. The idea was simple. Slaves, who knew where their bread and butter came from, would have a single focus of loyalty. They were also easy to obtain, since rival Turkish tribes were quite willing to sell off their prisoners, and sometimes their children, for profit. If slaves could be gotten young they could be appropriately educated and indoctrinated. They would thus be immune from the local partisan attachments that could make free troops so dangerous to a ruler. Turks, famous for their prowess as warriors as well as their physical attractiveness, were the most obvious choice for military slaves.

The use of Turkish slave soldiers quickly became fashionable, and the results were predictable. It did not take long for the leaders of the slave troops to discover that their services were indispensable and that they had become the real focus of power. The result was that they set themselves up as the guardians of the rulers they served, or sometimes as independent governors. Aḥmad ibn Ṭūlūn, the son of a slave, anticipated this pattern when in 868 he established his own rule in Egypt, paying only lip service to ʿAbbāsid sovereignty. The founders of the Ghaznavid dynasty in Afghanistan had been slave soldiers of the Sāmānid governors. Slave rulers continued the pattern, recruiting slave soldiers for themselves. The pattern was to become most refined and most successful in Egypt under the most enduring and glorious of the slave dynasties, the Egyptian Mamlūks (ca. 1260–1517), a dynasty we will meet again below.

Thus, through a combined pattern of nomadic migration, military conquest, and slave levies, the Turks became the military ruling class of the Islamic world. By the fourteenth century the historian Ibn Khaldūn saw Turks everywhere, and everywhere he saw them they were in power. Far from finding this distressing, however (they were, after all, his patrons), Ibn Khaldūn considered Turkish power a sign of God's mercy. When Islam was at its most vulnerable (Ibn Khaldūn is thinking of the Mongol threat) God brought the Turks to invigorate and protect it:

> It was by the grace of God, glory be to Him, that He came to the rescue of the True Faith, by reviving its last breath and restoring in Egypt the unity of the Muslims, guarding His order and defending His ramparts. This He did by sending to them, of this Turkish people and out of its mighty and numerous tribes, guardian amirs and devoted defenders who are imported as slaves from the lands of heathendom to the lands of Islam. This status of slavery is indeed a blessing . . . from Divine providence. (Ayalon 1988: 345)

When Ibn Khaldūn counted the Turks a gift of divine providence, he was writing with the clarity of hindsight. During the century following the Saljūq rise to power two separate infidel invasions, one from the west, the other from the northeast, faced the Muslims with the greatest externally induced crisis they had so far met with. The Turks, to Ibn Khaldūn's mind, had been the saviors of Islam in both cases.

The Crusades

In 1096, just four years after the death of Mālikshāh, while the Saljūq leadership was preoccupied in bitter struggles for power and succession, an army of heavily armored Frenchmen landed at Constantinople. From the perspective of European history we know, of course, that the arrival of the Crusaders was the culmination of a series of monumental events in Europe. From a Eurocentric perspective, the Crusades were a crucial turning point in the history of the continent, with enormous ramifications for the influence of the Church, the power of the papacy, and the religious and cultural unity of the continent. This was the first truly pan-European popular movement, and it was the Papal See's first and astonishingly successful public relations campaign.

The Muslims knew nothing of the motives of the Crusaders or the complex historical forces at work in Europe, nor would they likely have cared. From the Muslim perspective the Crusaders were simply *Faranj*, Franks, a designation that conveniently conveyed the sense of infidel, barbarian, and northern European in a single word. To the Muslims, the Franks were doing just what one would expect infidels and Christians to do – fighting Muslims and trying to seize Muslim territory. This was, after all, exactly what the Muslims had been doing to the Byzantine Christians for some centuries now. Not to put too fine a point on it, the medieval Muslims and the Crusaders had similar enough views of the world to understand each other well, and they are for that reason equally mystifying to modern people.

But even if the Franks were doing what was, from a Muslim perspective, expected of them, they still managed to come across as inordinately barbaric. In 1097 a Crusader army defeated a Turkish army at Nicaea. From there the Crusaders took a detour to Edessa, where they set up a fairly long-lasting kingdom, and then proceeded to take Antioch in 1098. In the winter of that year a Crusader army captured the Syrian city of Ma'arrat al-Nu'mān and began to earn a reputation for terror and treachery by promising amnesty then proceeding to massacre the population. The Crusader conquest of Jerusalem in July of 1099 cemented that reputation. The Crusaders massacred the residents of Jerusalem indiscriminately. Jews who took refuge in their synagogue were burnt alive.

After defeating a Saljūq army at Nicaea the Crusaders met with only local resistance. They had come, it turned out, at an exceptionally opportune time. The Saljūq leadership was concerned with its own conflicts to the east. The Fāṭimids in Egypt had softened the ground with their own invasion of Syria, leading at least one Muslim historian, Ibn al-Athīr, to suggest that they must have been in league with the Franks. The Ismā'īlīs were at the height of their terror-mongering. All in all, one could hardly have chosen a better time to conquer Palestine. The result was the establishment of a series of fairly durable

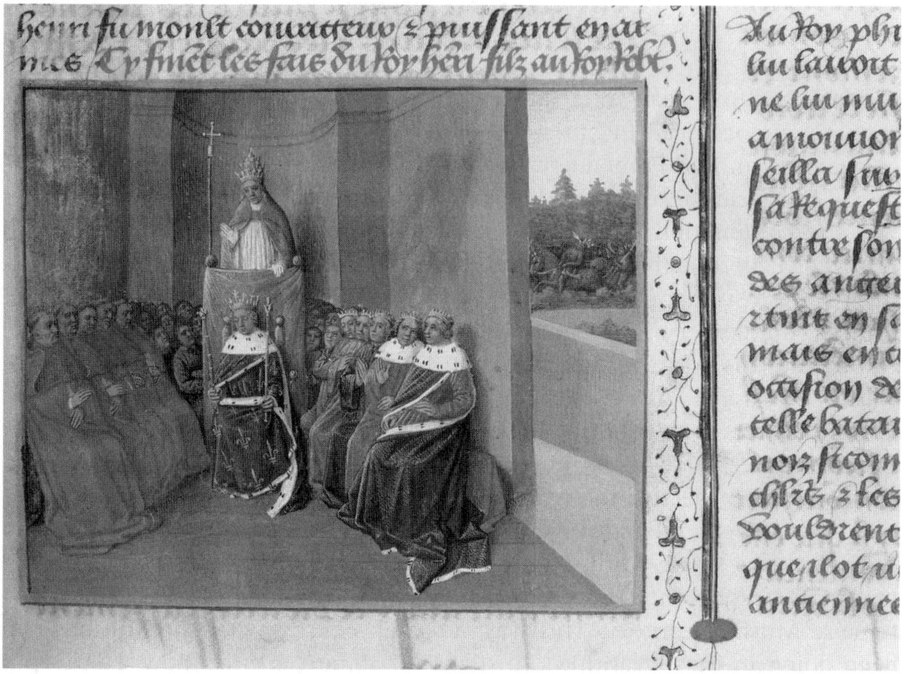

Figure 13.1 Pope Urban II preaching the Crusade at Clermont in the presence of King Philippe I of France (1053–1108) in 1095; from *Les Grandes Chroniques de France* (ca. 1640). Photo: Bibliotheque Nationale, Paris, France/The Bridgeman Art Library

Crusader states in Palestine and Syria, the kingdoms of Jerusalem, of Acre, and of Edessa chief among them.

One might reasonably expect that Muslims would be devastated and horrified by the success of this infidel incursion into the very heart of Muslim territory. In fact, contemporary Muslims seem to have responded with a degree of resignation. We have few contemporary Muslim accounts of the Crusaders, and we are therefore inordinately dependent on one of the most interesting, the memoirs of Usāma ibn Munqidh. Usāma's responses to the Crusaders may be idiosyncratic, but they are nonetheless intriguing for what they may suggest about Muslim responses to the invaders. The excerpts that follow are from Francesco Gabrieli's translation in his *Arab Historians of the Crusades.*

Usāma vacillated between amusement at the boorishness of the Franks and indignation at their barbarity. On the one hand, he expresses respect for their raw courage: "Among the Franks – God damn them! – no quality is more highly esteemed in a man than military prowess" (Gabrieli 1969: 73). On the other hand, he is shocked by their ignorance and barbarism. He describes with irony how a Frankish knight overruled a local doctor, ordering amputation for an abscess on the leg, and brain surgery for a woman with consumption. Both patients died immediately, and the Syrian doctor, a Christian, wryly reported, "I came away having learnt things about medical methods that I never knew before" (ibid. 76–7). His response to Frankish sexual mores is scandalized amusement. He recounts, for example, the report of a bath attendant:

> One day a Frankish knight came in. They do not follow our custom of wearing a cloth round their waist while they are at the baths, and this fellow put out his hand, snatched off my loin cloth and threw it away. He saw at once that I had just recently shaved my pubic hair. "Salīm!" he exclaimed. I came toward him and he pointed to that part of me. "Salīm! It's magnificent. You shall certainly do the same for me!" And he lay down flat on his back. His hair there was as long as his beard. I shaved him, and when he had felt the place with his hand and found it agreeably smooth he said: "Salīm, you must certainly do the same for my Dama." In their language Dama means lady or wife. He sent his valet to fetch his wife, and when they arrived and the valet had brought her in, she lay down on her back, and [he] said to me: "Do to her what you did to me." (Gabrieli 1969: 78)

Other anecdotes indicate how quickly the Crusaders adapted to their new environment. Usāma reports being invited to dine at a retired Crusader's villa where he was given the assurance that the knight never served Frankish food, and never allowed pork into his house. On another occasion he was rescued by veteran Templars from a newcomer, fresh from Europe, who had observed him praying, jumped on him, picked him up, and faced him east, exclaiming, "That is the way to pray." He expresses shock at the ignorance of the man, but he also recounts the profuse apologies of the other knights, who had obviously adapted to a religiously pluralistic environment (Gabrieli 1969: 80).

The boundaries between Crusader and Muslim territory and culture are porous, and Usāma seems to move freely between them. He reports developing a close friendship with at least one Crusader knight, who invited Usāma's son to take a tour of Europe with him. Usāma found the suggestion unthinkable, although he declined politely (Gabrieli 1969: 82–3). On another occasion he was involved in the ransom of prisoners, showing that he moved freely between Muslim and Crusader rulers and castles (ibid. 80–2).

In one of the most telling and poignant anecdotes, Usāma is troubled by the piety of Christian monks because it seems to reflect badly on Muslim piety: "The sight of their piety touched my heart, but at the same time it displeased and saddened me, for I had never seen such zeal and devotion among the Muslims." Subsequently, a friend took him to visit some ṣūfīs, however, and he was reassured: "I gave thanks to almighty God that there were among the Muslims men of even more zealous devotion than those Christian priests" (Gabrieli 1969: 83–4).

This last anecdote is striking because it reveals a rare chink in Usāma's cultural armor. The overwhelming tone of Usāma's account is one of amused superiority. The conclusion can be generalized. In none of the Muslim accounts of the Crusaders do the Franks come across as a serious threat. They are detestable barbarians, boorish infidels, they are in every way inferior to Muslims, but they are in no way a real danger. To the contrary, they fit all too well into the patterns of Syrian life and politics – another set of petty principalities that just happens to be ruled by infidels. The stories of well-adjusted Crusaders assimilating to Muslim practices further reinforce the sense of confidence: if the Crusaders are not driven out of Muslim territory, they will inevitably be absorbed into Islamic culture. The best of them can clearly see the superiority of Islam. The Crusaders are to be despised but hardly to be feared.

Usāma's confidence was well founded. Crusader kingdoms lasted until the late thirteenth century, when the fall of Acre in 1291 effectively put an end to the Crusader era in Palestine. After having lived in Palestine for two centuries the Crusaders left surprisingly little behind other than ruined castles. These are, admittedly, imposing and a boon to the tourist trade, but they are hardly a living legacy. The Crusaders took a good deal back with them in the way of language, culture, and science, but they left little behind other than the historical memory of their venture. The memories of the Crusades were like a time bomb, however, which was destined to go off in the future. At the time, they were a minor irritation, not a real threat at all. A much greater threat was looming, however, and the terror of that threat would be shared by Muslims and Christians alike.

The Mongols

In 1218 the governor of Khwārazm-shāh, a Muslim state centered in present-day Uzbekistan, rounded up a party of 450 Muslim merchants who had come from Mongol territory and had them killed. They were, he was convinced, Mongol spies. The Mongol emperor, Chingiz Khān, dispatched three envoys to demand reparations. The governor, who must have felt either extraordinarily confident or else suicidal, had one of the envoys killed and sent the other two back without their beards, a pointed insult.

The Mongol reprisal, in 1219, was swift, brutal, and virtually unopposed. The ruler of Khwārazm-shāh, 'Alā' al-Dīn Muhammad, abandoned his army and fled. Mongol armies proceeded to pillage and terrorize Transoxania and Khurāsān with impunity. Their motive was not conquest, but simple revenge, and their brutality was staggering and unprecedented. The surrender of the city of Merv in February 1221, recounted by Juvaynī, was typical:

Figure 13.2 Ghenghis Khan. Photo: National Palace Museum, Taipei, Taiwan/ The Bridgeman Art Library

> The Mongols ordered that, apart from four hundred artisans whom they specified and selected from amongst the men and some children, girls and boys, whom they bore off into captivity, the whole population, including the women and children, should be killed, and no one, whether woman or man, be spared. The people of Merv were then distributed among the soldiers and levies, and, in short, to each man was allotted the execution of three or four hundred persons. (Juvaynī 1958: 162)

Then the walls were destroyed, the citadel leveled, and the mosque of Abū Ḥanīfa set on fire. The same happened in Balkh. Nīshāpūr held out under siege for almost a year, but in April 1221 the entire population of the city was annihilated and Chingiz Khān gave the order that the city was to be leveled. Juvaynī concisely summarizes the horror with a quote from an escapee from Bukhārā, one of the few cities that had any escapees: "They came, they sapped, they burnt, they slew, they plundered and they departed" (Juvaynī 1958: 107).

Mongol brutality was not motivated purely by cruelty, but by the logic of terror. If the residents of a city were massacred, the next city was much more likely to surrender. Cities which surrendered without bringing Mongol casualties were consistently spared, but any harm done to a Mongol was met without mercy. In fact, the pattern of the Mongol conquests followed quite logically from the Mongol worldview, which was fairly simple and reflected a nomad's values: the world was divided into herds (the agrarian populations of the world) and herdsmen (the Mongol army). Agrarian populations were cattle to be owned, controlled, and milked by their Mongol masters. Some among the subject populations were more useful than others, and might be promoted to the level of auxiliaries to the Mongol ruling class, but in general the rest of humanity existed to be exploited (Fletcher 1986: 42–3).

Expansion and conquest followed necessarily from this worldview, but what enabled the Mongols to actually implement this pattern on a large scale were the peculiarities of the steppe environment. Mongol tribal society was one of the most thoroughly military societies that has so far existed. Every male was a trained warrior – there was no division of labor. The model for war was the hunt. As horse nomads the Mongols were highly mobile, and as pastoralists they could move their livelihood with them. The Mongol empire grew from a militaristic, super-tribal confederation which came into existence for the sole purpose of enabling the Mongol tribes to do together what they could not do alone – efficiently wrest wealth from neighboring agrarian societies. There was no reason for tribal leaders to willingly sign on and surrender autonomy to a super-tribal leader except for what it would get them, and what it got them was ever-expanding wealth and pastureland. Joseph Fletcher reasons that there was a certain inevitability to what happened next. Since there was no reason for the existence of such an empire except to prey on the rich, settled lands, once Chingiz Khān consolidated a confederation in 1206, invasion inevitably followed. And once started, a continual pattern of invasion and conquest was necessary to justify the empire's continued existence. Consequently, the Mongol army was the empire's most important institution: without the army the empire was impossible; without an ever-expanding empire, the army could not be held together (Fletcher 1986: 32–3).

Once the Mongol army had started, in other words, it was rather hard to stop. After the devastating incursions into Khurāsān of 1220 and 1221, Muslim lands were spared the attention of the main Mongol army for three decades because the Khāns were busy elsewhere. After Chingiz Khān's death in 1227 the empire was divided into four pieces under the overall leadership of Chingiz Khān's successor, the Great Khān Ögedei. The main action over the next decade was in Russia and eastern Europe, which the so-called Golden Horde attacked between 1237 and 1241. Ögedei's death in 1241 cut the campaign short, but the Golden Horde remained in control of vast stretches of territory. The Golden Horde comes into our story at a later point because the whole lot of them converted to Islam en masse under Özbeg (1313–41).

The conversion of the Mongols was still in the future, however, and meanwhile the Mongol leadership set its sights on the Islamic lands once more. The Great Khān Möngke – who succeeded Ögedei, but only ten years after his predecessor's death and following a long succession struggle – sent his brother Hülegü on a campaign into the Middle East. Hülegü had three goals. His primary mission was the suppression of the Nizārī Ismāʿīlī assassins, possibly in response to rumors of an attempt to send a band of assassins to kill the Great Khān. His secondary goal was to obtain the submission of the caliph in Baghdad, or to destroy him. Hülegü also seems to have had a third, more personal goal: to set up his own kingdom (Morgan 1986).

The first goal was speedily accomplished. In 1256 the last Nizārī assassin leader surrendered and obligingly led the Mongols from fortress to fortress, persuading his followers to do the same; the assassins of Persia were thus completely wiped out. This might have been, as Gibbon called it, "a service to mankind" (Gibbon 1902, 7: 126), but Hülegü quickly made up for it. In 1258 he moved on Iraq. His summons to the caliph to submit was refused, and the city was sacked. In a letter to the king of France the conqueror himself reported that 200,000 were killed. The last ʿAbbāsid caliph was wrapped in a carpet and kicked to death – apparently the Mongols had scruples about shedding royal blood.

In 1260 Hülegü moved on Syria, taking the Ayyūbid kingdoms of Aleppo and Damascus. The Crusader prince of Antioch joined forces with the Mongols, and was excommunicated for his treason. Egypt should have been next, but that very year the Mongol juggernaut came to an abrupt halt when the Mongol army was dealt a surprising defeat at the hands of the Egyptian Mamlūks. The unexpected reversal at the battle of ʿAyn Jālūt (the "Spring of Goliath," near Nablus in Palestine) marked the end of Mongol expansion in the Near East. The battle itself was probably less decisive than two other factors. First, Hülegü himself had already withdrawn on news of Möngke's death, and he had left his general to suffer the defeat. Second, the Mongols had by now discovered that Syria offered insufficient pastureland for Mongol-sized armies (Morgan 1986).

The victory at ʿAyn Jālūt was the deliverance that Ibn Khaldūn had credited to the Turks and to divine providence. From 1260 on, the Near East was divided between Mamlūks and Mongols. The Mamlūks took Syria and the Mamlūk general Baybars became the real founder of Mamlūk power. The Mamlūks also gained the prestige of becoming protectors of Islam. They subsequently tried to capitalize on this important role by inventing a caliphate. Persia and Iraq continued under Hülegü and his successors as the empire of the Īlkhāns.

The Impact of the Mongol Invasions

Modern historians have argued over the extent of the devastation wrought by the Mongols. Bernard Lewis in particular thinks that the effects of the Mongol conquest have been greatly exaggerated (Lewis 1973: 179–98). It is true that Muslim historians exaggerated the numbers of those killed. Estimates for the number killed at the city of Herāt, for example, vary from 1.6 million to 2.4 million, although the city could not possibly have held so many. Similarly 1.7 million are supposed to have died at Nīshāpūr. But even if there could not possibly have been more than a million residents in thirteenth-century Nīshāpūr, quibbling over the numbers misses the main point: however many there were, they were all killed. Given the totality and brutality of the massacres, this quibbling over numbers only displays a callousness toward the human and psychological tragedy felt by contemporary observers. Better, as Morgan suggests, to take the inflated numbers as evidence of the state of mind created by the invasions. This was, as he says, "a disaster on a grand and unparalleled scale" (Morgan 1986: 74).

While the short-term impact was unprecedented, the long-term effects of the conquests are harder to compute. Mongol brutality was unevenly distributed. Southern Iran was spared and the Mongols never reached Egypt and North Africa. Even some cities directly in the Mongol path recovered quickly. In March 1220 Juvaynī described Bukhārā as "a level plain." But by the time he wrote his history in the 1250s he could exclaim that "today no town in the countries of Islam will bear comparison with Bukhārā in the thronging of its creatures, the multitude of . . . wealth . . . the flourishing of science and the students thereof and the establishment of pious endowments" (Juvaynī 1958: 108). By that time the Mongols of Iran had reformed themselves, and as Hodgson comments, "They destroyed in a grand manner, they built in a grand manner too" (Hodgson 1974, 2: 405).

But while cities might be destroyed and rebuilt quickly enough, the agricultural economy of Iran was more fragile. Khurāsān before the conquests was described as rich, fertile, and flourishing. It has never matched that description since. Because the area has few rivers, agriculture is precariously dependent on an ancient and ingenious system of underground irrigation channels, qanāts, which tap the water of underground springs. Qanāts require constant maintenance, and the decline of the population and general disruption of the Mongol conquests severely disrupted this system (Morgan 1986: 80–1). The Mongols, of course, would not have much cared; they wanted pastures, not farms.

It is clear, then, that the Mongol conquests seriously disrupted patterns of economic life in Iran and central Asia. The Mongols have often been blamed for much more: blighting the development of Islamic intellectual life, engendering a deep conservatism in religious culture, and causing a turning inward from which Islam never recovered. In reality, however, what is most striking about the aftermath of the Mongol conquests is just how resilient Islam turned out to be.

A comparison with the Arab conquests is a temptation too strong to resist. Both conquests were breathtaking in speed and scope, both the work of nomads of warrior stock. In both cases the conquerors were held together by a strong sense of ethnic superiority, and a religious law. Yet for all of these similarities, the differences are even more striking, and in the differences is our chief lesson. The Arabs, for all that they were influenced by the Near Eastern environment, never lost their language, their sense of roots, or their distinct religious identity. They did not become Jews, Christians, or Zoroastrians and they did not adopt Greek as their language. The result of their stubbornness was a new synthesis and a fundamental transformation of the civilization and religious culture of the Near East. By contrast, the Mongols were religiously and culturally conquered by Islam. When the īlkhānid ruler Ghazan Khān converted to Islam in 1295 and the Golden Horde followed suit two decades later, Islam had won the war. The tenor of Mongol rule began to change immediately. Ghazan reformed Mongol administration to undo the worst of the exploitation of his predecessors. He revived the old Persian political theory which placed justice on purely pragmatic grounds: "If you commit extortion against the peasants, take their oxen and seed, and cause their crops to be consumed, what will you do in the future?" (Morgan 1986: 167). He introduced reformed rates and methods of taxation, he reformed coinage and weights, he overhauled the judicial system, and he introduced incentives for recultivation. The Muslims had not just outlasted the Mongols, they had absorbed, coopted, and utilized their strength.

The result was a new Islamic–Mongol synthesis, which was the seed of a significant renewal within Islamic culture. Once they had converted, the Mongols fit right in. Joseph Fletcher argues, quite plausibly, that the Mongols became Muslims (rather than Christians or Confucians) because Islam provided such a perfect fit (Fletcher 1986: 43–5). Here was a religion and a civilization a nomad could love. Islam required very little of her new rulers. The Mongol penchant for power did not need to be reined in, so long as that power was put to use in the name of Islam and against anarchy. Muslim chroniclers, horrified by the destruction wrought by the Mongol armies, had no qualms about putting their literary skills to work for Mongol rulers and cannot hide their grudging admiration for Mongol displays of brute power. Such power could only come from God, and in the words attributed to a pious Muslim by Juvaynī, "There is no point resisting omnipotence" (Juvaynī 1958). The Muslims already expected military rule to be the norm. The destruction of the institution of the caliphate was a blow, but it was the destruction of a prized fiction, not a real institution. Of the great Islamic institutions described in part III of this book – the caliphate, the law, the intellectual tradition of Islamic theology and ṭarīqa ṣūfīsm – only the caliphate was dealt a death blow. Arguably it was dead already. And even if the institution of the caliphate was destroyed, the ideal of a universal caliphate lived on until the early twentieth century when Atatürk, the founder of modern Turkey, finally put even its ghost to rest.

Fletcher argues, in other words, that the Mongols, after they got over their early excesses, were quite at home clothed in Islam. In fact, it might be argued that they reinvigorated an old pattern, putting military might back into the hands of nomadic warriors. Ibn Khaldūn, a first-hand witness to Mongol power in its later manifestations under Timūr and the most brilliant analyst of society that the Islamic world has so far produced, certainly thought so. It might be argued that the Mongols cleared the deck, so to speak, making it possible once again to conceive of wide-scale political unity. Consequently, they readied the way for the emergence of the three great Islamic empires of the sixteenth century, those of the Ottomans, Safāvids, and Mughals. All three of these empires were inspired and invigorated by the Mongol legacy, as we will see in the next chapter.

But having conquered the Mongols, did Islam sink into conservatism and lose its intellectual creativity? Even a superficial overview of the era that follows suggests otherwise. The immediate aftermath of the conquests was the age of the most celebrated of Persian ṣūfī poets, Jalāl al-dīn Rūmī (d. 1273). It was also the era of Naṣiruddīn Ṭūsī, a scientist, polymath, and reinvigorator of Twelver Shīʿīsm. The Mongol period was just the beginning of the Mamlūk dynasty, which brought a century of brilliant prosperity to Egypt and lasted for two and a half centuries. This was the period of the great Ḥanbalī reformer Ibn Taymiyya (1263–1328). It was also a time of enormous geographical expansion for Islam – the conversion of East Bengal took place in the fourteenth century, and Islam became well established in the Indonesian archipelago during the fifteenth century. The late fourteenth and early fifteenth centuries provided the environment for the great Persian poet Ḥāfiz (d. 1389), for the historian and brilliant social analyst Ibn Khaldūn (d. 1406), and al-Jīlī (d. 1428), who extrapolated Ibn al-ʿArabī's thought. This was the period of Jalāl al-dīn Suyūṭī (d. 1505), a scholar of encyclopedic range, and of al-Maqrīzī (d. 1442), the great Egyptian historian. If these were living in a period of decline, someone should have told them.

Resources for Further Study

On the Saljūqs, see the *Encyclopaedia of Islam* (*EI*) article, "Saldjūkids," by C. E. Bosworth, and Gary Leiser, *A History of the Seljuks* (1988). For the social and intellectual context of the Saljūq period, see Richard W. Bulliet, *The Patricians of Nishapur* (1972), and for a broader historical context see David Morgan,

Medieval Persia 1040–1797 (1988). On the phenomenon of slave soldiers see the *EI* articles, "Ghulām" and "Mamlūk," and David Ayalon, *Outsiders in the Lands of Islam* (1988).

For a general overview of the Crusades, see Jonathan Riley-Smith, *The Oxford Illustrated History of the Crusades* (1995). It has become all the rage to view the Crusades from an Arab perspective and there are now several studies. The most recent is Carole Hillenbrand, *The Crusades: Islamic Perspectives* (1999), which is profusely illustrated but falls short on useful analysis. Francesco Gabrieli, *Arab Historians of the Crusades* (1969), brings together translations from Muslim sources, and Amin Maalouf, *The Crusades through Arab Eyes* (1984), is an entertaining read, but not to be relied on as a work of research. For the end of the Crusader era, see P. H. Newby, *Saladin and his Time* (1983).

The best general introduction to the Mongols is David Morgan, *The Mongols* (1986). Morgan's article on the Mongols in *EI* presents a summary of his arguments. Other essential surveys are J. J. Saunders, *The History of the Mongol Conquests* (1971) and Rene Grousset, *Empire of the Steppes* (1970). For a popular introduction to the Mongols, with accompanying video series, see Robert Marshall, *Storm from the East* (1993). In my treatment of the Mongols here I have been especially influenced by Joseph Fletcher's provocative questions in "The Mongols: Ecological and Social Perspectives" (1986). For a skeptical perspective on the amount of damage done by the Mongol armies, see Bernard Lewis, "The Mongols, the Turks and the Muslim Polity" (1973). For an early Muslim account of the conquests, see Juvaynī's *Genghis Khan: The History of the World Conqueror* (1997). For the Mongol–Mamlūk conflict see Reuven Amitai-Preiss, *Mongols and Mamlūks* (1995). On Ibn Khaldūn, see Muhsin Mahdi, *Ibn Khaldun's Philosophy of History* (1957), and the translation of his *Muqaddimah* by Franz Rosenthal (Ibn Khaldūn 1969).

14
REVIVAL AND REFORM

At the beginning of the sixteenth century, while the Islamic legal scholars we met in chapter 10 were busy wrangling over the permissibility of coffee and coffee shops, the political environment of Islam changed dramatically in ways that shaped the Muslim experience over the next three centuries and also deeply influenced Muslim responses to the West in the nineteenth century. In particular, sixteenth-century Muslims witnessed a complete redrawing of the map of their world with the rise of three great empires – the Ottoman, the Safāvid, and the Mughal – all rooted in the Mongol–Turkish synthesis and all of them spectacular in their accomplishments. The evidence of the grandeur of these empires is still visible in the architectural treasures of Istanbul, Iṣfahān, Agra, and Lahore.

The Ottoman, Safāvid, and Mughal Empires

In 1453 a clan of Turkish warriors or ghāzīs conquered Constantinople, ended eleven centuries of Byzantine rule, and completed the job the Arabs had left unfinished in the seventh century. The conquest of Constantinople (henceforth Istanbul) opened the door for the expansion of Islamic rule into southern Europe. It also brought enormous prestige to the conquerors, the clan of Osmān (Arabic: 'Uthmān), who achieved what other Muslims had tried and failed at for eight centuries. Their leader, Mehmed, earned the title "the Conqueror," and the power of the Osmānlī family rapidly grew. Mehmed's successors

Figure 14.1 The Sulaymāniyya mosque in Istanbul. Photo: Photo © MaxFX/Shutterstock

consolidated Osmānlī rule in Anatolia and extended it into the Balkans. In 1517 Selīm "the Inexorable" (or "the Grim" depending on which side you were on) defeated the Egyptian Mamlūks in Syria. Suddenly the Ottomans, as Europeans called the family of Osmān, had themselves an empire that was astonishingly similar in size and extent to the pre-Islamic Byzantine empire. At the height of Ottoman power under Sulaymān "the Lawgiver" (also known as "the Magnificent"), who reigned for forty-six years from 1520 to 1566, the empire encircled the Black and Red Seas, and encompassed three-quarters of the Mediterranean coast. The Ottomans ruled over vast numbers of non-Muslim subjects, and the Turkish armies were the terror of Europe. In 1529 Sulaymān's forces laid siege to Vienna, and would certainly have taken it had their troops not been so eager to get home before winter.

While the Ottomans were expanding into Europe, a rival Muslim empire was growing in Persia. In 1501 the leader of a radical Shīʿī ṣūfī order conquered Tabrīz, set himself up as ruler, and pronounced Twelver Shīʿīsm the creed of the state. Ismāʿīl thus became the founder of the Safāvid empire and

Figure 14.2 The Friday congregational mosque in Iṣfahān. The mosque dates from the ʿAbbāsid period, but was added to, restored, and rebuilt, especially in the Saljūq and Safāvid periods. Photo: Bernard O'Kane/Alamy

the most successful and intolerant Shīʿī ruler since the fall of the Fāṭimids. Ismāʿīl seems to have aimed at no less than the complete destruction of Sunnī Islam, and in the territory that came fully under his control he was astonishingly successful. He enforced the ritual cursing of the first three caliphs, Abū Bakr, ʿUmar, and ʿUthmān, as usurpers, disbanded Sunnī ṭarīqas and seized their assets, faced Sunnī ʿulamāʾ with the choice of conversion, death, or exile, and imported Shīʿī scholars to replace them. The almost complete predominance of Twelver Shīʿīsm in modern Iran and southern Iraq is largely Shāh Ismāʿīl's doing.

Twelver Shīʿīsm might have come to dominate much more of the Islamic world if the newly emerging Ottoman state had not stood in Ismāʿīl's way. The Safāvī ṣūfīs had a significant following among the Turks of Anatolia, the so-called Qizil-bāsh ("Red Heads") who had a penchant for red turbans. In 1511 the Qizil-bāsh rose in rebellion against the Ottomans, but three years later, in 1514, the Ottoman Sulṭān Selīm decisively defeated the Safāvids, ending Shīʿī expansion. The Ottoman response to the Safāvid threat was to massacre the Qizil-bāsh and to persecute Shīʿī Muslims more generally. The

Figure 14.3 The Bādshāhi masjid in Lahore. Photo: © Chris Caldicott/Axiom

result was, for the first time, a sharp divide between Shīʿī and Sunnī Islam along geographical lines. The split deeply affected the ʿulamāʾ, who were ghettoized. Consequently, Shīʿī and Sunnī intellectual culture moved in different directions. The division also had a profound effect on the development of popular piety. In Safāvid lands the dominant religious form of Sunnī Islam, ṭarīqa ṣūfīsm, was replaced with popular Shīʿī piety, centered on the remembrance of the passion of Ḥusayn at Karbalāʾ and encouraging hatred of Sunnīs. Under the Safāvids the celebration of the passion of Ḥusayn during the month of Muḥarram came to be manifested in large-scale public rituals, including funeral processions, self-flagellation, and passion plays.

To the east the final piece in the puzzle was put in place by Bābur, an ambitious and resourceful descendant of Timūr. Forced out of central Asia by Uzbek expansion, Bābur based himself in Kabul and turned his attention to India. In 1526 he decisively defeated the Muslim rulers of Delhi at the battle of Pānīpat and the Mughal empire was born. During the long reign of Bābur's grandson Akbar (1556–1605) Mughal power expanded to include most of the Indian subcontinent. Under Akbar the Mughals came close to a policy of religious neutrality, making Akbar the poster child of later advocates of religious

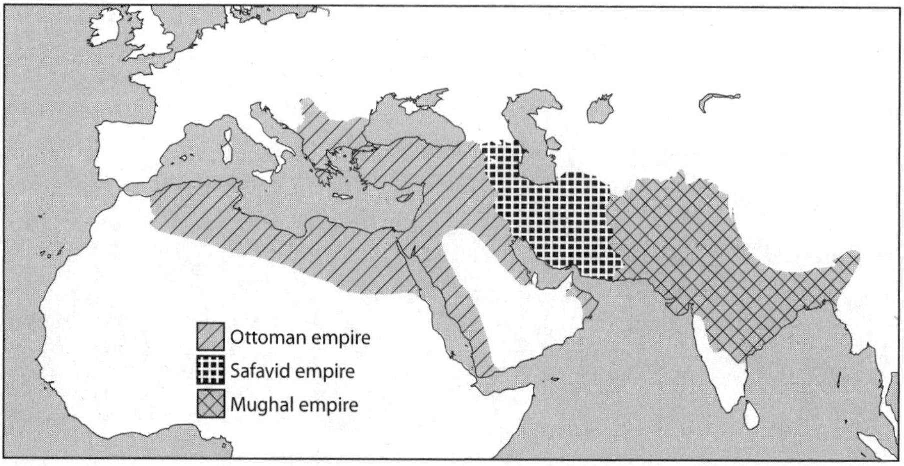

Map 7 The "Gunpowder Empires" ca. 1700 CE

tolerance and a favorite of Indian historians. Akbar abolished the head tax (jizya) on non-Muslims, prohibited Hindu girls from converting to Islam for marriage, set aside the death penalty for apostasy, and patronized the building of temples. He also engaged in religious experimentation, establishing a sort of private court ṭarīqa of his own and giving a hearing to spokesmen of every tradition, including Christians. Akbar's experiment with universalism did not last. His great grandson Awrangzēb, faced with a Hindu insurrection in the south, restored the jizya and generally adopted a hard line toward his Hindu subjects. Awrangzēb was the last of the great Mughal emperors. During his reign Mughal power was already in decline.

The Rise of European Power

The almost simultaneous rise of three great empires in the Islamic world is a striking enough convergence of events to mark the first three decades of the sixteenth century as an important historical watershed. The convergence becomes even more startling when we include European developments. In 1497 Vasco da Gama rounded the Cape of Good Hope, reaching India in 1498. During the following four decades Portuguese ships ruled the long-range sea routes to the Indian Ocean, paving the way for a European monopoly on long-range trade. Ferdinand Magellan's circumnavigation of the world between 1519 and 1522 showed that there would soon be no navigable port on earth out of range of European navies and merchant ships. In hindsight it is clear that the world economic and political context was on the verge of a major transformation.

The seeds of European expansion sown during these few decades at the beginning of the sixteenth century, although barely noticeable at the time, grew during the following centuries into full-blown imperialism. India felt the impact earliest: the Portuguese dominated the Indian Ocean and established coastal colonies in the sixteenth century, and the British took their place in the seventeenth century with the establishment of the British East India Company "presidencies" at Calcutta, Madras, and Bombay. In 1757 the company stumbled into the business of colonial rule when Robert Clive replaced the ruler of Bengal with a British puppet. By 1803 the British controlled Delhi, and the Mughal emperor became a marionette. Half a century later, in 1857, the British dispensed with the fiction of indirect rule, and India became the Jewel of the Empire.

For the Ottoman empire the first hint that something had changed in the world was a series of military and diplomatic reversals. The Ottoman army was driven back from Vienna in 1683 in a decisive enough way to show that it was falling behind European armies in technology and tactics. The peace of Karlowitz that followed in 1699 led to the loss of Hungary and the inescapable inference that the Ottomans were no longer invincible. Seventy-five years later the loss of invincibility had turned into a total rout. In 1774 at the treaty of Küçük Kaynarca Russia forced the Ottomans to their knees. The Russians gained not just Ottoman territory, but a naval presence in the Black Sea, trading rights, consulates wherever they liked, and the right to interfere in the empire at will as the protectors of Orthodox Christians. By the nineteenth century the Ottoman empire had been transformed from the terror of Christendom to the "Sick Man of Europe."

In Iran the impact of European power was felt less directly. The Safāvid empire imploded on its own with the invasion of the Afghan Nādir Shāh in 1722, who also did his best to destroy what remained of Mughal power, invading and sacking Delhi in 1739. Later in the century Iran enjoyed a period of relative independence and stability under Karīm Khān Zand (1750–79), but then became a pawn in the rivalry between Russia and Great Britain under the Qājār dynasty.

The Religious Environment

The trend toward European domination picked up speed in the nineteenth century, but to understand the range of Muslim responses to the challenge of European power in the nineteenth century, we need first to take stock of the religious mood during the preceding two centuries. As we have seen, the religious environment differed sharply from empire to empire. The Ottomans patronized a highly bureaucratic form of Sunnī Islam; the Safāvids became zealous promoters of Twelver Shī'īsm; and under Akbar the Mughals adapted their religious policy to the peculiar pressures of ruling an empire of Hindus. But beyond these obvious differences, significant changes were underway in the religious life of Muslims which would have an effect throughout the Islamic world. In particular, the place of the 'ulamā' and the institutional role of ṣūfīsm were undergoing changes throughout the Islamic world. During the same period movements on the fringes of the empires delivered the major institutions of Islam – the Islamic legal establishment and the ṣūfī orders – a forceful and violent critique.

The 'Ulamā'

The Ottoman rulers succeeded in absorbing the 'ulamā' into the structure of the state to an unprecedented degree. The Ottoman system was built upon the simple Mongol distinction between the rulers and the ruled. (In practical terms the difference was between those who paid taxes and those who spent them.) In this system the 'ulamā' formed their own hierarchy within the ruling class and were, in formal terms, part of the Ottoman army. Thus the title of the two chief judges of the empire was qāḍī-asker, judge of the army. Above the qāḍī-askers, the Shaykh al-Islām supervised a vast religious bureaucracy and shared equal status with the grand wazīr. At the highest level, along with the Shaykh al-Islām and the qāḍī-askers, the household of the sulṭān had two official prayer leaders, an official religious preceptor, a head astrologer, and a head physician. Forty-three qāḍīs divided into three levels served under the qāḍī-askers. A variety of grades of muftīs, prayer leaders, and preachers filled up the secondary ranks of the 'ulamā'. The system was formally a meritocracy, and the 'ulamā' were divided into twelve consecutive grades, with a formal system of certification marking the passage from one grade to the next. The Ottomans had successfully transformed the 'ulamā' into a religious bureaucracy, tied inextricably to the interests of the ruling class.

What the Ottoman 'ulamā' lost by way of independence was more than compensated for in wealth, power, and prestige. Like the other members of the 'askerī class the 'ulamā' paid no taxes, but they also enjoyed an additional unique privilege: they could pass on wealth to their descendants. Every other member of the army was, in formal terms, a slave of the ruling household and his property was subject to confiscation upon his death. Not so the religious scholars. Consequently, leading families worked hard to ensure that their sons entered the system. The 'ulamā' also supervised and benefited from the income of vast religious endowments (awqāf, sing. waqf). The Ottoman 'ulamā' made good use of these privileges, amassing enormous wealth and power. At the higher echelons of the hierarchy those in power also contrived to keep the wealth and power in the family, so to speak, and the most powerful 'ulamā' became, in effect, a hereditary aristocracy.

Like any wealthy, entrenched aristocracy many of the 'ulamā' proved to be rather resistant to any sort of change which might undermine their position. They had not only Islam to preserve, but also the institutions from which they derived their power, prestige, and livelihood. A powerful and hereditary bureaucracy is also not the normal breeding ground for great minds. There were notable exceptions, but they were swimming against the tide, and on the whole the religious bureaucracy of the Ottoman empire could be counted on to defend the status quo.

The 'ulamā' were not alone in having intertwined their fortunes with those of the state. Two major ṣūfī ṭarīqas, the Bektashiyya and the Mevleviyya, were also, in quite different ways, caught up in the intrigues of the ruling class. The Mevlevīs inherited a tradition of ingratiating themselves with the political authorities, and since they went out of their way to avoid making waves, they were well liked in the ruling establishment. The Bektashīs are a stranger case. From early on they had become closely tied to the Ottoman professional army, the Yeniçeri or Janissary Corps, which was formed from slave levies in the Balkans. The Christian background of the Janissaries accorded well with the quasi-Christian beliefs and practices of the Bektashīs, including belief in a "trinity" of God, Muhammad, and 'Alī, rites of confession and absolution, and veneration of saints common to both Christians and Muslims. The Janissaries became a powerfully entrenched conservative force in the empire until they were finally destroyed in 1826. Although the Bektashī religious outlook was far from orthodox, the Janissaries and the 'ulamā' found themselves to be allies during the eighteenth century in the common cause of resisting change.

The identification of the 'ulamā' with entrenched interests within the ruling class was not matched outside the Ottoman empire. Ismā'īl, founder of the Safāvid empire, had to recruit 'ulamā' from outside of Iran in order to build his Shī'ī state. This should have proven a golden opportunity to exert state control over religious scholarship, but Shī'ī scholars were doctrinally well equipped to resist threats to their independence. To begin with they were disposed to reject the ultimate legitimacy of any state not led by the twelfth imām. In addition, an internal squabble among Shī'ī 'ulamā' ended up reinforcing the independence of scholars. Shī'ī scholars were divided into two camps over whether religious authority was primarily textual (the Akhbārī position, which paralleled that of the Sunnīs) or whether it was vested in living scholars called mujtahids (the Uṣūlī position). Under the Safāvids the Uṣūlīs won out, and taught that each individual believer should submit to the authority of a particular living mujtahid. Twelver Shī'ī religious authority thus reached directly to ordinary believers and bypassed the state. This independence was further encouraged by the rapid breakdown of state authority in Iran during the eighteenth century.

The Mughal rulers also did their best to corral the 'ulamā' into serving state interests, but with only partial success. Akbar tried to overrule the 'ulamā' in the articulation and application of law, belatedly applying Ibn al-Muqaffa''s advice by putting himself in the place of the final arbiter in the interpretation of Sharī'a. Awrangzēb compiled his own collection of judicial rulings, the Fatāwā-yi 'Alamgīrī, in a similar attempt to make an end run around 'ulamā' monopoly on interpretation of the law. It is clear that 'ulamā' were closely involved with the state, but some of that involvement was by way of independent critique of state policy, as in the case of Aḥmad Sirhindī (discussed below), who ended up in prison for his pains. As with the Safāvids, the rapid decline of Mughal power in the eighteenth century left the 'ulamā' to fend for themselves, and they thus entered the modern period with their own institutions and accustomed to independence. It was an independence that would go in two different directions, however. As Barbara Metcalf shows in her *Islamic Revival in British India* (1982), two quite different kinds of religious institutions emerged. The first, represented by Lucknow's Farangī Maḥall, contented itself with the preservation of traditional learning in the midst of a tumultuous environment. A second line of 'ulamā', represent by Shāh Walī Allāh and his descendants, actively worked for the reform of Islam and the restoration of Muslim power.

Ṣūfī Reformers

Beginning in the sixteenth century ṣūfī ideas and institutions are widely rumored to have taken a sharp turn away from Ibn al-'Arabī's monism and toward a more sober, "reformist" brand of mysticism. An Indian ṣūfī, Shaykh Aḥmad Sirhindī (1564–1624), is usually identified as the initiator and representative figure in this trend, and the Mujaddidī branch of the Naqshbandī order, which he founded, its chief institutional manifestation. Fazlur Rahman, among the most highly respected modern scholars of Islam, labeled the result "neo-Sufism," and the label has stuck. In reality neo-Sufism should probably be seen simply as the result of the virtual saturation of Islamic culture by ṭarīqa ṣūfīsm, so that ṣūfī institutions came to encompass a wide range of Muslim tendencies, from the wild and ecstatic qalandar to the more or less sober respectability of the Naqshbandī ṣūfīs.

The Naqshbandī ṭarīqa, founded in Bukhārā in the fourteenth century, distinguished itself by insisting on silent dhikr and prohibiting music and dancing. It is also notable for encouraging engagement in the world, including the pursuit of wealth and political influence, and for fostering particularly strong master–disciple bonds. The Naqshbandiyya spread widely in central Asia, and had gained a significant following in India by the time of Akbar's death in 1605.

Early in his career Aḥmad Sirhindī was associated with Akbar's court and with Akbar's main adviser, Abū'l Faḍl. In 1600 he was initiated into the Naqshbandiyya and began making use of it as a platform for self-promotion. Tapping into millennial expectations aroused by the passing of the first thousand years of Islam, Sirhindī developed an elaborate theory of a renewer or mujaddid of the second millennium. The new millennium had ushered in the final stage in Islamic history, a time that would rival the time of the Prophet in glory and purity. The agent of this renewer would be the mujaddid, who would receive the mantle of responsibility to perform prophetic functions on earth. This mujaddid would be "a man of perfect knowledge" who is capable of fulfilling the task of the steadfast Prophet. We can catch echoes here of Ibn al-ʿArabī's idea of the "Perfect Man."

Sirhindī did little to disguise his own identity as the very mujaddid he proclaimed: "I am both the disciple of God and His desire," he wrote. "The chain of my discipleship is connected with God without any mediation. My hand is a substitute for the hand of God . . . Hence I am both the disciple of Muhammad the Messenger of God and His co-disciple." He claimed to occupy the ultimate office in mystical hierarchy, the Qayyūm, higher than the Quṭb and thus surpassing the position of Ibn al-ʿArabī. He claimed the mantle of prophetic action on earth with an audacious pun on his own name: "Muhammad," he proclaimed, "has become Aḥmad."

Aside from his rather daring claims for himself, there is little in Sirhindī's thought to suggest that he represents a new departure in ṣūfī ideas. His critique of excesses in ṣūfism and departures from the Sharīʿa do not go much beyond the standard Naqshbandī conservatism that he inherited, and his differences with Ibn al-ʿArabī, on whom he is heavily dependent, have been exaggerated. Yohanan Friedman's (1971) book on Sirhindī gives the impression that, far from representing a radical departure or a radical critique of theosophical ṣūfism, Sirhindī stands squarely within its tradition.

While his ideas may not be all that new, however, Sirhindī's activities suggest a shift in the self-perception of the ṣūfī's role vis-à-vis the political establishment. He is one of the first – or at least one of the most visible – in a line of ṣūfī dabblers in politics. Sirhindī's perception of his political role arises directly from his vocation. As mujaddid he has a responsibility to call rulers to account, to restore the Sharīʿa and generally to clean up the mess that he had inherited. The idea of the ṣūfī as reformer, which is implicit in the title "mujaddid," was a notion that Sirhindī's followers gave continuing life to with the establishment of the "mujaddidī" or "reformist" branch of the Naqshbandī ṭarīqa which spread widely through India, central Asia, and Turkey.

A century after Sirhindī's death the most notable Indian intellectual and ṣūfī of his time, Shāh Walī Allāh (1703–62), felt a similar burden to put things right in the world. Like Sirhindī, Shāh Walī Allāh was convinced he had a special vocation as a reviver of Islam, a conviction confirmed by visions. In one of these the Prophet's grandson Ḥusayn took Muhammad's mantle and placed it on Shāh Walī Allāh. "God granted to me the robe of revival and enabled me to give new vigor and guidance to this last age, laying a new foundation of present-day fiqh." Shāh Walī Allāh had a precocious intellect and his awareness of his superiority placed him firmly within the mystical tradition of self-promotion. "What a pity," he wrote, "that Plato has not seen the Greek philosophy I have!" His mystical ideas are dizzyingly complex, and represent a culmination of post-Ibn al-ʿArabī ṣūfīsm. But his sophisticated symbolic system, the "World of Prefiguration," which is populated with angels, angelic assemblies, and ṣūfī reformers, is still firmly rooted in medieval philosophical ṣūfīsm. It is hard to see his ṣūfīsm as a major departure from what came before.

Shāh Walī Allāh's political agenda was a good deal less complex than his mystical thought. During his lifetime Mughal rule in India disintegrated, and Shāh Walī Allāh responded in two ways. On the one hand, he actively lobbied for the return of strong Muslim rule, going so far as to invite the Afghan warlord, Nādir Shāh, to take over in Delhi. On the other hand, he laid the theoretical foundation for a new, more activist role for the ʿulamāʾ in the subcontinent by distinguishing between an external and an internal caliphate. It was the internal caliphate, represented by the ʿulamāʾ, that was responsible for maintaining the well-being of Islam even in the absence of strong political authority. The main task of the ʿulamāʾ, moreover, was to revive the intellectual legacy of Islam, especially by returning to the Sunna. Shāh Walī Allāh thus joined a number of Muslims in his generation who seem to have participated in a general revival of interest in the study of ḥadīth. Through his children and grandchildren, Shāh Walī Allāh's ideas continued to wield enormous influence among the ʿulamāʾ of the subcontinent.

Sirhindī, Shāh Walī Allāh, and those that followed them are significant because of the mood that they reflect. Despite their different circumstances it is clear to each that Islam is in a state of decline, in urgent need of renewal, and that they are uniquely gifted to do the job. Moreover, the means of renewal involves getting rid of innovations and taking the application of Islamic law more seriously. In other words, if Islam is in dire straits, the only possible explanation is that the Muslims have departed in some way from the true path. But the program that they offered as a solution was hardly revolutionary. To discover a much more radical appraisal of the state of Islam in the premodern period, we must see past the imperial ʿulamāʾ and the mainline ṣūfī ṭarīqas to events on the political fringes but at the spiritual center of the Islamic world, the Arabian peninsula.

The Wahhābī Movement

In 1740 a Ḥanbalī scholar in central Arabia, Muhammad Ibn 'Abd al-Wahhāb, launched a radical critique of contemporary religious practices and began preaching a return to absolute, unadulterated monotheism. For four years Ibn 'Abd al-Wahhāb was a voice in the wilderness, opposed as an extremist by other 'ulamā', including his own brother. In 1744 or 1745 his fortunes changed dramatically when he won over the local ruler of Najd, Muhammad ibn Sa'ūd (d. 1765). Under Ibn Sa'ūd's patronage, Ibn 'Abd al-Wahhāb gathered a community of Muwāḥḥidūn, defenders of the unity of God, who spread Ibn 'Abd al-Wahhāb's message with the tongue and with the sword. The result was the emergence of an extraordinary and enduring political-religious alliance, the Sa'ūdī–Wahhābī state.

Sa'ūdī–Wahhābī power grew rapidly within the Arabian peninsula, leading to conflict with the local leader in the Ḥijāz, the Sharīf of Mecca, beginning in the 1790s. In 1803, more than a decade after Ibn 'Abd al-Wahhāb's death, his followers conquered Mecca, lost it temporarily, then retook the city in 1806. Their stay in the Ḥijāz was brief but eventful. While there they destroyed tombs, demolished the birthplaces of the Prophet, 'Alī, Abū Bakr, and Khadīja, refused entry to the Syrian and Egyptian pilgrimage caravans, prohibited consumption of tobacco, leveled all buildings connected with "immoral" behavior, burned books that might in some way lead to idolatry, and abolished any special signs of recognition for descendants of the Prophet. The Wahhābī frenzy of purification was cut short by an Ottoman army led by the governor (and future ruler) of Egypt, Muhammad 'Alī, who retook Mecca in 1813 and destroyed the Sa'ūdī power base in central Arabia five years later. This, however, was by no means the end of the Wahhābī story. A second Sa'ūdī state emerged later in the nineteenth century, and in the twentieth century the Sa'ūdī–Wahhābī alliance took its third and final form under 'Abd al-Azīz ibn 'Abd al-Raḥmān Āl Sa'ūd (r. 1902–53), who conquered the Ḥijāz in 1924–5 and became the founder of the modern state of Sa'ūdī Arabia.

Ibn 'Abd al-Wahhāb's monotheistic zeal was not entirely his own invention. The Ḥanbalī school within which he was trained had a long tradition of zealous opposition to religious innovation stretching back to the founder of the movement, Aḥmad ibn Ḥanbal himself. Ibn 'Abd al-Wahhāb's true kindred spirit, however, was the thirteenth-century Ḥanbalī firebrand, Ibn Taymiyya. Ibn Taymiyya lashed out at just about every popular religious practice of his time, focusing his attacks especially on Shī'ism and ṣūfism. Two themes undergird Ibn Taymiyya's ideology: opposition to any show of devotion for a being other than God, which he held to be idolatry, and strict adherence to the teachings of ḥadīth. He moved in and out of favor with the Mamlūk rulers of Egypt and Syria, and spent a good bit of time in prison, but he seems to have been firmly convinced that state power was the key to purifying Islam and to "commanding good and forbidding evil." Ibn Taymiyya was a prolific writer and finally died in prison when his pen, paper, and ink were taken from him.

Like Ibn Taymiyya, Ibn ʿAbd al-Wahhāb preached an uncompromising doctrine of tawḥīd, the Unity of God. He taught that acceptance of the Unity of God was the foundational religious duty, and the proof of authentic belief was in deeds not words: a true monotheist must act like a true monotheist, and anyone who demonstrates devotion to any being other than God is, by definition, an idolater and a non-Muslim. It is no surprise that Ibn ʿAbd al-Wahhāb saw idolatry everywhere. Everywhere he looked so-called Muslims, under the influence of ṣūfī and Shīʿī piety, prayed, sought help, made vows, feared, and placed their trust in saints, saints' tombs, and relics. To Ibn ʿAbd al-Wahhāb it seemed that the Islamic world had returned to Jāhiliyya, the pre-Islamic period of idolatry and ignorance. It was his manifest duty (with the help of Ibn Saʿūd, of course) to wage jihād against the idolaters and to re-establish a purified Islamic polity.

Ṣūfīs and Shīʿite Muslims were not the only objects of Wahhābī polemics. Ibn ʿAbd al-Wahhāb also attacked the prevailing systems of Islamic law, accusing the ʿulamāʾ who maintained them of blind adherence to their own authorities at the expense of the pure teachings of the Qurʾān and Sunna. On this point Ibn ʿAbd al-Wahhāb was squarely within the Ḥanbalī tradition, which had always been the school most focused on ḥadīth and skeptical of the ijmāʿ of the scholars.

The Wahhābī movement has received credit and blame for far more than it actually accomplished. This is partly because agents of the British secret service found the label "Wahhābī" useful shorthand for just about any Muslim movement that threatened British interests. Thus the Wahhābīs have been credited with inspiring movements throughout the Muslim world that had no direct connection with the Arabian movement but seemed to display a vague family resemblance. Among the most interesting of these movements was the jihād movement of Sayyid Aḥmad of Rae Barēlī, the grandson of Shāh Walī Allāh. Sayyid Aḥmad's jihād more properly belongs in the category of Muslim reactions to European colonialism, which we will turn to in the next section, than in a discussion of trends in premodern Islam.

To sum up: from the sixteenth century to the eighteenth century a surprising number of different Muslims in different places concluded that things were not quite right with Islam, that renewal was needed, and that it was their job to set things right. These calls for renewal were motivated by widely varying circumstances, and the would-be reformers differed widely about what needed to be reformed. There are enough such calls for reform, however, to suggest a fairly widespread sense of malaise. There is little sign of the kind of confidence exuded by Usāma in the face of the Crusaders. And by the eighteenth century there was little excuse not to feel gloomy, for everywhere

Muslim political and military power seemed to be in decline or disarray. The mood was caught by nineteenth-century Muslims, and it would deeply influence the ways that many of them would respond to the European encounter.

Resources for Further Study

For a broad survey of developments in Islam during the period covered here, see John O. Voll, *Islam: Continuity and Change in the Modern World* (1982). On the Ottoman empire, see the many works of one of the deans of Ottoman studies, Halil Inalcik, especially *The Ottoman Empire: The Classical Age, 1300–1600* (1973), *Studies in Ottoman Social and Economic History* (1985), and *An Economic and Social History of the Ottoman Empire, 1300–1914* (edited with Donald Quataert, 1994). For a shorter, more accessible introduction to the Ottoman background, see Donald Quataert, *The Ottoman Empire, 1700–1922* (2000). Other useful studies include G. Goodwin, *A History of Ottoman Architecture* (1971), Michael Cook, *A History of the Ottoman Empire to 1730* (1976), and Stanford J. Shaw, *History of the Ottoman Empire and Modern Turkey* (1977).

For the Iranian background under the Safāvids and Qājārs, see P. Jackson and L. Lockhart, eds., *The Cambridge History of Iran*, vol. 6: *The Timūrid and Safāvid Periods* (1986), R. Savory, *Iran under the Safāvids* (1980), A. K. S. Lambton, *Qājār Iran: Eleven Studies* (1987), H. Algar, *Religion and the State in Iran, 1785–1906* (1969), and S. Bakhash, *Iran: Monarchy, Bureaucracy and Reform under the Qājārs, 1858–1896* (1978).

The best introduction to Islamic religious and intellectual trends in India and the Mughal empire is through the works of Aziz Ahmad, especially *Studies in Islamic Culture in the Indian Environment* (1969b) and *An Intellectual History of Islam in India* (1969a). For a fascinating window onto the world of the early Mughals, see *The Baburnama: Memoirs of Babur, Prince and Emperor* (Babur 1996), and for general historical background, Stephen Meredyth Edwardes, *Mughal Rule in India* (1930). The stunning architectural legacy of the Mughals is surveyed in G. Hambly, *Cities of Mughal India* (1977).

For developments in ṣūfism, much of the most useful work is focused on the lives of individual ṣūfīs. Important studies and primary sources include Yohanan Friedman, *Shaykh Ahmad Sirhindi* (1971), R. S. O'Fahey, *Enigmatic Saint: Ahmad ibn Idris and the Idrisi Tradition* (1990), S. A. A. Rizvi, *Shah Wali-Allāh and his Times* (1980), *Shah Wali Allāh, Sufism and the Islamic Tradition: The Lamahat and Sata'at of Shah WaliAllāh*, trans. G. N. Jalbani (1980), and Shāh Walī Allāh al-Dihlawī, *The Conclusive Argument from God*, translated by Marcia Hermansen (1996). For a study of the changing role of ṣūfī institutions, see B. G. Martin, *Muslim Brotherhoods in Nineteenth-Century Africa* (1976).

A foundational study of the changing role of the 'ulamā' in premodern and modern times is H. A. R. Gibb's *Islamic Society and the West: A Study of the Impact of Western Civilization on Moslem Culture in the Near East* (1950). This should be supplemented by the articles in Nikkie Keddie's *Scholars, Saints and Sufis* (1972b), and region-specific works on the 'ulamā', including E. N. Saad, *Social History of Timbuktu: The Role of Muslim Scholars and Notables 1400–1900* (1983), and Barbara Daly Metcalf, *Islamic Revival in British India: Deoband, 1860–1900* (1982). For the background to a particularly important African jihād movement, see M. Hiskett, *The Sword of Truth: The Life and Times of Shehu Usuman Dan Fodio* (1973), and for an introduction to the Wahhābī movement, see G. Rentz, "Wahhabism and Saudi Arabia" (1972).

15

ISLAM AND THE WEST

Napoleon's Invasion of Egypt

On June 28, 1798 a French armada under the command of Napoleon Bonaparte appeared off the Egyptian coast near Alexandria. Within less than a month the army of the Republic had crushed the Mamlūk army at the battle of the Pyramids, and Egypt was in French hands. The period of overt European colonialism had arrived, and for this reason 1798 is often taken as the marker for the beginning of modernity in the Middle East.

But was Napoleon's invasion really so significant? On the surface of it the expedition had little to do with Egypt or Islam and everything to do with the ongoing conflict between France and England. Since the French Revolution in 1789, England had been the chief thorn in the side of revolutionary France. Napoleon's Egyptian expedition had first been conceived as an "army of England" – a vast expeditionary force that would cross the Channel and invade. British naval power made direct invasion unrealistic, however, and the Egyptian expedition was conceived as a scheme to undermine British power indirectly, by putting France in a position to disrupt communications with imperial India.

Forces were mustered in great secrecy. The expedition was to involve more than 54,000 men and more than 300 ships, and up to the time of sailing the object of the expedition was to remain secret. On May 19, 1798 the armada set sail. The fleet interrupted its voyage at the island of Malta, where Napoleon put an official end to the Crusader era by taking the island from the last

Figure 15.1 Detail from the Battle of the Pyramids, July 21, 1798; oil on canvas by Antoine Jean Gros (1771–1835). Photo: The London Art Archive/Alamy

surviving order of Crusaders, the Hospitallers. On June 28 the army landed at Alexandria, and in July the Mamlūk army was destroyed.

The good fortunes of the French were short-lived. In August the British Admiral Nelson surprised and destroyed the French fleet in the battle of the Nile, one of the great naval battles of history. Nelson's reputation as a British naval hero was secured, and Napoleon's army was stranded in Egypt. Egyptian resistance hardened, and the French were faced with a fierce popular uprising in Cairo in October. An unsuccessful expedition north into Syria was a further setback, and by 1799 Napoleon had lost interest and, leaving his army behind, returned to France secretly. His generals immediately began to negotiate for the evacuation of French forces. In 1801 the French evacuated and a joint Ottoman–British force took over.

The whole adventure lasted only three years, and would seem to have had few enduring consequences. The Egyptians themselves were hardly impressed, despite a vigorous propaganda effort which presented Napoleon as a true Muslim come to liberate the Egyptians from their oppressors:

> In the name of God, the Merciful, the Compassionate. There is no god but God. He has no son, nor has he an associate in His Dominion. On behalf of the French Republic which is based upon the foundation of liberty and equality, General Bonaparte, Commander-in-Chief of the French armies makes known to all the Egyptian people that for a long time the Ṣanjaqs who lorded it over Egypt have treated the French community basely and contemptuously and have persecuted its merchants with all manner of extortion and violence. Therefore the hour of punishment has now come . . . O ye Egyptians, they may say to you that I have not made an expedition hither for any other object than that of abolishing your religion; but this is a pure falsehood and you must not give credit to it, but tell the slanderers that I have not come to you except for the purpose of restoring your rights from the hands of the oppressors and that I more than the Mamlūks, serve God – may He be praised and exalted – and revere His Prophet Muhammad and the glorious Qur'ān. And tell them also that all people are equal in the eyes of God and the only circumstances which distinguish one from the other are reason, virtue and knowledge. (Jabartī 1993: 28–9)

The Egyptian historian al-Jabartī, who chronicled the French invasion, was not impressed with the propaganda:

> They follow this rule: great and small, high and low, male and female are all equal. Sometimes they break this rule according to their whims and inclinations or reasoning. Their women do not veil themselves and have no modesty; they do not care whether they uncover their private parts. Whenever a Frenchman has to perform and act of nature he does so wherever he happens to be, even in full view of people . . . If he is a man of taste and refinement he wipes himself with whatever he finds, even paper with writing on it, otherwise he remains as he is. (Jabartī, 1993: 28–9)

One cannot help but be struck by the similarity between al-Jabartī's reaction and that of Usāma to the Crusaders six centuries earlier. Both found the foreigners barbarous, and found precious little to be learned from them. But if the French did not stay, and the Egyptians were not impressed, then how does 1798 rise to the level of historical watershed? At the simple level of military power, Napoleon's invasion taught a fairly clear lesson. European armies and navies could go where they pleased with impunity, and there was no power in the world of Islam that could hope to resist them.

There was also another side to the story. With Napoleon's army came another small army of scholars and scientists. They were young, enthusiastic, and recruited from the best French institutions. Among them were archeologists, architects, artists, astronomers, chemists, economists, mathematicians, engineers, naturalists, pharmacists, surgeons, and surveyors. They also brought with them a full printing press with more than thirty staff to operate it. Everywhere the French army went, these scholars fanned out. They set up an Egyptian Institute in Cairo, modeled after European scholarly institutes. And in the course of three years these scholars performed one of the most monumental feats of cataloging ever accomplished. They studied and recorded the archeology, geography, and natural history of Egypt in enormous detail. One of their finds in particular, the discovery of the Rosetta Stone, launched the entire field of Egyptology. The end result was twenty-eight massive volumes of the "Description of Egypt."

The Birth of Orientalism

Napoleon's expedition is sometimes called the birth of orientalism. The term orientalism, originally a simple label for European scholarship of the Orient, is now inextricably bound up with the work of Edward Said by that title. In his book Said argued relentlessly that Western scholarship of the Orient was an extension of European power. Scholarly activity rendered the "Orient" an object to be examined. Orientalism put knowledge at the service of power. In Said's analysis, Napoleon's invasion was one of the signature events in the development of orientalism.

One need not accept Said's argument uncritically to grasp the point that is of major relevance here. Western colonialism involved much more than military or political domination. Colonialism brought to bear the power of knowledge, economic power, the power to out-produce. In this sense, the Napoleonic expedition becomes fundamental to understanding what came next, and the nature of the challenge that Muslims were faced with in the modern world.

In the case of Egypt, what came next was a period of vigorous modernization and apparent independence under the ruler who is deservedly called the founder of modern Egypt, Muhammad ʿAlī. Muhammad ʿAlī was an Ottoman general of Albanian extraction. He arrived with the British–Ottoman force in 1801. By 1805 he was the semi-autonomous governor of Egypt. What followed was forty years of rapid modernization. Muhammad ʿAlī was the most successful modernizing ruler of his era in the Middle East. He built a highly efficient army of 160,000 troops. He built industrial works to equip his forces with everything from muskets to warships. He established training schools, including a school of medicine and a veterinary school.

Muhammad ʿAlī's apparent independence and strength were an illusion. The Egyptian economy was firmly within the orbit of Europe, and inordinately dependent on a single crop, cotton. And strong as he appeared, his armies were no match for the Europeans. After an Egyptian expedition into Syria threatened the survival of the Ottoman dynasty, the great powers intervened. The 1841 Treaty of London left Muhammad ʿAlī only a fraction of his former power.

Similar stories could be told about much of the Islamic world. After Napoleon's expedition there was no part of the Islamic world that was out of reach of European power. And if that power did not manifest itself in the form of military conquest or direct rule, it would nevertheless be felt in the spheres of the economy, industry, and education. And, of course, direct colonial rule spread rapidly. In 1830 the French took Algeria, and this time they stayed. In 1839 the British seized Aden, the French occupied Tunisia in 1881, and the following year the British took direct control of Egypt and the Sudan. Meanwhile the Ottoman empire was threatened in another direction by independence movements among Serbs, who rebelled in 1815, and Greeks, who fought a war for independence between 1821 and 1830.

Here were crusaders who could not be laughed off, Mongols who refused to be converted. How were Muslims to respond?

Jihād Movements

One of the first Muslim responses to European expansion was, quite naturally, a determination to throw the infidels out. But how? Activist resistance to colonial expansion took two quite different forms. On the political fringes of the Islamic world direct military resistance had a degree of success. In Bengal sometime after 1802, Ḥājjī Sharīʿat Allāh declared that India was no longer dār al-Islām but dār al-ḥarb, the abode of war, and announced a jihād against the British. In 1826 Sayyid Aḥmad of Rae Barēlī, a grandson of Shāh Walī Allāh, led his followers to India's northwest frontier, where he established a jihād state from which he attacked both the Sikh rulers of the Punjab and the British. His followers carried on sporadic jihād activity against the British through the 1890s. In the Sudan, Muhammad Aḥmad (d. 1885) – a charismatic religious leader who claimed the title of the Mahdī – shocked Europe by capturing Khartoum and killing the British hero General Gordon in 1885. The Mahdist state was crushed by Kitchener in 1899, but not before inspiring a generation of Muslims with anti-imperialist dreams. In North Africa an activist ṣūfī ṭarīqa, the Sanūsiyya, became a focus of resistance, first to the French, then to the Italians.

Such jihād movements were irritants, and they kept alive the fear of "Wahhābīsm" in European colonial councils, but they were only small ruptures in the strong net of European imperialism in which Muslims now found themselves trapped. By the late nineteenth century Europeans ruled in Indonesia, Malaysia, India, Egypt, Sudan, and much of North Africa. Persia was a puppet of the great powers and the Ottoman empire was reduced to a pawn in world affairs.

Al-Afghānī

Against this background the rather daunting challenge of arousing Muslim resistance to the West was taken up by Jamāl al-dīn al-Afghānī, one of the most colorful and elusive personalities of the nineteenth century. Al-Afghānī was a consummate conspirator and rabble-rouser, and since he seldom stayed in one place very long and was frequently at the center of some intrigue he is rather hard to pin down. His career takes us on a dizzying tour of the major Muslim leaders, centers of power, and intrigues of the nineteenth-century Islamic world.

We first hear of al-Afghānī in Afghanistan between 1866 and 1868, where he was allegedly trying to mobilize a jihād against the British. He next turns up in Istanbul during the period of reform known as the Tanẓīmāt, only to be deported in 1870 after delivering a controversial speech for which he was accused of heresy. From Istanbul he moved to Cairo, where he stayed for nine years and gathered a group of young disciples, among them Muhammad ʿAbdūh, who were to become the most important Egyptian intellectuals of their generation. He was expelled from Egypt in 1879 for his fiery political speeches, and moved on to India, where he opposed the modernism of Sayyid Aḥmad Khān. In 1883 he was briefly in London, then moved to Paris, where he engaged in a celebrated exchange with Ernest Renan and published an Arabic anti-imperialist journal with his Egyptian disciple, Muhammad ʿAbdūh. In the mid-1880s he was briefly involved in the political intrigues of Sir Wilfred Blunt. Shortly thereafter he offered his services to the Ottoman sulṭān, ʿAbd al-Ḥamīd II, as a sort of peripatetic anti-imperialist agent. In the late 1880s he spent two years in Russia, then moved on to Persia, where his activities helped to encourage a successful popular resistance to a British tobacco monopoly. ʿAbd al-Ḥamīd II invited him to Istanbul in 1892 and he remained there until his death in 1897 under the watchful eye of the suspicious sulṭān. He continued scheming to the end: one of his final intrigues was to incite the assassination of the Persian shāh, Naṣr al-Dīn.

Al-Afghānī's ideas are just as hard to pin down as his movements. He was an intellectual chameleon. Probably of Shīʿī origin, he passed as Sunnī by claiming Afghan birth. Although he was deeply influenced by the rationalist tradition of Islamic philosophy, and has been accused of atheism, he also posed as a defender of traditional Islam and bitterly attacked Sayyid Aḥmad Khān, whose religious ideas in some ways resembled Afghānī's. He espoused a reformed Islam, yet he cooperated with the most entrenched reactionaries. He passionately urged Muslims to unity, yet he was also an instigator of Egyptian nationalism. He sought the restoration of Muslim power, yet he promoted Hindu–Muslim cooperation against the British in India. Yet for all of his inconsistency, one

Figure 15.2 Jamāl al-dīn Al-Afghānī. Photo: Center for Islam and Science, Canada

theme in al-Afghānī's career makes sense of these contradictions. He was, through and through, an anti-imperialist and, like many activists, he was more concerned with finding effective means of arousing resistance than with maintaining intellectual consistency.

Sayyid Aḥmad Khān and ʿAlīgarh

The Indian reformer and anglophile Sayyid Aḥmad Khān had a completely different prescription for Muslims in the face of European imperialism. To his way of thinking the solution to the problem of Muslim weakness was not to resist imperialism, but to embrace the ways of the conqueror. "The well-being of the people of India, especially the Musulmans," he wrote, "lies in leading a quiet life under the benign rule of the British Government" (Donahue 1982: 40). The British in India were agents of the restoration of science and civilization to the Muslims, who had come to be "in comparison with the English

Figure 15.3 Sayyid Aḥmad Khān. Photo: Center for Islam and Science, Canada

as dirty, unclean wild beasts in the presence of beautiful, worthy men" (Robinson 2007: 106). This love for the British was accompanied, however, by the boldest reinterpretation of Islam of the nineteenth century.

Sayyid Aḥmad Khān's early career gave few hints of what was to come. His early religious writings are squarely within the mujaddidī ṣūfī tradition of Sirhindī and Shāh Walī Allāh: he expresses a devotion to the Sunna of the Prophet and an aversion to taqlīd, and he associated himself with the Ahl-i-Ḥadīth, who held that ḥadīth should be the major focus of religious authority for Muslims, and that existing law and practice should be reformed to accord with a literal reading of the tradition literature. The starting point of his thought was thus a desire to somehow restore a pure and unadulterated Islam, and he never abandoned the impulse. After the failure of the 1857 revolt against East India Company rule, Sayyid Aḥmad's search for "authentic" Islam took a more radical turn. He came into increasing contact with European missionaries and scholars, and partly under the influence of these encounters he began to question the authority of ḥadīth, arguing that the Qur'ān alone could be fully trusted to communicate the Prophet's legacy. Thus freed from the constraints of ḥadīth, he was free to interpret the Qur'ān in startling new ways. The jinn were not supernatural beings – for that would be contrary to reason – but an Arab tribe. The devil is not a real being, but a symbol of evil in human nature. Miracles are a result of the pious imagination and can be entirely explained by natural causes. There can be no contradiction between true Islam and modern science, for according to the maxim for which Sayyid Aḥmad is most famous, "Islam is nature and nature is Islam." Both the word of God, the Qur'ān, and the work of God, evident from nature, must be true. If they conflict then the word of God has been misunderstood.

Sayyid Aḥmad tried to combine his religious ideas with his conviction that the future of the Indian Muslims depended on embracing all things British with the founding of 'Alīgarh, a college devoted to educating the Muslim elite of British India. 'Alīgarh was a British boarding school where Indian Muslim boys learned to play cricket and to eat and dress like their colonial masters. It was also a path to secure jobs in the imperial government, and was hence lampooned in a famous poem:

> You seek to know what Aligarh is like?
> A distinguished stomach, call it right
> A stomach does take precedence, my friend
> But the main point is thought about our end.
> (Metcalf 1982)

'Alīgarh did nothing to further Sayyid Aḥmad Khān's dreams of reformation, however. Rather than teach a reformed and modernized Islam, Sayyid Aḥmad was forced by donors to remove himself from any involvement in the religious curriculum of the school, and traditional ʻulamāʼ were brought in to do the job.

The contrast between Afghānī and Aḥmad Khān is telling. Afghānī's impulse to reform Islam was diluted by his anti-imperialism; Aḥmad Khān's bold reinterpretation of Islam was tainted by his collusion with the British. The choice seemed to be between a jihād that left traditional Islam untouched in the interest of expediency, or a thoroughgoing reformation that looked a lot like embracing the enemy.

What the two shared is even more telling, and anticipates enduring trends. Both Afghānī and Aḥmad Khān were motivated by what might be called a revivalist impulse. Although they took that impulse in very different directions, they shared the assumption that the future of Islam can be best mapped out by looking to its past. For Afghānī, the glorious Muslim past to be revived was the rationalist tradition of the philosophers. For Aḥmad Khān, the past to be recovered was the tradition of the Muʻtazilites with their skepticism about ḥadīth and their tradition of metaphorical interpretation of the Qur'ān. Both assumed, in other words, that Islam had taken a wrong turn, and that the revival of the fortunes of the Muslims depended on returning to the intersection and following the path that should have been taken. The weakness of Islam, in other words, is the fault of Muslims, and the strength of Europe comes from having recovered what the Muslims abandoned.

Resources for Further Study

For al-Jabartī's account of Napoleon's invasion of Egypt see *Napoleon in Egypt: al-Jabartī's Chronicle of the French Occupation, 1798*, trans. Shmuel Moreh (1993). The most useful biography of Sayyid Aḥmad Khān is Christian Troll's *Sayyid Ahmad Khan: A Reinterpretation of Muslim Theology* (1978). Aziz Ahmad also focuses heavily on Aḥmad Khān's thought in his *Islamic Modernism in India and Pakistan, 1857–1964* (1967). For the wider context see Peter Hardy, *The Muslims of British India* (1972). The most prolific scholar on Afghānī has been Nikkie Keddie. See especially *An Islamic Response to Imperialism* (1968) and *Jamāl al-Dīn al-Afghānī: A Political Biography* (1972a). See also Elie Kedourie, *Afghānī and ʻAbdūh: An Essay on Religious Unbelief and Political Activism* (1966) and, for a broader overview of the modernist movement, Charles Adams, *Islam and Modernism in Egypt* (1933).

16
THE TURBULENT TWENTIETH CENTURY

Islam and Modernity

What has been the impact of modernity on Islam? A conventional approach to the question would be to present a catalog of the various Muslim responses to modernity, or "styles" of Islam. So, for example, we could describe how *adaptationists* like Sayyid Aḥmad Khān embraced (or were seduced by?) modernity; how *revivalists* like the Muslim Brotherhood's Sayyid Quṭb have reacted violently against modernity; how *modernists* like Fazlur Rahman have sought to define an Islam that is at once truly modern and authentic; how *conservatives* (traditional 'ulamā') have tried their best to ignore the modern world; and how *personalists* (read: ṣūfīs) have retreated to the safety of personal spirituality. There is some use to such schemes. They do offer a rudimentary explanation of some of the major conflicts and divisions among modern Muslims, and they at least remind us of the diversity of Islam.

When we begin to look more closely, however, the boundaries between the categories begin to blur. Modernists and revivalists, for example, begin to look a lot like one another, and sometimes the characteristics of the two "styles" seem to appear in a single person. It has been frequently pointed out, for example, that the great Indian Muslim poet and philosopher, Muhammad Iqbāl, whose theological and political ideas would make him a modernist by any measure, also has a fairly sharp revivalist side to him. One response is to form new, more precise categories. The absurd endpoint of such a process is predictable. There are also more serious grounds on which to criticize such categorizations. In particular these categories tend to leave the impression that

Muslims have done nothing in the twentieth century but react and respond to externally induced change.

I will adopt a somewhat different approach. The attempt to understand and categorize the various Muslim "responses" to modernity seems to me to ignore a prior question: what is it that Muslims are responding to? In other words, what changes has the modern world brought to Islam? My approach here will be to focus this question on each of the classical Islamic institutions surveyed in part III of this book: political institutions, Islamic law, Islamic theology, and ṣūfism. How has each of these institutions fared in the modern world? What has changed, and what has remained the same? We can begin with the pillar of classical Islamic political thought, the caliphate.

The Abolition of the Caliphate

In 1924 the Grand National Assembly of Turkey, urged on by the triumphant Atatürk, abolished the caliphate. The action should hardly have been necessary. As a real focus of political power, the caliphate had ceased to exist by the end of the tenth century. The ideal of the caliphate had continued to live on, however, and the later Ottoman sulṭāns, particularly ʿAbd al-Ḥamīd II (1876–1909), had not been shy about claiming the title of universal leader of the Muslims. This was a tricky proposition since the family of Osmān was patently not Arab, let alone descended from the Quraysh. The Ottoman hand was forced, however, by rivalry with European powers. In 1774, when the empress of Russia claimed to be the protector of all Orthodox Christians everywhere, the Ottomans naturally could not let the claim go unmatched, and they began calling the sulṭān "sovereign caliph of the Mahometan religion" (Enayat 1982: 53).

As it turned out, the Ottoman claim to the caliphate was taken rather more seriously outside of Ottoman domains than within. During World War I, Indian Muslim leaders in particular staked the whole of their anti-British campaign on the single issue of the caliphate. The resulting Khilāfat movement, centered on the call to come to the defense of the caliphate, was the first real mass mobilization of Indian Muslims and a significant turning point in the politics of the subcontinent. After 1919 the All-India Khilāfat Committee supplanted the Muslim League as the major force in Indo-Muslim politics, and the issue of the caliphate became a powerful tool for forging a sense that Indian Muslims shared a common cause and common grievance. And thus, ironically, it was Indian Muslims who raised the loudest objections to the abolition of the caliphate, and, to double the irony, the two Indian politicians who lobbied most vigorously for the restoration of the caliphate were a Shīʿīte, Amīr ʿAlī, and an Ismāʿīlī, the Aghā Khān.

Figure 16.1 Kemal Atatürk (1881–1938) and his wife Latifee Hanoun in the garden of their villa near Ankara, ca. 1923. Photo: Private Collection/Roger-Viollet, Paris/The Bridgeman Art Library

The irony was not lost on Atatürk. To his mind the Ottoman caliphate was nothing but a fiction around which his reactionary opponents could rally. Doing away with the caliphate was necessary if the sovereignty of the Turkish people, the pillar of Atatürk's political thought, was to mean anything. As long as the caliphate remained, Turkish popular sovereignty would remain vulnerable both to conservatives at home and to the demands of the caliph's Muslim subjects abroad. This was a burden Atatürk was unwilling for the Turks to bear, for

> in the whole of the Muslim world, the Turks are the only nation which effectively ensures the caliph's livelihood. Those who advocate a universal caliph have so far refused to make any contribution. What, then, do they expect? That the Turks alone should carry the burden of this institution, and that they alone should respect the sovereign authority of the caliph? This would be expecting too much [of us]. (Enayat 1982: 54)

His arguments for the abolition of the caliphate were simple and direct. The caliphate was intended simply as a utilitarian institution; the "real" caliphate had lasted for only thirty years; what passed for the caliphate in Islamic history was thus "fictitious" and sustained by force; the caliphate had outlived its purpose and Muslims were free to choose any suitable form of government.

Once gone, the caliphate had few mourners. Arab nationalists, in particular, who had chafed at Ottoman rule in Syria, Palestine, Iraq, and Arabia, were quite happy to see it go. To them the Ottoman claim to the caliphate had simply been an instrument of Turkish hegemony. If there was to be a caliph, then by all rights he must be an Arab. In fact the possibility of replacing Ottoman rule with an Arab caliphate became something of a rallying point for some Arabs. Well before the demise of the Ottoman empire the nationalist al-Kawākibī (d. 1902) proclaimed the virtues of Arab rulership and advocated a Qurayshi Arab caliph based in Mecca. Similarly, the 1916 Arab revolt that made Lawrence of Arabia a legend had been built in part on the caliphal pretensions of the Sharīf of Mecca. The latter soured nationalists on the idea of a revival of the caliphate, however, and they turned their attention in other directions.

Nationalism

The abolition of the caliphate finally put to rest al-Afghānī's dream of a pan-Islamic solution to the problem of imperialism. From this point on the Turks, the Arabs, the Indian Muslims, the Indonesians, and the Iranians would look to their own interests. It was a trend that Atatürk, for one, embraced with enthusiasm. Turkey was for the Turks; let the Arabs and the Indian Muslims see to their own interests. Few Muslims described the new reality so eloquently as the Indian Muhammad Iqbāl. "These lines clearly indicate the trend of modern Islam," he wrote. "For the present every Muslim nation must sink into her own deeper self, temporarily focus her vision on herself alone." Iqbāl saw a silver lining, however. The time would come when Muslim nations would be strong enough "to form a living family of republics" (Iqbāl 1999: 159).

Iqbāl's dream of an Islamic commonwealth was a dream for the future, however. Meanwhile, the nation-state was the default political pattern that Muslims would aspire to, and nationalism was the motivating principle underlying their struggles for independence. Nationalism had already set down roots in the Muslim world, but its early forms involved little more than appeals to patriotism in the face of British, French, or Dutch imperialism. Nineteenth-century Muslims like Muhammad ʿAbdūh saw nationalism as little more than a natural love of homeland that would stir their countrymen to rise in her defense. Nationalism at this level was an inevitable product of the colonial experience. If the Egyptians, Arabs, Indians, or Indonesians had felt no shared national identity before, they certainly did after the French, British, and Dutch consolidated their control. There is nothing quite like having one's land taken away to elicit a sense of common injury, the need for solidarity, and the development of a shared mythology to support that solidarity.

By the early twentieth century patriotism was no longer enough. As national aspirations were met and "nationhood" achieved, nationalists shifted their emphasis from the simple assertion and channeling of patriotic sentiment to concern for the grounds of national identity (Enayat 1982: 112). What could hold a nation together, in other words, once the bond created by a common enemy was gone? The consensus, especially among Arab nationalists, was that Islam alone was an insufficient bond. "Whoever will examine the evident facts and picture the map of the Muslim world," wrote Sāṭiʿ al-Huṣrī (d. 1964), "will have to concede that Arab unity is much easier to bring about than Muslim unity, and that this latter is not capable of realization, assuming that it can be realized, except through Arab unity" (Huṣrī 1982: 66). Unity, in other words, means political unity and must be distinguished from the spiritual unity of Muslim brotherhood. World religions, al-Huṣrī argued, have never been able to unify politically except in limited areas for a short time. The Egyptian nationalist Aḥmad Luṭfī al-Sayyid was more blunt in subordinating Muslim identity to Egyptian identity. "An Egyptian is one who recognizes no fatherland other than Egypt," he writes, and "our Egyptianness demands that our fatherland be our *qibla* and that we not turn our face to any other" (Luṭfi al-Sayyid 1982: 71–2). Turkish nationalists mirrored these sentiments. Iqbāl quotes approvingly the Turkish national poet, Ziya Gokalp: "The land where the call to prayer resounds in Turkish, where those who pray understand the meaning of their religion; the land where the Qur'ān is learnt in Turkish; where every man, big or small, knows full well the command of God; O Son of Turkey! That land is thy fatherland!" (Iqbāl 1999: 160). These ideas did not come out of nowhere. The continuing survival of the Ottoman empire and the fiction of the caliphate had masked a century's worth of the infiltration of political ideas from Europe. By the time the Ottoman empire dissolved, the ideas of nationhood, popular sovereignty, representative government, and parliamentary democracy had thoroughly permeated the Islamic world.

One critical question was still to be answered, however. In this new world of independent nation-states, where does Islam fit in? The abolition of the caliphate forcefully raised this question. Medieval Islamic political thought had been built around the ideal of a single unitary caliphate, and even if the ideal was seldom realized, the idea of the caliphate remained a powerful symbol. In particular, the investiture of local rulers by the caliph, however weak he might be, was a symbol of their allegiance to the ideals of Islamic law. In this way the political order was rendered legitimately "Islamic" and the guardians of the law could rest easy.

Secularism

In the new order of nation-states it was not at all clear that any role remained for the guardians of Islamic law. Atatürk's program, followed to varying degrees in other contexts, aimed at the complete disenfranchisement of the ʿulamāʾ, the destruction of traditional Islamic institutions, and the complete subordination of Islam to national goals and national institutions. His aim seems not to have been to do away with Islam, but to channel it and control its course – to tame it, so to speak – so that religion would coincide with his agenda for a modern, nationalist Turkey. Similar attempts to coopt and control religious institutions have become commonplace in the Islamic world, although nowhere has the experiment been quite so vigorously pursued as in Turkey. In Egypt, for example, the greatest bastion of traditional Islamic learning, al-Azhar, is a government-controlled institution, Muslim clerics are government employees, and sermons are written by bureaucrats. Consequently, when the regime of Gamāl ʿAbd al-Nāṣir became enamored of socialism, the major ʿulamāʾ agreeably espoused Islamic socialism. While the Egyptian pattern for handling the ʿulamāʾ falls short of the rigor and ruthlessness of Turkish policy, it nevertheless reveals a similar spirit.

But if the ʿulamāʾ were either to be disenfranchised or subordinated to the state, what was to take their place? In the absence of the caliphate, and with traditional Islamic institutions in decline or under attack, was there any role left for Islam in public life? If so, what was that role, what institutions would implement it, and who was to speak for Islam? This has been among the central battles among Muslims since the beginning of the twentieth century.

The battle began almost immediately after the abolition of the caliphate, and the first salvos were fired in Egypt. In 1925 a young graduate of al-Azhar, ʿAlī ʿAbd al-Rāziq, became the center of a storm after he published a treatise entitled, "Islam and the Basis of Government." ʿAbd al-Rāziq argued that the whole idea of the caliphate was without warrant in the Qurʾān or the Sunna. To make his case, ʿAbd al-Rāziq drew a sharp distinction between prophetic authority and political authority. "The Glorious Qurʾān," he writes,

> supports the view that the Prophet, peace be upon him, had nothing to do with political kingship . . . the Qurʾān clearly prohibits the Prophet, peace be upon him,

> from serving as a guardian of people, or their trustee, or a subduer . . . or a dominator . . . [he] had no rights over his people except of delivering the Message, and had he been a king, he would have had the right to govern his people. (Kurzman 1998: 32–3)

Thus, when Muhammad appeared to be wielding political authority, he was, in fact, simply acting as the messenger of God. The result is that the Prophet's exercise of authority establishes no precedent for later Muslims. Any authority he had was derived from his role as messenger of God and since there will be no more messengers that authority is vested in the message alone. This is not to be taken to mean that Muhammad somehow had less authority than a political ruler. In fact, his authority was more far-reaching, for "the status of the Message grants its carrier a wider authority than that which exists between ruler and ruled, and even wider than that of a father over his children" (Kurzman 1998: 30).

> He has patronage over that which is manifest and that which is latent in life, as well as the management of the affairs of body and soul, and our worldly and heavenly relationships. He directs the politics of worldly living and that of the next world . . . His orders to Muslims were obeyed; and his government was comprehensive. For nothing that the arm of government can reach is beyond the authority of the Prophet. (Kurzman 1998: 31)

The point is that the Prophet's authority is unique and not subject to reproduction or imitation. By this argument ʿAbd al-Rāziq seeks to strip away the very foundations of the caliphate, for the whole idea rested on the assumption that Muhammad's political authority could be passed on. Thus, while political authority is necessary, it does not depend on religious sanction. ʿAbd al-Rāziq's argument was not much different from that of the Turkish secularists. "Our Prophet," Atatürk argued, "has instructed his disciples to convert the nations of the world to Islam: he has not ordered them to provide for the government of these nations. Never did such an idea pass through his mind."

In ʿAbd al-Rāziq's view, Muslims should consider themselves free to establish forms of government of their own choosing. There is no one "Islamic" paradigm. Indeed, there is no necessary connection between Islam and government at all. Consequently, Muslims can and should do away with the old and bring in the new; they are "free to demolish the worn out system," to search out the best forms of government available, and to freely adopt European forms without any sense that this is somehow un-Islamic.

Perhaps what is most noteworthy about ʿAbd al-Rāziq's ideas is not his conclusions, but the basis of his argumentation. Secularism is a good thing, he argues, because a secular system is truly Islamic. He sets out, in other words, to defend a secular system of government on religious grounds, and he builds his case almost entirely on the Qur'ān and the life of Muhammad. Muhammad, he seems to suggest, was a good secularist. Not surprisingly these ideas did not go down well with the Egyptian religious establishment. ʿAbd al-Rāziq was officially condemned by al-Azhar, his diploma and judicial position were stripped from him, and his book was banned. Apparently the suggestion that Islam might have no official role in the new world of Muslim nation-states was perceived as a threat.

ʿAbd al-Rāziq's troubles indicate just what a hard sell "Islamic" secularism has turned out to be. The problem is partly a semantic one. The most natural translation of "secular" in Arabic was *lā-dīnī*, devoid of faith. The implication was not indifference to religion, but outright hostility. The Turks adopted a French word for secularism, describing the new state ideology as Laicism. Both the French background and the Turkish application of the idea emphasized disenfranchisement of traditional religious institutions and state control over religious affairs. In other words, what secularism patently did not mean to most Muslims was that the state would stay out of religious affairs. This was not a doctrine of separation or indifference, but of control, domination, and sometimes outright hostility to religious institutions. The zeal with which Atatürk pursued the destruction of traditional Islamic institutions in Turkey only reinforced this impression of hostility. The abolition of the caliphate was followed in quick order by the abolition of madrasas, the abolition of the system of religious courts, the banning of ṣūfī orders, and the outlawing of polygamy.

Destruction of the old institutions was only half of the program, however. What Atatürk and his disciples had in mind was a full-scale reformation. They aimed to transform Islam into a natural religion, conforming to reason and science, a national religion, akin to the Anglican Church, and a private religion. In a series of remarkable measures the Kemalists set out to implement these goals. Turkish replaced Arabic in the call to prayer, Sunday replaced Friday as the weekly holiday, Arabic script was replaced with Roman, and the vestiges of Islamic law were completely replaced with European-style civil and criminal codes. One of the oddest measures is also one of the most telling. The brimless fez was outlawed, and brimmed hats were required. It is impossible to perform ṣalāt wearing a brimmed hat.

One Turkish government report, never actually implemented, proposed a complete overhaul of Islamic worship. The report advocated clean, orderly, accessible places of worship with pews and cloakrooms. Worshipers should wear clean shoes to worship. The content of worship should also be changed:

> Measures should be taken to make worship beautiful, inspiring, and spiritual. For this reason we must prepare singers and imāms equipped with a fair knowledge of music. We must also have instruments of music in our places of worship. The need is urgent for modern and sacred instrumental music.

Islamic worship, in other words, should become very much like a Lutheran church service.

Such efforts to impose a reformation from the top down required a rather heavy-handed approach to government. As it turned out, it was not an approach that was compatible with democracy. After 1945, with the introduction of multi-party democracy in Turkey, traditional forms of religious expression showed their resiliency. The call to prayer reverted to Arabic, ṣūfī orders re-emerged, and Islamic educational institutions became popular. Many of the changes have had more lasting effect, however, particularly the secularization of the legal system, a point to which we will return below.

Secularism also took another form in the Islamic world. While the ideologies of secularism implemented in Turkey and advocated by ʿAbd al-Rāziq met with hostility, a great many Muslim states adopted a sort of secularism by default. If one takes oneself back in time to survey the nations of the Islamic world during the 1950s and 1960s it is difficult not to come away with the impression that Islam was a declining force in public and political life. The ideas that seemed to have life had little to do with Islam, although some effort might be made to justify them with Islamic vocabulary. This was the period, for example, when socialism was found alluring in many Muslim states. The regimes of Gamāl ʿAbd al-Nāṣir in Egypt, Sukarno in Indonesia, and Ayyūb Khān in Pakistan were secularist in all but name.

The Salafī Movement

The chief alternative to the secularist ideologies of Atatürk and ʿAbd al-Rāziq, or the secularism-by-default of Egypt, Pakistan, or Indonesia, was the rather nebulous idea of an Islamic state. Among Arabs this project was first taken up by a disciple of Muhammad ʿAbdūh, Rashīd Riḍa, and the so-called "salafī" movement of which he was the leading figure. Riḍa was a Syrian who moved to Cairo in 1897 and remained there for the rest of his life. He devoted his life's work to the dissemination and elaboration of the ideas of his mentor, Muhammad ʿAbdūh, and he published a magazine, *al-Manār*, which gained a remarkably widespread readership in the Muslim world.

On paper, Riḍa and the salafīs were committed to a restoration of an earlier golden age of Islam, the period of the pious ancestors, the "salaf al-ṣāliḥ." They limited this golden age to the very first generations of Muslims, and their program involved a return to the pure, unadulterated pattern of Islam reflected in the precedents set by the salaf. But this call to return to the past disguised a readiness to embrace a good deal that was modern. So, for example, in Riḍa's treatise on the caliphate (written just before its abolition) he argues that Islamic leadership is by its nature representative. The choosing of leaders, in other words, ultimately rests with the community. It is not difficult to see in Riḍa's work a clever justification of representative democracy couched in traditional Islamic terms. If the caliphate was to be restored it would be based on popular sovereignty. In fact, although his treatise is on the surface of it a discussion of the caliphate, he was actually preparing its death certificate. What the salafī position reflects, in reality, is a basic acceptance of European-inspired political institutions and ideas – the nation-state, parliaments, elections, representative democracy – and an attempt both to justify and to reshape such institutions and ideas so as to frame them as somehow legitimately "Islamic." Riḍa wants to find a place for the ʿulamāʾ in this system, but he sees them as representatives of the people. The chief mandate of such a state, what renders it Islamic, in fact, is the task of reintroducing Islamic law. This, therefore, becomes the single consistent theme among advocates of an Islamic state. An Islamic state is a state in which Islamic law is implemented. The problem that this leaves open is rather obvious: what does it mean to implement Islamic law? We will return to that question below.

The Muslim Brotherhood

The idea of the Islamic state was taken up and radicalized by one of the most remarkable and influential of modern Muslim movements, the Muslim Brotherhood. The Muslim Brotherhood, the Ikhwān al-Muslimīn, was founded in 1928 by Ḥasan al-Bannāʾ, an Egyptian schoolteacher and disciple of Rashīd Riḍa. The Brotherhood began as a youth organization, focused on religious instruction. While it used some of the language of ṣūfīsm, with al-Bannāʾ as supreme guide, it was also thoroughly modern, with organized cells and a highly developed leadership structure. Moreover, the Brotherhood was a grassroots movement that aimed at mass mobilization.

During the 1930s and 1940s events in Palestine transformed and radicalized the Brotherhood. Between 1936 and 1939 Palestinian Arabs organized a general strike in opposition to Jewish immigration and to the policies of the British administration in Palestine. The plight of the Palestinian Arabs attracted enormous sympathy in Egypt and elsewhere in the Muslim world, and after 1939 the Muslim Brotherhood became active in providing assistance, both humanitarian and military, to Palestinians. The fortunes and ideology of the Brotherhood continued to be closely tied to the issue of Palestine throughout its history. The establishment of the State of Israel in 1948 led to violent protests in Egypt in which the Brotherhood was implicated. The organization was banned in 1948 and al-Bannāʾ was assassinated in 1949. The Brotherhood's short-lived alliance with Gamāl ʿAbd al-Nāṣir and the Free Officers, who took power in 1952, was also forged by their partnership in Palestine. Much later, after the Arabs suffered a humiliating defeat at the hands of Israel in 1967, the Muslim Brotherhood was further radicalized.

Muslim Brotherhood political ideology rests on the simple demand for the establishment of an Islamic state. This is a demand that is shared by Pakistan's counterpart to the Muslim Brotherhood, the Jamā'at-i Islāmī. What has never really become clear, however, is what such an Islamic state would look like. According to the official Muslim Brotherhood program, Islam is defined as an all-encompassing system, and the implementation of Islam in the state would thus, presumably, be all-encompassing. The Brotherhood ideologues also held that the Islamic system that they advocated could be derived in its entirety from the Qur'ān and the Sunna of the Prophet. But beyond these hints, we get few details of a positive program. It is clear enough, to be sure, that the existing system is not Islamic, and it is equally clear that a thorough implementation of an Islamic system is the answer, but it is not at all clear what such a system will look like. This difficulty in outlining a detailed platform has been a widely shared characteristic of movements that, like the Muslim Brotherhood, have worked for a revival of Islam.

As it turns out, the absence of a positive program has not been much missed. Since the Brothers never actually succeeded in gaining power, they have enjoyed the luxury of never really having to grapple with the nitty-gritty questions of how to govern. Consequently, their creativity had to take other forms. Two innovations in particular can be credited to the Brotherhood. The first was a truly distinctive ideology of jihād and martyrdom. The second innovation, which originated with the founder of Pakistan's Jamā'at-i Islāmī, Abū'l A'lā' Mawdūdī, and was taken up by Sayyid Quṭb, was the idea of the modern jāhiliyya.

Jihād and Martyrdom

Brotherhood attitudes toward jihād and martyrdom were shaped on the battlefield in Palestine. It seemed to Ḥasan al-Bannā' that the idea of jihād had been emasculated both by ṣūfīs and modern Muslim apologists. Jihād was a God-given tool which seemed perfectly suited to the modern Muslim situation, but which modern Muslims had abandoned. Thus al-Bannā' called for a return to militant jihād, directed in the first instance at the British in Palestine. Along with this return to jihād he revived and restated the Islamic doctrine of martyrdom. Muslims, he said, should learn "the art of death." By this he meant that they should deliberately and purposefully plan how to make their deaths count for the cause of Islam. There is but a hair's breadth distance between this sort of teaching and the ideology of the modern suicide bomber. In all of this al-Bannā' comes close to reviving an old heresy. The Khārijites had been condemned, in part, for encouraging the "seeking of martyrdom." An even more significant departure from the classical tradition was the assertion that jihād, in the modern context, has become an individual rather than a collective duty. The pursuit of jihād is every Muslim's responsibility, and one cannot just sit back and hope that a professional army organized by the state will do the job for you. The reason is simple. Modern Muslim states are not truly Islamic, and they therefore have no legitimacy.

The situation of modern Muslims is like that of the Muslims in Arabia before the triumph of Islam. They live in a modern "jāhiliyya." There is no Islamic state to establish Islamic law or to raise armies. In such a situation it becomes the duty of every true Muslim to fight for the establishment of a true Islamic state. Moreover, the enemy is not external any more. The enemy is not just in Palestine, but is also represented by the godless regime at home. What we have here is what might be called a neo-Khārijite ideology: if the ruler is not a good Muslim, he is to be fought.

This negative assessment of the modern state takes us full circle. Muslim Brotherhood ideology leads in the end to an almost complete rejection of nationalism. There can be no solidarity with godless countrymen just because they share a homeland. One's countrymen are as bad as the infidels; in fact, many of them are infidels. The battle is thus not for one's nation. Rather, the battle is worldwide, and the enemy is everywhere. Solidarity is not based on national identity, but on religious ideology. Here we have the foundations for a sort of Islamic international.

From Sharīʿa to Secular Law and Back

The colonial era left traditional Islamic legal institutions in a shambles. According to the classical ideal the caliph was the symbol of the law, and the religious scholars were its guardians. Qaḍīs and muftīs were appointed by the state, and the interpretation and implementation of Islamic law was their domain. When the system had grown to maturity there was little call for innovation. Interpretation of the law was confined within the well-defined channels established by the four schools of law.

The European encounter changed all of this. The growing weakness of the Ottoman empire vis-à-vis Europe led to mounting pressure for reform, culminating between 1839 and 1876 in the Tanẓīmāt, a period of sustained reform and reorganization in the empire. Among the most important changes was the adoption of new European-style legal codes – a commercial code in 1850, and a new penal code in 1858. These legal reforms culminated with the promulgation of the Mejelle, an ambitious attempt to codify Ḥanafī law. Along with the introduction of legal codes came new "modern" courts to administer those codes, and a new legal bureaucracy. The complete disenfranchisement of the traditional legal scholars would not take place until the formation of the Turkish republic, but the reforms of the Tanẓīmāt were a move in that direction.

In regions that came under direct colonial rule the traditional legal structures suffered a more direct blow. When the French took Algeria in 1850 they introduced French legal codes. The British introduced their own legal codes in India in 1862, and the Sudan was under British law from 1899 onward. The result was that throughout much of the Islamic world the feature of Islam that had been the greatest symbol of the unity of Islamic civilization was virtually destroyed, and the main livelihood of the 'ulamā', the self-perceived guardians of Islam, was stripped from them.

Muslim Family Law

One area of law, however, remained relatively unchallenged. Family law was too hot for either Ottoman reformers or colonial administrators to handle. The closest that they came to tampering with laws of marriage, divorce, or inheritance was to attempt to systematize and publish the major legal rulings of a particular school so as to make them easier for modern-style courts to administer. The publication of Charles Hamilton's translation of an Islamic legal manual, the *Hedaya* (1791), was one such effort. The strange irony was that the caution of colonial administrators who didn't want to stir up unnecessary trouble inhibited any significant changes in family law during the colonial period. Some modern Muslim thinkers have complained, justifiably, that the colonial rule had a stultifying effect, preventing or discouraging the ordinary course of adaptation. In any case, Muslim nation-states emerged from the colonial period with a weird mixture of medieval family law and alien commercial and civil law. As a consequence, twentieth-century demands for Islamic legal reform have taken two apparently contradictory directions. On the one hand there has been strong pressure to "modernize" Muslim family law, and on the other hand a growing insistence on the "Islamization" of civil, commercial, and penal law.

Pakistan presents an interesting case in point. During the early 1960s under the influence of liberal ideas, Ayyūb Khān issued the Muslim Family Laws Ordinance of 1961. The ordinance severely limited polygamy by requiring that a husband prove in court that he can deal with all of his wives equitably; it made unilateral divorce by a husband much more difficult, and it removed what modernist Muslims considered to be an egregious inequity in the laws of inheritance. All of these changes involved significant innovations to the classical Islamic legal tradition. Most of the innovations have also been perceived to represent a significant improvement in the legal status of women.

By 1979 a very different sort of military leader, Zia al-Hāq, had come to power in Pakistan and introduced a series of legal reforms of a completely different stripe. Zia based his legitimacy on the claim that he had a mandate for the "Islamization" of Pakistan's legal system. In 1979 he proclaimed the introduction of an Islamic system, "Niẓām-i Islām." The heart of the new Islamic system was the reintroduction of "Islamic" criminal penalties. Thieves' hands were to be amputated, adulterers stoned, and those guilty of slander punished with flogging. Another major promise of the program was a phased plan to rid the economy of the curse of interest. Over the next few years the remainder of Pakistani law was to be reviewed for compatibility with Islamic law, and several institutions were established to oversee this work. (The most interesting was a Federal Shariat Court to which any Pakistani citizen could appeal if they came across a law that was un-Islamic and wished it to be struck down.)

On the surface of it the legal reforms of Ayyūb Khān and those of Zia al-Hāq went in opposite directions. The former moved to liberalize Islamic law, the latter to reintroduce it in conservative forms. Ayyūb's measures seemed to improve the legal situation for women, Zia's to seriously compromise it. But ironically, although the motives, directions, and effects were different, the basic methodological problem was very similar. In short, how is one to go about rebuilding Islamic law from scratch?

The challenges posed by this rebuilding have been reflected in a spirited and widespread debate among Muslims about the nature of religious authority and the sources of Islamic law. In a sense, modern Muslims have found themselves in a position akin to that of the early founders of Islamic jurisprudence. They are put in a position, in other words, of needing to rethink how to understand and apply the basic sources of religious authority.

Modern Qur'ān Interpretation

The challenge begins, of course, with the interpretation of the Qur'ān. To give a practical example, the Qur'ān seems to offer fairly specific guidance on two rather touchy issues which have direct relevance to women. On the question of inheritance, the Qur'ān lays out a simple rule: "God directs you as regards your children's inheritance: to the male a portion equal to that of two females" (4:11). The same sort of arithmetic is applied to the question of witnesses in court: "O you who believe! When you deal with each other, In transactions involving future obligations in a fixed period of time reduce them to writing . . . And get two witnesses, out of your own men, and if there are not two men, then a man and two women, such as you choose, for witnesses, so that if one of them errs, the other can remind her" (2:282). Neither of these verses seems particularly difficult to understand, and many medieval jurists had no trouble applying them in the most obvious way: women get half the inheritance of men, and their testimony in court is worth half that of a man. They also had no trouble understanding the reasoning behind the arithmetic: a woman is worth half a man.

Some modern Muslim men also see no difficulty with this reading, but on the whole the equation "one man equals two women" does not go over well in the modern world, especially among women. Two solutions seem possible. The first is exemplified by Iqbāl. "The share of the daughter," he writes, "is determined not by any inferiority inherent in her, but in view of her economic opportunities, and the place she occupies in the social structure of which she is a part and parcel" (Iqbāl 1999: 169). In other words, the reduced share of inheritance reflects a social situation in which women bear less financial responsibility than men. Having understood the reasoning, there can be no objection to the simple application of the rule. This has been the logic followed in contemporary Pakistani law. But Iqbāl's reasoning also suggests a second more courageous solution. If the reason that women receive half a share is a particular social and economic context, might not the rule change if the context changes? Where women enjoy social and economic equality, should not inheritance also be equal?

This kind of reasoning can be dangerous. In 1995 the Egyptian scholar Naṣr Abū Zayd was declared an apostate by an Egyptian court for this general sort of reasoning, and he and his wife were forced to flee the country. The problem is that this method of interpretation, which views the Qur'ān as shaped by particular historical and social contexts, clashes with a strong apologetic tendency in modern Islam which emphasizes the timelessness, eternal relevance, and perfection of the Qur'ān. If the Qur'ān is the perfect Word of God, how can its provisions be historically conditioned? Only a handful of modern Muslims have been willing to subject the Qur'ān to this kind of historical analysis, among them Muhammad Khalaf Allāh, Naṣr Abū Zayd, Fazlur Rahman, and Mohammed Arkoun.

The Problem of Sunna

While such reinterpretation of the Qur'ān is hardly mainstream, the situation is rather different in the case of the second source of Islamic law, the Sunna. The Sunna is the real stuff of Islamic law for the simple reason that the Qur'ān is rather limited in what it has to say on legal topics. Consequently, debates over religious authority center on the Sunna, which has come under attack in just about every conceivable way. Beginning with Sayyid Aḥmad Khān in the nineteenth century, some Muslims have rejected the authority of Sunna entirely, arguing for a return to the Qur'ān alone. This "scripturalism" is based largely on a negative assessment of the reliability of the ḥadīth literature. If the ḥadīth literature cannot be trusted, then there is no basis for knowledge of Sunna. Ghulām Aḥmad Parwēz in Pakistan and Maḥmūd Abū Rayya in Egypt took up this argument during the 1950s and 1960s.

The ideas of Parwēz and Abū Rayya were bitterly opposed. It is clear to most Muslims that to dispense with the Sunna is to undermine the very foundation of Islamic law, for the Qur'ān cannot stand alone. The challenge of deciding what is authoritative Sunna and what is not still remains, however, sometimes with significant consequences. For instance, both the Qur'ān and the ḥadīth prescribe penalties for adultery. Muslims who are concerned to reintroduce Islamic law are often confident that some penalty for adultery should be enforced. Unfortunately, however, there is a discrepancy between the Qur'ān and the Sunna on the precise penalty. While the Qur'ān prescribes flogging, the ḥadīth literature records that Muhammad ordered adulterers stoned. To complicate things, there are reports that a verse prescribing stoning actually was revealed, but was left out of the final version of the Qur'ān. Does the Sunna overrule the Qur'ān in this case? Modern Muslims disagree.

The problem, then, finally boils down to this: who gets to decide? On any given question of law, the results of scriptural interpretation and evaluation of the relevant ḥadīth reports could go many different ways. In the end the question becomes one of human interpretive authority. Who, in other words, speaks for God? Who has the authority to decide what is Islamic and what is not? The modern debate on this question has focused on two interconnected ideas in Islamic jurisprudence, ijtihād and ijmā'.

Ijtihād and Ijmā'

In classical Islamic jurisprudence ijtihād was not an independent source of law, but simply a description of part of the process of legal reasoning. When a scholar exerts effort, struggles, to discover the law of God, particularly when he applies the principle of analogy, he is engaged in ijtihād. Ijtihād is sometimes used as a synonym for qīyās. Mujtahids, those who engage in ijtihād, must be qualified, and if one is not qualified to be a mujtahid, then one is duty bound to follow the opinions of one's betters rather than setting out to give half-baked legal opinions. Safely keeping to precedent is called taqlīd.

In modern Islamic legal thinking the idea of ijtihād has been transformed from a minor to a major principle. It is, for Iqbāl, "the principle of movement in the nature of Islam" (Iqbāl 1999: 148). The idea of ijtihād has come to symbolize the possibility of progress, of change, and of the most basic reinterpretation of the Qur'ān and the Sunna. But even if the right of ijtihād is granted, the problem is not solved. Ijtihād is an individual activity, carries no weight on its own, and leads directly to the question of ijmāʿ. How is ijmāʿ to be realized in the modern world? Once again, the boldest ideas originate with Iqbāl. The modern legislative assembly, he argues, is the only possible form that ijmāʿ can take among modern Muslims. The process of interpreting and applying Islamic law, according to this way of understanding, becomes identical to the modern legislative process.

A New Kalām?

If the challenge of modern Islamic law is to enable Muslims to be good Muslims, the hope of modern Islamic theology is to persuade them that they have a faith worth keeping. The alluring heresies of the modern world are legion, and just as classical theologians sought to immunize Muslims against the appeal of error, so too have modern Muslim writers set out to defend and justify Islam in the face of modern intellectual challenges. Sayyid Aḥmad Khān laid out the agenda for the field. "Today we need," he wrote, "as in former days, a modern theology [ʿilm al-kalām] by which we either render futile the tenets of modern sciences or show them to be doubtful, or bring them into harmony with the doctrines of Islam" (Troll 1978: 311).

As it turned out, Sayyid Aḥmad's theological speculations seemed to have more to do with bringing Islam into harmony with infidel science than the other way around. He is most famous for his attempts at demythologizing Islam. He argued, for example, that Satan is a symbol of human evil, and denied the ontological existence of jinn or angels. Such ideas were more than his contemporary Muslims could handle. His motive seems to have been fairly simple, however, and that was to demonstrate that Islam was a religion that accorded fully with reason. The same could not be said, for example, of Christianity, and Sayyid Aḥmad began a commentary on the Bible to prove the point (Aḥmad Khān 1862 and 1865). In all of this Sayyid Aḥmad was true to the goals of the modern kalām that he proposed, even if his fellow Muslims failed to appreciate the effort.

Muhammad ʿAbdūh

A much more influential contribution to modern kalām came from Muhammad ʿAbdūh, al-Afghānī's Egyptian disciple. ʿAbdūh came to the task of updating Islamic theology with impeccable credentials. After his wilder days with al-Afghānī he settled down to become an establishment man. He was a product and representative of al-Azhar and must have felt the burden of upholding that tradition weighing on him as he wrote, for his *Theology of Unity* is anything but bold. By contrast with Sayyid Aḥmad's daring speculations, ʿAbdūh is cautious to a fault. On the question of free will and divine determinism, for example, a field which could probably have used some updating, ʿAbdūh refuses to engage, for "to discuss further the reconciliation between the Divine prescience and the Divine will, already proved, and the evident power of human choice, is to attempt to penetrate the secret of Qadar, or destiny. In this we are forbidden to involve ourselves. It is useless to busy our minds with what they can scarcely attain" (ʿAbdūh 1966: 63).

What our minds can attain, according to ʿAbdūh, is an assurance that Islam is a religion fully in accord with reason. In fact, the Qurʾān is the first revealed scripture in which "reason finds its brotherly place" (ʿAbdūh 1966: 31). Islam may contain that which transcends understanding, but it is nothing that reason finds impossible. In fact it is ʿAbdūh's elevation of reason more than anything that sets his work apart and that places him more with the philosophers than the Ashʿarīte theologians. Reason, he argues, is capable of discerning good and evil, and reason will demand the acceptance of Muhammad's prophethood.

Such appeals to reason by both Aḥmad Khān and ʿAbdūh are revealing of the time in which they lived. In nineteenth-century Europe confidence in reason was still off the charts, and for Muslim apologists this presented both a challenge and an opportunity. The challenge was to prevent Muslims from being persuaded that reason was somehow incompatible with Islam; the opportunity was to use the evident reasonableness of Islam to combat the missionaries of that most unreasonable of religions, Christianity. Reason and science, ʿAbdūh and Aḥmad Khān were convinced, were on the side of Islam.

Muhammad Iqbāl

By the time of Muhammad Iqbāl, the early twentieth century, the mood had changed, and the luster had worn off the idol of reason. Three great intertwined historical events separate Iqbāl from ʿAbdūh and Aḥmad Khān: World War I, the rise of communism, and the introduction of Turkish secularism. World War I, in particular, exposed the bankruptcy of European civilization, for in it the greatest achievements of Western science and technology were turned toward destruction. The contrast between East and West thus becomes a major theme of Iqbāl's poetry. The West represents dynamism, activity, intellect; the East represents heart, intuition, imagination, and humanity.

Thus Iqbāl was at once drawn to and repelled by the West. Educated at Cambridge, and deeply influenced by a stay in Germany during which he fell under the spell of Goethe, Iqbāl reveals a deeper understanding of the

Figure 16.2 Muhammad Iqbāl, Indian Muslim poet and philosopher who envisioned a separate Muslim state in the subcontinent. This photograph has become a symbol of Iqbal's iconic status as the intellectual father of Pakistan. Photo: Center for Islam and Science, Canada

currents of Western thought than any of his contemporaries. The dynamism of the West, in particular, attracts him. At the same time he warns of the seductive effect of Western ideas, the "dazzling exterior" of European culture that is liable to lure Muslims away from their spiritual center. Consequently, Iqbāl is grasping for a way to get at the principles that have led to Western success without taking with it the negative baggage: "I will take nothing from Europe except – a warning! You enchained to the imitation of Europe, be free, clutch the skirt of the Koran, and be free!" (Iqbāl 1966: 59).

Reason has thus lost its enchantment for Iqbāl. Where both Aḥmad Khān and 'Abdūh put the task of reconciling Islam and reason at the head of their agenda, Iqbāl was looking for another way of knowing, and he finds what he is looking for in the philosophical systems of Alfred North Whitehead and Henri Bergson.

Iqbāl's *Reconstruction of Religious Thought in Islam* takes us on a dizzying tour of early twentieth-century Western thought, encompassing Berkeley, Whitehead, William James, Einstein, Haldane, and Bergson. And where does it all lead to? God, the ultimate Ego, is not the static, changeless, transcendent being of the medieval philosophers and theologians, but a principle of infinite creativity and movement.

> God's life is self-revelation, not the pursuit of an ideal to be reached. The "not-yet" of man does mean pursuit and may mean failure; the "not-yet" of God means unfailing realization of the infinite creative possibilities of His being which retains its wholeness throughout the entire process . . . Thus a comprehensive philosophical criticism of all the facts of experience on its efficient as well as appreciative side brings us to the conclusion that the ultimate Reality is a rationally directed creative life. (Iqbāl 1999: 60)

In other words, God changes. The basic principles of the cosmos are creativity, change, movement. By laying this theological foundation, Iqbāl clears the way for what I take to be his major objective – a spirited defense of human freedom. "Does the ego then determine its own activity?" he asks. After a detour into German psychology Iqbāl gives his answers in the affirmative:

> The element of guidance and directive control in the ego's activity clearly shows that the ego is a free personal causality. He shares in the life and freedom of the Ultimate Ego who, by permitting the emergence of the finite ego, capable of private initiative, has limited this freedom of His own free will . . . Indeed Islam recognizes a very important fact of human psychology, i.e., the rise and fall of the power to act freely, and is anxious to retain the power to act freely, as a constant and undiminished factor in the life of the ego. (Iqbāl 1999: 109)

The determinism, indeed fatalism, that has marked Islamic thinking arises from the philosophers' misapprehension of God aided by an opportunist desire on the part of evil politicians to hide behind divine destiny.

In his final two chapters, "The Spirit of Muslim Culture" and "The Principle of Movement in the Structure of Islam," we finally see where Iqbāl is headed. Having discovered that movement, creativity, and evolution are the most basic principles of the cosmos, Iqbāl discovers that movement is exactly what Islam does best. In fact, the reason that Muhammad is the last of the prophets is that he represents the full coming to maturity of the human potential for creativity and freedom. "The Prophet of Islam," he writes,

> seems to stand between the ancient and the modern world. In so far as the source of his revelation is concerned he belongs to the ancient world; in so far as the spirit of his revelation is concerned he belongs to the modern world. In him life discovers other sources of knowledge suitable to its new direction. The birth of Islam . . . is the birth of inductive intellect. In Islam prophecy reaches its perfection in discovering the need for its own abolition. This involves the keen perception that life cannot for ever be kept in leading strings; that in order to achieve full self-consciousness man must finally be thrown back on his own resources. (Iqbāl 1999: 126)

In other words dynamism, the spirit of scientific inquiry, and creativity are all native to Islam – they are, in fact, its gift to humanity, for "all lines of Muslim thought converge on a dynamic conception of the universe" (ibid. 138). What does this mean in practical terms? The culminating chapter of the book, "The Principle of Movement in the Structure of Islam," is an analysis of what has gone wrong and a call for Muslims to embrace the dynamism of their heritage once again. For Iqbāl, the principle of movement in Islam is ijtihād, and it is only in Turkey, he tells us, that the spirit of ijtihād is truly alive.

The great modern scholar of Islam Hamilton Gibb implies, in his *Modern Trends in Islam* (1947), that Iqbāl's thought is a dead end. In many respects he is right. While Iqbāl's book is often read and quoted, especially in Pakistan, it is only his foray into legal thought that has been widely embraced and understood. The metaphysical analysis in Iqbāl's work is dauntingly complex, and draws on numerous strains of European thought that proved to be dead ends themselves. Consequently, his work can easily come across as quaint and dated.

This misses what is perhaps the most important point, however, that in the broad outlines of his ideas Iqbāl represents widespread trends in Muslim thinking in the modern period. In particular, he shares in a general rebellion amongst lay Muslims against the deterministic cast of Ashʿarīte theology. At the popular level this rejection of determinism finds expression in the frequent citation of a Qurʾānic verse that Iqbāl finds several excuses to quote: "Verily God will not change the condition of men, till they change what is in themselves" (13:14). Iqbāl is one participant, in other words, in a general reassertion of human freedom and revolt against determinism. Another manifestation of this trend has been the rehabilitation of the Muʿtazilites. This rehabilitation takes explicit form in some apologetic works, most notably Sayyid Amīr ʿAlī's *The Spirit of Islam* (1922). A more subtle form of what has been called neo-Muʿtazilism pervades the work of the modernist Fazlur Rahman. Although Rahman resisted identifying himself with the Muʿtazila, his opponents have not hesitated to do so, for he consistently and repeatedly defends human freedom and responsibility and the efficacy of human reason at the moral level.

The Vitality of Ṣūfīsm

So far it seems safe to conclude that the major institutions and intellectual traditions of Islam have shown remarkable resilience in the face of the challenges of modernity. Islamic political thought, legal ideas, and theological speculation have all demonstrated a surprising vitality. If we were to judge by the writings of both Muslim and non-Muslim scholars earlier in the century, we might expect ṣūfīsm to be the exception to this pattern. In 1950 the great scholar of Persian literature A. J. Arberry nostalgically recorded ṣūfīsm's epitaph. "Ṣūfīsm has run its course," he concluded, "and in the progress of human thought it is illusory to imagine that there can ever be a return to the point of departure" (Arberry 1950: 134). The time when ṣūfīsm dominated "the hearts and minds of learned and earnest men" had passed (ibid. 133).

Arberry at least mourned the demise of ṣūfīsm. Many modern Muslim writers have been far less sympathetic. Ṣūfīsm, especially in its more popular manifestations, has been blamed for the malaise and backwardness of Muslim societies. It has been blamed for encouraging an attitude of passivity and other-worldliness, and it has been dismissed as a source of superstition, or worse, heresy. Even Iqbāl, whose ideas are drawn from ṣūfī pantheism, laments that a "spirit of total other-worldliness in later ṣūfīsm obscured men's vision of a very important aspect of Islam as a social polity, and offering the prospect of unrestrained thought on its speculative side it attracted and finally absorbed the best minds in Islam" (Iqbāl 1999: 150).

Ṣūfīsm and the associated popular cults of dead saints would seem, on the surface of it, to be the manifestation of the Islamic tradition least adapted to modernity. An earlier generation of scholarship anticipated the passing of ṣūfīsm – at least in its public forms – as Islam experienced a wave of Protestant-style zeal. It is true that ṣūfī institutions are not what they once were. In Turkey the powerful orders were completely suppressed after the revolution. They were, after all, according to Atatürk's vision, dens of superstition and havens for reactionaries. In many other contexts the orders have been heavily regulated, their assets and leadership placed under the control of a state bureaucracy. Consequently, much of the economic and political power and prominence of institutional ṣūfīsm has been lost. The increasing prominence of revivalist and militant Muslim movements since the 1970s would seem to reinforce the impression that the manifestations of popular ṣūfīsm that remain are mere vestiges of superstition to be educated away, and that the future of Islam lies in other directions.

One does not have to be long in most any contemporary Muslim society (Saʿūdī Arabia excepted) to be persuaded otherwise. The influence of ṣūfīsm and ṣūfī ideas continues to be pervasive. Recent studies confirm this impression (e.g., Hoffman 1995; Buehler 1998). It is not uncommon in contemporary

Pakistan for well-educated professionals to visit and seek advice from pīrs. Ṣūfī shrines and festivals continue to be the focus of the most lively public religious activities. Ṣūfīsm might be compared to a powerful stream, sometimes forced underground, but still representing the most vital spiritual expression of modern Islam.

Resources for Further Study

On the transformation of Turkey under Atatürk, see Bernard Lewis, *The Emergence of Modern Turkey* (1961), and for a survey of the response to the abolition of the caliphate, see Hamid Enayat, *Modern Islamic Political Thought* (1982). Useful anthologies of primary documents include John Donohue and John Esposito, *Islam in Transition* (1982) and Charles Kurzman, *Liberal Islam* (1998). On ʿAbdūh and Riḍa, see Malcolm Kerr, *Islamic Reform* (1966), and on the Salafī movement more generally, David Dean Commins, *Islamic Reform: Politics and Social Change in Late Ottoman Syria* (1990). On Iqbāl, see Annemarie Schimmel, *Gabriel's Wing* (1963), and for a critique of modern Muslim religious ideas, including those of Iqbāl, see H. A. R. Gibb, *Modern Trends in Islam* (1947).

17

ISLAM IN THE TWENTY-FIRST CENTURY

Several years ago I began teaching a course called, "Islam in the Twenty-First Century." The title is an odd one. At the time I began teaching the course we were only two years into the century, and it was fairly obvious that we had no idea what directions Islam would take in the twenty-first century. To read a series of lectures offered in 1908 and entitled "Islam in the Twentieth Century" would likely provide a good bit of amusement. On the other hand, the course title raises an interesting question: has anything already changed in the new century that sets the experience of Muslims apart from what came before? Is there anything in the situation of Muslims in the twenty-first century that is fundamentally different from the situation they faced in previous centuries? The question can be put in personal and practical terms. In 1954 my parents traveled to Pakistan. They remained there to live and work for thirty-five years – more than a third of the twentieth century. How might someone in their shoes need to prepare differently today? What has changed?

Put this way, the answer seems all too obvious. On the morning of September 11, 2001, the world seemed to suddenly change. Western societies woke up to the significance of Islam in the world. Suddenly, the United States was at war, first in Afghanistan, then in Iraq, and finally in a sort of permanent war – a war with no predictable end – between the West and radical Islam. The repercussions of 9/11 continue to mount with no apparent end point. Among these repercussions: continuing war in Afghanistan and Iraq, the destabilization of Pakistan, the mobilization of Islamic radicals, a dramatic rise in the pattern of suicide bombings, a resurgence of Shīʿīte Islam and of Iranian ambitions, and increased Shīʿīte–Sunnī conflict. This is not the Islamic world that my parents entered in 1954. Theirs was a world in which the modernism of Sayyid Aḥmad Khān and the theological daring of Muhammad Iqbāl still seemed relevant, and a world in which Americans like them were, by and large, welcomed.

At one level, then, 2001 marks an historical turning point as significant as 1798 or 1914. Napoleon's invasion of Egypt in 1798 symbolically launched the eighteenth century and marked the beginning of modernity on the Islamic world; World War I ushered in the turbulent twentieth century with all of its political and ideological turmoil and launched the era of the nation-state; and the twenty-first century began on September 11, 2001. What, then, are the most pressing challenges facing the Muslim community in this new post-9/11 world?

The Challenge of Pluralism

At the start of this book I invited the reader to imagine a circle representing the set of all phenomena that fit under the rubric of Islam. How, I asked, can we determine what falls within the circle of Islam and what is excluded? For the outsider to Islam this represents an interesting academic exercise; for many contemporary Muslims, however, the problem is deeply practical. The problem of defining the boundaries of Islam (and deciding who has the authority to set those boundaries), the question of how wide and embracing (or how narrow and exclusive) the umma is, and the question of the relation of the circle of Islam to the circles of other faith communities – these represent the most searching questions faced by contemporary Muslims. In other words, the most urgent set of theological, ethical, and political problems faced by the Muslim community in the contemporary world is posed by the challenge of pluralism.

The situation faced by the Muslim community in the twenty-first century is in some ways fundamentally different from the situation described in the last chapter. The political challenge of modernity was colonialism, and the corresponding intellectual challenge was reason. Thus a central project of Muslim liberals and modernists was to establish that the circle of Islam and the circle of reason and science were not just overlapping, but identical. One could be a Muslim and be "modern" without any contradiction, for, as both ʿAbdūh and Aḥmad Khān had made clear, Islam is an eminently reasonable faith.

Muslims in the contemporary world continue to make the case for the rationality of Islam, but reason is no longer the central challenge they face. The yardstick of the postmodern world is not reason, but tolerance. The question most often posed by outsiders to Islam is not whether the claims of Islam are true and reasonable – a suitable religion for "modern" people; the new most frequently asked question is whether Islam is "a religion of peace." Are

Muslims, in other words, able to accept a place as one community among many? Are "Islamic" values compatible with a system of democratic pluralism, and with the ideology of pluralism that often accompanies it?

Pluralism as a sociological fact is nothing new, of course. Muslims have been facing the challenge of pluralism in this narrow sense from the very beginnings of Islam. The Near Eastern environment within which Islam was formed was anything but monocultural – it was a diverse and pluralistic society. Likewise the Ottoman and Mughal empires have often been heralded as models of well-managed religious and cultural diversity. What is new in the postmodern world is an increasingly dominant *ideology* of pluralism – an ideology that, as the Christian theologian Lesslie Newbigin argues, is suspiciously well adapted to a global consumer culture. This is an ethic of the supermarket, where choice is king, and where the customer is always right. Just as it would seem odd, not to say rude, to criticize the contents of one's neighbor's shopping cart, so too her religious beliefs. In postmodern consumerist culture religious belief systems are reduced to the same level as one's choice of breakfast cereal. One's own beliefs may be tasty and nourishing, but they are a matter of personal taste and experience. One may well recommend one's favorite cereal to others, but to suggest that another's preferred choice is actually poisonous will not do.

For Muslims, this postmodern challenge of pluralism cuts two ways. First, contemporary Muslims are faced with the problem of diversity within the Muslim community, and with the questions of how differences among Muslims are to be approached and how authority is to be constructed. How much diversity can be encompassed within Islam, and who is to decide? Second, the contemporary umma is faced with numerous other faith communities and ideological systems. How are Muslims to relate to those communities? The two problems are closely interrelated, and both are neatly illustrated by a controversy that arose among Muslims in Canada in 2002.

Twenty-First-Century Wahhābīsm

On December 25, 2002, a minor functionary at a mosque in the greater Toronto area distributed an email message that warned Muslims against greeting non-Muslims by wishing them a Merry Christmas. The message, sent from the Khālid bin al-Walīd mosque in Etobicoke, Ontario, reproduced a fatwa issued under the name of Muhammad al-Munajjid which held that congratulating the unbelievers on their religious festivals is absolutely forbidden (ḥarām) because such greetings amount to an affirmation of idolatry. Munajjid quotes from the Ḥanbalī scholar, Ibn al-Qayyim al-Jawziyya:

> Congratulating the Kuffār on the rituals that belong only to them is Harām by consensus, as is congratulating them on their festivals and fasts by saying 'A happy festival to you' or 'May you enjoy your festival,' and so on. If the one who says this has been saved from Kufr, it is still forbidden. It is like congratulating someone for prostrating to the cross, or even worse than that. It is as great a sin as congratulating someone for drinking wine, or murdering someone, or having illicit sexual relations, and so on. (www.alminbar.com/khutbaheng/9017.htm 1/29/2003)

The circulation of this fatwa in Toronto, as it turns out, was not an isolated incident – the ruling is widely distributed on the internet – nor is it difficult to trace its intellectual origins. The fatwa was issued by a Saʿūdī Arabian scholar, and it quotes liberally from two fourteenth-century Ḥanbalī scholars, Ibn Taymiyya and Ibn Qayyim al-Jawziyya. These characteristics, together with the content, mark it as a Wahhābī product. "Wahhābī" and "Wahhābīsm" are imprecise designations, sometimes abused, but the use of the terms is unavoidable. Here I take the term Wahhābīsm to refer to contemporary manifestations of radical Ḥanbalī ideological trends which resemble the ideology of the eighteenth-century scholar-activist, Muhammad Ibn ʿAbd al-Wahhāb, whom we met in chapter 14. Ibn ʿAbd al-Wahhāb proclaimed an uncompromising and rigorous monotheism, and called for a return to a pure Islam unadulterated by accretions (bidʿa). In practice this involved a rejection of all things ṣūfī, all things Shīʿīte, all veneration of saints or tombs, including those of the Prophet or his companions, and much of the Islamic intellectual tradition, including most theology and philosophy. The content of pure Islam is limited to that which can be justified by a narrow and rigorous interpretation of the Qurʾān and Sunna as they have been understood within the most radical tradition of Ḥanbalīsm. To put it in practical terms, Ibn ʿAbd al-Wahhāb and his intellectual heirs would have no difficulty rejecting most of what has been described in this book as deviant from true Islam.

An enduring political-religious symbiosis of the Saʿūdī ruling family and radical Ḥanbalī ulamāʾ in the Arabian peninsula has helped a version of Ibn ʿAbd al-Wahhāb's ideology not only to survive in the contemporary world, but to become wildly successful. The contemporary heirs of Ibn ʿAbd al-Wahhāb often claim no special allegiance to his teachings, claiming simply to represent the pure and timeless Islam in an unadulterated form. Thus they reject the term "Wahhābī," and claim simply to be part of a larger Salafī movement which aims at fidelity to the pure teachings of the early generations of Muslims, the Salaf al-Ṣāliḥ. But whatever the label, the survival and growth in the modern world of an ideology pioneered by Ibn ʿAbd al-Wahhāb and drawing on a common Ḥanbalīte intellectual heritage is undeniable.

Like their intellectual forebears, contemporary Wahhābīs draw the circle of Islam narrowly, and are thus most easily identified by what they oppose, including all manifestations of ṣūfīsm, all manifestations of Shīʿīte Islam, all forms of theological or philosophical discourse, most forms of music, and, in general, any idea, scientific or otherwise, that cannot be justified from the Qur'ān or the Sunna. Wahhābīs confidently assert that there is only one pure form of Islam, that this pure Islam can be known by means of simple adherence to the Qur'ān and the Sunna, and that all diversions from this unadulterated Islam must be vigorously opposed in favor of uniformity. Wahhābīsm, in short, is an ideology vigorously opposed to pluralism, whether that pluralism is within the circle of Islam or without. The circle of Islam is understood, within the Wahhābī worldview, as uniform; anything diverging from this uniformity is not Islam, and must be rejected. Moreover, it is not enough simply to reject alternative visions of Islam as wrong. One of the rallying cries of Wahhābīsm has been the Qur'ānic imperative to "command the right and forbid the wrong." Error and evil must not simply be avoided for the sake of one's own soul, they must be actively opposed, whether by argument or by force. The agent of choice for this job is the state, and it is thus incumbent upon the state to use its resources and coercive power to implement this vision of Islam.

But what if the state is unable or unwilling to fulfill this role? Or what if there is no legitimate Islamic state? It is questions like these that have brought extreme Wahhābīs together with the radical heirs of the Muslim Brotherhood in a new consensus on jihād and martyrdom. The majority tendency of the Islamic legal tradition is to constrain the waging of warfare within strict limits, and to define jihād as a function of the state. But as we saw in the last chapter, some modern Muslim thinkers, beginning with Ḥasan al-Bannā' and continuing through Sayyid Quṭb and his intellectual heirs, have argued that in the absence of a legitimate Islamic state jihād becomes the duty of Muslims as individuals. The most common form of this argument draws directly on the Ḥanbalī intellectual heritage, especially the writings of Ibn Taymiyya, who made a similar argument in the context of Mongol rule. Thus extreme tendencies within the Wahhābī tradition have come together with other trends in modern Muslim thought to produce a new cult of martyrdom. It is within this intellectual context that the suicide bombers of September 11 should be placed. There is perhaps no more emphatic rejection of pluralism than the willingness to kill and be killed as an uncompromising witness to the Truth.

The majority of Muslims and Muslim thinkers have no hesitation in rejecting such calls to violence. In fact, the system of ideas that justifies suicide bombings closely resembles the ideology of the early Khārijite heretics, a connection that more sober Muslim scholars have not been reticent about pointing out. The spread of Wahhābī ideas has given rise to a wide circle of sympathy, however, composed of Muslims who might reject the methods of the suicide bomber, but nevertheless applaud his goals. Since the 1970s, Wahhābī ideology has been systematically and energetically exported from Saʿūdī Arabia and the Gulf states to Muslim communities throughout the world, an enterprise financed by oil revenues. The means of dissemination of Wahhābī ideas have been various, including the financing of mosque-building programs, direct support of mosque functionaries, and the establishment and support of educational institutions. In the 1980s the program of "Islamization" inaugurated by Pakistan's military leader Zia ul-Haq was supported by Wahhābī money and manpower, and Wahhābī ideology was spread through the network of madrasas supported by the Zia regime. Wahhābī ideas have also been spread by guest workers from throughout the Muslim world who have come under the influence of such ideas while working in the Arabian peninsula. Saʿūdī control of the holy sites of Mecca and Medina and the administration of the Ḥajj only reinforces the pattern. Ironically, however, Wahhābīsm has also been aided by the Muslim diaspora in the West. Rima McGown's study of Somali immigrant communities in London and Toronto, for instance, demonstrated that in migrant communities diverse traditional and local religious symbols and sources of authority tended to be displaced by a more uniform "Islamic" religious identity (Berns McGown 1999: 228–37). McGown's conclusions coincide with anecdotal accounts of the increasing influence of Wahhābī-style Islam among Muslim immigrant communities.

Wahhābīsm, with its bold claim to represent the one true understanding of Islam, represents one important way of responding to the challenge of pluralism: to utterly reject the possibility that religious (or even cultural) diversity may be a good thing. The implications of such an ideology for Muslim relations with adherents of other religious traditions are made rather clear by the Toronto Christmas fatwa. Muslims may live among non-Muslims and put up with their infidelity for pragmatic reasons, but they must offer no sign of acceptance or approval of non-Muslim beliefs or practices. Moreover, the issue is clear-cut, and brooks no challenge. A line of authoritative scholars extending from Ibn Taymiyya to modern Ḥanbalī 'ulamā' has ruled that Muslims are not to compromise with the practices or beliefs of non-Muslims, and the consensus of these scholars is decisive.

Partly because of the resources and visibility of Wahhābī Islam in the modern world, non-Muslims are increasingly prone to identify "true" Islam with Wahhābī forms. Hence the idea that Islam is intrinsically at odds with Western values has spread widely, popularized by Samuel Huntington's "Clash of Civilizations" thesis, and reinforced by fear of terrorism since the attacks of September 11, 2001. There is a good chance, in other words, that the ordinary Western lay person, when she thinks of Islam, has in her mind a version of Islam which has been in some way colored by Wahhābī ideas. The more hawkish among Western commentators on the Islamic world regularly dismiss any divergence from the Wahhābī pattern as, at best, fringe ideas or movements which do not represent "true" Islam. This tendency to think the worst – to identify true Islam only with its most rigorous forms – has a distinguished pedigree reaching back at least to Lord Cromer, British High Commissioner in Egypt, who famously declared that "Islam reformed is Islam no longer." It is one measure of the success of Wahhābīsm that it has for so long and so successfully convinced many non-Muslims that it is the real thing.

Islamic Liberalism

There is, of course, another side to the story. The Qur'ān repeatedly insists that "there is no compulsion in religion" (2:256, 10:99, 18:29) and the phrase has become the prooftext of choice for Muslims who argue that Islam supports an ethic of tolerance and that Muslims can fully embrace pluralism. At the popular level this attitude can be illustrated by Muslim outrage at the Christmas fatwa. "If I can't wish you a Merry Christmas on your most holy day, what kind of relationship am I going to form with co-workers and neighbors and with schoolchildren?" asked a Pakistani Muslim interviewed by the *Toronto Star*. "This is the kind of thing that has to stop" ("Mosque Warns against saying Merry Christmas," *Toronto Star*, December 28, 2002). Officials at the mosque responded with embarrassment and quickly disavowed the email message, claiming that it was sent without authorization. Critics of the fatwa blamed it on the increasing influence of Wahhābīs in Toronto and talked of a "hijacking of Islam."

Such popular sentiments are given more sophisticated expression in the work of a growing number of self-designated Islamic "moderates" or "liberals". The defense of an Islamic liberalism rests on two primary arguments. First, Muslim liberals find in the Qur'ān a remarkably open attitude toward religious diversity. Fazlur Rahman, my own teacher at the University of Chicago, argued, for example, on the basis of Sūra 5 verse 48, that religious diversity is not just a necessary evil, but also a positive value:

> If God had so willed, he would have made all of you one community, but [He has not done so] that He may test you in what He has given you; so compete in goodness. To God shall you all return and He will tell you [the Truth] about what you have been disputing.

The value of different religions and communities, Rahman concluded, "is that they may compete with each other in goodness" (Rahman 1980: 167).

A more recent spokesmen for a liberal vision of Islam, Khaled Abou El Fadl of the UCLA Law School, makes a similar argument. "Qur'ānic discourse," Abou El Fadl argues, "can readily support an ethic of diversity and tolerance. The Qur'ān not only expects, but even accepts the reality of difference and diversity within human society" (2002: 15). He draws on a long list of Qur'ānic verses to support this argument:

> O humankind, God has created you from male and female and made you into diverse nations and tribes so that you may come to know each other. Verily, the most honored of you in the sight of God is he who is the most righteous. (49:13)

> If thy Lord had willed, He would have made humankind into a single nation, but they will not cease to be diverse . . . And for this God created them. (11:118–19)

> To each of you God has prescribed a Law and a Way. If God would have willed, He would have made you a single people. But God's purpose is to test you in what He has given each of you, so strive in the pursuit of virtue, and know that you will all return to God [in the Hereafter], and He will resolve all the matters in which you disagree. (5:49)

Such passages, according to Abou El Fadl, are a clear recognition of the reality and positive value of a multiplicity of religious convictions and laws.

How can such arguments for tolerance be reconciled with a host of apparently contradictory Qur'ānic data instructing Muslims to either fight or subdue and extract tribute from non-Muslims (e.g., 9:5 and 9:29)? Rahman and Abou El Fadl both apply a hermeneutic which subordinates particular commands of the Qur'ān to general principles. Specific commands in the text must be read not just in light of their particular context, but also in accordance with broader ethical and moral principles. The principle of a given command must be understood before that command can be appropriately applied in the new context inhabited by the interpreter. Thus, for both Abou El Fadl and Fazlur Rahman before him, the ethical values of the Qur'ān trump its particulars, and the particulars can only be understood against the backdrop of a full appreciation of Qur'ānic ethics.

This way of approaching the Qur'ān as a source of broad ethical principles makes it easy to characterize the core of the Islamic message as compatible with the central values of other monotheistic traditions, and even of broadly humanistic values. So jihād, for example, need not be warfare; rather, it may be taken to represent an unyielding moral and political commitment to the ongoing human struggle for justice and righteousness in the world. For Wahhābīs, by contrast, the core of the Islamic message is inseparable from its particulars. The issue between Wahhābīs and Islamic liberals reduces to a difference over the essential core of Islam. Is Islam, at its core, a broad system of morality and ethics? Or does it consist primarily of specific and unchanging divine commands? This ethical problem is in essence the same as the one raised by Plato's Euthyphro: "Is the pious or holy beloved of the gods because it is holy, or holy because it is beloved of the gods?" (*Euthyphro*, 435) The problem is an old one in Islamic ethics: do ethical categories like justice, kindness, mercy, or beauty have transcendental meaning, or are these subordinate to and defined by particular commands of the Qur'ān and Sunna?

A second argument in support of Islamic liberalism extends beyond scripture to appeal to the broader intellectual tradition of Islam. Liberals contend that the Islamic intellectual tradition not only encompasses a wide diversity of views, but also encourages and fosters this diversity. "The disagreement of the scholars," according to a famous tradition, "is a mercy to the community." Abou El Fadl (2001b) takes this tradition as the starting point for a passionate appeal for a spirit of tolerance within the Muslim community. The Islamic legal tradition, for example, institutionalizes diversity, first by accepting the four schools of law as equally valid, and then by tolerating a broad range of disagreement even within those four schools. The legal tradition thus strikes a balance between firm acceptance of the authority of revelation, which renders the struggle to understand that revelation meaningful, and a critical awareness of the fallibility of human interpreters of that revelation. If one goes beyond Islamic law to consider the intellectual traditions of Islamic philosophy and mysticism, the possible models for diversity within the bounds of Islam are vastly increased. The broad tolerance of the Islamic community through history is thus taken as a normative model in what might be seen as a uniquely contemporary application of the principle of ijmā'. What the community agrees on cannot be wrong, and mostly what the community seems to agree on is that there is a good deal of room for disagreement under the broad umbrella of Islam. Thus Fazlur Rahman sees a broad acceptance of diversity – a "catholic" spirit – as the definitive characteristic of Sunnī Islam.

The challenge of pluralism that Fazlur Rahman and Abou El Fadl respond to has been felt most acutely by Muslims in the West, and Islamic liberalism of the kind we have been describing here is in large part a product of the interaction of Muslim intellectuals with Western ideas and institutions. Fazlur Rahman was educated at Oxford, began his career at McGill University, and spent the most distinguished part of his career teaching at the University of Chicago. Similarly, Abou El Fadl works as an academic at UCLA, writes in English, and enjoys an appreciative audience among Western academics. For the most acute analysis of the situation of Western Muslims, however, we must look not to America, but to Europe and the controversial Swiss Muslim intellectual, Tariq Ramadan.

Islam in the West

In 2004 the University of Notre Dame, Indiana, appointed Tariq Ramadan to a prestigious chair in its Joan B. Kroc Institute for International Peace. The appointment represented something of a coup for Notre Dame. Ramadan is among Europe's leading Muslim intellectuals, and an outspoken advocate of Muslim integration into Western societies. Paul Donnelly of the *Washington Post* calls him "a Muslim Martin Luther." In July 2004, however, after Ramadan had already moved his belongings to the United States and enrolled his children in American schools, the Department of State revoked the work visa he had been issued two months earlier. The revocation invoked a provision of the Patriot Act that bans entry to foreigners who "endorse or espouse terrorist activity" (Buruma 2007).

Several months of public controversy over Ramadan and his ideas followed the visa revocation. Critics, among them many French intellectuals, accused Ramadan of anti-semitism, of supporting terrorism, and of cloaking an Islamist agenda in moderate garb. The French founder of Médecins sans Frontières (Doctors without Borders) called Ramadan "a most dangerous man." Fouad Ajami defended the visa revocation and excoriated Ramadan in the *Wall Street Journal*, arguing that "the liberty of an open society can never be a suicide pact, and the freedom of the academy is never absolute" (Ajami 2004). Critics argued that much of Ramadan's prestige was derived from ancestry. His grandfather was Ḥasan al-Banna', founder of the Muslim Brotherhood, and critics alleged that he has never repudiated his grandfather's ideas or distanced himself from his legacy.

So who is Tariq Ramadan, and why was he viewed as dangerous? The title of Ramadan's most widely read book, *Western Muslims and the Future of Islam* (2004), indicates his main concern. "Western citizens of the Muslim faith," he writes, "must think for themselves" and "Western Muslims must be intellectually, politically and financially independent" (2004: 6). His intellectual project is the articulation of a vision of Muslim engagement not just *with* the West, but *in* the West. Ramadan argues for full Muslim integration into Western societies; his is a vision in which Muslims can be fully Western without sacrificing Islam, and fully Muslim while still embracing Western identity and citizenship.

But how can Muslims willingly adapt themselves to a non-Muslim, presumably idolatrous, society? How are Muslims to reconcile themselves to Western culture and civilization for any other purpose than to replace it? As with Fazlur Rahman and Khalid Abou El Fadl, Ramadan begins with a distinction between universals, requiring no contextualization, and "social matters" in which the text "never allows itself, alone, to lay down a universal principle" (Ramadan 2004: 21). Basic Islamic religious practices and core values are fixed and universal, and therefore non-negotiable, but such core values are both limited and overlap with universal human values. Thus Muslims can and should affirm all that accords with Islamic values of truth, beauty, and justice in Western societies. But what of the specific social requirements of Islam encompassed by Sharī'a? In "human and social affairs," Ramadan argues, "People have complete discretion to experiment, progress and reform so long as they avoid what is forbidden" (ibid. 35). Moreover, even in the case of universals, context is determinative. The application of universal Islamic values will differ markedly in different societies and in different periods of history, for "Faithfulness to principles cannot involve faithfulness to the historical model because times change" (ibid. 36). Ramadan's argument leads to an apparently radical redefinition of Sharīʿa: "In Europe and in North America, as soon as one pronounces the shahada, as soon as one 'is Muslim' and tries to remain so by practicing the daily prayers, giving alms, and fasting, for example, or even simply by trying to respect Muslim ethics, one is already in the process of applying the Sharia, not in any peripheral way but in its most essential aspects." Thus the heart of Sharia is "personal, faithful commitment" (ibid. 33), and the law of God is reduced to doing one's best. Like Abou El Fadl, Ramadan argues that it is not results that matter so much as process. It is the methods of Islamic jurisprudence that are normative for Muslims, not particular positive rulings. And, again like Abou El Fadl, what Ramadan finds is that the methods of Islamic jurisprudence allow for both historical and cultural pluralism. The genius of the Islamic legal tradition is diversity.

In the field of international relations, Ramadan completely discards the binary division of the world into dār al-Islām and dār al-harb. In reality, he argues, Muslims are often safer and enjoy greater freedom in Western countries, and Western nations are therefore better qualified to be labeled dār al-Islām than most majority Muslim countries. Ramadan proposes two alternatives to the binary vision. The West, indeed the whole world, might be considered "dār al-dawa" – the abode of invitation, or even better, "dār al-shahāda" – the abode of witness. The latter articulates the responsibility of Western Muslims to bear witness to the truth of Islam, and makes it clear that this witness is not geographically limited, for "Muslims can now enter into the world of testimony, in the sense of undertaking an essential duty and a demanding responsibility – to contribute wherever they can to promoting goodness and justice and through the human fraternity" (Ramadan 2004: 77).

So far one might be excused for wondering what all the fuss is about. Ramadan is in continuity with the major trends in reformist Islam which run from Afghānī through Abdūh and Iqbāl to Rahman and Abou El Fadl. The originality of his contribution is in focusing his argument specifically on Western Muslims, and the bottom line of his argument is that Islam does not prevent Muslims from being at home in the West, nor should Western societies prevent them from being fully Muslim, for "Muslim citizens really are *citizens,* and they too have the right, within the framework of the national legislation, to be respected as *Muslims*" (2004: 100).

By now, for those familiar with the American religious environment, all of this should begin to sound curiously familiar. Ramadan sounds for all the world like an American evangelical Christian. Muslims are to be *in* the (Western) world, but not *of* it. They are to engage the culture without being coopted by it. They can and should appreciate all that is good, true, beautiful, and just in

Western civilization while never forgetting that they have a prophetic mission within the culture. Muslims must maintain a witness to truth and justice both within their home societies and in the world at large. Even the specific issues that Ramadan grapples with in the second part of his book would be familiar to any evangelical. Should Muslims send their children to separate schools, where they can get a truly "Islamic" education? Or should they engage the public educational system? In what does Muslim social responsibility consist? And how should a Muslim respond when the demands of conscience and citizenship are in apparent conflict?

Ramadan's vision is the most comprehensive Muslim answer to the challenge of pluralism yet to be articulated, and it amounts to a spirited defense both of pluralism within the Muslim community (Western Muslims can and must forge their own way) and of the possibility of full Muslim participation in a pluralistic society.

Why, then, is Ramadan controversial? Our analogy with American evangelicalism may provide a clue. Evangelicals from time to time strike similar fear in the hearts of secular Western intellectuals. Indeed, they are virtually incomprehensible to European intellectuals. Moreover, Evangelicals are especially troublesome when they learn to play the Western liberal game – engaging politically and culturally – without, however, giving up such illiberal positions as opposition to gay marriage or on-demand abortion. Similarly, Ramadan plays the liberal game and uses the rhetoric of liberalism without becoming satisfactorily liberal. Thus on some social issues he comes across as surprisingly conservative. He defends the wearing of the hijāb by Muslim women, for instance, and he consistently defends the legacy of his far from liberal grandfather. Of course the comparison must not be overstretched, but even the differences are telling. Unlike many American evangelicals who lean to the right on political and economic questions, Ramadan is decidedly left-leaning. And like many Christian Evangelicals, for whom support of Israel is an article of faith, Ramadan has been a consistent supporter of Palestinian causes. Thus *Western Muslims and the Future of Islam* ends up a curious mix of reformist methodology, traditional Muslim ethics, and left-leaning politics. An image of Muslim women wearing the hijāb while protesting the World Trade Organization might capture something of Ramadan's vision.

Ramadan represents a sort of post-fundamentalist vision – a Muslim evangelicalism – that offers a clear alternative to both Wahhābī totalitarianism and Westernized liberalism. For our purposes, Ramadan's work is a powerful indication of the enormous significance of the Muslim presence in the West. Ramadan's vision of a fully engaged Muslim community poses a significant challenge to Western liberalism. At the same time, the Western environment is shifting the course of Islamic thought in radically new directions. In practical terms the most dramatic of these new directions concerns gender issues.

Islamic Feminism

On March 18, 2005, a mixed gathering of about 125 Muslim men and women met in New York and performed Friday prayers under the leadership of Amina Wadud, Professor of Islamic Studies in the Department of Philosophy and Religious Studies at Virginia Commonwealth University. According to organizers this was a landmark – the first case in modern times of a woman leading men in public performance of ṣalāt. The prayers were not held at an established mosque, but on the grounds of the Cathedral of St. John the Divine in Manhattan, and they were the most dramatic act in a larger campaign by Muslim activists to assert the rights of women to equal treatment in American mosques. A chief organizer of the event, Asra Q. Nomani, who had already adopted civil rights-style tactics to challenge the unequal treatment of women at her hometown mosque in Morgantown, Pennsylvania, continued the campaign on a nationwide "Muslim Women's Freedom Tour." Opposition from within the Muslim community was vigorous. The event was accompanied and followed by protests and threats.

The woman-led prayer service in New York is one dramatic indicator of how rapidly the Muslim community is being shaped and challenged by the Western environment. Since 2005 imāms and leaders in mosques and Islamic centers have found themselves faced with determined, media-savvy activists unwilling to accept the status quo, and willing to make use of the American legal system to assert their rights. The campaign has had significant success, and has had a noticeable impact on the official positions of national Islamic organizations on the question of women's participation in public prayers.

At one level, these developments are not surprising. Muslim communities in the West are influenced by the same sociological forces that have challenged every religious community. As women receive better education and enjoy greater freedom, and as traditional family structures among immigrant communities adapt to the American environment, both men and women have questioned traditional limitations on women's religious practice. Moreover, these challenges are not limited to the West. Vigorous women's movements have arisen in Muslim communities throughout the world. Nor should we be surprised by the backlash of negative reaction as individuals and communities are threatened by change. From a sociological perspective neither the challenge nor the response is surprising. The interesting question, therefore, is not from whence Islamic feminism arises, or whether it has a future, but rather what impact Islamic feminism is having on how Muslims understand Islam.

The foundational article of faith for Islamic feminists is that Islam, rightly understood, does not and cannot support gender inequality. Therefore any practices or texts that appear to discriminate against women are, *ipso facto*, un-Islamic. The feminist intellectual project is to show that such practices as (forced) veiling, exclusion of women from prayers, exclusion of women from leadership positions, polygamy, unequal inheritance for women, and discrimination in laws of marriage or divorce, along with the texts that are used to support such practices, are not, in fact, Islamic.

Perhaps the simplest approach is exemplified by Fatima Mernissi's *The Veil and the Male Elite: A Feminist Interpretation of Women's Rights in Islam* (1991). For Mernissi, a French-educated Moroccan sociologist, the ḥadīth literature is the problem. Ḥadīth reflects what Mernissi calls "a tradition of misogyny" that is foreign to the actual practice or ethos of the Prophet. Misogynistic traditions are either rank fabrications – Mernissi puts most of the blame on a single transmitter of ḥadīth, Abū Hurayra – or the context of the ḥadīth report must have been misunderstood. In other words, Mernissi applies two strategies – ḥadīth criticism and historical contextualization. The aim of both is to free the Prophet and the Qur'ān of culpability for misogynist practices.

Mernissi does not entirely bracket the Qur'ān off from discussion. A central part of her argument is that the Qur'ānic verse most frequently invoked in support of the seclusion of women, Sūra 53 verse 33, has been misunderstood. The actual occasion for the revelation of this verse was specific to the Prophet. He had just married a new wife and Muslim men in the community were boorishly insensitive to his need for personal space. Thus Mernissi's primary strategy here is historical contextualization accompanied with the rejection of traditions which run contrary to her thesis, and that thesis can be summarized quite simply: the Prophet had such a positive record in his treatment of women that any evidence to the contrary is no evidence at all.

The weaknesses of Mernissi's approach are fairly obvious. First, she ignores the most problematic Qur'ānic verses, focusing most of her attention on ḥadīth. Second, her argument leads to the uncomfortable conclusion that the Muslim community was able to completely depart from the spirit of the Prophet's teaching in remarkably short order. Within a few years of the Prophet's death the misogynist tradition had taken over, not to face serious challenge until the modern period. In the end Mernissi's argument, although liberal on the surface, turns out to mirror fundamentalist methodology. One is prone to wonder who is likely to have the advantage on this particular playing field of ḥadīth criticism. While Mernissi plays well among American undergraduates in gender studies classes who are likely unfamiliar with the Islamic intellectual tradition, few Muslim scholars are likely to be swayed.

While Mernissi focuses on the ḥadīth literature and deals only in a cursory way with Qur'ānic texts, Amina Wadud's *Qur'an and Woman* takes the opposite approach. Wadud brackets off the ḥadīth literature and focuses her argument exclusively on the Qur'ān. In many respects her task is the easier one. She has no trouble, first of all, finding a solid foundation for gender equality in the language of the Qur'ān's creation narratives. She also has little trouble arguing that men and women are treated equally as ethical agents in the Qur'ān.

The Qur'ānic notion of taqwa (piety) trumps all superficial distinctions among human beings. In the end all that matters is the individual's response to God. Both of these arguments are plausible, although Wadud must ignore the Muslim exegetical tradition to make them. The argument starts to get mildly sticky when Wadud turns to images of paradise, which do seem rather more attractive to men than to women. The real challenge comes, however, toward the end of the book where Wadud takes on Qur'ānic passages which seem to establish the specific superiority of men over women. Sūra 4 verse 34 is especially problematic:

> Men are the protectors and maintainers of women, because Allāh has given the one more [strength] than the other, and because they support them from their means. Therefore the righteous women are devoutly obedient, and guard in [the husband's] absence what Allāh would have them guard. As to those women on whose part ye fear disloyalty and ill-conduct, admonish them [first], [Next], refuse to share their beds, [And last] beat them [lightly]; but if they return to obedience, seek not against them Means [of annoyance]: For Allāh is Most High, great [above you all].

Wadud argues that these verses do not support a universal or absolute superiority of men over women, but rather indicate a balance of responsibility between men and women in an ideal society. She reads the permission to the husband to beat his wife as a limitation on domestic violence – all of the prior steps must be followed first, and even then "this verse should be taken as prohibiting unchecked violence against females" (Wadud 1999: 76). The value that the Qur'ān seeks to protect here is marital harmony.

Wadud's overall strategy toward such problematic verses is "to restrict the meaning of many passages to a particular subject, event or context" (1999: 62) In other words, she seeks to contain the damage, arguing that verses with apparently negative implications for women are limited to specific contexts and must not be universalized. The argument, by now, should sound familiar. Rahman, Abou El Fadl, and Ramadan have all leaned heavily on this distinction between the universal and the particular, arguing that universal values trump particular commands or texts. Wadud applies the same argument; any particular command of the Qur'ān must be read against the background of a general principle of gender equality. Students to whom I assign Wadud's book usually have little difficulty identifying the weakness in this argument. When the Qur'ān calls men "managers" of the affairs of women, or permits men to take up to four wives, or tells them they may beat their wives (albeit lightly), this is not a mere human speaking. These are the words of God himself, and one cannot get much more universal than that. Moreover, by bracketing off of both the ḥadīth literature and the whole of the classical intellectual tradition – rereading the Qur'ān in isolation from Muslim intellectual history – Wadud raises the same question as Mernissi. What is one to do with Islam in history? This is, after all, a religion rooted in history which aims in some sense to transform the world by bringing human beings and societies into submission to God.

This last challenge is taken up, at least in part, in one of the most sophisticated recent works on Islam and gender, Khalid Abou El Fadl's *Speaking in God's Name: Islamic Law, Authority and Women* (2001b). Abou El Fadl adopts many of the same techniques as Mernissi and Wadud – ḥadīth criticism, historical contextualization, and the privileging of universals over particulars. The field of Abou El Fadl's analysis, however, is the whole hermeneutical tradition of Islamic law. He places himself within that tradition, utilizing, evaluating, and critiquing its hermeneutics and methods.

For Abou El Fadl, the law of God is not to be found in a fixed set of positive commandments, but rather in a process:

> The earmark of traditional Islamic methodology has been its open-ended and anti-authoritarian character. Fundamental to this character was an evolutionary process of exploration, investigation, and adjudication that, according to its own inner logic, resisted settlement or inertia. The law of God was fully embodied in the search for God's law. Islamic law consisted of a set of methodological approaches, normative principles, and positive commandments that were in a constant state of evolvement. (2001b: 170)

One is reminded here of Iqbāl. Islam is built for change, for constant evolution. And, like Iqbāl, Abou El Fadl makes much of ijtihād as the legal principle through which this evolutionary spirit finds practical expression. Unlike Iqbāl, however, Abou El Fadl has a thorough and sophisticated grasp of the classical sources of Islamic law. He invokes what he labels "post-Schleiermacher hermeneutic discourse" (2001b: 119), which raises fundamental questions about what or who determines the meaning of a text. The author? The text itself? The reader? The meaning of the fundamental Islamic texts, he argues, is not fixed. The Qur'ān and the Sunna are "open texts" and "works that leave themselves open to multiple interpretative strategies" (ibid. 146) Thus, "the text speaks with a renewed voice to successive generations of readers because its meaning is unfixed and actively evolving" (ibid.). In the end the interpretive community determines the meaning of a text, and interpretive traditions are constantly evolving. For Abou El Fadl gender issues are both the starting point and the practical application of these expressions of hermeneutical theory. He sets out, in other words, to establish a foundation on which arguments for feminist interpretation might be built.

It should be clear from this survey that Islamic feminism has implications that reach far beyond the particulars of women's mosque attendance, or inheritance rights. Fundamental issues of textual authority and interpretation are at stake, and the ramifications extend well beyond issues of gender. Feminism raises foundational questions about the authenticity and reliability of ḥadīth, about the interpretation of the Qur'ān, and about the nature of Islamic law. Moreover it is the pluralism of the modern Islamic community, and particularly its experience of the pluralism of Western societies, that makes these discussions both possible and urgent.

The Challenge of Islam

Clearly modern Islam has been deeply impacted by the presence of Muslims in the West and by the challenge of pluralism. Contemporary Muslims are faced with a rather striking range of alternative visions both for the place of Islam in a pluralistic world and for the place of pluralism in Islam. It would be a mistake to imagine, however, that the impact is only in one direction. The global presence of the Muslim community also poses a challenge to the world, and it seems to me that the most important lessons to be learned from the contemporary Muslim experience are related to this struggle to come to terms with pluralism. The very liveliness of the debate sets the Muslim community apart among the world's religious communities. For most Muslims, there is still a Truth with an upper-case "T" and an "Islam" with an upper-case "I" to be fought for – however broadly or narrowly these may be defined. Pluralism remains a problem for Muslims long after most other major religious communities have capitulated or taken refuge in private ghettos. The reason is simple. The Islamic tradition continues to hold out the ideal of a universal and all-encompassing system of ethics. Even for Muslim liberals the difference between right and wrong, justice and injustice, righteousness and unrighteousness, generosity and niggardliness is real, however difficult and fraught with uncertainty the effort to define these may be. For this reason the Muslim community offers a potent challenge to a postmodern ideology of pluralism.

GLOSSARY

adhān The call to prayer

'adl Justice; one of the distinctives of Mu'tazilite theology

ahl al-bayt Family of the Prophet, held in special honor by Shī'īte Muslims

Ahl-i-Ḥadīth Modern sect in the subcontinent which promotes uncritical obedience to prophetic ḥadīth

Aḥmadiyya Followers of the teaching of Ghulām Aḥmad of Qādiān, who claimed prophethood

Allāt Goddess of the pre-Islamic Arabs

amṣār (sing. **miṣr**) Garrison cities established by Arab conquerors

asbāb al-nuzūl Traditions describing the occasion on which a particular passage of the Qur'ān was revealed

Ash'arītes The dominant school of theology among Muslims which emphasizes the power and sovereignty of God

'askerī Military ruling class of the Ottoman empire encompassing the military, the 'ulamā', court officials, and nobility

athār Historical traditions

Avestas Zoroastrian scriptures

awā'il ḥadīth Traditions citing famous firsts

Azāriqa An extreme Khārijite sect

Bāb Shī'īte spokesman for the twelfth imām after his occultation

Badr 624 CE; Muhammad's first great victory over the Meccans

Baḥīra Christian monk who recognized the mark of prophethood on the young Muhammad

baqā' For some ṣūfīs the final stage of the mystic quest in which the ṣūfī returns from ecstasy to "continue" in God

baraka Spiritual power associated with holy people, places, or objects

barzakh Membrane or boundary separating two regions

Bektashiyya Ṣufī order of the Ottoman empire that venerated ʿAlī and was closely tied to the Janissaries

bidʿa Innovation; departure from Sunna

Chishtiyya Major ṣūfī order of the Indian subcontinent

dāʿīs Ismāʿīli missionaries

dalā'il al-nubuwwa Miracles that demonstrate to the validity of a prophet's mission

dār al-harb The abode of war, designating regions outside of Muslim rule

dār al-Islām The abode of Islam, designating regions ruled by Muslims

dhikr Remembrance of God; the central ritual practice of ṣūfīsm

dīwān System by which booty from conquests was distributed among Muslims

fanāʿ Passing away; the final stage in the ṣūfī quest

faqīr Freelance ṣūfī who embraces a life of poverty

fāsiq A Muslim who commits a grave sin

Fāṭimids Dynasty of Ismāʿīlī Shīʿītes that ruled a vast empire from Cairo, Egypt, during the tenth and eleventh centuries

fatwa The ruling of a muftī on a question of Islamic law; a fatwa is an individual opinion the authority of which is usually considered limited to the believer who requested the ruling. See also **ijtihād**

fiqh Understanding; the collective scholarly effort to understand and apply God's law

fitna Dissension; civil war

fuqahā' Scholars who engage in fiqh, the effort to understand God's law

fuṣḥā Classical Arabic

Fusṭāṭ Arab garrison city at the site of modern Cairo

Gemara Completion; rabbinic commentaries on the Mishna

ghayba Occultation; God's removal of the twelfth Shīʿīte Imām from the world

ghulām Slave; specifically a slave soldier. See also **Mamlūk**

Ghulāt Extremist Shīʿīte sects

ghusl Washing; major ablutions

gnosticism An imprecise catch-all term loosely applied to a variety of religious groups that deal in esoteric knowledge and tend to teach that matter is evil

ḥadīth A tradition that purports to transmit a saying, deed, or description of Muhammad. See also **Sunna**

ḥadīth literature The voluminous corpus of traditions about Muhammad preserved in a variety of literary forms

ḥadīth qudsī Traditions purported to be directly from Gabriel

Haggadah Jewish sacred narratives

Ḥajj Pilgrimage to Mecca; required of every able and financially capable believer once in his or her lifetime; one of the five pillars of Islam

Halakha Commandments in rabbinic Judaism

Ḥanafī A follower of the legal tradition of Abū Ḥanīfa; the most widely distributed of the four schools of law

Ḥanbalī A follower of the legal tradition of Ibn Ḥanbal

ḥarām Forbidden according to Islamic law

Hāshim Ancestor of Muhammad, namesake of the clan into which Muhammad was born, and putative founder of long-range Meccan caravan trade

hijāb Veil or covering; modest dress for women

Ḥijāz Western coastal region of the Arabian peninsula

Hijra Emigration; specifically Muhammad's emigration from Mecca to Medina, which marks the beginning of the Islamic era

Ḥimyar Pre-Islamic south Arabian kingdom

Hīra Capital of the pre-Islamic Lakhmid kingdom in southern Iraq

Ḥudaybiyya Site where Muhammad signed a ten-year truce with his Meccan adversaries

'ibādāt Acts of worship; the first division of Islamic law

Ibāḍīs Moderate Khārijites and the only Khārijite sect to survive into modern times

'Īd al-Adha The feast of sacrifice; the most important celebration of the Muslim calendar, coinciding with the pilgrimage

'Īd al-Fitr The first major religious feast of the Muslim calendar, coinciding with the end of the fast of Ramaḍān

'idda Waiting period before a divorce takes effect

ijmā' Consensus; a major principle of Islamic jurisprudence according to which the universal agreement of the community becomes a positive source of law

ijtihād Independent scholarly effort exerted in the attempt to understand and apply God's law; sometimes associated with the application of analogy or qiyās

Ikhwān al-Muslimīn The Muslim Brotherhood; an Islamic revivalist organization established by Ḥasan al-Bannā' in 1928

īlāf A word which appears in Qur'ān Sūra 106 and would no doubt enlighten our understanding of pre-Islamic Meccan trading patterns if we knew what it meant

Īlkhānids First of the Mongol dynasties to convert to Islam in 1295

'illa The reason or basis of a law

'ilm Knowledge, especially knowledge of religious sciences

imām A prayer leader and, by extension, the leader of the Muslim community; for Shī'ītes, a descendant of Muhammad possessing special knowledge and especially designated to lead the community

Imāmī Shīʿīsm The tradition of the majority of Shīʿīte Muslims who agree on twelve imāms, believe the twelfth has been hidden by God but will return in the future, and are sometimes called "Twelvers". See also **ghayba**

īmān Faith

Injīl Gospel

irāda Desire; specifically desire for God and one stage in the ṣūfī quest

ʿiṣma Purity; specifically the doctrine of infallibility applied to Muhammad and by Shīʿītes to the imāms

islam Submission

Ismāʿīlīs "Sevener" Shīʿītes who accept Ismāʿīl as the seventh imām and believe the imāmate continues through Ismāʿīl's line

isnād The chain of transmitters of a tradition given at the beginning of each ḥadīth

istiḥsān The application of personal judgment by a jurist to depart from strict application of qiyās

istiṣlāḥ Overruling the strict application of a legal rule for the sake of maṣlaḥa, the public good

iʿtikāf The practice of secluding oneself in a mosque for a set period

Jabrīyya Partisans of an extreme doctrine of divine determinism

Jaʿfarī fiqh The legal tradition of Twelver Shīʿītes

Jāhiliyya Time of ignorance preceding the rise of Islam; for some modern revivalists, any culture or civilization which is in rebellion against God

Jamāʿat-i Islāmī A revivalist organization founded in pre-partition India by Abū'l Aʿlā' Mawdūdī that became particularly influential in Pakistan

Janissaries The Ottoman professional army formed from slave levies in the Balkans

Jibrīl The angel Gabriel

jihād Struggle; in its most common usage, armed struggle on behalf of God

jinn Spiritual beings, created from fire, and mentioned frequently in the Qur'ān

jizya Head tax levied on non-Muslim subjects of the caliphate

Kaʿba Cube-shaped building in Mecca and center of Muslim pilgrimage

kāfir Unbeliever

kalām Dialectical theology

karāmāt Signs or graces; miracles performed by ṣūfī saints

Karbalā' Iraqī site of the martyrdom of the third Shīʿīte imām, Ḥusayn ibn ʿAlī

Kartīr Third-century Zoroastrian high priest

kasb Acquisition; a doctrine aimed at solving the ethical dilemma of divine determinism by asserting that humans acquire responsibility for deeds predetermined by God

Kaysaniyya Shīʿīte followers of Mukhtār and Muhammad ibn al-Ḥanafiyya after their deaths

Khalīfat Allāh Deputy of God; the title claimed by many early caliphs and claimants to the caliphate

Khalīfat Rasūl Allāh Deputy of the Prophet of God; the proper title of the caliphs according to religious scholars

khamr Wine; more specifically a beverage prohibited by the Qur'ān, the precise character of which is a matter of dispute

khanqah Ṣūfī lodge

Khārijites; Khawārij Those who withdrew from ʿAlī after the Battle of Ṣiffīn; a group of political-theological sects which emphasize works over faith

Khiḍr "The green one"; mysterious being mentioned in Qur'ān 18:60–82 and given mystical significance by many ṣūfīs

Khilāfat movement A movement of opposition to British rule and support for the Ottoman caliphate among Indian Muslims during World War I

madhhab Scholarly tradition or "schools" of jurisprudence; the four major madhhabs are the Ḥanafī, Malikī, Shāfiʿī, and Ḥanbalī

madrasa School or college

maghrib Geographical designation for the west, applied to north Africa; the fourth of the five daily prayers

maḥabba Love; a stage on the mystic quest

Mahdī Guided one; the title of the future Islamic leader who will establish justice; also, Sudanese leader who declared himself the Mahdī, defeated the British, and established a state in the Sudan

makrūh Discouraged according to Islamic law

malāma In ṣūfīsm, deliberately inviting blame or ridicule

Mālikī Adherent of the school of jurisprudence of which Mālik ibn Anas was the putative founder

Mamlūk Slave soldier; also, a brilliant Egyptian dynasty ruled by slave soldiers

Manāt Goddess in the pre-Islamic Arab pantheon

mandūb Recommended according to Islamic law

Manī Founder of Manichaeism

Manichaeism Missionary religion of Iranian origin characterized by a radical soul–body dualism

Ma'rib dam A centerpiece in the irrigation system of pre-Islamic Yemen

maʿrifa Gnosis; esoteric knowledge associated with the highest levels of ṣūfī experience

masjid Literally, place of prostration; mosque

maṣlaḥa Public interest; in Islamic law a principle which can override the strict application of a legal rule

maʿṣūm Pure; protected by God from major sin

matn The body of a ḥadīth report. See **isnād**

mawla (pl. **mawālī**) Clients; non-Arabs integrated into the Arab tribal structure by means of a patron–client system

Mejelle Ottoman codification of Ḥanafī civil law

Melitians Christian sect marked by a rigorous stand toward the readmission of apostates to the church

Mevleviyya "Whirling dervishes"; Sūfī brotherhood which traces itself to the poet Jalāl al-dīn Rūmī

Midrash "Exposition"; the interpretation and elaboration of Jewish scripture by means of oral tradition

miḥna Inquisition; the campaign, beginning in 833, by the ʿAbbāsid rulers al-Ma'mūn and al-Muʿtaṣim to impose Muʿtazilite dogma on the ʿulamā'

Minā Town near Mecca and an important station on the Ḥajj pilgrimage

Mishna The oral Torah; Jewish oral law believed to have been revealed to Moses at Mount Sinai, preserved and transmitted by rabbis, and codified during and after the third century

Monophysites Exponents of the doctrine that Christ had only a single divine nature

muʿāmalāt Division of fiqh concerned with obligations to other humans as opposed to obligations to God. See also **ʿibādāt**

mubāḥ Neutral action according to Islamic law

muftī A scholar who issues legal opinions in the form of fatwas

muḥaddithūn Scholars of ḥadīth

mujaddid Renewer of the faith

mujaddidiyya Branch of the Naqshandī ṭarīqa founded by Shaykh Aḥmad Sirhindī

mujāhada Striving; a stage on the mystic path

mujtahid A scholar who engages in independent effort, or ijtihād, to clarify a point of law

munāfiqūn Hypocrites; a major theme in the Qur'ān

Murji'a Those who postpone judgment about the ultimate fate of grave sinners, leaving the decision to God

muruwwa "Manliness"; the quintessential pre-Islamic Arab virtue

mutʿa Temporary marriage in Shīʿīte law

Muʿtazilites Theological movement that emphasized justice and human freedom

Muwaṭṭa' Legal treatise by the Mālik ibn Anas, founder of the Malikī school of fiqh

najāsa Ritual pollution requiring major ablutions for purification

Najrān Arabian oasis town with a significant Christian population in the pre-Islamic period

Nakhla Site of a famous raid by Muslims which violated the taboo on war during the month of Rajab

Nāmūs Appellation for Gabriel

Naqshbandiyya One of the most widely distributed ṣūfī brotherhoods, known for encouraging strict adherence to Islamic law and involvement in worldly affairs

naṣṣ In Shīʿīte Islam, the imām's designation of his successor
Negus Title of the ruler of Abyssinia
Neoplatonism Philosophical system associated with Plotinus which had an enduring influence on the development of Islamic philosophy and ṣūfism
Nestorianism One of three major branches of Christianity after the fifth century and the major Christian tradition of the Persian empire
Nizārī Ismāʿīlis The "assassins" of medieval legend who ruled mountain strongholds in Iran and Syria from 1090 to 1256
Pānīpat 1526 battle which established Mughal power in the Indian subcontinent
pillars of Islam Five ritual duties of Muslims. See **Ḥajj**; **Ramaḍān**; **ṣalāt**; **Shahāda**; **zakāt**
pīr Ṣufī master
qadar Divine power
qadariyya Partisans of free will
qāḍī Judge
Qāḍī-asker "Judge of the army"; title of the chief judges of the Ottoman empire
Qādiriyya Ṣūfī brotherhood traced to ʿAbd al-Qādir al-Gilānī
Qarmaṭīs Carmathians; established Ismāʿīlī states in Arabia and southern Syria
qaṣīda Ode; classical form of Arabic poetry
Qayyum Highest place in the hierarchy of saints; title claimed by Shaykh Aḥmad Sirhindī
qibla Direction of prayer
qiyās Analogical reasoning; a method of applying a known command from the Qur'ān or Sunna to a new case by means of analogy. See also **ijtihād**
Qizil-bāsh "Red heads"; partisans of Safāvid Shīʿīsm in Ottoman domains
Qur'ān Literally, recitations; the revelations received by Muhammad that together form the Muslim scriptures
Quraysh Muhammad's tribe and the dominant tribe of Mecca
Quṭb Axis or pole; title given to the head of the hierarchy of ṣūfī saints
Ramaḍān Name of he lunar month during which Muslims must fast from dawn to dusk; one of the five pillars of Islam
ra'y Independent judgment in Islamic law
Ridda wars Apostasy wars; Abū Bakr's campaign to subdue rebellious Arab tribes after Muhammad's death
Rifāʿiyya "Howling dervishes"; ṣūfī brotherhood famous for body piercing
ṣaḥīḥ Sound ḥadīth
Salafī A Muslim who claims to follow the example and teaching of the pious early generations of Muslims, the salaf al-ṣāliḥ, usually meaning the first three generations of believers

ṣalāt Prescribed worship; one of the five pillars of Islam

Saljūq Turks Turkish dynasty that sparked a Sunnī renaissance in the eleventh and twelfth centuries

samāʿ Literally, listening; ṣūfī music

samt Silence; a stage in the mystic quest

Sanūsiyya Activist ṣūfī order in North Africa that became a focus of anti-colonial resistance

Sāsānians Persian dynasty displaced by the Islamic conquests

Shāfiʿī School of Islamic jurisprudence traced to al-Shāfiʿī

Shahāda The Muslim confession of faith

Sharīʿa The totality of God's requirements for human behavior; Islamic law in its ideal form

Sharīf Noble

shaṭḥ Ecstatic utterances by ṣūfīs

shawq Mystic state of passionate longing for the beloved

shaykh "Elder"; a title of respect for a tribal leader or a ṣūfī master

Shīʿat ʿAlī Partisans of ʿAlī; Shīʿītes

Shīʿīte One of the partisans of ʿAlī

shirk Confusing something created with God; idolatry

Ṣifātiyya In Muslim heresiographies, those who attribute independent being to God's attributes

silsila Chain of transmitters of ṣūfī teaching

sīra Biography of Muhammad

ṣiyām Fasting

Siyāsat nāma Niẓām al-Mulk's advice to rulers

ṣūfī A Muslim mystic

ṣūfīsm Islamic mysticism

Suhrawardiyya Ṣufī order founded by al-Suhrawardī in Persia, but most successful in India

Sunna The example of the Prophet Muhammad, recorded in ḥadīth, which establishes normative precedent for Muslims; the second source of Islamic law

Sunnī A member of the majority community of Muslims, self-described as the ahl al-sunna wa'l jamaʿ, the people of the prophetic Sunna and consensus

Tabūk Oasis in northwest Arabia

taḥannuth Form of religious discipline practiced by pre-Islamic Arabis, including Muhammad

ṭahāra Ritual purity

ṭalab al-ʿilm Search for knowledge, pursued especially by scholars of ḥadīth

ṭalāq Divorce

Ṭālibān Theological students; puritanical movement Afghanistan and Pakistan

Talmud Collections of Jewish tradition and learning representing the culmination of rabbinic scholarship

Tanẓīmāt Period of sustained political and legal reform in the Ottoman empire 1839–76

taqiyya Pious dissimulation; a Twelver Shīʿite doctrine which allows followers of the imām to conceal their true beliefs

taqlīd Adherence to authoritative precedent

taqwa Piety; fear of God

ṭarīqa Ṣūfī order or brotherhood

taʿṭīl Stripping or negating God's attributes

tawakkul Trust; a stage in the mystic path

tawḥīd Oneness; the doctrine of God's absolute unity

tayammum Use of clean earth to perform ablutions when water is unavailable

Torah Pentateuch; first five books of the Hebrew Bible

Twelvers The majority branch of Shīʿītes who recognize twelve imāms

ʿubūdīya Servanthood; a stage on the mystic path

Uḥud Battle (625) in which the Muslims were defeated by the Meccans and the Prophet was wounded

ʿulamāʾ Muslim religious scholars

umma The community of Muslims

uṣūl al-fiqh The sources of Islamic law, especially the Qur'ān, the Sunna of the Prophet, qiyās, and ijmāʿ

Uṣūlīs Branch of Shīʿīte ʿulamāʾ that held that religious authority is vested primarily in living scholars, the mujtahids, as opposed to texts

ʿUzza Goddess in the pre-Islamic Arab pantheon

Wahhābī Member of a puritanical political-religious movement originating in eighteenth-century Arabia and named for its founder, Muḥammad Ibn ʿAbd al-Wahhāb

waḥī Revelation

walī Friend or trusted one; for ṣūfīs a friend of God, or saint; in marriage, the bride's closest male relative who acts as marriage guardian

wilāya Friendship with God; sainthood

wird Devotional exercises assigned to a disciple by a ṣūfī shaykh

wuḍūʾ Minor ablutions

Yathrib Oasis town; pre-Islamic designation of Medina

Zabūr Psalms

Ẓāhirīs Extinct school of fiqh famous for adhering strictly to the plain meaning of scriptural texts

zakāt Poor-tax; one of the five pillars of Islam

Zanādiqa Epithet applied to a variety of heresies that seemed connected with pre-Islamic Persian religion

ẓannī Conjectural

Ẓarūra The principle of necessity according to which a rule of Islamic law is suspended in extreme circumstances

Zaydīs Politically quiescent branch of Shīʿīte

Zoroastrianism Dualistic religion founded by Zoroaster that become the official religion of pre-Islamic Persia

zuhd Asceticism

ẓuhr Second of the five daily prayers, performed after midday

BIBLIOGRAPHY

ʿAbdūh, Muhammad. 1966. *The Theology of Unity*. Translated by I. M. Cragg. London: George Allen & Unwin.

Abou El Fadl, Khaled M. 2001a. *And God Knows the Soldiers: The Authoritative and Authoritarian in Islamic Discourses*. Lanham, MD: University Press of America.

Abou El Fadl, Khaled M. 2001b. *Speaking in God's Name: Islamic Law, Authority and Women*. Oxford: Oneworld.

Abou El Fadl, Khaled M. 2002. *The Place of Tolerance in Islam*. Boston, MA: Beacon Press.

Abrahamov, Binyamin. 1998. *Islamic Theology: Traditionalism and Rationalism*. Edinburgh: Edinburgh University Press.

Abu-Rabiʿ, Ibrahim M. 1996. *Intellectual Origins of Islamic Resurgence in the Modern Arab World*. Albany: State University of New York Press.

Adams, Charles C. 1933. *Islam and Modernism in Egypt*. Oxford: Oxford University Press.

Adams, Charles J. 1977. *A Reader's Guide to the Great Religions*. New York: Free Press.

Addas, Claude. 1993. *Quest for the Red Sulphur: The life of Ibn ʿArabī*. Translated by P. Kingsley. Cambridge: Islamic Texts Society.

Afnan, Soheil M. 1958. *Avicenna: His Life and Works*. London: Allen & Unwin.

Ahmad, Aziz. 1967. *Islamic Modernism in India and Pakistan, 1857–1964*. Oxford: Oxford University Press.

Ahmad, Aziz. 1969a. *An Intellectual History of Islam in India*. Edinburgh: Edinburgh University Press.

Ahmad, Aziz. 1969b. *Studies in Islamic Culture in the Indian Environment*. Oxford: Clarendon Press.

Ahmad, Aziz, and G. E. von Grunebaum. 1970. *Muslim Self-Statement in India and Pakistan, 1857–1968*. Wiesbaden: Otto Harrassowitz.

Aḥmad Khān, Sir Sayyid. 1862 and 1865. *Tabyīn al-Kalām: The Mohamedan Commentary on the Holy Bible*, 2 vols. Ghazeepore: author's imprint.

Ahmed, Akbar S. 1992. *Postmodernism and Islam: Predicament and Promise*. London: Routledge.

Ajami, Fouad. 2004. "Tariq Ramadan." *Wall Street Journal*, September 7.

Algar, Hamid. 1969. *Religion and the State in Iran, 1785–1906*. Berkeley: University of California Press.

Amīr Ali, Syed. 1922. *The Spirit of Islam*. London: Christophers.

Amitai-Preiss, Reuven. 1995. *Mongols and Mamlūks: The Mamlūk–īlkhānid War, 1260–1281*. Cambridge: Cambridge University Press.

Amitai-Preiss, Reuven, and David O. Morgan, eds. 2000. *The Mongol Empire and its Legacy*. Leiden: E. J. Brill.

Anderson, Norman. 1976. *Law Reform in the Muslim World*. London: Athlone Press.

Arberry, A. J. 1950. *Sufism: An Account of the Mystics of Islam*. London: Allen & Unwin.

Arberry, A. J. 1955. *The Koran Interpreted, by Arthur J. Arberry*. New York: Macmillan; London: Allen & Unwin.

Arberry, A. J. 1957. *The Seven Odes: The First Chapter in Arabic Literature*. London: George Allen & Unwin.

Arberry, A. J. 1964. *Aspects of Islamic Civilization as Depicted in the Original Texts*. London: George Allen & Unwin.

Arjoman, S. A. 1984. *The Shadow of God and the Hidden Imam: Religion, Political Order and Social Change in Shi'ite Iran from the Beginnings to 1890*. Chicago: University of Chicago Press.

Arkoun, Mohammed. 1994. *Rethinking Islam: Common Questions, Uncommon Answers*. Translated by R. D. Lee. Boulder, CO: Westview Press.

Ash'arī, Abū'l Ḥasan 'Alī al-. 1940. *Al Ibānah 'an uṣūl ad-diyānah* (The Elucidation of Islam's Foundation). Translated by Walter C. Klein. New Haven, CT: American Oriental Society.

Ash'arī, Abū'l Ḥasan 'Alī al-. 1953. *The Theology of al-Ash'arī: The Arabic Texts of al-Ash'arīs Kitāb al-Luma' and Risālat Istiḥsān al-khawḍ fī 'ilm al-kalām*. Translated by R. J. McCarthy. Beyrouth: Impr. catholique.

Atiyeh, George N. 1975. *The Contemporary Middle East 1943–1973: A Selective Annotated Bibliography*. Boston, MA: G. K. Hall.

'Aṭṭār, Farīd al-Dīn. 1966. *Muslim Saints and Mystics*. Translated by A. J. Arberry. Chicago: University of Chicago Press.

'Aṭṭār, Farīd al-Dīn. 1993. *The Conference of the Birds: A Philosophical Religious Poem in Prose*. Translated by C. S. Nott. Boston, MA: Shambhala.

Awde, Nicholas. 2000. *Women in Islam: An Anthology from the Qur'ān and Hadīths*. Richmond, UK: Curzon.

Ayalon, David. 1988. *Outsiders in the Lands of Islam: Mamluks, Mongols and Eunuchs*. London: Variorum.

Ayoub, Mahmoud. 1984. *The Qur'ān and its Interpreters*. Albany: State University of New York Press.

A'zamī, Muhammad Muṣṭafa. 1985. *On Schacht's Origins of Muhammadan Jurisprudence*. Riyadh, Saudi Arabia: King Saud University; New York: Wiley.

A'zamī, Muhammad Muṣṭafa. 1992. *Studies in Early Hadīth Literature: With a Critical Edition of Some Early Texts*. Indianapolis: American Trust Publications.

Babur, Emperor. 1996. *The Baburnama: Memoirs of Babur, Prince and Emperor*. Translated by W. M. Thackston. Washington, DC: Freer Gallery of Art.

Bacharach, Jere L. 1984. *A Middle East Studies Handbook*. Seattle: University of Washington Press.

Bakhash, S. 1978. *Iran: Monarchy, Bureaucracy and Reform under the Qājārs, 1858–1896*. London: Ithaca Press.

Balādhūrī, Ahmad ibn Yahyā. 1916, 1924. *The Origins of the Islamic State*. Translated by P. K. Hitti. New York: Columbia University Press.

Baldick, Julian. 1989. *Mystical Islam: An Introduction to Sufism*. London: I. B. Tauris.

Baljon, J. M. S. 1961. *Modern Muslim Koran Interpretation*. Leiden: E. J. Brill.

Bede, the Venerable. 1969. *Bede's Ecclesiastical History of the English People*, ed. Bertram Colgrave and R. A. B. Mynors. Oxford: Clarendon Press.

Bell, Richard. 1926. *The Origin of Islam in its Christian Environment*. London: Macmillan.

Bell, Richard. 1970. *Bell's Introduction to the Qur'ān*. Revised and enlarged by W. Montgomery Watt. Edinburgh: Edinburgh University Press.

Berns McGown, Rima. 1999. *Muslims in Diaspora: The Somali Communities of London and Toronto*. Toronto: University of Toronto Press.

Binder, Leonard. 1988. *Islamic Liberalism, a Critique of Development Ideologies*. Chicago: University of Chicago Press.

Black, Antony. 2001. *The History of Islamic Political Thought*. New York: Routledge.

Bosworth, Clifford. 1967. *The Islamic Dynasties: A Chronological and Genealogical Handbook*. Edinburgh: Edinburgh University Press.

Boullata, Issa J. 1990. *Trends and Issues in Contemporary Arab Thought*. Albany: State University of New York Press.

Böwering, Gerhard. 1980. *The Mystical Vision of Existence in Classical Islam: The Quarānic Hermeneutics of the Ṣūfī Sahl At-Tustarī (d. 283/896)*. Berlin: de Gruyter.

Boyce, Mary. 1990. *Textual Sources for the Study of Zoroastrianism*. Chicago: University of Chicago Press.

Bravmann, M. M. 1972. *The Spiritual Background of Early Islam: Studies in Ancient Arab Concepts*. Leiden: E. J. Brill.

Brockelmann, Carl. 1947. *History of the Islamic Peoples*. New York: G. P. Putnam's Sons.

Brown, Daniel. 1996. *Rethinking Tradition in Modern Islamic Thought*. Cambridge: Cambridge University Press.

Brown, Peter. 1971. *The World of Late Antiquity*. New York: Harcourt, Brace, Jovanovich.

Buehler, Arthur. 1998. *Sufi Heirs of the Prophet*. Columbia: University of South Carolina Press.

Bukhārī, Muhammad ibn Ismā'īl. 1996. *The English Translation of Ṣahīh al Bukhārī with the Arabic text*. Translated by M. M. Khān. Alexandria, VA: Al-Saadawi Publications.

Bulliet, Richard W. 1972. *The Patricians of Nishapur*. Cambridge, MA: Harvard University Press.

Bulliet, Richard W. 1979. *Conversion to Islam in the Medieval Period: An Essay in Quantitative History*. Cambridge, MA: Harvard University Press.

Burton, John. 1990. *The Sources of Islamic Law: Islamic Theories of Abrogation*. Edinburgh: Edinburgh University Press.

Burton, John. 1994. *An Introduction to the Hadīth*. Edinburgh: Edinburgh University Press.

Buruma, Ian. 2007. "Tariq Ramadan Has an Identity Issue." *New York Times Magazine*, February 4.

Chelkowski, P. J., ed. 1979. *Ta'ziyeh: Ritual and Drama in Iran*. New York: New York University Press.

Chittick, William. 1980. *A Shi'ite Anthology*. Albany: State University of New York Press.

Chittick, William. 1998. *The Self-Disclosure of God: Principles of Ibn al-'Arabī's Cosmology*. Albany: State University of New York Press.

Chodkiewicz, Michel. 1993. *Seal of the Saints: Prophethood and Sainthood in the Doctrine of Ibn al-'Arabī*. Translated by L. Sherrard. Cambridge: Islamic Texts Society.

Cole, J. R., and N. Keddie. 1986. *Shi'ism and Social Protest*. New Haven, CT: Yale University Press.

Commins, David. 1990. *Islamic Reform: Politics and Social Change in Late Ottoman Syria*. New York: Oxford University Press.

Cook, Michael, ed. 1976. *A History of the Ottoman Empire to 1730*. Cambridge: Cambridge University Press.

Cook, Michael. 1981. *Early Muslim Dogma: A Source-Critical Study*. Cambridge: Cambridge University Press.

Cook, Michael. 1983. *Muhammad*. Oxford: Oxford University Press.

Cook, Michael. 2000. *The Koran: A Very Short Introduction*. Oxford: Oxford University Press.

Corbin, Henry. 1993. *History of Islamic Philosophy*. Translated by L. Sherrard. London: Kegan Paul International.

Cormack, Margaret, ed. 2002. *Sacrificing the Self: Perspectives on Martyrdom and Religion*. Oxford: Oxford University Press.

Coulson, Noel J. 1964. *A History of Islamic Law*. Edinburgh: Edinburgh University Press.

Cragg, Kenneth. 1971. *The Event of the Qur'ān: Islam in its Scripture*. London: Allen & Unwin.

Cragg, Kenneth. 1985. *The Pen and the Faith: Eight Modern Muslim Writers and the Qur'ān*. London: Allen & Unwin.

Crone, Patricia. 1987a. *Meccan Trade and the Rise of Islam*. Princeton, NJ: Princeton University Press.

Crone, Patricia. 1987b. *Roman, Provincial and Islamic Law: The Origins of the Islamic Patronate*. Cambridge: Cambridge University Press.

Crone, Patricia, and Michael Cook. 1977. *Hagarism: The Making of the Islamic World*. Cambridge: Cambridge University Press.

Crone, Patricia, and Martin Hinds. 1986. *God's Caliph: Religious Authority in the First Centuries of Islam*. Cambridge: Cambridge University Press.

Daftary, Farhad. 1990. *The Ismā'īlīs: Their History and Doctrines*. Cambridge: Cambridge University Press.

Donner, Fred McGraw. 1981. *The Early Islamic Conquests*. Princeton, NJ: Princeton University Press.

Donner, Fred McGraw. 1998. *Narratives of Islamic Origins: The Beginnings of Islamic Historical Writing*. Princeton, NJ: Darwin Press.

Donohue, John J., and John L. Esposito, eds. 1982. *Islam in Transition: Muslim Perspectives*. Oxford: Oxford University Press.

Duchesne-Guillemin, J. 1983. "Zoroastrian Religion." In *The Cambridge History of Iran*, vol. 3, part 2. Cambridge: Cambridge University Press.

Dutton, Yasin. 1999. *The Origins of Islamic Law*. Richmond, UK: Curzon.

Edwardes, Stephen Meredyth. 1930. *Mughal Rule in India*. Oxford: Oxford University Press.

Elad, A. 1992. "Why Did 'Abd al-Malik Build the Dome of the Rock? A Re-examination of the Muslim Sources." In Julian Raby and Jeremy Johns, eds., *Bayt al-Maqdis: 'Abd al-Malik's Jerusalem*, part 1. Oxford: Oxford University Press for the Board of Faculty of Oriental Studies.

Eliade, Mircea, ed. 1987. *The Encyclopaedia of Religion*, 16 vols. New York: Macmillan.

Enayat, Hamid. 1982. *Modern Islamic Political Thought*. Austin: University of Texas Press.

Encyclopaedia of Islam, 2nd edn. 1960– . Leiden: E. J. Brill.

Encyclopedia of Islam and the Muslim World. 2004. New York: Macmillan Reference USA, Thomson/Gale.

Ernst, Carl W. 1985. *Words of Ecstasy in Sufism*. Albany: State University of New York Press.

Esack, Farid. 1999. *On Being Muslim: Finding a Religious Path in the World Today*. Oxford: Oneworld.

Esposito, John L., ed. 1995. *The Oxford Encyclopedia of the Modern Islamic World*. New York: Oxford University Press.

Fārābī, Abū Naṣr. 1985. *Al-Farabi on the Perfect State: Abū Naṣr al-Fārābī's Mabādi ārā ahl al-madīna al-fāḍila: A Revised Text with Introduction, Translation, and Commentary*. Translated by R. Walzer. New York: Oxford University Press.

Firestone, Reuven. 1990. *Journeys in Holy Lands: The Evolution of the Abraham-Ishmael Legends in Islamic Exegesis*. Albany: State University of New York Press.

Fletcher, Joseph. 1986. "The Mongols: Ecological and Social Perspectives." *Harvard Journal of Asiatic Studies* 46, 11–50.

Frank, Richard. 1978. *Beings and their Attributes: The Teachings of the Basrian School of the Mu'tazila in the Classical Period*. Albany: State University of New York Press.

Frend, W. H. C. 1982. *The Early Church*. Philadelphia, PA: Fortress Press.

Friedman, Yohanan. 1971. *Shaykh Ahmad Sirhindi*. Montreal: McGill University, Institute of Islamic Studies.

Frye, Richard Nelson. 1963. *The Heritage of Persia*. Cleveland, OH: World Publishing.

Fyzee, Asaf A. A. 1949. *Outlines of Muhammadan Law*. Oxford: Oxford University Press.

Gabrieli, Francesco. 1969. *Arab Historians of the Crusades*. Translated by E. J. Costello. London: Routledge & Kegan Paul.

Gatje, Helmut. 1976. *The Qur'ān and its Exegesis*. Translated by A. T. Welch. Berkeley: University of California Press.

Geertz, Clifford. 1968. *Islam Observed: Religious Developments in Morocco and Indonesia*. New Haven, CT: Yale University Press.

Gervers, Michael, and Ramzi Jibran Bikhazi, eds. 1990. *Conversion and Continuity: Indigenous Christian Communities in Islamic Lands, Eighth to Eighteenth Centuries*. Toronto: Pontifical Institute of Mediaeval Studies.

Ghazālī. 1953. *The Faith and Practice of al-Ghazālī*. Translated by W. M. Watt. London: G. Allen & Unwin.

Ghazālī. 1980. *Freedom and Fulfillment: An Annotated Translation of Al-Ghazālī's al-Munqidh min al-dalāl and Other Relevant Works of al-Ghazālī*. Translated by R. J. McCarthy. Boston, MA: Twayne.

Ghazālī. 1982. *The Recitation and Interpretation of the Qur'ān: Al-Ghazālī's Theory*. Translated by M. A. Quasem. London: Kegan Paul International.

Ghazālī. 1997. *The Incoherence of the Philosophers.* Translated by M. E. Marmura. Provo, UT: Brigham Young University Press.

Gibb, H. A. R. 1947. *Modern Trends in Islam.* Chicago: University of Chicago Press.

Gibb, H. A. R. 1950. *Islamic Society and the West: A Study of the Impact of Western Civilization on Moslem Culture in the Near East.* Oxford: Oxford University Press.

Gibb, H. A. R. 1963. *Arabic Literature: An Introduction.* Oxford: Clarendon Press.

Gibb, H. A. R. 1969. *Mohammedanism: An Historical Survey,* 2nd edn., revd. Oxford: Oxford University Press.

Gibbon, Edward. 1902. *The Decline and Fall of the Roman Empire,* 7 vols. London: George Bell & Sons.

Gilsenan, Michael. 1982. *Recognizing Islam: Religion and Society in the Modern Middle East.* London: Croom Helm.

Goitein, S. D. 1955. *Jews and Arabs: Their Contacts through the Ages.* New York: Schocken Books.

Goldziher, Ignaz. 1973. *Muslim Studies,* 2 vols. Translated by C. R. Barber and S. M. Stern. Chicago: Aldine.

Goldziher, Ignaz. 1980. *Introduction to Islamic Theology and Law.* Translated by A. Hamori. Princeton, NJ: Princeton University Press.

Goodwin, G. 1971. *A History of Ottoman Architecture.* Baltimore, MD: Johns Hopkins University Press.

Grabar, Oleg. 1996. *The Shape of the Holy: Early Islamic Jerusalem.* Princeton, NJ: Princeton University Press.

Graham, William A. 1977. *Divine Word and Prophetic Word in Early Islam: A Reconsideration of the Sources with Special Reference to the Divine Saying or Hadith Qudsi.* The Hague: Mouton.

Grousset, Rene. 1970. *Empire of the Steppes: A History of Central Asia.* Translated by N. Walford. New Brunswick, NJ: Rutgers University Press.

Guillaume, Alfred. 1980. *The Traditions of Islam.* Oxford: Oxford University Press.

Haeri, Shahla. 1989. *Law of Desire: Temporary Marriage in Shi'i Iran.* Syracuse, NY: Syracuse University Press.

Hallaq, Wael. 1997. *A History of Islamic Legal Theories: An Introduction to Sunnī uṣūl al-fiqh.* Cambridge: Cambridge University Press.

Hallaq, Wael. 1993. "Was al-Shāfi'ī the Master Architect of Islamic Jurisprudence?" *International Journal of Middle Eastern Studies* 25, 587–605.

Halm, Heinz. 1991. *Shi'ism.* Edinburgh: Edinburgh University Press.

Hambly, Gavin. 1977. *Cities of Mughal India.* New Delhi: Vikas.

Hamidullah, Muhammad, trans. 1968. *The First Written Constitution in the World: An Important Document of the Time of the Holy Prophet.* Lahore: Sheikh Muhammad Ashraf.

Hamidullah, Muhammad. 1977. *Muslim Conduct of State.* Lahore: Sheikh Muhammad Ashraf.

Hardy, Peter. 1972. *The Muslims of British India.* Cambridge: Cambridge University Press.

Hasan, Ahmad. 1970. *The Early Development of Islamic Jurisprudence.* Islamabad: Islamic Research Institute.

Hattox, Ralph S. 1988. *Coffee and Coffeehouses: The Origins of a Social Beverage in the Medieval Near East.* Seattle: University of Washington Press.

Hawting, Gerald R. 1999. *The Idea of Idolatry and the Emergence of Islam: From Polemic to History*. Cambridge: Cambridge University Press.

Hawting, Gerald R. 2000. *The First Dynasty of Islam: The Umayyad Caliphate AD 661–750*. London: Routledge.

Hawting, Gerald R., and Abdul-Kader A. Shareef. 1993. *Approaches to the Qur'ān*. London: Routledge.

Haykal, Muhammad Ḥusayn. 1995. *The Life of Muhammad*. Translated by Ismā'īl al-Fārūqī. Plainfield, IN: American Trust Publications.

Hazard, Harry W. 1954. *Atlas of Islamic History*. Princeton, NJ: Princeton University Press.

Hillenbrand, Carole. 1999. *The Crusades: Islamic Perspectives*. Chicago: Fitzroy Dearborn.

Hirenstein, S., and M. Tiernan, eds. 1993. *Muhyiddin Ibn Arabi: A Commemorative Volume*. Shaftesbury, UK: Element Books.

Hiskett, M. 1973. *The Sword of Truth: The Life and Times of Shehu Usuman Dan Fodio*. New York: Oxford University Press.

Hitti, Philip Khuri. 1963. *History of the Arabs*. London: Macmillan; New York: St. Martin's Press.

Hodgson, Marshall. 1955. *The Order of the Assassins*. The Hague: Mouton.

Hodgson, Marshall. 1974. *Venture of Islam*, 3 vols. Chicago: University of Chicago Press.

Hoffman, Valerie J. 1995. *Sufism, Mystics, and Saints in Modern Egypt*. Columbia: University of South Carolina Press.

Holt, P. M., and Ann K. S. Lambton, eds. 1970. *The Cambridge History of Islam*. Cambridge: Cambridge University Press.

Hopwood, Derek, and Diana Grimwood-Jones. 1972. *The Middle East and Islam: A Bibliographical Introduction*. Zug, Switzerland: Inter Documentation.

Hourani, Albert. 1983. *Arabic Thought in the Liberal Age*. Cambridge: Cambridge University Press.

Hourani, Albert. 1991. *A History of the Arab Peoples*. Cambridge, MA: Belknap Press of Harvard University Press.

Hourani, George. 1985. *Reason and Tradition in Islamic Ethics*. Cambridge: Cambridge University Press.

Hujwīrī, 'Alī ibn 'Uthmān. 1959. *The Kashf al Mahjūb: The Oldest Persian Treatise on Sūfism*. Translated by R. A. Nicholson. London: Luzac.

Humphries, Stephen. 1991. *Islamic History: A Framework for Inquiry*. Princeton, NJ: Princeton University Press.

Huṣrī, Sāti'al-. 1982 "Egyptianness." In John Donahue and John Esposito, eds., *Islam in Transition: Muslim Perspectives*. Oxford: Oxford University Press.

Hussain, J. M. 1982. *The Occultation of the Twelfth Imam: A Historical Background*. London: Muhammad Trust.

Ibn al-'Arabī. 1980. *The Bezels of Wisdom*. Translated by R. W. Austin. New York: Paulist Press.

Ibn al-Kalbī. 1952. *The Book of Idols, Being a Translation from the Arabic of the Kitāb al-asnām*. Translated by N. A. Faris. Princeton, NJ: Princeton University Press.

Ibn al-Naqīb, Ahmad. 1994. *Reliance of the Traveler: The Classic Manual of Islamic Sacred Law 'Umdat al-Salik*. Translated by N. H. Keller. Beltsville, MD: Amana Publications.

Ibn Isḥāq, Muhammad. 1955. *The Life of Muhammad: A Translation of Ibn Isḥāq's Sīrat Rasūl Allāh*. Translated by A. Guillaume. New York: Oxford University Press.

Ibn Khaldūn. 1969. *The Muqaddimah: An Introduction to History*. Translated by F. Rosenthal. Princeton, NJ: Princeton University Press.

Ibn Rushd. 1994. *The Distinguished Jurist's Primer: A Translation of Bidāyat al-mujtahid*, 2 vols. Translated by I. A. Nyazee. Reading, UK: Garnet.

Ibn Ṭufayl, Muhammad ibn 'Abd al-Malik. 1972. *Ibn Tufayl's Haqq ibn Yaqzān*. Translated by L. E. Goodman. New York: Twayne Publishers.

Inalcik, Halil. 1973. *The Ottoman Empire: The Classical Age, 1300–1600*. Translated by N. I. Imber. London: Weidenfeld & Nicolson.

Inalcik, Halil. 1985. *Studies in Ottoman Social and Economic History*. London: Variorum.

Inalcik, Halil, and Donald Quataert. 1994. *An Economic and Social History of the Ottoman Empire, 1300–1914*. Cambridge: Cambridge University Press.

Iqbāl, Muhammad. 1966. *Javīd Nāmā*. Translated by A. J. Arberry. London: George Allen & Unwin.

Iqbāl, Muhammad. 1999. *The Reconstruction of Religious Thought in Islam*. Lahore: Sheikh Muhammad Ashraf.

Izutsu, Toshihiko. 1966. *Ethico-Religious Concepts in the Qur'ān*. Montreal: McGill University Press.

Izutsu, Toshihiko. 1987. *God and Man in the Koran*. Salem, NH: Ayer.

Jabartī, 'Abd al-Raḥmān. 1993. *Jabartī's Chronicle of the French Occupation, 1798*. Translated by Shmuel Moreh. Princeton, NJ: Marcus Wiener.

Jackson, P., and L. Lockhart, eds. 1986. *The Cambridge History of Iran*. Cambridge: Cambridge University Press.

Jansen, J. J. G. 1974. *The Interpretation of the Koran in Modern Egypt*. Leiden: E. J. Brill.

Johansen, Baber. 1988. *The Islamic Law on Land and Rent*. London: Croom Helm.

Jones, A. H. M. 1986. *The Later Roman Empire, 284–602: A Social, Economic and Administrative Survey*, vol. 2. Baltimore, MD: Johns Hopkins University Press.

Juvaynī, 'Alā al-Dīn. 1958. *History of the World Conqueror*. Translated by J. A. Boyle. Manchester: Manchester University Press.

Juvaynī, 'Alā al-Dīn. 1997. *Genghis Khan: The History of the World Conqueror*. Translated by J. A. Boyle. Seattle: University of Washington Press.

Juynboll, G. H. A. 1969. *The Authenticity of the Tradition Literature: Discussions in Modern Egypt*. Leiden: E. J. Brill.

Juynboll, G. H. A. 1983. *Muslim Tradition*. Cambridge: Cambridge University Press.

Kaegi, Walter Emil. 1992. *Byzantium and the Early Islamic Conquests*. Cambridge: Cambridge University Press.

Kassis, Hanna. 1983. *A Concordance of the Koran*. Berkeley: University of California Press.

Katsh, Abraham Isaac. 1954. *Judaism in Islam: Biblical and Talmudic Backgrounds of the Koran and its Commentaries: Suras II and III*. New York: Bloch.

Keddie, Nikkie. 1968. *An Islamic Response to Imperialism*. Berkeley: University of California Press.

Keddie, Nikkie. 1972a. *Jamāl al-Dīn al-Afghānī: A Political Biography*. Berkeley: University of California Press.

Keddie, Nikkie, ed. 1972b. *Scholars, Saints and Sufis*. Berkeley: University of California Press.

Kedourie, Elie. 1966. *Afghānī and 'Abdūh: An Essay on Religious Unbelief and Political Activism in Modern Islam*. London: Frank Cass.

Kelsay, John, and James Turner Johnson, eds. 1991. *Just War and Jihad: Historical and Theoretical Perspectives on War and Peace in Western and Islamic Traditions*. Westport, CT: Greenwood Press.

Kennedy, Hugh. 1986. *The Prophet and the Age of the Caliphs*. London: Longman.

Kerr, Malcolm. 1966. *Islamic Reform: The Political and Legal Theories of Muhammad ʿAbduh and Rashīd Riḍā*. Berkeley: University of California Press.

Khadduri, Majid. 1955. *The Islamic Law of Nations: Shaybani's Siyar*. Baltimore, MD: Johns Hopkins University Press.

Kister, M. J. 1980. *Studies in Jāhiliyya and Early Islam*. London: Variorum.

Knysh, Alexander. 2000. *Islamic Mysticism: A Short History*. Leiden: E. J. Brill.

Kohlberg, Etan. 1991. *Belief and Law in Imami Shi'ism*. Aldershot, UK: Variorum.

Kritzeck, James, ed. 1975. *Anthology of Islamic Literature*. New York: New American Library.

Kurzman, Charles. 1998. *Liberal Islam: A Sourcebook*. New York: Oxford University Press.

Lambton, A. K. S. 1981. *State and Government in Medieval Islam*. Oxford: Oxford University Press.

Lambton, A. K. S. 1987. *Qājār Iran: Eleven Studies*. London: I. B. Tauris.

Landen, Robert G. 1970. *The Emergence of the Modern Middle East: Selected Readings*. New York: Van Nostrand Reinhold.

Lapidus, Ira. 1988. *A History of Islamic Societies*. New York: Cambridge University Press.

Leiser, Gary. 1988. *A History of the Seljuks: Ibrahim Kafesoglu's Interpretation and the Resulting Controversy*. Carbondale: Southern Illinois University Press.

Lester, Toby. 1999. "What is the Koran?" *Atlantic Monthly*, January.

Lewinstein, Keith. 2002. "The Revaluation of Martyrdom in Early Islam." In Margaret Cormack, ed., *Sacrificing the Self: Perspectives on Martyrdom and Religion*. Oxford: Oxford University Press.

Lewis, Bernard. 1961. *The Emergence of Modern Turkey*. Oxford: Oxford University Press.

Lewis, Bernard. 1966. *The Arabs in History*. London: Hutchinson.

Lewis, Bernard. 1967. *The Assassins: A Radical Sect in Islam*. London: Weidenfeld & Nicolson.

Lewis, Bernard. 1973. *Islam in History: Ideas, People, and Events in the Middle East*. Chicago: Open Court.

Lewis, Bernard. 1973. "The Mongols, the Turks and the Muslim Polity." In *Islam in History: Ideas, Men and Events in the Middle East*. London: Alcove Press.

Lewis, Bernard, ed. 1987. *Islam: From the Prophet Muhammad to the Capture of Constantinople*. New York: Oxford University Press.

Lewis, Bernard. 1993a. *Islam and the West*. Oxford: Oxford University Press.

Lings, Martin. 1976. *The Qur'ān: Catalogue of an Exhibition of Qur'ān Manuscripts at the British Library, 3 April–15 August 1976*. London: World of Islam Publishing, for the British Library.

Lings, Martin. 1983. *Muhammad: His Life Based on the Earliest Sources*. New York: Inner Traditions International.

Luṭfi al-Sayyid, Aḥmad. 1982. "Egyptianness." In John Donahue and John Esposito, eds., *Islam in Transition: Muslim Perspectives*. Oxford: Oxford University Press.

Lyall, Charles James. 1981. *Translations of Ancient Arabian Poetry, Chiefly Pre-Islamic, with an Introduction and Notes*. Westport, CT: Hyperion Press.

Maalouf, Amin. 1984. *The Crusades through Arab Eyes*. New York: Schocken Books.

McAuliffe, Jane Dammen. 1991. *Qur'ānic Christians: An Analysis of Classical and Modern Exegesis*. Cambridge: Cambridge University Press.

McChesney, R. D. 1991. *Waqf in Central Asia*. Princeton, NJ: Princeton University Press.

MacDonald, Duncan Black. 1903. *The Development of Muslim Theology, Jurisprudence, and Constitutional Theory*. New York: Scribner's.

MacDonald, Duncan Black. 1909. *The Religious Attitude and Life in Islam*. Chicago: University of Chicago Press.

McDonough, Sheila. 1970. *The Authority of the Past: A Study of Three Muslim Modernists*. Chambersburg, PA: American Academy of Religion.

Madelung, Wilfred. 1982. *Religious Trends in Early Islamic Iran*. Albany, NY: Bibliotheca Persica.

Madelung, Wilfred. 1985. *Religious Schools and Sects in Medieval Islam*. London: Variorum.

Mahdi, Muhsin. 1957. *Ibn Khaldun's Philosophy of History*. Chicago: University of Chicago Press.

Mahdi, Muhsin, ed. 1963. *Medieval Political Philosophy*. Glencoe, IL: Free Press.

Makdisi, George. 1981. *The Rise of Colleges: Institutions of Learning in Islam and the West*. Edinburgh: Edinburgh University Press.

Marmura, Michael E., ed. 1984. *Islamic Theology and Philosophy: Studies in Honor of George F. Hourani*. Albany: State University of New York Press.

Marshall, Robert. 1993. *Storm from the East*. Berkeley: University of California Press.

Martin, B. G. 1976. *Muslim Brotherhoods in Nineteenth Century Africa*. Cambridge: Cambridge University Press.

Massignon, Louis. 1994. *The Passion of Al-Ḥallāj: Mystic and Martyr of Islam*. Translated by H. Mason. Princeton, NJ: Princeton University Press.

Māwardī, ʻAlī ibn Muhammad. 1996. *The Ordinances of Government: A Translation of al-Ahkām al-Sultāniyy w. al-Wilāyāt al-Dīniyya*. Translated by A. H. Wahba. Reading, UK: Garnet.

Mernissi, Fatima. 1991. *The Veil and the Male Elite: A Feminist Interpretation of Women's Rights in Islam*. New York: Addison-Wesley.

Metcalf, Barbara Daly. 1982. *Islamic Revival in British India: Deoband, 1860–1900*. Princeton, NJ: Princeton University Press.

Mir, Mustansir. 1987. *Dictionary of Qur'ānic Terms and Concepts*. New York: Garland.

Momen, Moojan. 1985. *An Introduction to Shi'i Islam: The History and Doctrine of Twelver Shi'ism*. New Haven, CT: Yale University Press.

Morewedge, Parviz. 1979. *Islamic Philosophical Theology*. Albany: State University of New York Press.

Morewedge, Parviz. 1992. *Neoplatonism and Islamic Thought*. Albany: State University of New York Press.

Morgan, David. 1986. *The Mongols*. Oxford: Blackwell.

Morgan, David. 1988. *Medieval Persia 1040–1797*. London: Longman.

Morony, Michael G. 1984. *Iraq after the Muslim Conquest*. Princeton, NJ: Princeton University Press.

Motzki, Harald. 1991. "The Muṣannaf of Abd al-Razzāq al-Sanʻānī as a Source of Authentic āḥadīth of the First Century A.H." *Journal of Near Eastern Studies* 50, 1–21.

Muir, William, Sir. 1897. *The Mohammedan Controversy, Biographies of Mohammed*. Edinburgh: T. & T. Clark.

Musallam, B. F. 1983. *Sex and Society in Islam*. Cambridge: Cambridge University Press.
Muslim ibn al-Ḥajjāj. 1994. *Ṣaḥīḥ Muslim bi sharḥ al-Nawāwī*. Cairo: Dār al-Ḥadīth.
Nasir, Jamal J. 1986. *The Islamic Law of Personal Status*. London: Graham & Trotman.
Netton, I. R. 1982. *Muslim Neoplatonists*. London: George Allen & Unwin.
Neusner, Jacob. 1968. *History of the Jews in Babylonia*, 5 vols. Leiden: E. J. Brill.
Newby, Gordon. 1988. *A History of the Jews of Arabia*. Columbia: University of South Carolina Press.
Newby, P. H. 1983. *Saladin and his Time*. London: Faber & Faber.
Nicholson, Reynold Alleyne. 1914. *The Mystics of Islam*. London: George Bell.
Nicholson, Reynold Alleyne. 1921. *Studies in Islamic Mysticism*. Cambridge: Cambridge University Press.
Nicholson, Reynold Alleyne. 1959. *The Kashf al-Mahjūb of al-Hujwīrī*. London: Luzac.
Nicholson, Reynold Alleyne. 1998. *A Literary History of the Arabs*. New York: Kegan Paul International.
Niẓām al-Mulk. 1978. *The Book of Government: or, Rules for Kings: The Siyar al-muluk or Siyasat-nama of Nizam al-Mulk, translated from the Persian by Hubert Darke*, 2nd edn. London: Routledge & Kegan Paul.
Nomani, Asra Q. 2005. *Standing Alone: An American Woman's Struggle for the Soul of Islam*. New York: HarperSanFrancisco.
Noth, Albrecht. 1994. *The Early Arabic Historical Tradition: A Source-Critical Study*. Princeton, NJ: Darwin Press.
O'Fahey, R. S. 1990. *Enigmatic Saint: Ahmad ibn Idris and the Idrisi Tradition*. London: Hurst.
Ormsby, Eric. 1984. *Theodicy in Islamic Thought: The Dispute over Ghazālī's "Best of All Possible Worlds."* Princeton, NJ: Princeton University Press.
Padwick, Constance. 1996. *Muslim Devotions: A Study of Prayer-Manuals in Common Use*. Oxford: One World.
Parrinder, Edward Geoffrey. 1976. *Jesus in the Qur'ān*. London: Sheldon Press.
Pearson, J. D. 1958. *Index Islamicus, 1906–1955*. London: Mansell.
Pellat, Charles. 1976. *Ibn al-Muqaffaʿ: (Mort vers 140/757), "Conseilleur" du calife*. Paris: Maisonneuve et Larose.
Pentz, Peter. 1992. *The Invisible Conquests: The Ontogenesis of Sixth and Seventh Century Syria*. Copenhagen: National Museum of Denmark.
Peters, F. E. 1973. *Allāh's Commonwealth: A History of Islam in the Near East, 600–1100 AD*. New York: Simon & Schuster.
Peters, F. E. 1991. "The Quest of the Historical Muhammad." *International Journal of Middle East Studies* 23, 291–315.
Peters, F. E. 1994a. *Mecca: A Literary History of the Muslim Holy Land*. Princeton, NJ: Princeton University Press.
Peters, F. E. 1994b. *Muhammad and the Origins of Islam*. Albany: State University of New York Press.
Peters, F. E. 1994c. A *Reader on Classical Islam*. Princeton, NJ: Princeton University Press.
Peters, J. R. T. M. 1976. *God's Created Speech*. Leiden: E. J. Brill.
Peters, Rudolph. 1996. *Jihad in Classical and Modern Islam*. Princeton, NJ: Markus Wiener.
Powers, David. 1986. *Studies in Qur'an and Hadith: The Formation of the Islamic Law of Inheritance*. Berkeley: University of California Press.

Quataert, Donald. 2000. *The Ottoman Empire, 1700–1922*. Cambridge: Cambridge University Press.

Qushayrī, ʿAbd al-Karīm al-. 1990. *Principles of Sufism*. Translated by B. R. von Schlegell. Berkeley, CA: Mizan Press.

Raby, Julian, and Jeremy Johns. 1992. *Bayt al-Maqdis: ʿAbd al-Malik's Jerusalem*. Oxford: Oxford University Press for the Board of Faculty of Oriental Studies.

Rahman, Fazlur. 1958. *Prophecy in Islam*. London: Allen & Unwin.

Rahman, Fazlur. 1965. *Islamic Methodology in History*. Karachi: Central Institute for Islamic Research.

Rahman, Fazlur. 1972. *Islam*, 2nd edn. Chicago: University of Chicago Press.

Rahman, Fazlur. 1980. *Major Themes of the Qur'ān*. Minneapolis, MN: Bibliotheca Islamica.

Rahman, Fazlur. 1982. *Islam and Modernity: Transformation of an Intellectual Tradition*. Chicago: University of Chicago Press.

Ramadan, Tariq. 2004. *Western Muslims and the Future of Islam*. Oxford: Oxford University Press.

Rentz, G. 1972. "Wahhabism and Saudi Arabia." In Derek Hopwood, ed., *The Arabian Peninsula: Society and Politics*. London: George Allen & Unwin.

Retsö, Jan. 2003. *The Arabs in Antiquity: Their History from the Assyrians to the Umayyads*. London: RoutledgeCurzon.

Riley-Smith, Jonathan. 1995. *The Oxford Illustrated History of the Crusades*. Oxford: Oxford University Press.

Rippin, Andrew. 1988. *Approaches to the History of the Interpretation of the Qur'ān*. Oxford: Clarendon Press.

Rizvi, S. A. A. 1980. *Shah Wali-Allāh and his Times*. Canberra: Ma'rifat Publishing House.

Robinson, Neal. 1991. *Christ in Islam and Christianity*. Albany: State University of New York Press.

Robinson, Francis. 2007. *Separatism among Indian Muslims: The Politics of the United Provinces' Muslims, 1860–1923*. Cambridge: Cambridge University Press.

Rodinson, Maxime. 1980. *Muhammad*. Translated by A. Carter. New York: Pantheon Books.

Rodinson, Maxime. 1991. *Europe and the Mystique of Islam*. Seattle: University of Washington Press.

Roolvink, R. 1957. *Historical Atlas of the Muslim Peoples*. Cambridge, MA: Harvard University Press.

Rosenthal, Franz. 1975. *Gambling in Islam*. Leiden: E. J. Brill.

Rosenthal, Franz. 1990. *Greek Philosophy in the Arab World*. Brookfield, VT: Variorum.

Rubin, Uri. 1995. *The Eye of the Beholder: The Life of Muhammad as Viewed by the Early Muslims: A Textual Analysis*. Princeton, NJ: Darwin Press.

Saad, E. N. 1983. *Social History of Timbuktu: The Role of Muslim Scholars and Notables 1400–1900*. Cambridge: Cambridge University Press.

Sachedina, Abulaziz Abdulhussein. 1981. *Islamic Messianism: The Idea of the Mahdi in Twelver Shi'ism*. Albany: State University of New York Press.

Sachedina, Abdulaziz Abdulhussein. 1988. *The Just Ruler in Shīʿite Islam: The Comprehensive Authority of the Jurist in Imamite Jurisprudence*. New York: Oxford University Press.

Sahas, Daniel J. 1972. *John of Damascus on Islam. The "Heresy of the Ishmaelites."* Leiden: E. J. Brill.

Saunders, J. J. 1971. *The History of the Mongol Conquests*. London: Routledge.

Sauvaget, Jean. 1965. *Introduction to the History of the Muslim East: A Bibliographical Guide*, ed. Claude Cahen. Berkeley: University of California Press.

Savory, R. 1980. *Iran under the Safāvids*. Cambridge: Cambridge University Press.

Schacht, Joseph. 1950. *The Origins of Muhammadan Jurisprudence*. Oxford: Clarendon Press.

Schacht, Joseph. 1964. *An Introduction to Islamic Law*. Oxford: Clarendon Press.

Schimmel, Annemarie. 1963. *Gabriel's Wing*. Leiden: E. J. Brill.

Schimmel, Annemarie. 1975. *Mystical Dimensions of Islam*. Chapel Hill: University of North Carolina Press.

Schimmel, Annemarie. 1980. *Islam in the Indian Subcontinent*. Leiden: E. J. Brill.

Schimmel, Annemarie. 1982. *As Through a Veil: Mystical Poetry in Islam*. New York: Columbia University Press.

Schimmel, Annemarie. 1985. *And Muhammad is His Messenger: The Veneration of the Prophet in Islamic Piety*. Chapel Hill: University of North Carolina Press.

Sells, Michael A. 1989. *Desert Tracings: Six Classic Arabian Odes*. Middletown, CT: Wesleyan University Press.

Sells, Michael A., ed. 1996. *Early Islamic Mysticism: Sufī, Qur'ān, Miraj, Poetic and Theological Writing*. New York: Paulist Press.

Sells, Michael A. 1999. *Approaching the Qur'ān: The Early Revelations*. Ashland, OR: White Cloud Press.

Serjeant, R. B. 1981. *Studies in Arabian History and Civilization*. London: Variorum.

Shāfiʿī, Muhammad ibn Idrīs. 1961. *Islamic Jurisprudence: Shāfiʿī's Risāla*. Translated by M. Khadduri. Baltimore, MD: Johns Hopkins University Press.

Shahīd, Irfan. 1984a. *Byzantium and the Arabs in the Fourth Century*. Washington, DC: Dumbarton Oaks Research Library and Collection.

Shahīd, Irfan. 1984b. *Rome and the Arabs: A Prolegomenon to the Study of Byzantium and the Arabs*. Washington, DC: Dumbarton Oaks Research Library and Collection.

Shahīd, Irfan. 1988. *Byzantium and the Semitic Orient Before the Rise of Islam*. London: Variorum.

Shahīd, Irfan. 1989. *Byzantium and the Arabs in the Fifth Century*. Washington, DC: Dumbarton Oaks Research Library and Collection.

Shahīd, Irfan. 1995. *Byzantium and the Arabs in the Sixth Century*. Washington, DC: Dumbarton Oaks Research Library and Collection.

Shāhrastānī, Muhammad ibn ʿAbd al-Karīm. 1984. *Muslim Sects and Divisions: The Section on Muslim Sects in Kitāb al-milal wa 'l-nihal*. Translated by A. K. Kazi and A. K. Flynn. London: Kegan Paul International.

Shaw, Stanford J. 1977. *History of the Ottoman Empire and Modern Turkey*. Cambridge: Cambridge University Press.

Shehadi, F. 1983. *Metaphysics in Islamic Philosophy*. Delmar, NY: Caravan Books.

Shiblī Nuʿmānī. 1979. *The Life of the Prophet*, 2 vols. Translated by M. Tayyib Bakhsh Budayuni. Lahore: Kazi Publications.

Siddiqi, Muhammad Zubayr. 1993. *Hadīth Literature: Its Origin, Development and Special Features*. Cambridge: Islamic Texts Society.

Sirriyeh, Elizabeth. 1999. *Sufis and Anti-Sufis: The Defense, Rethinking and Rejection of Sufism in the Modern World*. Richmond, UK: Curzon.

Sivan, Emmanuel. 1985. *Radical Islam: Medieval Theology and Modern Politics*. New Haven, CT: Yale University Press.

Smith, Margaret. 1959. *Readings from the Mystics of Islam*. London: Luzac.

Sprenger, Aloys. 1869. *Das Leben und die Lehre des Mohammed*. Berlin: Nicolai.

Spuler, Bertold. 1960. *The Muslim World: A Historical Survey*. Leiden: E. J. Brill.

Stowasser, Barbara Freyer. 1994. *Women in the Qur'ān: Traditions and Interpretation*. New York: Oxford University Press.

Sweetman, James Windrow. 1947. *Islam and Christian Theology: A Study of the Interpretation of Theological Ideas in the Two Religions*. London: Lutterworth Press.

Ṭabarī, Abū Ja'far Muhammad b. Jarīr al-. 1987. *Commentary on the Qur'ān*. Oxford: Oxford University Press.

Ṭabarī, Abū Ja'far Muhammad b. Jarvr al-. 1992. *The Battle of al-Qādisiyyah and the Conquest of Syria and Palestine: AD 635–637/AH 14–15*. [*Tārīkh al-rusul wa-al-mulūk*, vol. 12.] Translated by Y. Friedmann. 40 vols. Albany: State University of New York Press.

Ṭabarī, Abū Ja'far Muhammad b. Jarvr al-. 1993. *The Challenge to the Empires*. [*Tārīkh al-rusul wa-al-mulūk*, vol. 11.] Translated by Khalid Yahya Blankinship. Albany: State University of New York Press.

Ṭabāṭabā'ī Muhammad Ḥusayn. 1975. *Shi'ite Islam*. Translated by S. H. Nasr. Albany: State University of New York Press.

Thomas, David. 1992. *Anti-Christian Polemic in Early Islam: Abu 'Isa al-Warraq's "Against the Trinity."* Cambridge: Cambridge University Press.

Tibi, Bassam. 2001. *Islam Between Culture and Politics*. New York: Palgrave.

Trimingham, J. Spencer. 1971. *The Sufi Orders in Islam*. Oxford: Clarendon Press.

Troll, Christian. 1978. *Sayyid Ahmad Khan: A Reinterpretation of Muslim Theology*. New Delhi: Vikas.

Udovitch, Abraham. 1970. *Partnership and Profit in Medieval Islam*. Princeton, NJ: Princeton University Press.

Vaglieri, Veccia. 1993. "Ghādir Khumm." In *Encyclopaedia of Islam*, vol. 2. Leiden: E. J. Brill.

Vauchez, André, ed. 2000. *Encyclopaedia of the Middle Ages*. Chicago: Fitzroy Dearborn.

Voll, John O. 1982. *Islam: Continuity and Change in the Modern World*. Boulder, CO: Westview Press.

Voll, John O., and John Esposito. 1991. *The Contemporary Islamic Revival: A Critical Survey and Bibliography*. New York: Greenwood Press.

Von Grunebaum, Gustave E. 1953. *Medieval Islam*, 2nd edn. Chicago: University of Chicago Press.

Von Grunebaum, Gustave E. 1962. *Modern Islam*. Berkeley: University of California Press.

Von Grunebaum, Gustave E. 1970. *Classical Islam*. Chicago: Aldine.

Von Grunebaum, Gustave E., ed. 1971. *Theology and Law in Islam*. Wiesbaden: Harrassowitz.

Wadud, Amina. 1999. *Qur'an and Woman: Rereading the Sacred Text from a Woman's Perspective*. Oxford: Oxford University Press.

Waines, David. 1995. *An Introduction to Islam*. Cambridge: Cambridge University Press.

Wakin, Jeanette. 1972. *The Function of Documents in Islamic Law*. Albany: State University of New York Press.

Walī Allāh, al-Dihlawī, Shāh. 1980. *Shah Wali Allāh, Sufism and the Islamic Tradition: The Lamahat and Sata'at of Shah Wali Allāh*. Translated by G. N. Jalbani. London: Octagon Press.

Walī Allāh, al-Dihlawī, Shāh. 1996. *The Conclusive Argument from God*. Translated by M. Hermansen. Leiden: E. J. Brill.

Walzer, Richard. 1953. "Islamic Philosophy." In Sarvapelli Radhakrisnan, ed., *History of Philosophy: Eastern and Western*. London: Allen & Unwin.

Wansbrough, John E. 1977. *Quranic Studies: Sources and Methods of Scriptural Interpretation*. Oxford: Oxford University Press.

Wansbrough, John E. 1978. *The Sectarian Milieu*. Oxford: Oxford University Press.

Watt, W. Montgomery. 1948. *Free Will and Predestination in Early Islam*. London: Luzac.

Watt, W. Montgomery. 1953. *Muhammad at Mecca*. Oxford: Clarendon Press.

Watt, W. Montgomery. 1956. *Muhammad at Medina*. Oxford: Clarendon Press.

Watt, W. Montgomery. 1961. *Muhammad: Prophet and Statesman*. London: Oxford University Press.

Watt, W. Montgomery. 1962. *Islamic Philosophy and Theology*. Edinburgh: Edinburgh University Press.

Watt, W. Montgomery. 1973. *The Formative Period of Islamic Thought*. Edinburgh: Edinburgh University Press.

Waugh, Earle H. 1989. *The Munshidin of Egypt: Their World and their Song*. Columbia: University of South Carolina Press.

Weiss, Bernard. 1992. *The Search for God's Law: Islamic Jurisprudence in the Writings of Sayf al-Dīn al-Āmidī*. Salt Lake City: University of Utah Press.

Wensinck, A. J. 1932. *The Muslim Creed: Its Genesis and Historical Development*. Cambridge: Cambridge University Press.

Widengren, G. 1983. "Manichaeism and its Iranian background." In *The Cambridge History of Iran*, vol. 3, part 2. Cambridge: Cambridge University Press.

Wolfson, Harry Austryn. 1976. *The Philosophy of the Kalam*. Cambridge, MA: Harvard University Press.

Yarshater, Ehsan, ed. 1968. *The Cambridge History of Iran*. Cambridge: Cambridge University Press.

Yūsuf 'Alī. 1989. *The Meaning of the Holy Qur'ān*, 6th edn., revd. Beltsville, MD: Amana Publications.

INDEX